THE EDDIE CANTOR STORY

**BRANDEIS SERIES IN AMERICAN
JEWISH HISTORY, CULTURE, AND LIFE**

Jonathan D. Sarna, Editor

Sylvia Barack Fishman, Associate Editor

For a complete list of books that are available in the series,
visit www.upne.com

David Weinstein
The Eddie Cantor Story: A Jewish Life in Performance and Politics

David G. Dalin
Supreme Court Jews: From Brandeis to Kagan

Naomi Prawer Kadar
*Raising Secular Jews: Yiddish Schools and Their Periodicals
for American Children, 1917–1950*

Linda B. Forgosh
Louis Bamberger: Department Store Innovator and Philanthropist

Gary Phillip Zola and Marc Dollinger, editors
American Jewish History: A Primary Source Reader

Vincent Brook and Marat Grinberg, editors
Woody on Rye: Jewishness in the Films and Plays of Woody Allen

Mark Cohen
Overweight Sensation: The Life and Comedy of Allan Sherman

David E. Kaufman
*Jewhooing the Sixties: American Celebrity and Jewish Identity —
Sandy Koufax, Lenny Bruce, Bob Dylan, and Barbra Streisand*

Jack Wertheimer, editor
The New Jewish Leaders: Reshaping the American Jewish Landscape

Eitan P. Fishbane and Jonathan D. Sarna, editors
Jewish Renaissance and Revival in America

Jonathan B. Krasner
The Benderly Boys and American Jewish Education

Derek Rubin, editor
Promised Lands: New Jewish American Fiction on Longing and Belonging

DAVID WEINSTEIN

THE EDDIE CANTOR STORY

A JEWISH LIFE
IN PERFORMANCE
AND POLITICS

To The Meyerstein Family,

Thank you!

Best Wishes,
Saul West
12/3/2017

BRANDEIS UNIVERSITY PRESS Waltham, Massachusetts

Brandeis University Press
An imprint of University Press of New England
www.upne.com
© 2018 Brandeis University
All rights reserved
Manufactured in the United States of America
Designed by Richard Hendel
Typeset in Chaparral, Transat, and Matra
by Passumpsic Publishing

For permission to reproduce any of the material in this book,
contact Permissions, University Press of New England, One Court Street,
Suite 250, Lebanon NH 03766; or visit www.upne.com

Library of Congress Cataloging-in-Publication Data
NAMES: Weinstein, David, 1967– author.
TITLE: The Eddie Cantor story: a Jewish life in performance and politics /
    David Weinstein.
DESCRIPTION: Waltham, Massachusetts: Brandeis University Press, 2017. |
    Series: Brandeis series in American Jewish history, culture, and life |
    Includes bibliographical references and index.
IDENTIFIERS: LCCN 2017019187 (print) | LCCN 2017033438 (ebook) |
    ISBN 9781512601343 (epub, mobi, & pdf) |
    ISBN 9781512600483 (cloth: alk. paper)
SUBJECTS: LCSH: Cantor, Eddie, 1892–1964. | Entertainers — United
    States — Biography.
CLASSIFICATION: LCC PN2287.C26 (ebook) |
    LCC PN2287.C26 W46 2017 (print) | DDC 791/.092 [B] — dc23
LC record available at https://lccn.loc.gov/2017019187

5 4 3 2 1

CONTENTS

Acknowledgments   ix

Introduction   1

1   IMMIGRANTS, CRIMINALS, AND ACTORS (1892–1908)   7

2   A VAUDEVILLE EDUCATION (1908–1916)   18

3   THE JEWISH WISE GUY (1916–1919)   31

4   A SNAPPY HEADLINER (1919–1923)   47

5   MAKIN' WHOOPEE WITH ZIEGFELD (1923–1930)   64

6   VOICE OF THE DEPRESSION (1929–1938)   83

7   RADIO WITH A JEWISH ACCENT (1931–1938)   107

8   THE FIGHT AGAINST NAZISM (1933–1939)   126

9   CANTOR GOES TO CHURCH (1939–1941)   148

10   IT'S TIME TO SMILE AGAIN (1941–1945)   165

11   POSTWAR STRUGGLES (1945–1950)   181

12   THE LAST COMEBACK (1950–1952)   195

13   FADING AWAY (1952–1964)   212

Epilogue: Eddie Cantor's Legacy   230

Notes   239

Index   291

ACKNOWLEDGMENTS

I never saw Eddie Cantor perform live. He died a few years before I was born. I first experienced Cantor through *The Colgate Comedy Hour* programs on which he starred during the early 1950s. I found a few of these shows on videotape while I was researching my previous book: *The Forgotten Network: DuMont and the Birth of American Television* (2004). I had associated Cantor primarily with vaudeville and Broadway of the 1910s and 1920s. I was surprised to see Cantor headlining a popular television program many years after his vaudeville days. Even though he was a little past his prime on *The Colgate Comedy Hour*, Cantor's charisma, energy, and ability to connect with audiences impressed me. I wanted to know more about this performer. After I finished *The Forgotten Network*, I turned my attention to Cantor.

I immersed myself in primary materials and scholarship covering more than seventy years of American social, cultural, and political history. Fortunately, I had many wise mentors and experts to guide me in this research and writing. I am especially grateful to the following people for reading portions of this manuscript, sending me archival treasures, and sharing their vast knowledge about everything from Lower East Side history to the modern publishing industry: Margaret Bausman, Lila Corwin Berman, Hasia Diner, Tom Doherty, Brian Gari, Grace Hale, Jeff Hardwick, Daniel Horowitz, Ari Y. Kelman, Alan Kraut, Lisa Moses Leff, David Margolick, Jonathan Markovitz, Michael McGerr, Cynthia Meyers, Howard Pollack, Jennifer Porst, Kathy Fuller Seeley, Lauren Sklaroff, Sean VanCour, Jennifer Hyland Wang, Steve Whitfield, and the Wolkin family.

I benefited from opportunities to deliver talks about Eddie Cantor and participate in seminars hosted by the following groups and organizations: the American University Judaic Studies Program, the Association for Jewish Studies, the Baltimore–DC Media Studies Group, B'nai Israel Congregation (Rockville, Maryland), the Radio Preservation Task Force, the Smithsonian Institution National Museum of American History Colloquium, the Society for Cinema and Media Studies, and the Wisconsin Center for Film and Theater Research. I thank the coordinators, fellow panelists, and attendees of these programs for engaging in lively discussions about Eddie Cantor and his world.

I am lucky to work with a great group of supportive friends and colleagues at the National Endowment for the Humanities (NEH), a vibrant intellectual environment. In addition, the agency's Independent Study, Research, and Development (ISRD) program granted me time to conduct archival research. The views that I express in this book do not represent those of the NEH or the federal government.

A Montgomery County (Maryland) Arts and Humanities Council grant facilitated a valuable research trip to Los Angeles and San Francisco.

In writing *The Eddie Cantor Story*, I had the opportunity to explore terrific libraries and archives. Thanks to the NEH Library (Donna Mc-Clish); the American Jewish Historical Society (Boni J. Koelliker and Susan Woodland); Oviatt Library Special Collections and Archives, California State University, Northridge (David Sigler); the Library of Congress Recorded Sound Research Center (Bryan Cornell, Karen Fishman, and David Sager); Archives and Special Collections, Loyola Marymount University (Clay Stalls); the National Center for Jewish Film (Lisa Rivo); the New York Public Library for the Performing Arts (Annemarie van Roessel); the Paley Center (Mark Ekman and Jane Klain); SAG-AFTRA (Valerie Yaros); the Shubert Archive (Maryann Chach and Sylvia Wang); the Film and Television Archive, University of California, Los Angeles (Mark Quigley); Library Special Collections, University of California, Los Angeles (Annie Watanabe-Rocco); the Bancroft Library, University of California, Berkeley (Chris McDonald); Special Collections and University Archives, University of Maryland Libraries (Michael Henry and Chuck Howell); the Wisconsin Center for Film and Television; and the YIVO Institute for Jewish Research (Gunnar Berg and Fruma Mohrer). Special thanks to Milt Larsen for generously making his personal Eddie Cantor collection available to me and to Carol Marie for her kind and resourceful work in uncovering and sharing so many great materials from this collection.

An earlier version of chapter 8 was previously published in *American Jewish History* (December 2010). Thanks to the journal and to Dianne Ashton for her editing of this essay.

Phyllis Deutsch at University Press of New England/Brandeis University Press is a great editor. I especially appreciate her enthusiasm for the project, wise suggestions for revision of the manuscript, and expert guidance through the different stages of publication. Thanks, also, to the skillful team that prepared the manuscript for publication, including the production editor, Susan Abel, and the copyeditor, Elizabeth Forsaith.

Sleater-Kinney, the Mekons, Neil Young, and the Fastbacks provided a steady soundtrack when I needed a break from Tin Pan Alley. In addition, this music inspired me to think more deeply about fandom, celebrity, nostalgia, and other concepts that are central to this book.

Special thanks to Ellie Weinstein and Sara Weinstein for their curiosity about Eddie Cantor and recommendations for alternative titles ("The Jewish Cantor" received strong consideration). I also thank Sara and Ellie for showing me the joys of being a dad and for enticing me away from Eddie Cantor.

Through my many years of writing this book, Rachel Weinstein's questions, ideas, comments, and copyediting prompted me to clarify my thinking and writing. Rachel's most important contributions to this book are harder to describe. I thank Rachel for her love, support, encouragement, and willingness to choose family vacation spots based on their proximity to Eddie Cantor landmarks and archives.

This book is dedicated to the memories of Susan Flatt and Steve Weinstein.

THE EDDIE CANTOR STORY

INTRODUCTION

or more than forty years, Eddie Cantor was one of America's most popular and recognizable entertainers. The child of Russian immigrants, Cantor grew up in a series of small tenement apartments on New York's Lower East Side. He was orphaned at age three with no siblings and raised by his maternal grandmother. Cantor used show business as a vehicle for social and economic mobility. From the 1910s through the 1950s, he headlined in theater, film, radio, and television. A versatile master of promotion and merchandising, Cantor spun off numerous products, including hit records, best-selling books, board games, campaign buttons, and even Eddie Cantor cigars. Cantor's immense popularity across different media, his pride in his Jewish heritage, and his engagement with pressing political issues distinguished him from other stars of his era.

This is a book about how Cantor (1892–1964) starred on America's biggest stages while also identifying as a Jew. It was not easy for Cantor to reconcile his "Jewish" and "American" personas. During the first half of the twentieth century, Jews in all areas of professional life were very careful in how they revealed and claimed Jewish identities. Jews in the entertainment industry faced particular challenges in expressing aspects of Jewish religion, culture, and politics. Many show business executives, producers, singers, and actors quietly shed their Jewish backgrounds and did not call attention to the fact that they were Jewish.[1] Cantor was different. Rather than effacing his Jewish identity, he embraced it by incorporating Jewish perspectives in his work on and off the stage. Cantor's story provides a new way of understanding the possibilities and parameters of Jewish expression in popular culture.

Cantor filled his routines with Jewish phrases, allusions, jokes, songs, and stories. The sly actor frequently did not mark this material as "Jewish." Instead, he relied on attentive audiences to interpret his coded performances. Jews and non-Jews who were familiar with Jewish culture and politics appreciated Cantor in ways that were not accessible to other audience members.[2] When speaking at charity benefits and writing for the Jewish press, Cantor was more direct about Jewish social and political issues. But because of his celebrity status, boundaries between different platforms collapsed. For example, bold condemnations of antisemitism that Cantor delivered at Hadassah fund-raisers merited coverage in the major daily newspapers and weekly newsmagazines. Sometimes this attention helped Cantor's career and enhanced his image among non-Jews. Other times, this scrutiny damaged Cantor's reputation before the non-Jewish public, including his radio sponsors.

The Eddie Cantor Story's first five chapters focus on Cantor's Lower East Side childhood, his climb through the ranks of vaudeville, and his stardom on Broadway during the late 1910s and the 1920s. These chapters highlight the ways in which Cantor's experiences as a Jew informed his performance style. Cantor mostly presented light music and comedy, though his work had a satirical edge and frequently poked fun at conventional social mores. Cantor also commented on politics. For example, he was among the first and most persistent stage critics of Henry Ford and nativism. Offstage, Cantor headlined charitable benefits and led the actors' union in its 1919 strike against producers. Starting in the early 1930s, Cantor's topical humor and offstage activism increased in response to the Great Depression and growing antisemitism in the United States and Europe. This book's focus shifts accordingly. The later chapters examine how Cantor made social issues, especially Jewish concerns, more central to his public persona.

Throughout his career, Cantor usually demonstrated good instincts in balancing music, comedy, and politics. But he occasionally antagonized audience members or radio sponsors who did not want his politics to intrude on their entertainment. With his proud combination of New Deal liberalism and fervent anti-Nazism, Cantor provoked adversaries to question his loyalties. Some implied that he was a communist sympathizer. Others charged that he placed Jewish interests over American interests in advocating for refugees and opposing antisemitism during the 1930s. Cantor crafted strategies for defusing these kinds of accusations while remaining popular with Jewish and non-Jewish audiences across the political spectrum.

From today's perspective, Cantor's fame may seem odd. Some of his music and comedy appear to be nostalgic, antiquated, or offensive. It is difficult to look beyond the caricatured homosexuality from *Whoopee!* (1930) and the racism of the blackface makeup in which Cantor per-

formed throughout his career. In addition, Cantor portrayed effeminate nebbishes, fast-talking salesmen who slipped into Yiddish, and
wisecracking city kids enjoying illicit sex and illegal booze. Today these
roles would not pass muster with the Anti-Defamation League or social
media commentators sensitive to negative images of Jews. This music
and comedy also seem incompatible with Cantor's liberal politics and
his philanthropic activity, which valued tolerance and decency. For example, Cantor performed in blackface through the early 1950s, even
though he frequently participated in campaigns opposing prejudice
and discrimination. He also railed against antisemitism while playing
characters that perpetuated stereotypes of weak Jewish men. *The Eddie
Cantor Story* explores these contradictions through careful analysis of
Cantor's performances and the popular reception of his work. Cantor was a crafty actor who defied easy labels. Within a particular play,
show, or film, he would both perpetuate and undercut racial and ethnic
stereotypes. More broadly, this book examines Cantor's blackface and
ethnic comedy in the context of changing performance practices and
social attitudes about race, stereotypes, and Jewish expression.

Historical context is essential for understanding Cantor in relation to
American Jewish history. Even seemingly simple terms such as "Jewish
culture" and "Jewish community" did not hold consistent meanings for
Cantor and his audiences. The "community" was never monolithic, and
it shifted over time. Jews built identities based on a set of fluctuating
and overlapping categories, including social class, gender, politics, religious observance, country of origin, occupation, and geographic loca-
tion. For example, the American Jewish community, circa 1910, included
rural peddlers, urban garment workers, wealthy German bankers, Yid-
dish-speaking socialists, poor immigrants, acculturated lawyers, Orthodox Jews, and many other social groups. A snapshot of the community
would have looked very different twenty years earlier, in 1890, or twenty
years later, in 1930. As a celebrity, Cantor crossed social boundaries.
He identified as a working-class child of Russian immigrants from the
Lower East Side, but he also mingled comfortably with the German-
Jewish elite that headed communal associations and philanthropies.
Given the diversity of American Jews, *The Eddie Cantor Story* does not
measure Cantor according to a single ideal of "Jewishness." Instead, this
book examines how Cantor presented his perspectives and experiences

Harry S. Truman (right), with George Jessel (center) and Cantor at a 1957 Israel Bonds dinner celebrating Cantor's sixty-fifth birthday.

as a Jew, on and off the stage, and how audiences responded to these Jewish expressions.

More than any other Jewish actor of his stature, Cantor assumed a responsibility to help his coreligionists in America and abroad through offstage activism. Cantor regularly crisscrossed the country, speaking at local synagogues, charitable federations, and Hadassah meetings. While his show business peers occupied their late nights at Hollywood parties or New York nightclubs, and their days sleeping off the previous night's excesses, Cantor appeared at charity banquets. He met with religious and lay leaders, shook hands, took pictures, signed autographs, and listened to endless roll calls naming donors. When it was his turn at the microphone, Cantor did not sing or joke. Instead, he delivered powerful political statements and moving fund-raising solicitations. Cantor also granted interviews exclusively for the Jewish press and wrote articles under his byline. These pieces were not mere reprints of the standard promotional fare that publicists created for actors. Cantor analyzed social problems from a Jewish perspective and recommended courses of action on complex, divisive subjects, such as antisemitism, Zionism, economic inequality, the New Deal, and threats to civil liberties.

In strategically choosing his political causes and battles, Cantor blurred the line between altruism and self-interest. He used the infrastructure of Jewish charities, including large membership meetings and public service radio programs, as platforms from which he addressed problems that were important to him. Given the many tensions within Jewish communal politics and philanthropy, some leaders may have disagreed with Cantor's positions, but few criticized him publicly. After working with so many different people and organizations, Cantor built a strong reputation among American Jews. This remarkably loyal Jewish fan base served him well during low points in his career. Charitable events, in the Jewish community and beyond, also provided Cantor with the opportunity to build personal and professional relationships with leading philanthropists, clergy, politicians, and government officials. Cantor shared the head table at fund-raising banquets with everybody from Rabbi Stephen Wise to Eleanor Roosevelt. The actor also demonstrated his patriotism through his associations with well-established organizations such as the American Legion and the Red Cross.

Letters from statesmen over the years attest to Cantor's success at positioning himself as a respected activist and iconic American figure whose significance transcended the comedy stage and partisan politics. In 1938 Franklin Roosevelt acknowledged his "old friend" and quoted Cantor in an important radio statement on the growing threat of Nazism.[3] Nineteen years later, when Cantor turned sixty-five, former president Harry S. Truman was the featured speaker at the actor's birthday party: a benefit for Israel Bonds. Richard Nixon, then vice president, didn't attend in person, but he sent a letter of congratulations, praising Cantor's "humanitarian achievements." Nixon added a handwritten postscript: "The Nixons always enjoy you whether in the movies, on TV, radio, or in person!"[4] Shortly after Cantor's seventy-second birthday, on February 3, 1964, he received a formal commendation from President

Lyndon Johnson for his lifetime of humanitarian service. Since a heart condition prevented Cantor from traveling across country to the White House, California Governor Edmund G. Brown visited the ailing actor's Beverly Hills home and delivered the citation.

By 1964 Cantor had come a long way from the Lower East Side tenement where he began his life. *The Eddie Cantor Story* chronicles this journey.

1 IMMIGRANTS, CRIMINALS, AND ACTORS (1892–1908)

The Lower East Side of the 1890s was a brutal neighborhood, but Isidore "Izzy" Iskowitz had little say in where he spent his childhood. Iskowitz, who later become known as Eddie Cantor, was born in a small Eldridge Street apartment on January 31, 1892.[1] Two years earlier, his parents, Meta Kantrowitz and Mechel Iskowitz, had emigrated from Russia. Meta and Mechel were part of a wave of more than a half-million Jews who arrived in the United States between 1870 and 1898. Most began their lives in America like Cantor's parents: without much money, in a Lower East Side tenement. More than three hundred thousand Jews lived in the small section of Lower Manhattan by 1893.[2]

When Meta and Mechel arrived in New York, they reunited with two of Meta's brothers who had immigrated earlier. Meta's mother, Esther Kantrowitz, left Russia to join her children in 1891, when Meta was pregnant with Eddie. The Kantrowitz family's life in America was difficult and at times tragic. Eddie's mother, Meta Kantrowitz Iskowitz, died of lung disease on July 26, 1894, when her son was two years old.[3] Soon thereafter, Eddie lost his father Mechel, an aspiring musician. Cantor tells a moving story in *My Life Is in Your Hands* (1928), the first of two autobiographies that he published, about his father's final moments. Mechel, bedridden and suffering from pneumonia, plays the violin for as long as he can. Suddenly, the music stops and Mechel's eyes close. Little Eddie looks at his father and then asks Grandma Esther with a whimper, "Why don't papa play no more [music]?" Esther answers, "He's asleep, mine child . . . You're an orphan, woe is me! Alone in the world!"[4]

Is the story true? Possibly. Mechel Iskowitz may have died of pneumonia in late 1894 or early 1895, as Cantor later recounted. Or Mechel may have abandoned his son and built a new life elsewhere. In addition to providing a sympathetic description of his father's final moments, Cantor portrayed Mechel as a "lovable ne'er-do-well" who had little interest in finding working or earning money. After his wife died, Mechel "grew restive, nervous, excited. He wandered the streets constantly." Cantor's characterizations of his father suggest that Mechel was not prepared to support his mother-in-law and his young son. Mechel may have left Esther and Eddie, rather than assuming responsibility for their care.[5] In fact, Jewish immigrants deserted their families with alarming frequency.[6]

Given the lack of extant documentation, it is impossible to ascertain when and how Cantor's father died. More broadly, most of Cantor's early life must remain a mystery to historians. Our knowledge is filtered through Cantor's memories and his self-interest as a celebrity who carefully crafted his public image. Except for a few stray census records, there are no primary sources or even interviews with people who knew Cantor as a child to confirm the actor's accounts of his coming-of-age in New York. Cantor's autobiographies, two essay collections, interviews, and comedy sketches about his youth, created and modified over his years in the spotlight, mix fact with fiction. His entertaining, surprising recollections of his early life should not be taken too literally; however, these stories illustrate how Cantor saw himself and how he wanted the public to see him. Cantor used childhood anecdotes to explain and amplify different aspects of his star persona. He highlighted his rise from poverty, identity as a Lower East Side Jew, familiarity with violent street life, and practicality in pursuing a career in show business.

Cantor recalled that after his father's death, he and his Grandma Esther, about sixty years older than Eddie, struggled "to keep some sort of food in our stomachs and a roof over our heads." They rented a series of apartments in dark, crowded, stuffy Lower East Side tenement buildings. A two-room basement dwelling on Henry Street, their home for the longest period of time, was so cold that Eddie and Esther would nail down the windows so no air could get in. Cantor later wrote, "We'd go to sleep literally drugged from lack of oxygen." In 1903, when Cantor was eleven, the rent of nine dollars became too steep, and the family moved from Henry Street to a cheaper tenement on Market Street. Sixteen families shared a single toilet, located in the yard. "If you had to wait in line, you skipped it," Cantor wrote. They soon returned to Henry Street.[7]

Cantor's recollections of his bleak living conditions are consistent with scholarly research about the Jewish Lower East Side during the

Cantor in 1900 at the age of eight.

1890s and 1900s. For example, the historians Annie Polland and Daniel Soyer recreate the sights and sounds of a typical tenement hallway: "the aroma of a neighbor's cooking, the screeching of toddlers, odors of chamber pots, the brisk footsteps of a contractor bringing in the next bundle of clothes to be assembled, a Yiddish conversation among third-floor housewives, echoes of children's street games from street or roof, and the never-ending hum of sewing machines." Outdoors offered a reprieve, if the weather was not too hot or cold, but the dense city streets still reeked of sewage, garbage, and the rotting carcasses of dead horses and other animals.[8]

Eddie and Esther shared their small apartments with a revolving group of eight or nine Polish girls who were central to the family's livelihood. Esther ran an employment agency for immigrants, providing temporary lodging until she could find work for them as maids. She received a dollar or two for each placement. Cantor's entrepreneurial grandmother also peddled candles and safety pins and worked as a *shadchen*, or matchmaker, introducing the girls to potential husbands. Esther collected a fee, usually twenty-five dollars, if the couple married. She sometimes received invitations to the weddings, which gave her the opportunity to stuff her pockets with food for young Eddie. In watching his grandmother's matchmaking, Cantor learned to take a cynical view of love and marriage, a theme of "Makin' Whoopee" and other popular Cantor songs of the 1920s. Writing in 1957, he recalled that as a child, marriage meant money: "Every couple looked to me like a potential pair of shoes or a pair of pants."[9]

Eddie slipped into a life of destructive delinquency while Esther was busy earning enough money for food and rent. At age six, the boy wandered the streets all night with older children, singing popular songs, making noise, and getting into trouble. A little later, he learned to steal food from pushcarts. More traumatically, Cantor was hit with a brick hurled during a gang fight, leaving him unconscious and lying in a pool of blood. He was unable to walk for several months. The beating left a permanent scar across his forehead. Still, Eddie continued to court trouble. At age twelve, he carried a gun and burglarized shops as part of a gang. "Being the skinniest and most agile of the younger boys, I was employed to crawl through narrow bars and fanlights to open doors and secret passages for the marauders," he later explained.[10]

Devotion to work, young Eddie, and Judaism defined Grandma Esther's life. Though Cantor later respected Esther's piety, he did not have warm memories of childhood Judaic experiences. Esther prepared a hot meal and lit candles every Friday night to celebrate Shabbat with her young grandson. But the boy would sneak out of the apartment and walk the streets until midnight. The punishment on the rare occasions when Esther was able to catch him: Eddie would have to stay home and

Cantor in 1948 with a framed portrait of Grandma Esther in the background.

join Esther in synagogue the next day. Esther paid for Eddie's religious schooling in preparation for his bar mitzvah at the Orthodox Pike Street Synagogue. However, the boy skipped his lessons until shortly before the ceremony, when he asked the rabbi to help him prepare a speech so that he did not disgrace his grandmother. Cantor "added quite a few things to the speech when the rabbi wasn't looking. In the

......

Orthodox shul, the women sit upstairs, so I looked up at my grand-mother, intoning, 'There sits my grandmother, she has been my father and my mother.' It was the only time she saw me on stage." In addition to this sentimental nod to Esther during his biggest stage performance to date, Cantor's other memory of the event is that the synagogue care-taker stole a watch that Esther gave Eddie as a bar mitzvah gift. The bar mitzvah story from *Take My Life* (1957), his second autobiography, is one of the actor's few references to synagogue attendance.[11]

Despite Cantor's antipathy to Jewish rituals, aspects of his Judaic education under Esther remained with him throughout his life. Can-tor drew on his knowledge of the religion as fodder for stage comedy and occasionally used the High Holidays to make more serious political statements. Cantor strongly identified as a Jew, though he rarely fol-lowed traditional religious laws and practices. In his 1959 book *The Way I See It*, Cantor traced his lifelong observance of "certain food taboos of the Jewish faith" to habit and tradition, rather than religious convic-tion: "Having been brought up in a strictly Kosher home, I never tasted ham, bacon, pork, or any sort of shellfish as a kid. Later, I just continued to eat what I'd always eaten." He explained that "rules and regulations obscure, even smother, the spirit" of religion.[12]

Instead of following Judaic commandments, Cantor and many other working-class Jewish kids of his generation, the children of immigrants, learned the value of quick wits and a good sales pitch. They knew how to take care of themselves in streets that could be violent. Cantor some-times crossed the line from self-defense to brutality. When a teacher challenged the thirteen-year-old Cantor to joke less and improve his grades, Cantor hit the man in the jaw, knocking him unconscious. Can-tor then dropped out of school. Esther did nothing to try to reverse his decision.[13] Perhaps she hoped that Eddie would begin to earn money. It was not unusual for a working-class child to forgo secondary education. In 1909, the year that Cantor would have graduated from high school, only 8 percent of all seventeen-year-olds nationally earned a diploma. Children typically dropped out at age thirteen or fourteen so that they could work full-time and contribute to the family's expenses. Immi-grant Jewish families saw education as a vehicle for social mobility, but many also were dependent on the extra income that working children could provide.[14]

After Cantor left school, he did not bring money home to his grandmother. At this point, Cantor later observed sardonically, he felt ready "to retire and spend my remaining days in leisure [and] comfort."[15] He recounted his recalcitrant early teenage years: "truant from school, pilferer of pushcarts, hooligan, street fighter, liar — to [Esther] I was Itchik [Cantor's' nickname] and she loved me no matter what."[16] Cantor tested this devotion. When Eddie was thirteen years old, he stole a purse from one of Esther's servant girls, and then disappeared for a week, living in a cheap Bowery flophouse. He returned home, scared of punishment, to find Esther thrilled that he was safe. Cantor explained his grandmother's perspective, "Better a live criminal than a dead little popeyed kid."[17]

The man who became one of America's most benevolent and respected entertainers earned pocket money as a teenager working for local gangsters. One hoodlum paid Eddie three dollars a day to look tough and guard scab workers during a strike. The job served as an ironic introduction to labor politics for the future president of the Screen Actors Guild. A little later, at the instigation of another local gangster, Cantor borrowed a gun and threatened a rival suitor of his future wife, Ida Tobias.[18] Cantor believed that show business miraculously saved him from prison or an early death on the streets. As he wrote in *My Life Is in Your Hands* (1928), during the "vague, formative years I vacillated, drifted between impulses to act and amuse and a desire to slouch around street corners, hang out in poolrooms, join guerilla gangs, and become a gangster's tool. Who could tell, by looking at a group of East Side youngsters, which would become a Gyp the Blood or Lefty Louie and which a Marcus Loew or Irving Berlin?"[19] Cantor's stories about the brutal Lower East Side reminded his audiences that he had traveled a rough road before he found stardom. Cantor and other Jewish actors and songwriters softened their working-class accents and embraced America, but the experiences of Cantor while growing up were very different from those of most middle-class theatergoers. Though Cantor was playing the role of a weak hypochondriac in *Whoopee* when he released *My Life Is in Your Hands*, beneath the stage makeup stood a tough guy.

Throughout his career, Cantor portrayed variations of the rebellious, independent, scrappy Lower East Side kid, suspicious of authority and eager to battle those who stood in his way. Away from the spotlight, he tussled over money and artistic control with the most powerful figures in the industry: network executives, sponsors, theatrical producers, and studio heads. In addition, the writers and supporting talent who worked with Cantor on radio told stories of his egomania and demanding requirements.[20] The longtime announcer Harry von Zell explained that people who worked with Cantor "will say he [Cantor] was sometimes a difficult man. That he sometimes tended to be aggressive and rather stubborn, and rather cantankerous. In all honesty, I have to say that Eddie could be difficult. Eddie was what you'd call a fighter." Von Zell attributed this aspect of Cantor's character to his childhood on the Lower East Side: "What people have to know about a man like Cantor is what makes him a fighter. Here is a man who from the very first day he could react intellectually or emotionally to anything, he had to fight to exist. No mother. No father."[21]

For a typical Lower East Side boy who ended his formal education around the age of thirteen, socially acceptable vehicles for building a career included learning a craft or starting a business. These paths were not open to Cantor, who had no money or apparent skills beyond his gift for gab. The orphan had nobody looking out for him except for a grandmother who could not help him find work. Esther did not have a vocation or business to share, and she did not speak English. She and Eddie talked together in Yiddish. Cantor later spoke the language of Jewish immigrants onstage for a laugh from time to time, but Yiddish was not valuable to him as a teenager.[22] He also lacked the patience and discipline to take an entry-level factory or clerical job and work his way up. For example, having left school, he handled mail at a local insurance company, but was fired two weeks into the job for stealing postage stamps. After this, Cantor remembered, "It took me two years to decide that I wanted another [job]."[23]

Without better options, Cantor half-heartedly attempted to break into show business. He played occasional weddings, bar mitzvahs, and social clubs with a friend, Dan Lipsky, having fun and hoping that amateur performances would lead to professional engagements. The young men wore silly costumes and delivered bits from vaudeville sketches. Always hustling, Cantor supplemented his income at these affairs by suckering grooms into dice games. Cantor used loaded dice. His partner Lipsky soon "deserted the stage for a job in an engineer's office, while I began to flounder once more," Cantor recalled.[24]

In 1908, at age sixteen, Cantor watched cronies such as Lipsky find work while he lived on the streets, slept on tenement roofs, and relied on handouts for his next meal. At the urging of friends, tired of giving him food and money, Cantor decided to try his luck at Miner's Bowery Theater. Built in 1878, Miner's had a reputation for raucous, merciless crowds. The "amateurs" at Miner's and similar small-time venues included low-level professionals who competed for prize money: a modest five dollars and all the loose change they could scoop up from the stage. If the performers failed, they would be pulled offstage with a giant hook. Aspiring vaudevillians hoped that a manager or agent might discover them.[25] Cantor later recalled that Miner's "was my first appearance on a regular stage; it marked a big moment in my life. But all it meant to the Eddie of that time was a hook and a dollar."[26]

By the time of Cantor's stage debut, Izzy preferred the more Americanized "Edward" or "Eddie," and Cantor's Grandma Esther had shortened the family name from "Kantrowitz" to "Cantor." At Miner's and throughout his career, taking the stage as a "cantor" did not hide the actor's ethnicity, but Cantor did not see his Jewish-sounding last name as a liability.[27] At Miner's, his first name was more of a problem. When the announcer introduced him, Cantor remembered hearing "a loud, derisive laugh" because "Edward" sounded feminine to the rough crowd. "Any man whose name wasn't John, Jim, or Harry had no right to live. And here was a thing coming out under the perfumed misnomer of 'Edward' and it probably wore embroidered garters."[28]

Cantor impersonated comedians who were popular locally and had distinctive traits that were easy for the fledgling performer to mimic and his audience to recognize. His repertoire included Cliff Gordon, who made satirical political stump speeches with a German accent; Harry Thompson and Walter Kelly, who performed similar acts as judges presiding over comedic courts; and Junie McCree, who affected the slow drawl of a drug addict.[29] Not surprisingly, given his childhood poverty and his limited opportunities to attend theatrical shows, Cantor had never actually watched these actors. Cantor later recalled that he "had seen their imitators" and gathered his material from them. At the end of the night, Cantor lined up onstage alongside other amateurs who had survived "the hook" given to unsuccessful acts. The announcer pointed to each act, while the crowd voted for the winner with noise and applause. Cantor, the gritty local kid with the girlish name, won the five-dollar prize.[30]

As he thought about how he would earn a living, Cantor recognized that show business offered the most promise. He was not alone. Other Jewish actors and songwriters made a similar calculation. Irving Berlin, George Burns, and Joe Smith and Charlie Dale (Smith and Dale) all grew up on the Lower East Side around the same time as Cantor. George Jessel, the Marx Brothers, Ed Wynn, Al Jolson, Sophie Tucker, and Fanny Brice lived in similar working-class Jewish neighborhoods in New York or other East Coast cities, a half-step up the economic ladder from the Lower East Side. Despite slight differences in their financial status, nobody had much money growing up. They saw people like them working on local stages. Why not try their luck as actors?

Circa 1910, New Yorkers who wanted to break into "show business" worked in the theater industry, which had multiple, ascending levels: amateur hours, burlesque, small-time vaudeville, big-time vaudeville, and the "legitimate" stage revues of Broadway and other large theaters. Each level provided more money and prestige. Singers, dancers, comedians, magicians, and assorted novelty acts clustered in vaudeville, where there was a demand for talent and they could earn a decent living. In 1912, for example, one thousand theaters across the country booked top-line and mid-level vaudeville acts, generating combined annual revenue of $100 million. Another four thousand presented "small-time" entertainers.[31] George Burns, four years younger than Cantor, followed a similar route from the Lower East Side to vaudeville, radio, film, and television. Burns later wrote of vaudeville, "If a performer had fourteen good minutes he could work six years without changing a word or playing the same theater twice."[32] Fledgling entertainers also worked at weddings, saloons, and county fairs.

Working-class kids, especially Jewish and Irish youths, did not flock to the theater out of a burning desire to express themselves artistically. They embraced stage life so they could make money. Though Jews encountered prejudice in other fields, the entertainment business presented few such obstacles. Producers knew that audiences would pay to see skillful performers, regardless of religion or ethnicity. In addition, aspiring actors such as Cantor needed little or no capital to break into show business. Singing and acting jobs paid a little more than other options, such as street peddling and entry-level clerical or service work, and vaudeville dangled the possibility of making big money quickly.[33] Top stars commanded at least $2,500 per week. Even the small-time circuits paid performers between $20 and $150 per week.[34] The Marx Brothers, who began their show business careers around the same time as Cantor, learned about the economic potential of the stage at a young age. Their mother Minnie Marx immigrated to America with her family from Germany as a teenager around 1880. She watched her younger brother, Al Shean, find fame as part of the comedy duo Gallagher and Shean. Driving her sons to pursue careers in show business, Minnie asked, "Where else can people who don't know anything make so much money?"[35]

Novice performers could earn a few dollars onstage as they dreamed of headlining big-time venues, but the lowest rungs of show business did not offer steady work. In between acting jobs, aspiring entertainers such as Cantor and Burns drifted among small clerical, manufacturing, and retail positions.[36] In addition, the road from amateur hours to big-time vaudeville wound through countless small towns and third-rate theaters operated by shifty managers and producers. In 1908, at the age of sixteen, Cantor stood ready to go down this road.

2 A VAUDEVILLE EDUCATION
(1908–1916)

rom 1908 to 1916, Cantor worked his way up from amateur hours through vaudeville to Broadway. As he traveled around the United States and Canada with other actors, and delivered hundreds of performances in different kinds of cities and venues, Cantor learned about the art and the business of popular entertainment. Over these eight years, he also began to develop a distinctive comedy style, which included the use of blackface. Cantor's show business apprenticeship began west of New York City.

In December 1908, Cantor joined a touring company: the producer Frank Carr's *Indian Maidens* burlesque show, which played small towns in Pennsylvania and West Virginia. Cantor earned a decent salary of fifteen dollars a week, though the job with the third-rate production proved to be a rough introduction to professional theater. The road manager absconded with the troupe's money about a month into the tour, leaving Cantor and his fellow actors stranded. Eddie wired his grandmother for the train fare home.[1]

Cantor had recovered from the experience by the summer of 1909, when he worked as a singing waiter at Carey Walsh's saloon on Coney Island. He and the other waiters scampered through the packed restaurant balancing trays full of beer as they fielded requests for popular songs. After living on the streets of the Lower East Side and working low-level amateur shows and burlesque houses, Cantor was not fazed by the rough but manageable crowd at Carey Walsh's. He later explained, "While bottles were thrown occasionally, the guests aimed only at one another, never at the entertainers." Ever sensitive to his audience, Cantor knew that patrons had traveled several hours to reach Coney Island, where they expected a fun-filled time: "They were mostly people who could spare only one day in the week for fun, and they had to get it quick in concentrated doses."[2]

As the tourists shouted requests, Cantor learned to think, and sing, quickly on his feet. "It was a guest's inviolate right to request a particular

Cantor in 1908, as he began his career in show business.
Courtesy of Magic Castle/Milt Larsen.

song, and it was the singing waiter's duty to know it," he wrote.[3] Cantor was accompanied on the piano by Jimmy Durante, a son of Italian immigrants who had also grown up on the Lower East Side. When Cantor and Durante didn't know a song, the two men faked it. Durante improvised a melody, while Cantor energetically made up words to fit the song's title. If a patron called Cantor on the ruse, Cantor innocently asked whether there were two songs with the same title. "The question always planted a doubt in the mind of the guest and he felt compensated," Cantor remembered. "For at least he had heard the mate to his favorite number. It was a good drill in extemporaneous acting and had many variations."[4]

Cantor recalled amassing four hundred dollars working at Carey Walsh's.[5] At age seventeen, for the first time in his life, he had money saved, though the funds did not last very long. When the summer ended, Cantor returned to the Lower East Side from Coney Island and managed to squander his entire bankroll during one very bad evening with the family of Ida Tobias, the woman he wanted to marry. Invited to the wedding of Ida's sister Minnie as Ida's date, the eager young man spared no expense to impress Ida and her father. Eddie arrived in fine clothes, rented an automobile, and freely bought champagne for the guests. Most daringly, he approached David Tobias, Ida's father, about marrying Ida. Knowing that Tobias did not approve of acting, Cantor claimed that he had built his bankroll as a successful restaurant manager, but he still hoped to become a professional performer. Tobias responded with an ultimatum: "If you don't forget acting, you'll have to forget Ida." Tobias further urged Cantor to save enough money to open a men's clothing store. Cantor recalled that he and Ida "barely spoke" as he drove her home in the rental car after Minnie's wedding, because she agreed with her father.[6] Tobias represented the common view among Lower East Side Jews that entrepreneurship represented a more economically viable and socially prestigious means of earning a living than acting. Growing up with Grandma Esther, however, Cantor had been able to ignore these kinds of expectations. Now he had a difficult choice to make: either secure a legitimate job or lose Ida.

Under the influence of Ida and her father to find respectable work, Cantor bounced between entry-level office and clerical positions after he returned from Coney Island at the end of the summer of 1909. He also pursued stage roles without much luck, since his limited experience and repertoire did not match his grand ambitions. In a 1920 interview, one of the first in which Cantor discussed his early career, he recalled trying to approach Broadway producers and theater managers at this time: "I had picked the biggest managers in New York with whom to land a job among the principles in their productions. But I didn't land, not just then."[7]

In 1910 Cantor met George Jessel, who became a lifelong friend, at an audition for *Benches in the Park*, a new play that Gus Edwards was preparing. The composer of popular standards "By the Light of the Silvery Moon" and "School Days," Edwards produced a series of big-time vaudeville shows featuring precocious kids who sang, danced, and joked. Cantor was a scrawny eighteen-year-old who looked younger than his age. Jessel, only twelve, was almost as experienced as Cantor, having appeared at the Imperial Theatre, a movie house in East Harlem that occasionally featured singers such as Jessel and other live vaudeville acts.[8] Edwards was prepared to hire both Jessel and Cantor, but *Benches in the Park* never made it to the stage. Cantor and Jessel occasionally performed on the same bills with different acts in 1910 and 1911, before reuniting on Edwards's *Kid Kabaret* in September 1912.[9]

Soon after the audition for Edwards, Cantor landed a small role with Bedini and Arthur, a well-known novelty act that featured juggling and parodies of more serious plays. In *Madame Ten*, a spoof of the climactic courtroom scene in the melodrama *Madame X*, Cantor played a witness who testified in rapid-fire French. While Jean Bedini and Roy Arthur usually worked as a duo, their production of *Madame Ten* included seven speaking parts plus extra spectators, jurymen, and officers. *Madame Ten* ran for five weeks, from late May through early July 1910, at Hammerstein's Roof Garden theater, one of the top vaudeville venues in Manhattan. Around the time that Cantor joined them, Bedini and Arthur were playing on bills with Gus Edwards's acts. Edwards may have recommended Cantor to Bedini. Cantor reunited with Bedini and Arthur for a longer, more prominent stint the following summer.[10]

Cantor was still looking for regular stage work in February 1911, when the agent Joe Wood gave him an opportunity to perform at small houses in upstate New York. The actor played towns such as Auburn, Utica, Rome, and Mechanicsville, with ticket prices ranging from ten cents to a quarter. At this stage of his career, Cantor's comedy routine consisted of stolen jokes and impressions of better-known vaudevillians. Acts such as Cantor's appealed to small-town audiences that had not seen the originals, and Cantor began to earn short but favorable newspaper reviews and features.[11] An unnamed writer from the *Utica Sunday Tribune* interviewed Cantor, reporting that the young comedian preferred the "intelligent and responsive up-state audiences" over the Broadway crowds "that are eaten up with ennui and too blasé to smile."[12] The article illustrates the willingness of Cantor, or a publicist speaking for him, to ingratiate himself with local audiences. It also reflects Cantor's enthusiasm over his new opportunity to perform a series of shows.

Cantor used the upstate engagements to sharpen his comedy routine before signing with the People's Vaudeville Circuit. Joseph Schenck, who managed People's Vaudeville, emigrated from Russia with his family as a teenager in 1893 and settled on the Lower East Side. Schenck later became a top Hollywood producer and studio executive, but at the time, he ran a string of third-rate theaters in Brooklyn and northern New Jersey. Though the spaces were small and admission was cheap, the work with Schenck was a step up for Cantor because it offered him an opportunity to perform in and around New York, the hub of vaudeville. Cantor played People's Vaudeville from May to July 1911. At Schenck's urging, Cantor freshened his act with new costumes and accents, so that audiences would not tire of him when he returned to the same venues on the small circuit. First Cantor performed with a German accent, then a Jewish one, then in blackface. Of these different stage images, Schenck liked blackface the best.[13]

Blackface was widely accepted in vaudeville. Most performers who came of age during the 1910s—including Cantor, Sophie Tucker, George Burns, and George Jessel—appeared in blackface early in their careers. In addition, such headliners as Al Jolson, Eddie Leonard, and Frank Tinney made blackface central to their stage personas. Theater owners did not fear that their box office would suffer if they offended African-Americans. Many venues did not allow black patrons. Other theaters segregated seating, forcing blacks to enter from back entrances and take seats in upper balconies.[14] Powerless as consumers, blacks were subject to vicious caricatures that presented them as lazy, vain, sexual, primitive, dangerous, and ridiculous. Even vaudevillians such as Cantor, who did not purvey the most noxious stereotypes, sanctioned and perpetuated a performance style that demeaned African-Americans.

The systemic exploitation at the core of blackface is striking to people today. In search of a few laughs and desperate to distinguish themselves from competitors, white actors furthered their careers by donning makeup that exaggerated the looks and behavior of another race of people. In his 1953 chronicle of vaudeville, the former performer and *Variety* columnist Joe Laurie Jr. explained that "working in white face demanded a personality, which many of the guys didn't have, but when blackened up with a big white mouth they looked funny and got over easier."[15] During the 1910s, however, white performers saw the makeup as a benign theatrical convention that enhanced their marketability and public appeal.

Cantor described his early blackface appearance as a combination of happenstance and ambition to present a fresh, modern look. Initially, he worried that the burnt cork makeup would get into his eyes and irritate them. He left "amateurishly large circles" around his eyes, but "out of this blunder was born a new idea." He decided to cover his makeup flaw with a pair of white-rimmed glasses, which accentuated Cantor's naturally wide "banjo eyes" and referenced a popular culture stereotype that rendered blacks ridiculous, childlike, and fearful. Cantor's makeup perpetuated these negative images of African-Americans, and he sometimes played characters that exhibited these traits. But he also softened and altered standard blackface caricatures by revealing his distinctive personality and acting skill beneath the blackface masks. "The spectacles gave me a look of intelligence without straining my face. Unwittingly I had added an intellectual touch to the old-fashioned darky of the minstrel shows," he later explained. "By putting on glasses the sooty spirit of the cotton fields was brought up to the twentieth century. I brought my negro friend up North and tailored him nattily in a wasp-waisted coat, white socks, and patent leathers. There was just a trace of cotton fluff in his ears, but the night-club rhythm danced in his eyes. I leaped with both feet into the new creation."[16] Cantor retained this look when he performed in blackface over the years, but he varied his costume by adding or removing his hat, bow tie, or glasses.

Cantor appeared in a handful of promotional photos and sheet music during the late 1910s and early 1920s holding a banjo, a symbol of South-

Cantor in his standard blackface costume, circa 1917.
Courtesy of UCLA Library Special Collections.

ern minstrelsy, though reviewers do not describe him using this prop onstage. In his vaudeville and Broadway performances, Cantor did not play the banjo, and he rarely sang of the old South. Instead, he developed a sophisticated, original Jewish blackface character. He spoke in his natural, working-class New York accent, but used careful diction and a grandiose vocabulary that contrasted with standard blackface dialect. Moreover, playing against images of blacks as physically aggressive or violent, Cantor's character was alternately effete, cowardly, intellectual, and modern. The actor's dark skin and wide eyes conditioned audiences for a traditional blackface performance, but his speech, clothes, and actions were urban and Jewish.

Cantor was not alone in putting a distinctive stamp on blackface. Under the black cork, most comedians performed "as themselves," without presenting stereotypical black accents, mannerisms, and talk about a mythical South. Looking back on his time in vaudeville, George Burns remembered, "Performers wearing blackface didn't imitate blacks, most of them spoke in their ordinary voices. The only thing that blackface meant was that the person wearing it was working in show business."[17] Joe Laurie Jr. also recalled that blackface comedians simply wore black makeup "and talked 'white.' No dialect, didn't even try, in fact some of them told Hebe [Jewish] stories in blackface."[18]

After Cantor's stint with People's Vaudeville ended in the summer of 1911, his blackface character found a home with Bedini and Arthur. Cantor rejoined the comedy juggling act for nearly a year. Bedini and Arthur performed in the country's largest vaudeville theaters. Jean Bedini, who was in charge of the act, had the novel ability to catch a turnip dropped from 150 feet above him, though he only practiced the trick on occasion. Arthur, in blackface, served as a silent comedian. Cantor made the most of his opportunity to work with them.

Initially, Cantor ran errands for the two men offstage; however, Bedini soon gave the ambitious assistant bit roles, which Cantor milked for laughs. In one skit, Bedini slid a plate off his arm and caught it. Arthur tried to mimic him, smashing the dish. Cantor recalled, "Then I took another plate, slid it down my arm, caught it with ease, and snapped my fingers scornfully at Arthur. Arthur pursued me with a hammer and I exclaimed, 'He means to do me bodily harm!' It was the first time any audience had heard a negro speak such Oxford English, and it was the first line I spoke on the big time. From that moment on, Arthur and I developed into a sissy-bully team, he the boor and I the cultured, pansy-like negro with spectacles."[19]

Bedini gave the unpredictable young comedian freedom to join the act onstage whenever he wanted to do so. Audiences liked Cantor's deadpan recitations of bad poems and his burlesques of female headliners. He wore blackface and women's clothing, delighting the audience when he needed a laugh by dropping his dress. Cantor did not invent this kind of female impersonation and sexual caricature in blackface. It came out of a broader nineteenth-century minstrel tradition. Cantor never indicated that he was aware of this tradition, though Bedini and Arthur had explored female impersonation before Cantor joined the act.[20] While not unique, Cantor's "cultured negro" in drag was novel enough to attract notice in the trade press. A short March 1912 *Variety* review affirmed that the "Bedini and Arthur act with the 'cissy' coon did extremely well."[21] A July 1912 *Variety* piece similarly referenced the "'cissy' in blackface" act.[22]

Cantor was learning to craft roles and performances that held multiple meanings and worked on different levels. On the one hand, Cantor's blackface parodies did not threaten mainstream white audiences. A poor, slight, bug-eyed Jewish kid wearing blackface and a skirt ranked low on the social hierarchy. Audience members could feel superior to Cantor while they watched his antics running from Arthur, parodying the mannerisms of the upper class, or hiking up his skirt. On the other hand, by blending Jewish, blackface, and female impersonation styles, Cantor was difficult to classify and somewhat menacing. He experimented with different identities and behavior that theatergoers dared not try in their own lives. Cantor was starting to build a persona that harnessed the power, energy, and unpredictability of live theater. From the time of his youth, he had a strong rebellious streak. With Bedini and Arthur, Cantor learned that he could become popular while cultivating this tough, anarchic aspect of his personality. He did not have to merely imitate other performers or tame his image for mainstream audiences. Some people might laugh *at* him; others would laugh *with* him. Cantor retained this lesson over the years as he used different roles, especially his evolving Jewish blackface character, to cross barriers and frustrate attempts to classify him according to standard social and cultural categories.[23]

Recognizing Cantor's growing popularity, Bedini retitled the act, "Bedini and Arthur, Assisted by Eddie Cantor" in early 1912.[24] Bedini, a stage veteran, also wrote new material for Cantor. Vaudeville became Cantor's passport to a world well beyond the East Side of Manhattan. As he rode the train from town to town, Cantor grew as an actor and a person. Bedini and Arthur toured as far west as Nebraska and south to New Orleans, playing two shows daily on the national Keith and Orpheum vaudeville circuits. They worked the major houses, including Hammerstein's Victoria in New York. As George Burns, who played similar venues, noted, "The [big-time] theaters were beautiful . . . Everything about the big-time was better; the ticket takers, the backstage crew, the huge orchestra, the acts, even the audience."[25] Whereas growing up, Cantor could barely afford the price of a vaudeville ticket, he now had the opportunity to watch seven or eight new acts at each venue where Bedini and Arthur performed. Cantor observed countless jugglers, acrobats, magicians, singers, comedians, and actors. He shared the stage with headliners such as Eva Tanguay, Harry Houdini, Belle Baker, and Fanny Brice, who later costarred with Cantor in the *Ziegfeld Follies*.[26]

During his early years in vaudeville, Cantor learned how to conduct himself professionally. Whereas such contemporaries as George Jessel and Groucho Marx pepper their memoirs with racy stories of romantic liaisons on the road, Cantor discusses his acting and the costars who helped him improve his craft. While touring the western United States and Canada in 1913, Cantor became friends with Will Rogers, who performed rope tricks on several bills with *Kid Kabaret*. Cantor remembered, "The cowboy was the first guy I'd ever met from west of the Bronx and I worshipped him."[27] Through Rogers, Cantor learned that his New York, Jewish culture held exotic appeal beyond the Lower East Side: "I bought [Rogers] his first kosher meal and showed him strange worlds hidden in the slums that he was intensely interested in but had never seen before. The extreme East and far West met and liked each other."[28] Rogers mentored Cantor four years later when they reunited in the 1917 *Ziegfeld Follies*.

In September 1912, Cantor used his success with Bedini and Arthur as a springboard to a featured role in the producer Gus Edwards's new show, *Kid Kabaret*. Cantor remained with *Kid Kabaret* through April 1914. At age twenty, he was the oldest member of the talented troupe, which featured Jessel and George Price. The cast members, including Cantor, were not well known at the time. People came to the show primarily because of Edwards's reputation as a producer, songwriter, and talent scout. The act's premise: when a boy's parents go out for the evening, the boy, played by Eddie Buzzell, invites his friends over to put on a show. The thirty-seven-minute skit, long by vaudeville standards, mainly showcased the musical talents of the fourteen kids. Cantor, in blackface, played the family's wisecracking butler. "Mine was a good part, there's always sympathy in the theater for anyone in a servile capacity; and when I'd talk back to my little Master Buzzell the audience loved it," Cantor remembered.[29] In one scene, Cantor imitated two more famous blackface performers: Eddie Leonard and emerging star Al Jolson. Cantor received top billing and the most stage time, since his character, the butler, announced each act.[30]

After *Kid Kabaret* concluded its national tour in the summer of 1914, Eddie Cantor and Ida Tobias married. By this time, Cantor had established himself in vaudeville, though he was more familiar to theater managers and show business insiders than he was to audiences. The young actor was working regularly, and he managed to save much of what he earned. He recalled that he purchased a ring for Ida and still had twenty-five hundred dollars in the bank. Yet Ida's father only grudgingly approved of the marriage. He threw the couple a small wedding in the Tobias family apartment. After the wedding, the couple honeymooned in England for a little over a month. Cantor managed to pick up some stage work while he was in London.[31]

When the Cantors returned to America in July 1914, Eddie and Ida moved into a new home: a one-room annex to Ida's sister's apartment in the Bronx. Eddie began to craft a new act, teaming with veteran straight man Al Lee.[32] Cantor and Lee debuted their act, "Master and Man," in October 1914, with Cantor in blackface and Lee in natural makeup. Cantor's new agent, Max Hart, who managed several headliners, united the two actors. Cantor and Lee did not receive top billing in the big-time vaudeville houses that they played across the country from 1914 to 1916. However, they usually earned a few positive lines from reviewers while supporting bigger names, such as Nora Bayes, Eva Tanguay, Frank Fogarty, and Eddie Leonard. As the featured comedian in a two-man act, Cantor attracted more critical attention than in his previous roles with

Bedini and Arthur and *Kid Kabaret*. He had the luxury of performing original material that fit his emerging persona: an oddball Jewish kid from the streets of New York. Cantor combed through popular humor magazines, adapting jokes for the seventeen-minute act. In addition, he purchased material from an established writer, James Madison, who worked with several headliners, including Al Jolson. Cantor and his fellow comedians also knew Madison as the publisher of *Madison's Budget*, a twice-yearly magazine with gags, anecdotes, and sketches that entertainers could use onstage for free.[33]

While other vaudevillians relied on outlandish costumes and accents, Cantor appeared in street clothes, talked in his natural voice, and told jokes that built on everyday experiences. As far as Cantor knew, he was the first blackface comedian to perform "without dialect and without comedy clothes."[34] He started the act with a few minutes of patter about the First World War, which had begun the previous summer, including a joke in which he proudly combined his blackface and Russian Jewish heritage. Alluding to his given name of Iskowitz, Cantor told Lee that with the war on, he was ready to fight for his "mother country, Russia." He explained, "Darkest Russia . . . my relatives are all in the war. My father's General Petrovich, my uncle's General Ivanovich. Then there's eczema—another itch."[35] Routines about funny Russian names did not pass for sharp political satire, even by the polite standards of 1914. However, Cantor's interest in the day's news, which continued throughout his career, distinguished him from many other vaudevillians, who repeated variations on their familiar jokes and routines from one season to the next or stole similar material from other performers. *Variety* appreciated Cantor's topical references, describing the opening "talk on the war" as "pertinent and to the point."[36]

Cantor continued his routine with bits that highlighted his quirkiness. For example, he originated a joke around this time that he often repeated later. His poor father, he explained, was in prison. "After all, no matter how much the boss likes you, you can't work in a bank and bring home samples."[37] On one level, the joke seems silly. Everybody knows it is illegal to steal money from the bank. But, like much of Cantor's humor, the line has a clever twist, as the audience pauses to connect "samples" to "stolen money." Cantor's delivery left little time for reflection. The rapid talker with a working-class New York accent embodied the image of the kind of slick city kid who really could have a parent in prison.

As he had with Bedini and Arthur, Cantor served as an anarchic presence onstage, interrupting Lee's singing with jokes and non sequiturs. Cantor later described his role as "strictly a nut act." When it was his turn to sing, he chose novelty pop songs, such as "The War in Snyder's Grocery Store" and "Down in Bom-Bom Bay," sometimes adding his own comical lyrics.[38] An appreciative *Variety* reviewer interpreted Cantor's off-kilter approach as "cissy stuff,'" explaining that it was "unusual in blackface." The critic concluded that Cantor helmed a "good comedy act, and out of the beaten rut."[39] Others also recognized Cantor's use of blackface as the act's most distinctive and successful comedy device. The *New York Clipper* described Cantor as "the funniest blackface working the vaudeville thing today."[40]

Cantor used his reputation as a blackface performer to graduate from vaudeville in 1916. The producer Oliver Morosco gave Cantor a small part in a new production, *Canary Cottage*, slated for the more prestigious "legitimate" musical theater. In the bedroom farce, Cantor played a chauffeur, described in one review as "the negro with the exquisite vocabulary," a character similar to his blackface roles in vaudeville.[41] *Canary Cottage* played on the West Coast for several months, starting in May 1916, before moving to New York. On February 5, 1917, *Canary Cottage* opened on Broadway, where it served as the inaugural production for the new, 1,009-seat Morosco Theater. By the time *Canary Cottage* reached Manhattan, Cantor was no longer with the show. Instead, he was onstage three blocks away from the Morosco, presenting a solo act at the New Amsterdam Theatre and working for America's top producer, Florenz Ziegfeld.[42]

3 THE JEWISH WISE GUY
(1916–1919)

uring the 1910s and 1920s, Florenz Ziegfeld's annual *Follies* and a companion show, the rooftop *Midnight Frolic*, delighted audiences with beautiful girls, spectacular sets, sophisticated sketches, and witty musical numbers. Ziegfeld also had a knack for spotting talent and poaching promising entertainers from lesser Broadway and vaudeville outfits. When Cantor joined the *Midnight Frolic* in October 1916, Bert Williams, Fanny Brice, W. C. Fields, and Will Rogers were featured players in the *Follies*.

The *Midnight Frolic* followed the revue format of the *Follies*, though it was shorter: a little under two hours, compared with the three-hour *Follies*. For the *Midnight Frolic*, Ziegfeld transformed the garden atop the New Amsterdam Theatre into a lavish nightclub. The spectacular set designer Joseph Urban's "magnificent draperies of yellow formed a canopy of gold over the main floor."[1] After taking in the *Follies* downstairs at the New Amsterdam, theatergoers could order drinks and a late supper while they indulged in a more intimate performance featuring a new set of chorus girls and comedians at the *Midnight Frolic*.

Before his big Ziegfeld debut on October 2, 1916, Cantor waited outside the theater "just breathing the air, watching the swells ride up in their Rolls-Royces. The broadcloth gleams, the jewels shine. These people are all going up on the Roof. They're my audience! Let me at 'em!"[2] Tickets to the rooftop, advertised as "The Meeting Place of the World," started at an expensive two dollars, with the better seats costing three dollars each. Ziegfeld reserved tables near the stage for VIPs, who enjoyed making splashy entrances.[3]

Despite the hefty ticket prices, the audience for Ziegfeld's shows included a variety of patrons who liked top-flight comedy, music, dancing girls, and the freedom that a night on the town offered. Tourists and socialites sat alongside gangsters and adulterers. Fostering a licentious atmosphere on stage and off, Ziegfeld's publicists spoke of the "businessmen" in the audience. These men experienced Broadway while their families stayed home or vacationed outside the city. Dangling the possibility that the couple sitting together in the next row might not be married (to each other), Ziegfeld even included a sketch in the 1920 *Ziegfeld Follies* depicting a "tired businessman" and the "girl with him" bantering about the show.[4] Given the expectations of theatergoers, Ziegfeld had the latitude to be brash and risqué. But the producer still had to be careful and could not be too aggressive in challenging genteel sensibilities. While he was with Ziegfeld, Cantor learned to craft popular performances strategically so that he could appeal to multiple audiences and tastes. Cantor employed these lessons throughout his career.

The two-part *Midnight Frolic*, in which Cantor made his Broadway debut, lasted until 1:45 in the morning. It featured seventeen scenes, most of them filled with flirtatious chorines singing, dancing, and thrilling the patrons gawking from nearby tables. The show included one nonmusical scene, described in the program only as "A New Nut." Even though he was not named in the program, Cantor fearlessly worked the crowd. He flaunted his background as a brazen Jewish wise guy from the city streets, a little rough around the edges, but funny and talented. With his slight build and unassuming appearance, Cantor joked about his anonymity while acknowledging his working-class accent and attitude. He started his routine, "Ladies and gentlemen, I'm not a regular actor. I work for a plumber in Hastings and yesterday something went wrong with the plumbing at Mr. Ziegfeld's house. He heard me singing in the bathroom and thought this would be a good gag. So it doesn't matter if you applaud or not. Tomorrow I go back to plumbing."[5]

After telling a few jokes, Cantor removed three cards from a deck and chose audience members to hold the cards high above their heads. Cantor's assistants were three prominent Broadway figures: William Randolph Hearst, Diamond Jim Brady, and Charles Dillingham, a producer who sometimes partnered with Ziegfeld. The power brokers continued to hold their cards awkwardly as the blackface Jewish comedian demonstrated his command of the room by strumming a broken ukulele and singing endless choruses of "Oh How She Could Yacki Hicki Wicki Wacky Woo," a risqué novelty song about a "hula" girl in Honolulu. Cantor remembered, "The audience began to howl, realizing that the cards had nothing to do with the act . . . I'd taken a big chance; it'd worked. As

I gathered up the cards the greatest thing in the world was happening —applause! I had stopped the show!" Lest there be any doubt about his humble, slightly disreputable origins, Cantor ended the routine with the self-deprecating, clever joke from his vaudeville act about his father stealing samples from the bank.[6] The irreverent little Jewish guy from the streets of the city won over an opening night crowd by teasing the most socially prominent audience members. Many in the audience knew the Lower East Side through photographs, newspaper articles, and sociological reports on crime and poverty by such urban reformers as Jacob Riis and Lewis Hine. The crowd expected Cantor to be tough. He didn't disappoint them.

Vaudeville performers such as Cantor, though experienced in playing big theaters, toiled beneath the cultural radar of Broadway's critics and patrons. When he made his Ziegfeld debut, the "new nut" did not merit more than a line or two in opening night reviews of the show. Critics did not reference Cantor's previous stage appearances or his card trick with the distinguished theater patrons, though the *Dramatic Mirror* reported that Hearst "beamed with his customary good nature" throughout the *Midnight Frolic*.[7] The lavish sets and graceful Ziegfeld girls commanded more critical attention, but Cantor established his place in the show through his wit and energy. As in vaudeville, critics noted Cantor's similarity to Al Jolson, who, in 1916, was starring in *Robinson Crusoe Jr.*, which featured a Hawaiian novelty song, "Yacka Hula Hickey Dula," like the one that Cantor performed in the *Midnight Frolic*. The comparisons to Jolson helped Cantor. Given Jolson's enormous popularity, and his long-term contract with the rival Shubert outfit, Ziegfeld saw the value in signing a similar Jewish blackface singer-comedian. Cantor's seemingly spontaneous jokes and easy interactions with the audience also evoked less-obvious comparisons to Will Rogers, who starred in the *Midnight Frolic* of 1915 before joining the *Follies* the next year. By 1916 Rogers was known more for his topical monologues, and occasional verbal sparring with celebrities in the audience, than for the rope tricks that he performed in vaudeville when Cantor first met him three years earlier. Cantor later remembered that he learned the importance of updating his act with topical jokes from watching Rogers during this time.[8]

Cantor's slot on the bill was a tryout. Before opening night, the actor had not yet secured a long-term contract. The young performer did not remain a free agent. The day after his *Midnight Frolic* debut, Cantor received a telegram from Ziegfeld: "Enjoyed your act, you'll be here a long time."[9] Cantor played the roof for twenty-seven weeks, and then moved into the *Ziegfeld Follies* when the new edition opened in the summer of 1917. He signed a two-year contract with Ziegfeld, earning four hundred dollars a week plus considerable "side income" playing parties all over Manhattan. "One night I would entertain at the Vanderbilt home, and the next night at a Bronx lodge dinner," Cantor recalled. "It was excellent drill at impromptu performance and swift adaptation to surroundings."[10] Cantor and his family, which now included his wife, Ida, and two daughters, Marjorie (born 1915) and Natalie (born 1916), could move from the apartment they shared with Ida's sister in the Bronx to their own space nearby. Over time the homes would grow bigger, as would Cantor's family, which numbered five daughters after the births of Edna (1919), Marilyn (1921), and Janet (1927).

In January 1917, when Cantor was still with the *Midnight Frolic*, Esther Kantrowitz died. Eddie made contributions in his grandmother's memory to the Jewish Hospital of Brooklyn, ensuring that "some equally poor and destitute soul may get the relief that was denied her."[11] He also took out small display advertisements in *Variety* on the anniversary of Esther's death and around Yom Kippur, modifying the traditional Jewish practice requiring children to recite the Mourner's Kaddish prayer in synagogue on the anniversary of a parent's death and to participate in a Yizkor memorial service each year on major holidays.[12] Yizkor advertisements in *Variety*, which other actors also purchased, epitomized the way performers balanced religious and secular practices. Jewish actors were not an observant lot, but most were familiar with Judaic law and felt a connection to the religion. They referenced holidays or rituals, such as Yizkor memorials, talking among themselves or on the insider pages of *Variety*, but did not speak about Judaism as openly on vaudeville or Broadway stages during the late 1910s. Non-Jewish audiences did not know enough about Judaism, and these theatergoers wanted entertainment that spoke to them more directly. Cantor did not mention the death of Esther or pay tribute to his immigrant grandmother from the stage in 1917. Starting with his 1928 autobiography, however, he frequently wrote about her strength and kindness. He also expressed

Cantor shares a copy of his autobiography, *My Life Is in Your Hands* (1928), with Florenz Ziegfeld.

regret that Esther "never had the satisfaction of knowing I had attained a measure of success."[13]

The 1917 *Ziegfeld Follies* celebrated the pleasures of urban America. The show began with an "Arabian Nights" sketch, featuring a harem of chorus girls in skimpy costumes, as a young man bets his future father-in-law that New York offers more excitement in a day than Baghdad does in 101 nights. The revue continued with a series of dance numbers, sketches, and solo star performances, some more connected to the New York theme than others. Cantor, Bert Williams, Fanny Brice, and Will Rogers each chose music or delivered monologues for their own "specialties," solo scenes of approximately ten minutes each, performed in front of the curtain while the stage crew changed the elaborate sets.

The spectacular finale to the first act, "The Episode of Patriotism," featured Gene Buck and Victor Herbert's rousing "Can't You Hear Your Country Calling." It drew more critical attention than any comedy sketch. With the United States having entered the war in Europe in April 1917, a little over two months before the *Ziegfeld Follies* premiered on Broadway, the timely "Can't You Hear Your Country Calling" urges the audience to "answer the call" and "fight for peace." Paul Revere rides a white horse across the stage, joining George Washington, Woodrow Wilson, and chorus girls representing the Allied nations. The number closes with a fleet of battleships moving forward toward the audience. The orchestra plays "The Star-Spangled Banner," and an enormous American flag unfurls across the ceiling of the vast auditorium. Cantor did not appear in this scene, but he absorbed Ziegfeld's lesson that audiences and critics liked a little patriotism mixed with their risqué songs and routines.[14]

Cantor and Fanny Brice performed a song-and-dance duet, "Just You and Me." While wearing blackface, the two Jewish stars from New York promise each other: "Through the cotton fields we'll wander. Happy we will be. Soon the wedding bells will chime, for just you and me." The number generated little critical attention, perhaps because it cast the comedians in ill-suited straight rolls, as Southern blacks, singing an unremarkable romantic ballad. The sketch marked the only time in her long stage career that Brice appeared in blackface. While Cantor was more comfortable in blackface, which he also wore in his other sketches, he rarely performed these kinds of Southern plantation songs.[15]

For his solo set, Cantor chose "The Modern Maiden's Prayer" and "That's the Kind of a Baby for Me." The two light, topical numbers commented on the modern, autonomous "new woman," no longer content with domesticity. Cantor soon recorded both songs for Victor records. In his working-class New York accent, Cantor delivered a Jewish street kid's response to the more traditional, innocent Victorian songs of cuddling, courtship, and marriage, such as "Pretty Baby" (1916) and "Me and My Gal" (1917), which remained popular.[16] With his slight appearance, big eyes, and youthful demeanor, Cantor seemed innocent. Yet his well-timed cynicism and surprisingly sexual innuendo let audiences know that he was not as chaste and pristine as he seemed.

Of Cantor's two songs, "That's the Kind of a Baby for Me," by the journeymen songwriters J. C. Egan and Alfred Harriman, made the biggest splash. Cantor's performance brought the act to "a riotous finish," according to *Variety*.[17] In February 1918, when Cantor was still singing "That's the Kind of a Baby for Me" on a national tour of the *Follies*, the song's publishers purchased a *Variety* advertisement quoting the great Ziegfeld himself: "'That's the Kind of a Baby for Me' was not only an instantaneous hit on the opening night of the Follies, but the greatest hit the *Ziegfeld Follies* has ever had."[18] As rendered by his newest star, the song epitomized the world that Ziegfeld created in the *Follies*. Cantor and Ziegfeld gleefully disregarded the typical Victorian middle-class emphasis on thrift, self-denial, and chastity.[19]

In "That's the Kind of a Baby for Me," Cantor surveys the New York nightlife of gold diggers, kept men, racial segregation, and conspicuous consumption. Cantor describes a new neighbor in his apartment building. Her "dreamy eyes" have "made a hit" with him. The singer goes around town with this wealthy and "awfully wild" lady. He appreciates the modern woman's independence. She pays for their evenings out at Broadway shows and nightclubs. The sources of her money: alimony checks and a rich father. Cantor can barely contain his excitement. On the recording, his voice cracks at one point. Elsewhere, the nasal, New York–accented delivery flies off key, stretching "baby" into a short yodel. By the end of the song, Cantor is positively gleeful over his good fortune as the woman takes him for a ride in her limousine.[20]

Cantor's light song pokes fun at popular fears and stereotypes of both black and Jewish sexuality. The short, hyperactive Jewish actor in blackface costume hardly fit the popular ideal of the dapper, handsome playboy. Cantor's romp around the city with a high-society divorcée took nerve and violated sexual taboos. Given the racial prejudice and segregation on Broadway and throughout the city, Cantor's character would not have dared to be seen around town with a wealthy white woman in real life.[21]

In his music and comedy sketches, Cantor frequently inserted himself into places where Jews were not always welcome: tony nightclubs, corporate boardrooms, and the Old West. He used these fantasies of breaking social barriers to reveal discriminatory mores and practices. Fanny Brice was a model and a mentor for this kind of humor. For example, in Brice's solo scene from the 1917 *Follies*, she posed as a "Yiddish-Egyptian maid" to parody the modern dancer Ruth St. Denis. In other celebrated songs and sketches during the late 1910s and early 1920s, Brice played a Jewish Indian ("I'm an Indian," 1918), a Jewish art model ("Rose of Washington Square," 1920), and a Jewish ballet dancer ("Becky Is Back in the Ballet," 1922). Together, Brice and Cantor presented a fresh style of Jewish comedy that occasionally exaggerated Jewish mannerisms or perpetuated stereotypes, but also challenged audience members who were uncomfortable with Jews.[22]

The key to the success of "That's the Kind of a Baby for Me," Cantor remembered, was that "he had adopted a fast, lighting style of song delivery."[23] The satirical observations flew by quickly in his unbridled performances from this time, allowing Cantor to sneak in sexual innuendo and, later, political commentary or Jewish jokes. Audience members didn't have a chance to become angry or offended. Cantor's snappy singing and dancing distinguished him from other performers and became essential to his charm and appeal. The charismatic actor provided a jolt of chaotic, anarchic energy, in contrast to the more measured routines that surrounded him in the revues.

In addition to the two songs in his "specialty" set, Cantor costarred in a sketch with Bert Williams, a *Follies* veteran. Born in the British West Indies, Williams's family immigrated to New York City when Williams was a child. Darkening his skin with blackface makeup, the singer and comedian starred in several editions of the *Ziegfeld Follies*, beginning in 1910. Cantor's association with Williams, known for his sophistication on and off the stage, inverted the typical racial roles of the time, with Cantor, the eager apprentice, learning about comic timing and the power of understatement from the stage master. Cantor appreciated the opportunity to watch and work with Williams every night. He later wrote of Williams, "As a performer, he was close to a genius. As a man, he was everything the rest of us would like to have been." Cantor viewed his friend and mentor as a "master of pantomime," who taught him about physical comedy. He explained that Williams "was a miser with gestures, never raising his hand six inches if three would suffice."[24]

In his 1917 *Follies* skit with Williams, Cantor returned to what he described as his "cissy blackface" character. Williams, a porter at Grand Central Station, awaits the arrival of his son Cantor, a college football star. Cantor remembered, "After these fond expectations, I entered, slight and effeminate, with white-rimmed glasses and mincing step." Cantor speaks to Williams in a "girlish treble" and shows off the latest dance steps, to the dismay of Williams.[25] In addition to presenting a different kind of blackface character from the young man-about-town of Cantor's solo act, the sketch satirized the college experience. Cantor's portrait of a shallow, dim college boy suggests that kids attended college to date, dance, and party—a common concern during the 1920s.[26]

Following the New York run in the summer of 1917, the entire Ziegfeld Follies company embarked on the show's annual tour, covering fifteen cities in the East, Midwest, and Canada through April 1918. The show played to capacity audiences, even though most seats cost $2.50, top dollar at the time.[27] On tour, Cantor contributed to the *Follies'* patriotic theme by adding "The Dixie Volunteers," a new song by Edgar Leslie and Harry Ruby. Leslie was best known at that time for co-writing the lyrics to "For Me and My Gal." Ruby, age twenty-two, played piano in vaudeville while trying to establish himself as a songwriter.[28] Both composers had grown up in New York and worked on Tin Pan Alley, but that did not stop them from writing a paean to the Southern soldier preparing for war in the proud tradition of "fighting men like Stonewall Jackson and like Robert E. Lee." The nostalgic myth of the brave, honorable Southerner who fought nobly to protect his region's institutions dominated public discourse about the war and its legacy during the 1910s. The country celebrated the semicentennial of the Civil War with a series of reunions and exhibitions. Surviving black soldiers had no place in these national commemorations. For example, the historian David Blight described the large 1913 Gettysburg event as a "Jim Crow reunion, and white supremacy might be said to have been the silent, invisible master of ceremonies."[29]

In "The Dixie Volunteers" Cantor uses his blackface makeup and rebellious image to remind audiences that not everybody had a say in the recent commemorations of the Old South. As with much of Cantor's stage work during this time, the satire is nuanced. The actor leaves room for different interpretations. On a literal level, playgoers could enjoy

"The Dixie Volunteers" as a simple patriotic song. But in his persona as a modern wise guy with a sharp sense of irony, Cantor also prepares his audience not to take him literally. Singing in a New York accent, Cantor praises the "peaceful sons" of the South heroically enlisting to fight in World War I. The incongruous sight of the slight blackface comedian from the Lower East Side "giving three cheers to the Dixie volunteers," probably while playfully rolling his big eyes, presents a different perspective on the history and legacy of the Southern military ideal.[30]

After touring with his first *Ziegfeld Follies*, Cantor returned for the 1918 edition, along with Fields and Rogers, joining new costars Ann Pennington and Marilyn Miller. The *Follies* opened on Broadway on June 18, 1918, and went on the standard national circuit from September 1918 to May 1919. As in 1917, Cantor sang two songs and delivered a short monologue during his solo act, titled "Fresh from the Bronx," an allusion to his newcomer status as well as the New York borough with a large Jewish population.[31] "But after the Ball Was Over," Cantor's risqué opening night song, tells the story of a young man who has his choice of female company at the end of the night, despite his apparent lack of social skills: "In the hall at the ball he would sit all alone / But every night the girls would fight to take him home."[32] *Variety*'s Sime Silverman praised Cantor's "personality" and style, asserting that "as far as comedians go, he is the backbone and hit of the show."[33]

Cantor also earned universal praise for his comedy in another skit, "The Aviator's Test." He plays a weak young military recruit at an entrance exam. The performance enabled Cantor to showcase his skills at using his flexible body for laughs. Cantor remembered, "I received a grueling physical examination at the hands of Frank Carter. He whacked and banged me, clapped me together and pulled me apart like an accordion and did everything but twine me around like a spool. It was the first physical comedy scene I ever played and turned out to be the biggest hit of the show."[34]

Cantor did not use blackface in "The Aviator's Test." Instead, he appeared in standard theatrical makeup and clothes, which accentuated his natural skin tone and features. Cantor and the press referred to this natural image as "whiteface" to distinguish it from blackface.[35] This whiteface look expanded Cantor's acting repertoire by freeing him to develop a fresh set of facial and body movements and to play different

The star-filled cast of the 1918 *Ziegfeld Follies*. From left: W. C. Fields, Will Rogers, Lillian Lorraine, Cantor, and Harry Kelly. Courtesy of Magic Castle / Milt Larsen.

kinds of characters. Cantor appreciated the importance of appearing onstage without blackface for the first time since 1911. Always willing to take chances in new roles and media, Cantor realized that he needed to expand his repertoire and change his image. He had resolved that "old Black-face must die. In a moment of emergency, I had put on his dark mask and he had helped me to success. Now the audience knew only this cork-smeared face, while I stood hidden behind it wondering what would happen if the blacking came off." Ziegfeld initially did not want Cantor to shed his familiar makeup. The producer relented only after Cantor threatened to quit the show. When he took the stage in whiteface, Cantor recalled, "It was the first time that I felt revealed to the audience and in personal contact with it."[36]

Though "The Aviator's Test" represented a career-changing opportunity for Cantor because he performed in natural whiteface makeup, most critics did not note the change in his appearance. Here, as in other productions during this time, reviewers were more interested in Cantor's characterizations, songs, and overall delivery. It was not unusual for *Ziegfeld Follies* stars to change their looks over the course of a show. Rogers, for example, also had a blackface turn in the 1918 *Follies*, as did Brice in the previous year's edition. In addition, blackface was only one element of Cantor's stage persona. His funny, charismatic performance as the prospective aviator overshadowed the recognition, by critics and audience members alike, that the scene was an important departure. Reviewers praised the sketch's "good, rollicking, belly-shaking slapstick" and topical parody of "Uncle Sam's new rigid tests for the flying men."[37]

Cantor saw "The Aviator's Test" as a model for one of his most celebrated scenes, "At the Osteopath's," which debuted in June 1919 as part of the new edition of the *Follies*. Cantor wrote the routine with Rennold Wolf, his collaborator on "The Aviator's Test," and used it as a reliable crowd-pleaser in later plays, films, radio, and television programs through the early 1950s, when the physical demands of the sketch became too great.[38] In whiteface, Cantor portrays Percival Fingersnapper, a young man who visits a shady, sadistic osteopath, Dr. Cheeseborough Simpson, played by veteran straight man George LeMaire (born Meyer Goldstick).[39] Dr. Simpson interviews Percival and then adjusts him in a raucous scene.

As with the aviator sketch, "At the Osteopath's" combines topical satire, witty dialogue, and daring physical comedy. Critics recognized the skit as a "burlesque of osteopathy treatment," which had grown in popularity during the early twentieth century.[40] The unconventional practice promoted natural healing and promised that back treatments could cure a host of maladies and illnesses. Osteopathy lacked credibility among many authorities, including the American Medical Association, the federal government, and the military, which refused to commission osteopaths as medical officers during World War I.[41] As a practitioner of alternative medicine and a dubious figure in the eyes of many audience members, the osteopath served as an ideal comic foil for the typical Cantor character, toggling between innocence and street savviness.

Even as Dr. Simpson bends and twists him during "At the Osteopath's," Cantor is quick with a knowing wisecrack. During the examination, Dr. Simpson asks Cantor's character, Percival, "How are the joints?" When he hears "joints," Percival immediately thinks of night-clubs, rather than his body: "I don't know. I am a stranger in town." Percival ogles the pretty office stenographer but does not seem choosy. Dr. Simpson offers Percival advice for managing headaches. "Why don't you do as I do?" suggests the doctor. "When I have a headache I go home and my wife kisses me, the headache disappears." Percival replies, "What time will your wife be home?" As the patient submits to the treatment, and the two men roll around together in a slapstick wrestling match, Percival exclaims to the doctor, "Kiss me!" The command only causes additional tussling and pain for Cantor's character.[42]

Is Percival gay? Is he straight? Is he looking for a quick fling or something more lasting? Cantor made this kind of ambiguous sexuality central to his stage and film roles through the mid-1930s. He frequently portrayed effeminate, unmarried characters who flirted with both men and women, sometimes while wearing dresses. Within a particular play or even a scene, he would swing from the naïve and bashful young man, unaware that he is the object of somebody's affection, to the joyful, hungry hedonist. From the time that he emerged as a "nut job" on vaudeville, featuring a "Jewish blackface" character, Cantor challenged popular expectations and defied easy classifications. By masquerading as a black, Jewish, gay man, Cantor signaled his identification with social outsiders and his refusal to assimilate into white, middle-class Victorian culture.[43] Yet these masquerades usually lasted for only a short scene or even a quick line or two before Cantor switched to another persona more compatible with social conventions.

Through his shifting stage identities, Cantor demonstrated his playfulness before middle-class audiences that enjoyed risqué, transgressive humor onstage.[44] The actor's flirtations with homosexuality and bisexuality anticipated the "pansy craze" of the late 1920s and early 1930s. Audiences flocked to Broadway plays and nightclubs featuring shows with gay characters and scenes. The historian George Chauncey tied the new, widespread acceptance of gay subculture to Prohibition. The Eighteenth Amendment prohibiting the sale of alcohol was ratified in 1919 and began to be enforced under the Volstead Act in 1920, creating a social world of speakeasies and illegal drinking. Middle-class people demonstrated their sophistication and distinguished themselves from narrow-minded Prohibitionists by embracing "transgressive" urban nightlife.[45] Even before Prohibition went into effect, Cantor and Ziegfeld recognized that theatergoers out on the town at the *Ziegfeld Follies* were receptive to unconventional perspectives on morality and sexuality.

Cantor's effeminate jokes and mannerisms built on stereotypes not only of homosexuals, but also of overly intellectual emasculated Jewish men.[46] With "The Aviator's Test" and "At the Osteopath's," Cantor presented two similar stock characters from Jewish folk culture: the *schlemiel* and the *nebbish*. These figures are hapless, simple, clumsy, inept victims. As the literary scholar Ruth Wisse explained, the schlemiel's masculinity is "thoroughly extinct. The traditional male virtues such as strength, courage, pride, and fortitude are prominent only in their absence." The nebbish, described by the writer Leo Rosten alternately as the "twin brother" and "first cousin" of the schlemiel, is a "nonentity." A nebbish, writes Rosten, "is the kind of person who always picks up what a shlemiel knocks over."[47] More than any other comedian of the 1920s and 1930s, Cantor brought these archetypes to American popular culture, where they have continued to circulate and influence later performers, such as Jerry Lewis, Woody Allen, Rick Moranis, and Jason Alexander.

Some audience members may have laughed at Cantor's weak Jewish man being pummeled onstage. However, Cantor also subverted this stereotype. In "At the Osteopath's" and other stage roles through *Whoopee*, he made the nebbish attractive, especially in contrast to the dim, nasty, corrupt brutes who served as his antagonists. Rather than ridiculing his nebbishes, Cantor's playful, empathetic characterizations invited the audience to laugh along with him. Cantor mitigated his nebbish roles with self-reflexive distancing devices. He breaks character in "At the Osteopath's" by making wisecracks in the midst of the chaotic beating, reminding the audience that he is really okay and the skit is all in good fun. In discussing the appeal of "At the Osteopath's" and similar scenes, Cantor later observed, "Audiences love to see somebody knocked and battered about to the point of insensibility so long as they feel he isn't really getting hurt. But if they suspect that the punishment has passed the point of fun, they suddenly stop laughing and even show resentment."[48] For the poor orphan who grew up learning that he could win people's sympathies and admiration with stories of resilience in the face of adversity, the nebbish with flashes of *chutzpah*, or nerve, put money in the bank.

The contortions, tumbles, and snappy comments drew attention to Cantor's versatile acting skills and reestablished his masculinity. Somebody that talented and funny could hardly be a schlemiel. Cantor won universal praise for his physical comedy in "At the Osteopath's." The critic Heywood Broun described the scene as "furiously amusing all the time. It was perhaps as fine a slapstick sketch as we have ever seen in the theater." John Corbin, a drama critic for the *New York Times*, observed that Cantor was "uproariously acclaimed by the audience and never failed to delight his admirers."[49]

In "At the Osteopath's" and his other *Follies* roles, Cantor gave his characters a sly sexual appeal that undercut the image of the hapless schlemiel. The star perfected his "innocently lecherous character," as described by the music historians Philip Furia and Michael Lasser, in his specialty act from the *Ziegfeld Follies* of 1919, performed in blackface. Cantor sang the topical, fast-paced "You Don't Need the Wine to Have a Wonderful Time" by Harry Akst and Howard E. Rogers, a response to the ratification of the Eighteenth Amendment. It was one of several Broadway show tunes mocking the idea that conservative legislators could stop the rollicking good times in the city. Cantor's character sings of his preference for women over cocktails: "Lots of people like a cordial after dessert, but give me something cordial that is wrapped in a skirt." The *New York Evening Sun* critic quoted the line approvingly. With his knowing smile, rolling eyes, and sly vocals, Cantor made these songs seem sexual and dangerous, though the lyrics still fell within socially acceptable boundaries. During this phase of his career, under the tutelage of Ziegfeld and a stable of creative and experienced writers, Cantor mastered the art of sexual innuendo.[50]

Irving Berlin's "You'd Be Surprised," Cantor's other song from the specialty segment, was a perfect fit for his persona as the young man who was not as innocent as he seemed. Indulging his taste for comedy that upended audience expectations, Cantor tells a risqué story about the unassuming Johnny and his girlfriend, Mary. Johnny doesn't have much going for him in terms of looks or brains. When Mary's friends wonder why she is with him, she slyly endorses Johnny's hidden qualities as a lover. A typical line is, "He isn't much as a dance, but when he's taking you home / You'd be surprised." Since "advertising pays," soon Johnny is very popular, and Mary's friends have similar explanations for their affection toward Johnny: "He isn't much in the light, but when he gets in the dark / You'd be surprised."[51]

Cantor allowed Berlin to help him with the song's delivery before the opening. The two Lower East Side natives had been friends since Cantor emerged from the *Midnight Frolic* in 1916. Always eager to test material and gauge audience reaction before he opened a show, Cantor took the initiative to secure bookings under assumed names in uptown theaters, so that he could "spot the deadwood and eliminate it." Berlin attended one of these shows. "At this time, I still sang every song running up and down the stage," Cantor remembered. Berlin advised Cantor not to move so much when delivering the new song. Instead, Cantor relied on his big eyes and shocked facial expression to deliver the punchline, "You'd be surprised." He also enhanced the song's deadpan, risqué humor by lingering over the lyrics, stretching out words such as "surprised," and singing about Johnny's charms from Mary's perspective.[52]

"You'd Be Surprised" became one of Cantor's biggest hits and one of the most popular songs of late 1919 and early 1920, selling nearly nine hundred thousand records and eight hundred thousand pieces of sheet music.[53] It was also one of the last songs he would sing in the *Ziegfeld Follies* until 1923. At the height of his popularity, in August 1919, Cantor became active in the Actors' Equity strike against Ziegfeld and other theater owners. The strike contributed to a rift between the famed producer and his biggest star.

4   A SNAPPY HEADLINER
(1919–1923)

o protect themselves from exploitative theater managers, a group of 112 actors formed the Actors' Equity Association (AEA or "Equity") in 1913. Even with their new organization, the performers were unable to win significant concessions from the main organization of theater owners and producers: the Producing Managers' Association (PMA). The actors' demands included the recognition of Equity and extra pay for Sunday and holiday matinee performances. In the summer of 1919, Equity members affiliated with the American Federation of Labor (AFL) and voted to strike any theater affiliated with the PMA. The strike began on August 6, 1919, and quickly built momentum over the next two weeks, as one New York venue after another closed. Cantor, elected to Equity's leadership council in November 1918, initiated a walkout of the *Ziegfeld Follies*, enlisting costars Van and Schenck, Eddie Dowling, and Ray Dooley to join him. The New Amsterdam Theatre, home of the *Follies*, went dark on Wednesday, August 13. While Ziegfeld threatened to mount a new edition of the *Follies* without these headliners, the AFL called on other theatrical workers to strike along with the actors.[1] Cantor later explained, "The *Follies* had to close. Even if they could have put on a show without us, the AF of L had joined the strike and tied up the stagehands and electricians." A furious Ziegfeld served the striking stars with a series of injunctions and lawsuits, but he could not force them back to the stage.[2]

Cantor responded by affirming his alignment with the union, evoking his Lower East Side roots: "I am with the Equity Association and will go back to the cloak and suit trade if they lose in their fight against the manager."[3] As the strike continued, Cantor positioned himself alongside the rank-and-file workers, despite his high salary and the risks to his career. At an August 18, 1919, Equity benefit show, he recited a short poem illustrating his pro-union allegiances: "Ashes to ashes and dust to dust, tell me the manager actors can trust."[4] Cantor had little to gain financially from the union's efforts to achieve recognition and improve basic wages and working conditions. He later wrote, "There was no question of personal profit. It was a spirited movement to elevate the profession as a whole, and the more fortunate actors made sacrifices freely that their less fortunate associates should gain a measure of protection."[5]

For the first time, Cantor used his position as a celebrity to promote an offstage social issue. He demonstrated an ethos forged on the streets of New York growing up: sympathy for the underdog, bitter anger at the indignities of poverty, and loyalty to his peer group, which had evolved from his neighborhood "gang" to the everyday actors with whom he shared the stage. Shortly before he went on strike, Cantor demonstrated this working-class solidarity: "Mr. Ziegfeld and [the producer A. L.] Mr. Erlanger are fine men, and they pay me a lovely salary, but they don't associate with me. The people who associate with me call me 'scab.'"[6]

As the labor action evolved into street theater and attracted attention in daily newspapers and the trade press, Cantor led the media-savvy actors in parades, impromptu demonstrations, and benefit performances. The AEA held nightly shows at the Lexington Theater featuring a revolving cast of America's biggest theatrical stars, including Cantor, Ethel Barrymore, Lionel Barrymore, Marie Dressler, Frank Tinney, and W. C. Fields. Cantor remembered the fervor of those shows: "We played twelve performances in six days and were eager to do more. We made bonfires of our emotions and swept our audiences in a blaze of excitement. It was the greatest week in our lives."[7] In its review of the August 25, 1919, benefit performance, the *Dramatic Mirror* noted that Cantor "won a rousing welcome when he pranced out in his accustomed Ziegfeldian manner" and sang "I've Got My Captain Working for Me Now," which he also performed in the *Follies*. Fields, then appearing in *Midnight Frolic*, reprised a golfing routine that he first introduced on the Ziegfeld stage. The fact that the striking headliners were using this material to benefit the union served as a further insult to Ziegfeld.[8]

The strike ended after four weeks, on September 6, 1919, with the PMA agreeing to the actors' demands for union recognition, the implementation of a standard eight-performance week, and assurances that the producers would abandon damage suits against the strikers.[9] Cantor returned to work in the *Ziegfeld Follies*, honoring his contractual obligation to perform on Broadway and in the subsequent national tour through the end of May 1920. However, Ziegfeld remained angry at the actor who had become a star under his patronage. Cantor recalled, "Ziegfeld didn't speak to me again . . . He'd have no more to do with me. He felt that because I was a member of Equity Board, I'd had more to do with the strike than the others."[10]

Despite the acrimony, in April 1920, Cantor signed a long-term contract with Ziegfeld that raised his salary to eight hundred dollars a week. The deal enabled the producer to retain one of Broadway's most popular stars. In return, Ziegfeld agreed to graduate Cantor from the *Follies* and headline him in a new musical, to be determined, that fall. Cantor later claimed that Ziegfeld had promised that he would costar with popular actress Marilyn Miller in *Sally*, which opened in December 1920 and became a hit. The powerful producer never fulfilled this obligation.[11] Cantor performed in the new *Ziegfeld Follies* of 1920 during the show's first week in New York, in July 1920, but refused to continue, hoping to pressure Ziegfeld to move forward with the new show. While Cantor waited, the producer further aggravated the situation by claiming that Cantor owed him 50 percent of the revenue from the star's increasingly lucrative record sales. Earlier that year, in February 1920, Cantor signed a five-year agreement with Emerson Records for $220,000. It was the largest record deal ever awarded to a Broadway or vaudeville performer.[12]

On August 28, 1920, Cantor and Ziegfeld voided their contract. Ziegfeld issued a short statement explaining, "It is impossible to hold Cantor to his contract on account of his business methods." Cantor replied that he had won the battle by forcing Ziegfeld to free him: the producer had not met his contractual obligation to have Cantor star in a musical.[13]

Writing in 1928, Cantor believed that his labor activism was the chief factor in damaging his relationship with Ziegfeld and causing him to lose the part in *Sally*: "By joining my less fortunate colleagues to aid their cause I had definitely surrendered this opportunity, which, as the figures afterward proved, would have yielded me nearly four hundred thousand dollars. But I had sincerely enjoyed the sacrifice and felt more than repaid for my share in the triumph of Equity."[14] Cantor overstated his sacrifice. While his participation in the strike certainly strained his relationship with Ziegfeld, it also enhanced the actor's image. After receiving a great deal of positive publicity, Cantor emerged as a selfless and principled supporter of actors' rights. Over the years, Cantor continued to advocate for actors and, more broadly, to influence public opinion through his celebrity status.

By 1920 Cantor had reached a level of stardom that offered him opportunities for more money, recognition, and creative control than Ziegfeld was willing to offer. The savvy performer was ready to move on. As a free agent, Cantor briefly considered going on a vaudeville tour. He decided, instead, to sign with Ziegfeld's rivals: the Shuberts. In addition to producing Broadway musicals and revues, the organization headed by brothers Lee and J. J. Shubert booked hundreds of theaters across the country. The Shuberts had a long association with Al Jolson, who starred in ten different productions at the Winter Garden and other New York theaters during the 1910s and 1920s. The Shubert brothers were stingy compared to Ziegfeld and had a reputation for hiring third-rate writers, mounting shows with shabby sets, and scaling down casts by replacing New York actors before going on the road with shows. Still, Cantor and his agent, Max Hart, negotiated a lucrative contract with the Shuberts, which paid Cantor 10 percent of the gross box office receipts, with a guaranteed salary of a whopping $1,250 per week through June 1, 1923. Cantor frequently exceeded the contractual guarantee, with the weekly box office regularly hitting $20,000 and the headliner receiving $2,000. He made more money in one week than the average American worker earned in a year. In addition, he supplemented his income playing after-hours private parties.[15]

Cantor starred in two similar revues for the Shuberts. *Midnight Rounders* (November 1920 through January 1922) toured the country but did not have any Broadway dates. *Make It Snappy* (February 1922 through June 1923) had a successful run at the Winter Garden and played in twenty-one other cities. For the first time, Cantor's name and talent carried an entire show.

While the Shuberts prepared Cantor's first production, *Midnight Rounders*, Cantor performed in another play, *Broadway Brevities*, for two months in the fall of 1920. *Broadway Brevities* opened to strong business at the Winter Garden, breaking the box office record for a single performance with a $5,400 gross take on the first Saturday night. Though most critics liked Cantor, the rest of the show received mixed reviews for its flawed writing, pacing, and set design. Despite the drawing power of Cantor and two other former Ziegfeld stars, George LeMaire and Bert Williams, ticket sales slowed after the first month.[16]

In their otherwise enthusiastic reviews of Cantor's performance, critics disliked the star's vulgarity. While the headliner's *Ziegfeld* act featured suggestive body movements and lyrics, he crossed the line to more explicit and offensive sexual content in *Broadway Brevities* and the production that followed, *Midnight Rounders*. The *New York Clipper*, an entertainment weekly, commented on the "vulgarity" of one of Cantor's comedy scenes and was even more critical of his solo performance later in the show: "Eddie Cantor sang a few special songs that had nothing to do with clean subject matter and should not be relied upon, it seems to us, to create approval for this talented comedian. Besides, the show already contains enough vulgarisms to mar its acceptance by a wide patronage." The *New York Clipper* and other newspapers did not quote the offensive songs or routines.[17]

When Cantor went on the road with *Midnight Rounders*, critics connected "blue" elements of his act to his native city at a time when New York symbolized urban decadence and licentiousness. Writing about Cantor, the *Hartford Courant* critic explained, "He has, of course, played in New York shows so much that he has come to think that nothing is really funny to an audience that doesn't have some suggestion of evil or some possible double meaning for those who like that sort of thing —which is rather a pity for theatre audiences that can be highly amused by a clever, nimble comedian who sings pretty well and knows how to make his effects, even without any dirt thrown in."[18]

Critics and audiences appreciated Cantor's jabs at conventional Victorian mores and conventions as long as he didn't go too far.[19] Actors, speakers, and writers had to watch their words when the subject was sex, lest they offend audiences and even risk censorship or arrest for violating local obscenity laws. In addition, organizations such as the Anti-Defamation League of B'nai B'rith (ADL), dominated by the more established German Jews, fought negative Jewish stage images, including perceptions that Jews were "vulgar."[20] For a young actor who had grown up in a working-class neighborhood and spent his formative professional years touring the country with vaudeville troupes, it was difficult to distinguish between acceptably risqué and dangerously offensive humor. Whether writing letters to the *Jewish Daily Forward*, debating free love and contraception in cafes, or exchanging street-corner quips about promiscuous boarders who rented rooms in family homes, Lower East Side Jews were comfortable talking about sex. In addition, during his youthful romps around Lower Manhattan, Cantor would have encountered all sorts of ribald, licentious activity.[21] Before he signed with the Shuberts, Ziegfeld guided Cantor and kept him out of trouble. Without Ziegfeld's counsel, Cantor faltered at first, though he corrected himself for *Make It Snappy* (1922) and later productions.

Cantor recycled old favorites alongside new material in *Broadway Brevities*. His most popular scene was a reprise from the previous year's *Follies*: a variation of the osteopath routine in a dentist's office with his former *Follies* partner LeMaire. Cantor performed in an additional comedy sketch, also in whiteface. He then switched to blackface for his solo turn: a monologue and three songs. Soon after opening night, at LeMaire's urging, Cantor dropped the blackface entirely in select performances for the first time in his career. In a statement issued during the run of the show, Cantor touted the new look: "I admit that I had no faith in the experiment and thought I would be back to my old make-up before the week was over. To my surprise the scenes which I played in whiteface went remarkably well, and I got some results which had not been possible in the disguise."[22]

Despite Cantor's attempts to change his stage image, audiences expected to see Cantor in the burnt cork makeup. Citing his experience with *Broadway Brevities*, Cantor believed that people would complain if he tried to perform in natural makeup for an entire show. "We got about forty letters from people who seemed to think they hadn't gotten their money's worth," he said in a 1922 interview. The actor remained frustrated with the public's demand for blackface: "I do the same stuff with or without it [blackface], but folks have me pegged as a blackface man and a blackface man I've got to be . . . I don't myself quite understand why people will laugh more at a joke delivered in blackface than the same [joke] without the burnt cork. But they do." Cantor also blamed his record labels, Emerson and Columbia, for using blackface pictures of him to advertise his records.[23]

By the early 1920s, Cantor's image as a blackface performer had crossed media, encompassing theater, records, sheet music, and print advertisements. At this point, even if he had wanted to stop using blackface entirely, it would have been too commercially risky for him to do so. Cantor experimented with performance styles and personas throughout his career, but he made changes cautiously, always sensitive to his audiences. In *Midnight Rounders* and later productions during the 1920s, Cantor wore whiteface for most of the night, freeing him to portray different types of characters with a fuller range of facial expressions. The actor used blackface more selectively and strategically to satisfy audiences with light songs and jokes similar to his familiar Ziegfeld specialty acts. The segments lasted approximately fifteen minutes, and he usually presented them at the end of his performances.

Cantor distinguished his blackface character, which was not intended to imitate black people or evoke black culture, from the traditional Southern minstrel figure. In a June 1923 newspaper interview, conducted a week after *Make It Snappy* completed its fifteen-month run at theaters across the country, he explained, "While the first blacking up was done to resemble a negro, gradually another impulse came and the whole matter of blacking up was idealized. It was realized that to black up meant practically the elimination of facial expression. That was a handicap to the player . . . Practically the only reminder of the negro is in the use of such songs, as 'mammy' songs, and purely incidental things which had their origin in the American negro."[24]

For Cantor and his *Make It Snappy* collaborators, the old minstrel style was passé. In the prologue to *Make It Snappy*, two theatergoers, a husband and wife, speak with an usher about the night's performance. The man wants to know who is starring in the show.

The usher replies, "Eddie Cantor, a blackface comedian."

The wife comments, "Oh, I like that. Now we will hear some of those darky tunes."

The husband answers, "All the blackface comedians I have seen of late talk Jewish."[25]

Cantor's performance of "My Yiddisha Mammy" illustrates the way he revealed his Jewishness beneath the blackface makeup. Cantor featured the song on opening night of *Make It Snappy* at the Winter Garden Theatre on April 13, 1922. Though he did not receive many publishing credits, Cantor coauthored "My Yiddisha Mammy" with Jean Schwartz, who wrote several other numbers in *Make It Snappy*, and lyricist Alex

Cantor was featured on the sheet music for "My Yiddisha Mammy" (1922). Courtesy of Billy Rose Theatre Division, New York Public Library for the Performing Arts.

Gerber.[26] "My Yiddisha Mammy" starts out like a traditional mammy song, "down South, where the Swanee River flows" and the "cotton grows." After a few additional lines about Southern mammies, Cantor upends the audience's expectations: "I've got a Mammy / But she don't come from Alabammy / Her heart is filled with love and real sentiment / Her cabin door is in a Bronx tenement." Cantor's Jewish mammy has "never been where the sweet magnolia grow / She don't play a banjo or ukulele." Instead, in a clever rhyme with "ukulele," Cantor reveals that his mammy's lullaby is "Eli, Eli," a song that originated in the Yiddish theater in 1896 and by the early 1920s had moved to vaudeville and popular recordings, becoming one of America's best-known Jewish songs. This choice of music, a symbol of Jewish authenticity, explains why Cantor loves his "Yiddisha mammy."[27]

From the stage of the Winter Garden, Al Jolson's symbolic home, Cantor's song parodies Jolson's sentimental paeans to plantation life. Cantor's admission that he is Jewish, and his pride in Jewish culture, challenges the authenticity of Jolson and other performers who masqueraded as sons of the Deep South while truncating their Jewish backgrounds.[28] Cantor's proud affection for his Jewish "mammy" may have inspired Jack Yellen and Lew Pollack to write their more sincere and sentimental "My Yiddisha Momme," which has become a staple of American Jewish popular music since Sophie Tucker first performed it in 1925.

Cantor constantly swapped "My Yiddisha Mammy" and other music in and out of his repertoire. The *Make It Snappy* orchestra knew seventeen different Cantor songs at any given time, even though the star sang only a handful of these each night. By varying his selections, Cantor kept *Make It Snappy* interesting for himself and audience members who liked the show so much that they returned for multiple performances. As one of the two most popular Broadway singers from the era, rivaled only by Jolson, Cantor had his choice of material. After Cantor performed a song onstage, the sheet music was certain to feature his image, and the song stood a good chance of becoming a hit, especially if the headliner recorded the music. Professional song pluggers, working for music publishers, desperately stalked Cantor while he toured, hoping to find him in his dressing room or hotel. In addition to giving the star a good selection of new material, these salesmen quietly paid performers such as Cantor to sing their songs.[29]

The star chose music that allowed him to present the familiar character and style from *Ziegfeld Follies* specialties. During *Midnight Rounders*, he introduced audiences to "Margie," written by Benny Davis, Con Conrad, and J. Russel Robinson.[30] A love song with a cynical twist, "Margie" became a staple of Cantor's repertoire throughout his career. Cantor starts the song as the wry narrator, addressing the audience: "You may talk about your love affair / Here's one I'd like to tell to you / All night long they sit upon the stairs / He holds her close and starts to coo." Cantor then takes the part of the lovesick young man courting Margie, a lady who seems ambivalent at best. He implores her: "Don't forget your promise to me / 'Cause I have bought the home and ring and everything." In the end, Cantor sounds defeated: "I know who inspired that song / Another good man has gone wrong / Oh Margie, Margie, it's you."[31]

Shubert's opening night press release emphasized the New York settings and credited Cantor for collaborating with the writer Harold Atteridge to create the sketches. Critics raved over Cantor's depictions of city people. Alexander Woollcott praised the star's "hilariously funny" portraits of typical New Yorkers. Gilbert Seldes also singled out these urban caricatures, commending Cantor's "ingenuity" and "courage." Echoing Cantor's argument that the star was free to be himself without the blackface mask, Robert C. Benchley observed, "In place of the neurotic Negro appeared a Jewish boy with large, bewildered eyes and mild manner, an apologetic calm superseding the offensive assurance and, oddly enough, a considerably more sanitary batch of songs and jokes."[32]

Benchley's calm "Jewish boy" also had a more aggressive side. Cantor wrote a sketch for *Make It Snappy* in which he plays a slick-talking, bootlegging cab driver fleecing a farmer from out of town. Cantor first steals the man's watch and then beats the visitor, demanding payment for illegal booze. A policeman steps in, but rather than protecting the hapless rube, the officer prepares to arrest the farmer for stiffing the cabbie. The farmer pleads with the officer to send a telegram to his wife, "Mrs. Cyrus Shapiro." Suddenly the tone shifts. The policeman introduces himself as Morris Cohen, and the three men bond over their shared religion. Cantor's character returns the watch. The scene ends with the men speaking in Yiddish as they chase a newsboy selling the *Dearborn Independent* offstage.[33]

Cantor's hustling Jewish cab driver would have been familiar to urban theatergoers; but the sketch also reveals other Jewish figures, subverting audience stereotypes. In addition, the scene highlights the characters' affinities based on shared Jewish backgrounds and common enemies. The topical jab at the *Dearborn Independent*, an influential magazine with a weekly circulation of more than a half million, targets the newspaper's publisher, Henry Ford. A hero to many because of his success as a pioneering car manufacturer, Ford also emerged as the nation's foremost purveyor of nativist antisemitism. In May 1920, the *Dearborn Independent* launched a notorious campaign positing a worldwide Jewish conspiracy to control banking, promote Marxism, and undermine Christianity. "Jewish interests were held responsible for a decline in public and private morals, for intemperance, for high rents, short skirts, rolled stockings, cheap movies, vulgar Broadway shows, gambling, jazz, scarlet fiction, flashy jewelry, night clubs, and so on," wrote the Ford biographer David L. Lewis.[34] In articles decrying "Jewish manipulators of the public mind," the *Dearborn Independent* made Jews agents and symbols of broader social transformations, including booming cities that were growing more racially and ethnically diverse.[35]

Cantor takes his shot at Ford carefully, as a quick joke at the end of the sketch. He never says the name "Henry Ford," mentioning only the newspaper. Cantor could not be too political or too Jewish for his audience. Yet in chasing the *Dearborn Independent* off his stage, Cantor's message was simple: if Henry Ford and his followers did not like short skirts, movies, Broadway, and Jews, that was their problem. Cantor and his people did not need Ford's blessing. Ford's America was changing. Cantor represented the future. Jews heard this message. As the *Boston Jewish Advocate* columnist Max H. Newman wrote, Cantor "is a sincere and earnest Jew and has a way of assailing anti-Semitism in his plays that is more powerful than the written word."[36]

The taxi sketch, "My Yiddisha Mammy," and other performances from *Make It Snappy* marked an evolution in Cantor's style and a new direction for Jewish stage comedy. Without actually using the word "Jewish," Cantor crafted routines that commented on contemporary life from a Jewish perspective. The actor's accent, Yiddish phrases, politics, subject matter, and attitude marked him as a proud and unapologetic Jew from New York, navigating the modern city. Through his comic characters and his own success on the country's biggest stages, Cantor promoted the message that Jews belonged in America. The actor's ease with his religious identification and his casual references to Jewish culture challenged the older image of the "stage Jew." This character type was defined by bulging eyes, a putty nose, a heavy Yiddish accent, ill-fitting clothes, dishonest business practices, uncontrollable lust for money, and a newcomer's understanding of the basic tools required to navigate daily life. The grossest negative images were fading by the late 1910s owing to the changing tastes of performers and audiences as well as protests by Jewish groups such as the ADL. However, comedians such as Monroe Silver, best known for his "Cohen on the Telephone" routines, continued to present lightweight novelty routines that relied primarily on funny Jewish accents and the old stock Jewish characters. Similarly, popular acts such as Smith and Dale made Jewish accents, puns, and malapropisms central to their comedy. The stereotypes also persisted in the films of actors George Sidney, Max Davidson, and Sammy Cohen. The image of the stage Jew and parodies of greenhorns were growing increasingly irrelevant and antiquated for Cantor and his audience. In addition, always aware of the dangers of typecasting, Cantor did not want to be known primarily as a "Jewish comedian" or a dialect specialist.[37]

By the 1920s, Jews had become central to the economic and social life of New York. In 1920, more than 1.6 million Jews lived in the city's five boroughs, representing approximately 29 percent of the city's overall population.[38] Jewish culture became more hip and fashionable through such figures as Cantor and Fanny Brice. Broadway theatergoers, regardless of whether they were Jewish, understood the quick, funny Jewish and Yiddish references by modern comedians, or at least they pretended that they did. For example, the critic Alan Dale noted that the opening night audience had no trouble decoding the smattering of Yiddish in Make It Snappy: "The programme contains no glossary for the edification of the uninitiated, but last night's audience seemed to include none of those. The gently bubblesome Hebraism that effervesced so persistently was vastly appreciated. No glossary was necessary."[39]

In "Joe's Blue Front," the most widely praised and important sketch of the Shubert years, Cantor portrayed another Jewish character: a fast-talking tailor named Moe. Cantor and his costars performed "Joe's Blue Front" in both Midnight Rounders and Make It Snappy. "Joe's Blue

Front" is set in a Lower Manhattan suit shop. As Moe, Cantor forms a quick-witted and aggressive team with the shop's owner, played by Joe Opp. They relentlessly foist their apparel and accessories on an overwhelmed customer, known in the program only as "The Prospective Victim." The rumpled prospect with a high-pitched voice, played by Lew Hearn, wants to purchase "a nice, classy suit . . . college boy style."

Moe and the owner employ creative, entertaining pitches as they keep pushing clothes that the customer doesn't want or need. For example, the first possibility, which the owner describes in a Yiddish inflection, is "a very handsome English walking suit, the latest cut, comes right straight from the Piccadilly." The customer begins walking around, then blurts out, "There's a nail sticking me in the back," referring to a painful irregularity in the garment.[40]

Moe jumps in with a smile on his face: "That's not a nail. That's our own invention. You know how you go into a restaurant and you hang up your hat and your umbrella and you get indigestion because you think someone's going to steal it? This is our own invention." Cantor grabs a hat and umbrella as he talks and hangs it on the long hook protruding from the customer's upper back. "Now, you take your umbrella and your hat and you hang it up and nobody can steal it from you. Now go ahead. Take a walk," he urges the customer. Hearn takes a few hesitant steps, with the hat and umbrella dangling from his back, as the tailor continues his banter. "You'll take the suit," he concludes, before slipping it off Hearn and moving to new items, including a comically oversized hat, a shirt that is the wrong color, and other absurdly big or small clothes. "Joe's Blue Front" ends with the customer buying a ridiculous "sailor suit," explaining, "I'll take anything to get out of here."

"Joe's Blue Front" showcases the timing, physical comedy, and quick wit of Cantor and his costars. It also presents a menacing character, more akin to *Make It Snappy*'s hustling taxi driver than Cantor's more innocent roles, while satirizing a common urban experience. Whether as a patient, a cab driver, or a tailor, Cantor mined the awkward frustrations of seemingly banal everyday situations and encounters. Without explicitly referencing Moe's ethnicity, Cantor also presented a strong Jewish character: one that incorporated elements of the stereotypical pushy Jewish salesman, but also showcased confidence and toughness. The critic Gilbert Seldes praised "the whole-heartedness of Cantor's

Cantor with Lou Hearn and Joe Opp (left to right) in the "Joe's Blue Front" sketch from *Midnight Rounders* (1920). Courtesy of Billy Rose Theatre Division, New York Public Library for the Performing Arts.

violence — essentially the bullying of a coward who has at last discovered some one weaker than himself."[41] Cantor's edgy wise guy modeled a style of jittery, aggressive American Jewish comedy that remained popular through figures such as the Marx Brothers, Milton Berle, Don Rickles, Mel Brooks, Jerry Seinfeld, and Larry David. In addition, his Yiddish phrasing and rhythms became a hallmark of Jewish humor, rendering even mundane or insulting dialogue funny.

Cantor kept "Joe's Blue Front" alive across theater, film, radio, and television, ensuring his character's standing among comedy aficionados. In 1949 Berle reprised "Joe's Blue Front" on his television variety show, playing Cantor's role opposite Hearn. After the broadcast, Hearn, like Cantor a veteran of vaudeville who grew up on New York's Lower East Side, tussled with Cantor over who originated and wrote "Joe's Blue Front." Their dispute was never resolved.[42] In 2012 director Martin Scorsese pronounced the sketch "the essence of Jewish comedy." Scorsese made a "direct link" between Cantor's style and that of the British comedian Sacha Baron Cohen, who starred in Scorsese's film *Hugo* (2011) and played more provocative characters in other films and television programs.[43]

Even with his rough edges, Cantor's Moe is likeable, charming, and appealing to audiences. To capitalize on the popular character, demonstrating creative merchandising and promotion, the Shuberts partnered with local clothing stores. When the show came to town, newspaper advertisements featured the tagline "Eddie Cantor Could Sell 'Em" and the name of the shop. Retailers told readers about "Joe's Blue Front," the hit of *Midnight Rounders*. Hinting at the character's ethnicity, the ads placed Moe's fictional shop on Baxter Street, a small block in Lower Manhattan known for its cheap clothing stores owned by Jewish merchants. The advertisements praised Hearn's taste in asking for a "belt in the back" and promised that customers would be able to find all kinds of suits at their local shops. In Kansas City, Rothschild's went a step further, claiming that when the actors were not performing, they wore the Society Brand Clothes available at Rothschild's.[44]

Retailers clamored to associate with Cantor because he electrified crowds. His audiences in New York and other cities, including a mixture of tourists and locals, ventured into downtown theaters for a night of excitement. Cantor didn't disappoint them. He sang, danced, joked, rolled his eyes, clapped his hands, and allowed audiences to bask in the aura of one of the country's most powerful and popular entertainers. In a review of *Midnight Rounders*, the *Chicago Tribune* critic Sheppard Butler described Cantor's command of the stage from the minute the show opened: "Cantor, an eager entertainer, leaps into the fray from a seat in the front row with an avowal that he is 'God's gift to the amusement world' and quickly becomes the life of the party."[45]

Cantor confidently combined his experienced craftsmanship with a youthful freshness and spontaneity. Whether he introduced a new song, improvised a line, or delivered scripted material with his typical jaunty pleasure, he gave audiences what they wanted: a witty, funny, spontaneous, risqué night out at a hit Broadway revue. Like other successful Jewish performers, Cantor grew up in a world that valued speed, quick wits, and ambition. He incorporated the bustle of the Lower East Side into a style that resonated with audiences across the country. The *Variety* editor-publisher Sime Silverman linked Cantor's charismatic appeal to his energetic delivery: "Eddie Cantor, under his blackface, has a galloping personality. When he's moving about, his magnetism increases, although there when standing still. His system of song delivery is movement, rushing, swinging arms, and action, while the arms keep moving when he stands quiet to talk. He tells a story as well as he sings a song, a rare combination."[46] Even the slangy titles of plays such as *Midnight Rounders* and *Make It Snappy* reflected the restless, urban sensibility that Cantor brought to the stage. "All the peppiest of American language originates with the vaudevillian and the cartoonist," the actor said proudly in 1923.[47] Though Cantor was not a kid when *Make It Snappy* opened in 1922, his charisma and attitude signaled the thirty-year-old's alignment with the emerging youth culture of the 1920s, which celebrated raw energy and rebellion against social constraints.[48]

Cantor's youthful irreverence onstage carried over into his offstage dealings with J. J. Shubert, one of the most important and powerful producers in the 1920s. Shubert could be tyrannical, but Cantor was not intimidated by him. Throughout his career, Cantor attempted to mold all aspects of the productions in which he starred. He was not the kind of actor who came to the theater a few minutes before showtime, played his part, and then left for the night. The star frequently clashed with producers because of his strong opinions. In *Midnight Rounders* and

Make It Snappy, Cantor battled with Shubert over ticket prices, casting decisions, production values, choices of venues, the quality of the promotional flyers, and Shubert's lack of personal involvement in the productions. The fact that Cantor made valid points, based on his nightly observations and strong stage instincts, did not mollify Shubert. The producer was incensed that his star, who also had a financial interest in the show, attempted to call the shots in areas that usually came under the purview of the producer.[49]

By early 1923, after nearly three years of tense backstage negotiations with J. J. Shubert, Cantor did little to hide his frustration. The irreverent and spontaneous performer used his stage platform to disparage the Shuberts during several performances of *Make It Snappy*, while plotting the next phase of his career. With his contract set to expire on June 1, 1923, Cantor considered several options, and he even signed a short-term contract to appear on the Keith vaudeville circuit; however, he most wanted to reunite with Ziegfeld. As Cantor later wrote, "Mr. Ziegfeld was class. The Shuberts were just show business."[50] Knowing that Ziegfeld remained angry from their battles in 1919 and 1920, the crafty actor appealed to the producer's vanity. In March 1923, Cantor took out a full-page ad in *Variety* highlighting the box office success of *Make It Snappy*, which had recently played in Chicago opposite Ziegfeld's *Sally*. Cantor's ad featured a blurb from the *Chicago Tribune*'s review of his show: "EDDIE CANTOR AT $3.30 IS KEEN COMPETITION TO 'SALLY' AT $4.40." Within a week of the advertisement's appearance, Ziegfeld called Cantor long distance, offering to have him star in a musical comedy. "Not a word about the strike or ill feeling," Cantor recalled. On May 15, 1923, while Cantor was still appearing in *Make It Snappy*, Ziegfeld announced that he and Cantor had signed a long-term contract.[51] Eddie Cantor was returning to the *Ziegfeld Follies*.

5 MAKIN' WHOOPEE WITH ZIEGFELD (1923-1930)

n June 4, 1923, when Cantor rejoined the *Follies*, he had a window of three weeks in which he could also play other venues before an exclusivity clause came into effect. Rarely one to refuse work, Cantor presented a twenty-minute vaudeville act in local theaters, taking an early slot on the bills so that he could still appear in the *Follies* later the same night. The irreverent performer brought back his jokes about the Shuberts, prompting J. J. Shubert to write a furious letter to Cantor representative Daniel Lipsky. The producer sputtered about Cantor's ingratitude, "ignorance and stupidity," while attempting to maintain his dignity: "No man can go upon the stage and openly insult us as he [Cantor] has done repeatedly since he closed with us."[1] Continuing his more openly Jewish topical humor from *Make It Snappy*, Cantor also targeted well-known antisemites. He received many letters "warning him to keep quiet about the Ku Klux Klan and Henry Ford when he is on the stage," according to *Variety*.[2] Threats to "keep quiet," whether from white supremacists or theatrical producers, usually provoked the brawler in Cantor.

The young star's growing political awareness and eagerness to take on nativism distinguished him from other major comedians, who steered clear of controversial politics, reserving topical routines for safe and popular subjects. Prohibition or President "Silent Cal" Coolidge lent themselves to easy satire before supportive audiences. The Ku Klux Klan (KKK) represented particular challenges because of the difficulty of finding humor in its racism, anti-Catholicism, and antisemitism. The KKK also threatened touring performers with violence, boycotts, and verbal confrontations. The early 1920s saw a rise in nativist sentiment and support for the KKK. Estimates placed the Klan's membership at between four and five million in 1924, including US congressmen and state officials from both major political parties. Most performers had no need to alienate audiences or make trouble for themselves. In contrast, Cantor jibed about the Klan and Ford throughout the 1920s.[3]

Cantor performed his solo specialty act and three comedy skits in Ziegfeld's new summer 1923 *Follies* show, which featured dancer Ann Pennington and the comedy team of Gallagher and Shean. According to the *Evening Mail* reviewer James Craig, Cantor "stopped the show" with the upbeat "My Girl Uses Mineralava (That's Why I'm Her Beau)," one of the few songs in his career for which Cantor received sole writing credit.[4] Always looking for ways to make a little extra money, Cantor creatively endorsed a facial mud mask for women in the midst of a *Ziegfeld Follies* production. Cantor tells the story of his girl, who "has no looks and is only four feet high," but Mineralava transformed her skin. The song pokes fun at Mineralava and marketing: "Her face was wrinkled couldn't beat it / Looked like it was 'cordian pleated / But since she uses / Mineralava I love her so."[5] This early example of commercial advertising on the Broadway stage modeled a promotional style that became more popular on radio, where Cantor and other comedians integrated creative and occasionally irreverent sponsor pitches into their programs. Cantor formed an independent music publishing company in partnership with Mineralava, perhaps intending to write additional songs for the cosmetics firm and other manufacturers, but no sequels followed.[6]

The Cantor-Ziegfeld collaboration that summer paved the way for Cantor to star in *Kid Boots*: his first "book show" with a single narrative integrating the music and dialogue, as opposed to Cantor's previous revues comprising a series of sketches. After four weeks of out-of-town previews, *Kid Boots* debuted on Broadway on New Year's Eve 1923 and added to Cantor's string of critical and commercial successes. He played the title character in nearly five hundred Broadway performances through February 1925, and then went on a national tour for fifteen months until May 1926.[7]

Joseph McCarthy, who wrote the music to *Kid Boots* with partner Harry Tierney, approached Cantor and Ziegfeld with the idea for a play set at a tony Palm Beach country club. Cantor plays Boots, a nickname earned through his activities as the club's resident bootlegger. Boots also serves as the chief golf caddy, gambler, hustler, and dispenser of advice about life, love, and women. The story revolves around two young golf pros, Randolph Valentine (Robert Barrat) and Tom Sterling (Harry Fender), who face each other for the club championship and the hand of Polly Pendleton (Mary Eaton), the pretty daughter of a wealthy member. Critics did not take the "mixed up" plot all that seriously. As one wrote, "The story moves along pleasantly, without supplying any undue strain upon the mental acumen of the onlooker."[8]

Two productive librettists, Otto Harbach and William Anthony McGuire, wrote the book for Kid Boots, with an assist from Cantor. Harbach authored twelve different Broadway shows between 1923 and 1926 alone, the years that Kid Boots played in New York and around the country. Ziegfeld hired the experienced writer to help McGuire, who had several theatrical credits, but had not yet written a musical at the time of Kid Boots. McGuire's recent success with Six Cylinder Love (1921), a popular comedy that poked fun at a young couple's love of cars and consumerism, served as his primary calling card. After the success of Kid Boots, McGuire wrote sketches and books for nine different Ziegfeld shows, including Whoopee. He also worked on two Cantor films: The Kid from Spain (1932) and Roman Scandals (1933).[9]

McGuire had a knack for drafting light stories, breezy dialogue, and the kind of snappy one-liners that Cantor liked. McGuire also incorporated Cantor's ideas, showing the kind of malleability that was important for anyone who wished to have a long working relationship with Cantor. As the headliner and the focus of attention, Cantor revised scripts, inserted gags, and suggested plotlines. For example, he told the Kid Boots writers to rework his osteopath act and set it in the women's locker room of the country club. Harbach and McGuire wrote a raucous scene in which a club member, Dr. Josephine Fitch (Jobyna Howland), applies electric shock to Cantor's character and then tries to heal him on the osteopath's table, located in the locker room. Cantor later recalled, "It was the best physical comedy scene I have ever played, and Jobyna Howland did her part so well that I always had real aches and pains when it was over."[10] Cantor delivered several additional jokes to Harbach and McGuire each day. "Both playwrights looked bored at my literary efforts, and [initially] spurned the lines because they were mere jokes and had nothing to do with the play," he recalled. The writers reconsidered, and Cantor's contributions "turned out to be among the biggest laughs in the show."[11]

Dr. Josephine Fitch (played by Jobyna Howland) receives a golfing lesson from Boots (Cantor) in *Kid Boots* (1923). Courtesy of UCLA Library Special Collections.

In addition to recycling the chiropractor bit, *Kid Boots* includes a version of the tailor scene in which a snooty club member wants to buy a blue sweater from the pro shop. After making the man's head spin, Boots persuades him to buy a red cap instead. In reflecting on the scene, Cantor explained how he drew upon successful sketches from his repertoire while keeping the material fresh for audiences: "Once a comedian has struck certain styles of comedy that suit him, it is interesting to follow the many variations he devises, so that he can use the same idea and yet conceal it."[12] Theatrical audiences and critics across the country, who might see a popular entertainer's new show once every couple of years, expected stars to reprise familiar gags.

Cantor continued to joke about nativist threats in *Kid Boots*, probably adapting quips from his solo vaudeville performance earlier that year. In one sequence, Boots banters with his friend Tom: "Do you know my idea of perfect harmony? To see a baseball game between the Ku Klux Klan and the K of C [Knights of Columbus] with a negro umpire for the benefit of Jewish War Relief."[13]

After imagining the Klan supporting Jewish war victims in Europe and Palestine, Cantor's character turns his attention to Ford: "Yesterday I was twenty-six and I put five dollars down on a Ford. Not that I care anything for Henry socially. I figured out that if he ever gets to be the president it won't do any harm to be in right. And Tom—think of it —if he ever does get to be president of this country everybody will own a Ford—then can you imagine some smart Jewish fellow who invents a FORD SWATTER so he can sock 'em down."[14] Cantor's shots at the KKK and Ford, while not his funniest or sharpest satirical lines, made the important symbolic statement that he was not afraid of these threats to Jews and other racial and ethnic minorities. Through his jaunty barbs, Cantor subtly positioned himself alongside the politicians, newspapers, and activists who opposed Ford and the KKK. As in the taxi scene from *Make It Snappy*, the quick lines may have held special meaning for Jews, but slipped by others. Nativist politics are not central to the lightweight plot of *Kid Boots*, which is more concerned with puncturing country club pretensions and the hypocrisy of Prohibition.

Despite the thin story and unremarkable music, *Kid Boots* sparkled in areas that mattered more to critics and audiences. It featured singing, dancing, chorus girls in skimpy outfits, risqué jokes, topical references, and most important, Eddie Cantor. The star used his two-and-a-half-year run with *Kid Boots* to solidify his popular persona as the funny, likeable, street-smart wise guy who is not above a little criminal activity. Dressed in a bow tie, high socks, and baggy plaid pants in which he hides his liquor, Boots looks and sometimes acts the part of a clownish caddy. But Cantor's personality towers over the role and dominates the play. As the *New York World* observed approvingly, Cantor could not disappear into the character of Boots: "Technically speaking, Eddie was not supposed to be himself at all. Accurately speaking, he could not even seem to be someone else."[15]

The charismatic actor had blended his "real life" and stage personas since his vaudeville days. But his self-reflexivity reached a new level in *Kid Boots* and provided a model for later plays, films, and radio programs. When the country club members decide to throw an elaborate party, the featured entertainer is none other than "Mr. Eddie Cantor of the Ziegfeld Follies." In his role as himself, rather than Boots, Cantor dons blackface for the only time in the play to perform his specialty music and comedy routine.[16] The performance segment gave Cantor an opportunity to interpolate one or two new jazzy songs each night. His selections included the breezy, risqué "Charley, My Boy" and "If You Knew Susie," which he released as popular recordings and retained in his repertoire for the rest of his career.[17]

Cantor's decision to appear in blackface for only one scene did not make big news. Most critics did not comment on his makeup. Those who did wondered why he had chosen to put on blackface for earlier roles, recognizing that the star did not transition into an African-American character through the makeup. For example, the *Chicago Tribune* critic wrote, "I've never been able to understand the blacking up of Cantor, Mr. Jolson, and some of the other popular funmakers, for they are Negroid in nothing else and venture not at all into characterization."[18] By the early 1920s, blackface had fallen out of favor with other performers for aesthetic, not political, reasons: like Cantor, they felt that the burnt cork was too much of a novelty and limited their roles. However, the makeup was so central to Cantor's persona that he could not abandon it. In *Kid Boots* and subsequent productions, blackface functioned much like the chiropractor and tailor skits: as tools for satisfying theater patrons with fondly remembered bits from Cantor's early days.

During the early 1920s, the Jewish press and its readers recognized the Broadway headliner from the Lower East Side as a Jewish-American success story. Cantor appeared in newspapers' surveys of prominent Jews in business and popular entertainment, which helped readers identify fellow Jews while also instilling a sense of pride at the group's growing social mobility and economic prosperity. Countless Americans, regardless of ethnicity, appreciated entertainers such as Jolson, Brice, and Cantor. But these performers held special meaning for Jewish audiences. Their popularity supported a pluralistic ideal in which Jews were central to the nation's cultural life and demonstrated the positive contributions of Jews to America.[19]

The achievements of Jews in all strata of show business countered antisemitic charges about the pernicious influence of Jews in film and theater. Writing in the *Sentinel*, the Chicago Jewish weekly, the journalist Jack Lait pointed to Cantor and other "celebrities of the boards," who revealed "the breadth of talent and personality sprinkled through the Hebrews in America." Lait thundered that "Henry Ford's hired liars" labeled these Jewish success stories "a menace and a shame. The truth is that the Jew is the most daring theatrical spectator, the most artistic theatrical producer, the most effective stage entertainer."[20]

Jewish newspapers covered stars' activities in the Jewish community, including charitable benefits and donations to Jewish causes. These articles had a practical function: to publicize local fund-raising campaigns and events featuring celebrities. They also contributed to the positive image of Jews that many within the Jewish community, including industry executives and performers themselves who were in the line of antisemitic fire, wanted to foster.[21] In 1924 the *Pittsburgh Jewish Criterion* commended Cantor and other actors for forming the Jewish Actors Guild, which provided emergency financial aid to actors and raised money for other Jewish charities. The newspaper appreciated the importance of these kinds of public embraces of Jewish identity, predicting that involvement in the guild could lead to "active participation in other Jewish causes." Alluding to Ford, the newspaper also perceptively wondered whether "anti-Jewish agitation" induced "young men like Cantor" to become involved with Jewish issues, rather than hiding their "Jewish origin."[22] In the coming years, the fight against antisemitism fueled Cantor's Jewish communal activism.

Philanthropic activity also enabled Cantor to enhance his image, as a Broadway comedian, among Jews. Cantor was well aware of biases against show business. For many years, he remembered the stinging criticisms of his profession by his father-in-law, David Tobias. For example, Cantor recalled in 1957, "Ida's dad said all actors were bums. He didn't want any bums in his family. He wanted me to go into a legitimate business."[23] As the working-class son of Russian immigrants who could seem vulgar onstage and would seemingly do anything for a laugh, Cantor did not fit the ideals of the German-Jewish establishment, which included bankers, lawyers, businessmen, and intellectuals. Cantor's working-class Jewish style undermined the more dignified, acculturated image that influential organizations such as the American Jewish Committee wanted to present and also alarmed prominent Jews who were not active in the Jewish community, but had built careers in other areas of American life. For example, the journalist Walter Lippmann wrote an article in the *American Hebrew* charging that Jews were responsible for fostering antisemitism. He criticized the conspicuous spending and taste of the "rich and vulgar and pretentious Jews of our big cities" and the values of the poor, who had "lost their ancient piety and acquired no new convictions."[24]

Cantor's frequent involvement in charitable benefits provided opportunities for the Broadway actor to demonstrate his good taste and values. He also mingled with Jewish leaders and supported shared causes. In May 1920, Cantor entertained at a fund-raiser to help Jews who had suffered during the European war and its aftermath. Others on the dais included the wealthy philanthropists Walter N. Rothschild and Felix M. Warburg.[25] This war relief work provided useful experience for Cantor's more extensive refugee activism during the 1930s. He urged a Maryland audience in February 1922 to donate to the American Jewish Relief Campaign, using appeals to transnational Jewish responsibilities that foreshadowed his later speeches on behalf of Jews fleeing Nazi Germany: "If the Jews of Baltimore realize that this money is to be used to save hundreds of thousands of Jews in Eastern Europe from death and starvation, there is no doubt that the half million dollars will be raised with ease."[26] Later that month, Cantor appeared at a war relief dinner in Brooklyn. His fellow speakers included New York State Supreme Court Justice Mitchell May and businessman Nathan S. Jonas, who became a close friend and mentor to Cantor.[27]

Other major charitable campaigns of the early 1920s focused on the urgency of providing basic food, shelter, and medical assistance to new immigrants. Cantor did less work with the many philanthropies conducting this domestic relief, though he occasionally appeared alongside prominent figures at local Jewish federation galas. Cantor made assistance to children more of a priority. The actor keenly remembered his difficult childhood and appreciated his good fortune to be able to live and work in America. In October 1920, the actor celebrated National Apple Week by distributing apples to orphans.[28] The next year, he escalated his activities, organizing and headlining a concert for the Home for Jewish Children in Boston. A *Boston Jewish Advocate* article previewing the show illustrates the way philanthropy heightened Cantor's image in the Jewish community: "Cantor is a Jew who is proud of the fact. Off the stage, he impresses those who meet him as a dignified, calm, and serene gentleman." The article also referenced Cantor's empathy with the needy because of his experiences growing up on the Lower East Side.[29]

In May 1921, Cantor announced that he was sending twenty-five city boys to Surprise Lake Camp, a haven for poor city kids located fifty miles north of Manhattan in Cold Spring, New York. Cantor spent two happy summers at the camp as a teenager. Sending children to summer camp was not the most pressing need facing Jews. But Cantor's lifelong commitment to Surprise Lake Camp and the Jewish charity that ran the camp, the Educational Alliance, gave him an opportunity to repay the organization. In addition, this philanthropy reinforced several aspects of his public persona: loyalty, concern for orphans, recognition of his humble beginning, and advocacy for the importance of cultural experiences along with food and shelter.[30]

Moving beyond his charitable work, Cantor boldly asserted his Jewish identity when he postponed the opening night of his *Kid Boots* engagement at the Woods Theatre in Chicago, originally slated for September 27, 1925, because it fell on Kol Nidre, marking the start of Yom Kippur. Instead, he opened the next night, after the holiday had ended. Cantor recognized the symbolic importance of Kol Nidre. The decision about whether to perform on the holy day, a focal point of 1925's new Broadway hit, *The Jazz Singer*, soon became a litmus test by which Jews who lived in the public eye demonstrated their Jewish identification. The actor affirmed that, on this day, his religious obligations and symbolic position as a Jewish celebrity outweighed obligations to his producer, fellow actors in *Kid Boots*, and audiences that might appreciate an extra Chicago show. This was a risky position for a Broadway star to take in 1925. Actors fervently devoted themselves to their professions, not their religions. Producers did not schedule opening nights around Jewish holidays.

As with many of his Jewish statements during this time, Cantor carefully spoke to other Jews without alienating non-Jewish audiences. Cantor revised the opening date early enough for the theater to announce his new (post–Kol Nidre) premiere date well before the tickets went on sale. No shows were canceled at the last minute. The daily newspapers in Chicago and elsewhere wrote nothing about the change in date, which drew coverage only in *Variety* and the Jewish press.[31] *Variety* did not approve of Cantor's decision to postpone opening night, violating the great show business maxim that the show must go on. Its initial coverage of the cancellation underscored Cantor's vanity, rather than his piety: "Cantor said it had been a lifelong ambition of his to become sufficiently important to open or not to open and get away with it." The newspaper contrasted Cantor's postponement with the professionalism of another Jewish star, Willie Howard, who opened a different play in Chicago on Kol Nidre. According to the article, Howard would have preferred to postpone the performance, but his producers, the Shuberts, convinced the actor that "it would be wrong of him to disappoint his public by not opening."[32]

Cantor received more support from the local Jewish community. Chicago rabbi S. Felix Mendelsohn commended Cantor for his stance in the weekly *Sentinel*, a Jewish newspaper. Mendelsohn highlighted Cantor's symbolic importance to Jews and non-Jews: "We wish to assure Eddie that the Jewish people is very proud of him for the stand he has taken in this matter. He has proved to the world once again that whenever a principle is involved, money means nothing to the real Jew. We should also like to remind Eddie that for the financial loss which he sustained by refusing to play Yom Kippur eve he has already made up in self-respect which he gained for himself and for his people."[33]

Two weeks later, the *Sentinel* published a short letter from Cantor in which the entertainer thanked the rabbi for his support and affirmed his desire to draw attention to the strong character of American Jews.

Cantor also fired another salvo in his ongoing fight against antisemitism: in this case, the stereotype of the money-hungry Jew. He wrote to Mendelsohn, "I believe you are right when you say that most of the Jews hold principle above money, and such an act as mine brings it to light."[34] Cantor's cancellation of opening night and his subsequent explanation in the *Sentinel* represented his most direct and thoughtful affirmations of his Jewish identification up to that time. His newspaper statement provided a rare example of a secular celebrity using the tiny Jewish press to address his fellow Jews about putting religious faith above career expectations. As major national figures, with egos to match, other headliners had outgrown the Jewish press and expressed little interest in opposing stereotypes. In addition, the actor avoided the potential embarrassment to himself, and offense to his Jewish followers, of an opening night on Kol Nidre.

Variety soon changed its position on Cantor, recognizing the support and affection that the actor had earned by postponing the premiere. In a more favorable follow-up less than three months later, the weekly reported that Cantor had received "one of the grandest ovations and sendoffs ever accorded any person" when he appeared at a Chicago Jewish Federation banquet. "As a mark of respect, everyone in the room arose at his introduction, arose when he left, and at his departure, Julius Rosenwald and Jacob Loeb announced that he [Cantor] was one of the outstanding Jews of America and extolled his virtue, his efforts, and his work."[35]

Aside from losing a night of box office receipts, Cantor and Ziegfeld did not suffer financially. In October 1926, after Cantor had completed his long Broadway run (489 performances) and a twenty-one-city tour of the country, Paramount Pictures capitalized on the popularity of Cantor and *Kid Boots* by releasing an adaptation of the play. The sixty-minute silent film shares little with the hit musical beyond the title, lead actor, and a country club setting for some scenes. Cantor plays a tailor's assistant who gets mixed up with a millionaire (Lawrence Gray) and a pretty girl (Clara Bow). The critic Robert E. Sherwood aptly described *Kid Boots* as an "extraordinarily silly comedy with one of the worst plots in history," but the film provided a vehicle for flirtation, slapstick chases through city streets, mountainside cliffhangers, and other physical comedy at which Cantor excelled. Cantor performed silent versions of the familiar tailor and osteopath scenes, along with several new gags and routines. Sherwood and other critics excused the weak plot because of Cantor's acting skills. As Sherwood wrote, "Rhyme, reason, continuity, and logic may be utterly forgotten when Eddie Cantor embarks on his breathless gags. And there is an ample sufficiency of these." *Variety* similarly praised Cantor's "sense of natural comedy," predicting a successful career in the movies.[36]

After the success of *Kid Boots*, Cantor returned to Hollywood in January 1927 and started production on his second and final silent feature film, *Special Delivery*, released in April 1927. Cantor plays a mailman who captures a wanted con man. *Special Delivery* offered a thinner plot and fewer good scenes for Cantor than *Kid Boots*. In a typical lukewarm review of the film, the *Motion Picture News* critic Laurence Reid wrote, "They haven't done so well by Eddie Cantor in his successor to 'Kid Boots,' though there's no denying the piece has its share of laughs." The review went on to praise Cantor, but noted the "poor arrangement of scenes" and continuity problems in *Special Delivery*.[37] The year after the release of *Special Delivery*, Cantor assessed the film even more harshly, explaining that he wrote the original story for *Special Delivery* "as a less hokey vehicle only sparsely interspersed with gags." But by the time the film made it to the screen, "everything between laughs was cut out, giving the hoppy, hiccup effect of a comic strip or a stale-joke book . . . I saw my brain-child get its brains knocked out and I had to be an accomplice in the crime."[38] Still, *Special Delivery* did not hurt Cantor's reputation. Theater owners reported that the film did good business nationally. As *Variety* explained of the Los Angeles run, "With star well known and liked here, audience sort of condoned the weak moments of this screen opus."[39]

While Cantor filmed *Special Delivery*, he suffered from fatigue, weight loss, and chest pains, diagnosed as pleurisy. He recuperated for several weeks in the spring before returning to the stage in the *Ziegfeld Follies* of 1927. With music by Irving Berlin, the *Follies* enabled the star to showcase his full range of talents and infuse the performances with the contagious energy and charisma that live audiences loved. In addition to providing a better creative platform than silent film, the return to Broadway gave Cantor a higher salary. Whereas Cantor earned $4,000 a week in Hollywood, Ziegfeld offered him $4,500 plus a percentage of the box office receipts.[40]

As the sole headliner of the 1927 *Ziegfeld Follies*, Cantor sang, danced, and joked for nearly two hours each night. He co-wrote the sketches with Harold Atteridge, who had worked on *Midnight Rounders* and *Make It Snappy* for the Shuberts. The production demonstrated Cantor's comic versatility while building on established characters and types. Cantor played a clerk in a pet store, selling dogs much the same way he sold suits as a tailor. His other roles ranged from an inept ballet dancer to Mayor Jimmy Walker to a Jewish pilot from New Jersey. In Cantor's parody of Charles Lindbergh's solo transatlantic flight, Lindbergh becomes the similar-sounding Ginsberg, proud pilot of *Mosquito — The Spirit of New Jersey*. In his autobiography, published the following year, Cantor compared the sketch to the osteopath routine, except "the physical punishment took the form of a mental examination" by a major in charge of pilots at the airfield. When the officer asks Ginsberg whether he received a (military) commission, Ginsberg slips into Lower East Side salesman mode: "No, a straight salary." Like Lindbergh, Cantor's Ginsberg has sandwiches packed for the long trip, but the Jewish pilot decides to cancel the flight when he discovers that they are all ham sandwiches.[41]

Cantor remained with the *Ziegfeld Follies* from August 1927 through the end of January 1928, when he had to leave the show because he was, again, stricken with pleurisy. The actor spent time recuperating in Palm Springs, California; the Battle Creek Sanitarium in Michigan; and the Great Neck, New York, home that his family was renting. Never one to take a full vacation, Cantor used the period offstage to tell the writer David Freedman his life story, inaugurating a productive and profitable writing collaboration.[42] A fellow child of the Lower East Side, Freedman had a knack for churning out lively stories and witty gags. As writing partners from 1928 to 1934, Cantor and Freedman produced the screenplay for the film *Palmy Days* (1931), weekly radio scripts for *The Chase and Sanborn Hour*, and five books.

The autobiography, *My Life Is in Your Hands* (1928), emphasizes Cantor's rough childhood, love for Ida, and passion for show business. These aspects of his life story remained central to his persona for the rest of his career. Cantor does not allow his Jewish identification to overwhelm his image as an "American" stage star. *My Life Is in Your Hands* does not disclose Cantor's given name, "Isidore Iskowitz," which sounded much more foreign and a little more Jewish than "Cantor." Eddie's father in the book is "Michael Cantor," and "Grandma Esther" has no surname. Cantor and Freedman judiciously recall characteristic Jewish texts or experiences, but they rarely use the word "Jewish," relying on readers to understand this context. For example, the authors reference the Talmud on the first page of the book, and they frequently name streets and landmarks on the Jewish Lower East Side of Manhattan.

With *My Life Is in Your Hands* completed and ready to be released later in the year, Cantor began rehearsals for his new Ziegfeld show, *Whoopee*, in the fall of 1928. *Whoopee* extended Cantor's string of critical and commercial stage successes. Out-of-town previews in Pittsburgh and Washington, DC, set box office records for those cities. When tickets went on sale in Washington, the National Theatre opened at dawn, anticipating heavy advance sales, and quickly sold out. In New York, *Whoopee* premiered at the New Amsterdam Theatre on December 4, 1928, and remained there through November 1929, when it toured the country.[43]

The musical boasted many elements that appealed to audiences: Cantor, Ziegfeld, and a breezy story based on *The Nervous Wreck* (1924), a hit comedy by the Pulitzer Prize–winning playwright Owen Davis. Set in the West, *The Nervous Wreck* makes fun of tough guys, marriage, and trends in psychology. The main character, played by Cantor in the musical, is a likeable hypochondriac from Pittsburgh named Henry Williams. The heroine, Sally Morgan, tricks Henry into helping her escape an arranged marriage to a violent sheriff, Bob Wells. In adapting *The Nervous Wreck* for the musical stage, the Ziegfeld house writer William Anthony McGuire retained the central characters, the plot, and several scenes. McGuire added typical Ziegfeldian elements: snappy jokes, pleasant music, pretty girls, flashy costumes, and ornate sets.

McGuire also introduced a new character, Wanenis, who is part Indian. Sally cannot cross racial lines and marry Wanenis, her true love. In a plot twist, McGuire removes this barrier. Black Eagle, the Indian chief who raises Wanenis, claims that Wanenis is really white and that he was secretly adopted by the Indians as a child. Despite Black Eagle's revelation, some characters in the play are not ready to accept Wanenis as white. In the play's final scene, Cantor's character, Henry, delivers a brief statement opposing prejudice: "What's so terrible about being a little bit Indian? Look at Senator [Charles] Curtis, our newly elected vice-president. He's part Indian. And what's wrong with my friend Bill Rogers, you got to love him, and who in the world is going to walk up to Jack Dempsey and say 'to Hell with the Indians.'"[44] The play ends with an elaborate dance routine, the "Whoopee Ball." Sally marries Wanenis. Henry marries his nurse, Mary, and adopts a baby, as the cast reprises the song "Makin' Whoopee." In later radio and stage productions, Cantor frequently inserted serious observations about social problems, similar to his *Whoopee* character's remarks about prejudice. As in *Whoopee*, Cantor kept these comments brief and wrapped them around lighter fare, so that he did not antagonize audience members who disagreed with him or preferred breezy entertainment to weighty social commentary.

McGuire's script touches on issues of racial prejudice, miscegenation, and the poor treatment of Native Americans, but critics did not say very much about the play's politics. Nor did they take the contrived plot, including the marriages at the end, all that seriously. Instead, reviewers such as J. Brooks Atkinson of the *Times* appreciated *Whoopee* as a "gorgeous spectacle." In the big finale, wrote the *Washington Post* critic John J. Daly, "eight or ten Indian Lady Godivas come down the mountainside" riding real horses. "It is, as one of the first-nighters remarked, no time for dimming of the eyesight — and a spectacle of grandeur the like of which all the Indian chiefs who ever lived on the reservation of old never saw."[45]

Reviewers credited Cantor, along with the barely clothed chorus girls on horseback, for the play's success. Atkinson, for example, praised the headliner's versatility, proclaiming that Cantor "has never been so enjoyable as a comedian." Another opening night critic, Richard Lockridge of the *New York Sun*, similarly lauded Cantor's combination of star power and craftsmanship: "Even without Eddie Cantor's eyes, the rest of the show would roll. But I should hate to see it without him — hate not to watch that excellent clown building up his effect, gesture by gesture and word by word, until in the end everything he does and says is inexpressibly comic . . . His material is fair; he is delightful."[46]

As in other roles going back to his *Ziegfeld Follies* days of the late 1910s, aspects of Cantor's character, such as his physical weakness and hypochondria, perpetuated familiar Jewish stereotypes. In addition,

Cantor's persona made Henry Williams, whose religion is not identified in *The Nervous Wreck*, seem Jewish in *Whoopee*. But Cantor undercuts attempts to classify Henry or take the stereotypes too seriously. Over the course of the show, the character shifts among different occupations, personalities, sexual preferences, races, religions, and ethnicities. At one time or another he is white, black, Native American, Greek, Catholic, and Jewish, referencing Hebrew school.[47] *Whoopee* also includes a short variation on "Joe's Blue Front." Disguised as an Indian at a trading post, Henry barters with Underwood (Spencer Charters), a rich landowner. As they haggle, Cantor gradually moves from a typical Broadway Indian accent to a Jewish one. The two actors continue to improvise the negotiation, with Henry, the resourceful East Side salesman, getting the best of the deal.[48] Throughout his career, Cantor used these kinds of quick, funny, seemingly improvised bits to playfully highlight his Jewish background and his verbal facility.

The star broke character entirely to perform his specialty act in blackface. By late 1928, when *Whoopee* opened, blackface had become a nostalgic reminder of Cantor's skills as the consummate musical comedy performer. A thin premise sets the blackface scene. Henry is hiding from the sheriff in a stove. When Bob turns on the stove, Cantor pops out, covered in soot. Cantor interpolated songs and added new jokes to this segment throughout his run in *Whoopee*. He adapted this specialty routine for *A Ziegfeld Midnight Frolic* (1929), a short early sound film that provides a rich document of Cantor's solo act during this time. While he performs in blackface, he does not otherwise reference African-Americans. Instead, *A Ziegfeld Midnight Frolic* includes three songs from *Whoopee* and a short monologue with a sharp, clever joke about Henry Ford.

In July 1927, Ford issued a widely published statement apologizing to the Jewish people. He claimed that he had entrusted the *Dearborn Independent* to others and that, had he known about the newspaper's many antisemitic publications, he "would have forbidden their circulation." The historian Victoria Saker Woeste described Ford's statement, drafted by lawyer and American Jewish Committee president Louis Marshall, as "a masterful work of evasion draped in apparent contrition." While some major newspapers and members of the Jewish community accepted the apology because it effectively ended Ford's long and painful war against Jews, others, including Cantor, did not let the antisemitic industrialist off the hook so easily.[49]

In *A Ziegfeld Midnight Frolic*, Cantor announces with a mischievous smile, "I'm tickled that Henry Ford apologized to a race of people with whom I am very familiar." He then pauses and rolls his eyes upward, giving the audience time to align the joke with their knowledge of the news as well as Cantor's Jewish background. He continues, "And I know why Henry Ford was angry at the Jewish people in the first place. They got more for second-hand Fords than he was getting for new ones." Cantor's pride at Jewish acumen tweaks the insecurities at the heart of the antisemitic accusation that Jews controlled American business and finance. Cantor jokingly agrees that Jews are better businessmen than the nativists who resented them.[50]

Cantor ends his specialty act with the "Automobile Horn Song," a gyrating, eye-rolling tribute to "the only horn that has sex appeal." He generously gives the "boys" in the audience some advice for dealing with icy girls: "If you can't get by with scotch and rye / Then I'll loan you my . . ." — the rude horn from the orchestra finishes Cantor's sentence as he smiles and then runs offstage.[51]

Whoopee parodies conventional ideas about love, marriage, and masculinity. The stern sheriff Bob Wells (Jack Rutherford) stalks Sally Morgan (Frances Upton) and Henry, her accomplice. Bob represents the traditional masculine values: physical strength, violence, and relentless pursuit of his woman for marriage. In contrast, Henry gets the best of Bob through a different set of values, such as sensitivity and creativity, that were generally associated with women and Jews. Cantor's funny, decent, and gentle character seems baffled at the idea that people would go to so much trouble in the name of love. At different times, Henry seems attracted to men, women, and even a live calf, with which Cantor makes a big entrance in *Whoopee*'s opening scene. But echoing the streetwise cynicism of Cantor's earlier stage characters, Henry is wary of marriage.[52]

Cantor explains his caution in the song "Makin' Whoopee," by Gus Kahn and Walter Donaldson. He transforms from the sickly Henry Williams to a smooth and confident Broadway performer, backed by adoring chorus girls, introducing the impending wedding between Bob Wells and Sally Morgan. "Makin' Whoopee" starts with a snippet from

Cantor sings "Makin' Whoopee" in the film adaptation of *Whoopee!* (1930).

the "Wedding March," as Cantor begins his commentary: "Every time I hear that march from Lohengrin / I am always on the outside looking in / Maybe that is why I see the funny side / When I see a fallen brother take a bride / Weddings make a lot of people sad / But if you're not the groom, it's not so bad." Cantor then tells a wry, off-kilter love story: from wedding to boring domesticity to infidelity to pending divorce. After the judge sets alimony, Cantor counsels the philandering husband to stay with his wife: "You'd better keep her / You'll find its cheaper / Than making whoopee." Love brings the couple together, but cold economic calculation maintains the marriage.[53]

Offstage, Cantor had a more conventional view of marriage and a quieter life. He did not frequent the nightclubs and speakeasies of 1920s Manhattan, though he occasionally accepted work entertaining at after-hours apartment parties.[54] Other actors made the gossip columns and filled their memoirs with stories about chasing women, drinking booze, and consorting with mobsters. Al Jolson famously "stole" Ruby Keeler from Johnny "Irish" Costello.[55] The comedian Joe E. Lewis had his throat slashed by Chicago gangsters. Cantor's old friend George Jessel was especially active away from the stage. In his autobiography, Jessel talks about a pleasant dinner with Al Capone. Among their discussion topics was how frightened Cantor had been when he was forced to give a performance at Capone's home. Nucky Johnson, the gangland boss of Atlantic City who later served as the central figure in HBO's fictionalized *Boardwalk Empire* (2010–2014), hosted Jessel's wedding. Jessel explained that he "had often performed at [Johnson's] many benefits for the under-privileged."[56] In fact, Cantor did not enjoy a similar relationship with Johnson, though he appears as a friend of Johnson's and other gangsters in several episodes of the television drama.

While headlining in *Whoopee*, Cantor lived in suburban Great Neck with Ida and his five children, all girls. He and Ida remained married until her death in 1962. Though Cantor rarely discussed Ida in his interviews before *Whoopee*, perhaps worried that images of domesticity would clash with his licentious stage persona, he made his love for Ida and the girls more central to his public persona starting with the 1928 autobiography and his statements during the run of *Whoopee*. Even as he satirized marriage onstage, Cantor was transitioning to a more mature image as a family man and responsible citizen. In May 1929, at the age of thirty-seven, Cantor announced that he would retire from the stage when his contract with Ziegfeld expired and *Whoopee* closed in 1930. The actor had amassed a fortune on Wall Street. He asked, "Now that I am a millionaire, why should I tie myself down to time schedules and be prevented from following my own inclinations?"[57] He wanted to pursue philanthropic work and spend more time with his family. In January 1930, Cantor again declared that he was finished with live theater because of the rigors of nightly performing, affirming his desire to "tuck the kids into bed and tell them some genuine bedtime stories."[58]

Cantor kept his word about theatrical work. He occasionally committed to short engagements, but did not star in a play again until *Banjo Eyes* (1941). However, Cantor was not truly ready to swap stardom for bedtime stories. Instead, he was planning his next career moves. The economic Depression, sound film, and radio presented new opportunities.

6   VOICE OF THE DEPRESSION
(1929–1938)

As the 1920s ended, Eddie Cantor symbolized the decade's prosperity. Cantor and other celebrities flaunted the spoils of their wealth: fine clothes, big houses, expensive nights on the town, and flashy jewelry. Rather than resenting this conspicuous consumption, the public eagerly devoured gossip columns and fan magazines that provided glimpses of their favorite performers' fabulous lives.

For Cantor and many other Jewish performers, the children of immigrants who came of age in poor urban neighborhoods, wealth symbolized success. Cantor concludes his 1928 autobiography with a loving discussion of suburban real estate, rather than chronicling his most recent Broadway triumph in the *Ziegfeld Follies* of 1927 or his preparations for *Whoopee*. Cantor's family rented a "choicely appointed cottage" in tony Great Neck during the construction of his new mansion, rumored to cost $500,000. The temporary dwelling included "big grounds with a nice white fence all around, a vegetable garden, and garage space for several cars. It is quite a thing for one who has lived in a two-room basement on Madison Street," writes Cantor with a combination of pride and humility at his good fortune.[1]

Cantor lived opposite an estate belonging to Nathan S. Jonas, the founder of Manufacturer's Trust, one of America's largest financial institutions in 1928. Cantor visited his wealthy neighbor often, describing the older man as both a father figure and financial adviser. The orphan from the East Side knows that he has succeeded in America when Jonas dramatically hands him a financial statement and congratulates him on becoming a millionaire.[2]

On October 12, 1929, at the age of thirty-seven, Cantor moved from the rental property into his Great Neck dream house, which was now complete.[3] By then, it was clear that his plans to retire and live a quiet life would not go as planned. Throughout the fall of 1929, the stock market went on a long, steep decline. The last days of October were especially dramatic and volatile. On October 29, 1929, "Black Tuesday," panicked investors sold 16.4 million shares, a record volume for the New York Stock Exchange. By mid-November, when stocks hit their low for the year, the *New York Times* index of industrial stocks had fallen 50 percent from its high fewer than ten weeks earlier.[4] Rumors circulated that Cantor had lost $1 million in "paper profits." He was not alone.[5]

Variety greeted readers on October 30, 1929, with the front-page headline, "Wall St. Lays an Egg." The article conveys the shock and fear with which the entertainment industry reacted to the crash: "Many people of Broadway are known to have been wiped out. Reports of some in show business losing as much as $300,000 is not hearsay." An elderly vaudeville producer who had lost his life's savings "was found weeping like a child." Less sympathetically, *Variety* predicted that "any number of girls will probably have to give up expensive apartments and revise their manner of living."[6]

The prospects for a quick recovery seemed dim. *Variety* reported a dive in ticket sales for live theater, with New Yorkers "in no mood for high price amusement."[7] The trade magazine anticipated that all aspects of show business would be "depressed for months to come."[8] At the New Amsterdam Theatre on Broadway, where Cantor starred in *Whoopee*, box office receipts were off more than 30 percent in November 1929. After averaging $45,000 per week in gross sales before the crash, sales slumped to around $30,000. Therefore, Ziegfeld decided to take the show on the road for a national tour.[9]

Even before *Whoopee* closed on November 23, 1929, Cantor understood that the Jazz Age was over. New economic times demanded a fresh entertainment aesthetic. Nobody moved faster than Cantor. In the midst of the shock, panic, and misery around him, he remained cool, seized the opportunity, and remade his image from a beneficiary of the boom to a victim of the crash. Cantor took a commercial risk by presenting himself as the nation's leading jester in the wake of a disaster; however, his performances demonstrated his uncanny ability to anticipate public sentiment and deliver the kind of entertainment that the public wanted.

On Friday, October 25, 1929, at the end of a volatile week for the market, Cantor made a curtain speech about the economy from the stage of the New Amsterdam. Rather than remaining silent about his personal finances, like most other public figures, he daringly opened the post-*Whoopee* monologue by confirming the rumors of his losses that had been circulating around town: "Well, folks, they got me in the market just as they got everybody else." Cantor then continued his routine about the financial chaos, including one acidic observation that became part of Depression lore: "Nowadays, when a man walks into a hotel and requests a room on the nineteenth floor, the clerk asks him, 'For jumping or sleeping?'"[10]

The line perfectly encapsulated the hopelessness and despair that many experienced during the early years of the Depression. While the image of bankers plummeting to their deaths is more of an urban myth than a historical truth, the national suicide rate increased more than 20 percent between 1929 and 1933, from 13.9 to 17.4 per one hundred thousand.[11] Sydney Weinberg, a senior partner with Goldman Sachs at the time of the crash, looked back on the era: "I don't know anybody that jumped out of the window. But I know many who threatened to jump. They ended up in nursing homes and insane asylums and things like that. These were people who were trading in the market or in banking houses. They broke down physically, as well as financially."[12]

Two nights after his *Whoopee* curtain speech, on October 27, 1929, Cantor emceed the annual Jewish Theatrical Guild dinner at the ornate Commodore Hotel. The event attracted fifteen hundred people, including Mayor Jimmy Walker, Sophie Tucker, Ben Hecht, the agent William Morris, the Hollywood executive William Fox, and the guest of honor, George Jessel. New York radio station WMCA broadcast the program live. Cantor started the evening by joking about the economic turmoil that had shocked the nation: "If the stock market goes any lower, I know thousands of married men who are going to leave their sweethearts and go back to their wives." He continued, "As for myself, I am not worried, my broker is going to carry me; he and three other pall-bearers." Throughout the 1920s, Cantor made himself a symbol of fast money and upward mobility. But after the crash, he quickly reconfigured his act to minimize his wealth and empathize with people struggling financially. As he began to remake his persona, Cantor substituted gallows humor for his old lighthearted exuberance.[13]

Cantor did not single-handedly invent the idea of using darkly appropriate comedy to cope with the market crash. As stocks plummeted, show business insiders characteristically responded with anecdotes and quips, which Cantor quickly and skillfully exported from the street corners and backrooms of Broadway to living rooms across the nation. Cantor's friend Will Rogers presented a similar dry wit and populist perspective on greedy Wall Street financiers and hypocritical, incompetent politicians.[14] On October 25, 1929, the *New York Times* published a biting letter from Rogers with a chilling observation similar to one Cantor offered a few days later: "When Wall Street took that tail spin, you had to stand in line to get a window to jump out of, and speculators were selling space for bodies in the East River." Referencing stagnant crop prices and other economic difficulties with which Midwesterners contended throughout the 1920s, before the market crash, Rogers quipped, "Now they [Wall Street investors] know what the farmer has been up against for eight years."[15] The next day, Rogers described himself flying over the country, looking down on "prosperous towns," and deciding that the market crash would not affect most of the country, as it did New York. "Why an old sow and a litter of pigs make more people a living than all the steel and general motor stock combined," he wrote. "Why the whole 120,000,000 of us are more dependent on the cackling of a hen than if the Stock Exchange was turned into a night club. And New Yorkers call them rubes."[16]

Rather than talking of "old sows," "rubes," and divisions between urban and rural America, Cantor focused on shared struggles and common enemies. He quickly disseminated his sharp, topical comedy through every popular medium of the time.

On October 29, 1929, while the stock market was shattering records for trading volume, Cantor continued his campaign against Wall Street by recording his *Whoopee* monologue, which the Victor label quickly released as "Eddie Cantor's Tips on the Stock Market."[17] A few weeks later, Simon and Schuster published Cantor's latest Depression product: *Caught Short!: A Saga of Wall Street* (1929), a book of jokes and short narrative sketches, including some bits from the stage routine. *Caught Short!* was an immediate success, selling one hundred thousand copies in the first week and a total of five hundred thousand copies.[18] A *Variety* reviewer labeled Cantor "the flap-eared prophet of yesterday's tragedy," commending his "snappy writing" and timeliness in releasing the book "just when everybody is talking about the market."[19] In *Caught Short!,*

Cantor observes, "Nearly all of us made promises we can't keep on account of the turn in Wall Street. I promised my wife a rope of pearls. I can't get the pearls but I have the rope—and I'm thinking of using it myself." *Variety* recognized the commercial potential of Cantor's black humor, predicting that "Mrs. Cantor may yet get that rope of pearls."[20]

Cantor released five joke books between 1929 and 1932, three co-written with David Freedman, filled with seemingly autobiographical stories that melded fact and fancy. Similar in tone and style to his comic monologues, the publications helped Cantor present himself as the nation's "chief mourner of the late-lamented stock market," according to the *New York Times*.[21] The books sold for about a dollar each and made no pretentions at being high art. Cantor's publisher, Ray Long and Richard R. Smith, promoted *Your Next President!* (1932) with the one-line description: "NOT a literary treat—just one laugh after another."[22] Nevertheless, Cantor recognized the social and political importance of this empathetic, topical humor, which articulated the anger and frustration of those suffering during the economic collapse. While he was writing *Caught Short!*, the author told himself, "You owe it to the American public to hand them a snicker in their hour of Goldman-Sachs."[23]

Cantor occasionally needled Goldman Sachs from the stage and in print. More quietly, in February 1932, he launched a lawsuit against the firm, alleging that it "willfully and recklessly" squandered funds in purchasing stock, including Manufacturer's Trust, at artificially inflated values. Cantor personally lost $323,000 on his investments with Goldman Sachs, plus he covered the losses of friends. The suit remained in the courts through 1936, when the two sides reached a settlement that favored Goldman Sachs.[24] Aside from Goldman Sachs, Cantor did not target other prominent banks and investment houses with Jewish management. Most notably, Cantor spared the Bank of United States, founded by Joseph S. Marcus, a Jewish immigrant from Eastern Europe. The bank's well-publicized collapse in late 1930 devastated the many Jewish customers who had trusted the Bank of United States with their savings.[25]

With his many friends in New York's Jewish community, Cantor may have found it distasteful to laugh about the management, investors, small businesses, and working people who lost money in Jewish-led institutions, which were relatively small players in the nation's finances.

In addition, jibes from Cantor about Jewish banks may have fueled antisemitic accusations that Jews were responsible for the economic calamity. In a long 1936 article that studied Jewish participation in America's economic life, and countered charges of disproportionate Jewish influence in key industries, *Fortune* magazine found that "there are practically no Jewish employees of any kind in the largest commercial banks." Similarly, investment firms with Jewish ownership "do not compare in power with the great houses owned by non-Jews."[26]

The *Fortune* article hints at the deeper division between banks owned and operated by non-Jews, such as J. P. Morgan and Company, and the handful of Jewish-owned firms, most notably Kuhn, Loeb, and Co. Though Jewish and non-Jewish bankers did business together, they operated in different social, cultural, and religious worlds. Jews were excluded from the resorts and clubs frequented by the Morgan directors, which made the House of Morgan an inviting target for Cantor.[27]

In one of the sharpest sketches in *Caught Short!*, Cantor talks his way into the Morgan boardroom. The comedian puts on blackface and explains to the security guard, "I'm the Kuhn, of Kuhn, Loeb and Co."[28] In addition to making a punning reference to his blackface through the derogatory term "coon," the line signals Cantor's solidarity with the Jewish firms and articulates a populist anger at the power and folly of the nation's great banking houses. Cantor plays himself, the wisecracking Jewish comedian, rather than a stereotypical African-American, as he satirically reconstructs an actual closed-door meeting at the offices of J. P. Morgan and Company that made headlines in October 1929. Responding to record trading levels and sharp declines on Wall Street on the morning of October 24, 1929, five leading financiers met that afternoon. Thomas W. Lamont, senior partner at the Morgan firm, emerged from the meeting with the news that the financial system was fundamentally sound. Lamont also implied that it was a good time to invest in the market, asserting that many stocks had fallen too low. The banker's statement steadied stocks that day, but "Black Monday," the steepest one-day decline in market history, was only four days away.[29]

In Cantor's timely spoof, the hapless financiers make small talk about their cars and chauffeurs before they get to the "serious business" of the meeting: finding a new masseur for their country club. Without having addressed the precarious financial situation, the bankers emerge to find "a mob of frantic reporters" waiting to hear how they will respond to the "agonizing howls from the Stock Exchange across the street." According to Cantor, "That's where real leadership showed itself." In "slow measured tones," Lamont announces, "Everything is well in hand. We are entirely pleased with the situation. Conditions are basically sound." In Cantor's version of the story, investors are more savvy and skeptical of Lamont. After his pompous statement, "Reporters rushed to their telephones, and in a moment the market dropped ten points more."[30]

The topical comedy in *Caught Short!* satirizes the assurances by leading politicians, bankers, and industrialists at the height of the October crash that all was well with the economy. Yet Cantor also gently blames himself for trusting these authorities and trying to use the stock market to get rich quickly. Cantor identifies himself as a "comedian, author, statistician, and victim" on the title page and begins *Caught Short!* by focusing on his victimization: "My throat is cut from ear to ear. I am bleeding profusely in seven other places. There is a knocking in the back of my head, my hands tremble violently, and I have a sharp shooting pain all over my body . . . You can readily guess that I was in the market. Brother, I wasn't *in* the market: I was *under* it." A short "note about the author" appended to the manuscript assures readers: "As a financier and stock market operator [Cantor's] experience is intensely real and truly representative of the excitements and despairs of millions of his fellow Americans."[31]

The comedian exaggerated the direness of his circumstances for dramatic effect. The market crash represented, at most, a temporary financial setback. Cantor offset his bad investments with savings and other assets, including a marketable name and reputation as a top-flight entertainer, which enabled him to procure lucrative work on stage, radio, and film. Even in October 1929, the performer was drawing a salary of $5,000 a week from *Whoopee*, which toured the country, starting in Boston, through March 1930.[32] The traveling show interpolated quips about President Hoover and jokes from *Caught Short!* The *Boston Globe* reported that "even those in the audience who had been the hardest hit by the crash roared with laughter over his clever wise-cracks." When *Whoopee* reached Chicago in January 1930, the *Tribune* critic praised Cantor's "reckless" style, while expressing skepticism about his money troubles: "Mr. Cantor talks so much about the stock market that I'm convinced he didn't lose a dollar."[33]

After the *Whoopee* tour ended, Cantor went to Hollywood so he could star in the big-budget film version, for which he received more than $200,000.[34] Seeing his future in film, Cantor moved the family to Beverly Hills and tried to sell his newly constructed suburban estate in Great Neck. The December 1930 listing of Cantor's home, after the actor had spent more than a year lamenting his stock market losses, prompted rumors that Cantor needed money. Cantor did not dispel these rumors. He had no need to appear prosperous as so much of the country suffered. However, Cantor's former close friend and financial adviser, Daniel Lipsky, estranged from Cantor since the Wall Street crash, issued a statement that Cantor was doing well financially. The performer did not own stocks on margin. Cantor's losses, though real, did not require him to sell other assets, including the house in Great Neck. According to Lipsky, Cantor's jokes about being ruined in the market were for "stage purposes only and he is a highly prosperous man." In fact, according to a *New York Times* article, "Cantor's friends intimated that a million [dollars] was a conservative estimate of Cantor's fortune."[35] The actor earned approximately $450,000 the year after the market crash.[36] The commercial and critical success of the film version of *Whoopee*, released in the fall of 1930, further solidified Cantor's financial position. Starting in 1931, Cantor joked less about the decline in his personal fortunes and more about the state of the nation.

The movie *Whoopee!* closely followed the script of the Broadway production, though the producer Samuel Goldwyn and the writer William M. Conselman purged the raciest lines. *Whoopee!* cemented Cantor's national reputation as one of America's most popular comedians. Newspapers across the country raved about the production, especially Cantor. The *Atlanta Constitution* called Cantor "an uproariously funny little lad" and advised listeners to "forget that you have worries and troubles: just sit back and laugh your head off and have a good time. Cantor is a sure cure for the blues."[37] The *Variety* editor Sime Silverman presciently assured theater owners, especially those in smaller markets, of the film's box office appeal: "Not an iota of question about the b.o. return on this in the keys and good sized towns. There should be none in the sticks or tanks either. House managers can guarantee this to be [the] laugh picture in those places and make the town turn out for the opening. Rest of the stay will take care of itself."[38]

The many large and medium-sized cities in the East and Midwest, where Cantor regularly toured with his theatrical productions throughout the late 1910s and the 1920s, immediately embraced *Whoopee!* The movie was a hit in New York, Philadelphia, Cleveland, and Providence.[39] In Chicago, sales started slowly, "but everybody who saw [*Whoopee!*] liked [it], and told somebody else," according to *Variety*, giving the picture a strong closing figure.[40] Audiences also packed movie houses in cities outside Cantor's theatrical touring circuit, such as Portland, Denver, and Oklahoma City.[41] Theater owners in smaller markets staged creative promotions for the film. The Strand Theatre in Altoona, Pennsylvania, was "jammed from opening to closing" after employees blanketed the town with promotional cards and streamers.[42] In Louisville, Kentucky, Loew's theater manager Walter D. McDowell outfitted everybody from newspaper delivery boys to drugstore waitresses to school dance orchestras with "Cantor berets" and stenciled "See *Whoopee!*" on streets throughout the town.[43]

Not surprisingly given its popularity, *Whoopee!* provided a template for a series of Cantor vehicles featuring the same kinds of risqué jokes, sexy chorus girls, exotic settings, and lavish costumes. In the six successors to *Whoopee!* from 1931 to 1937, Cantor plays an effeminate young man without much money or social standing who finds himself in an alien land where local tough guys want to hurt him. The exotic settings for the lightweight, contrived stories include ancient Rome, Mexico, Egypt, and ancient Baghdad. In these metaphors for the immigrant experience, Cantor's naïve character learns to master new and dangerous situations, despite his initial confusion and weakness, through a combination of astonishing luck, savvy wisecracks, a strong sense of moral decency, and a propensity for leading lavish song-and-dance routines when all else fails. The big-budget productions include the occasional Yiddish phrase or quick Jewish quip, but Cantor also draws on Jewish cultural experience more subtly, through his series of likeable nebbish roles. The disadvantaged outsider became a staple of Jewish screen humor.[44]

In his widely cited *What Makes Pistachio Nuts?* (1992), the historian Henry Jenkins claims that *Whoopee!* "turned a modest profit based on its strong showings in several northern cities and its mild success elsewhere, but it failed to excite interest in 'the sticks' or in regional centers." Jenkins argues that the producer, Goldwyn, and the studio, United Artists, identified Cantor's Jewishness as a problem and engaged in a "de-Semitization campaign," forcing the actor to expunge "all overt acknowledgment of his ethnic identity" after *Whoopee!* so that he could appeal to filmgoers in "the hinterlands."[45] Jenkins understates the national popularity of *Whoopee!*, and he overstates the extent to which the studio made Cantor and his films less Jewish for rural audiences. Cantor's characters in the films that followed are similar to Henry Williams from *Whoopee!* However, Jenkins is correct in pointing out that studios found it difficult to include overtly Jewish material in the comedies of the early 1930s. In considering story ideas for Cantor's films, studio executives may have feared that explicitly Jewish characters and scenarios would have been too obscure for audiences unfamiliar with Jewish culture.

Beyond differences in regional taste, there were other reasons that 1930s films rarely featured Jewish characters and themes. After July 1934, the Production Code Administration (PCA) began to strictly enforce its code governing movie content. The code required that people of all nations be represented fairly and prohibited material ridiculing "any religious faith." Around this time, Jewish advocacy groups such as the ADL monitored Hollywood and worked closely with producers to eliminate stereotypical images of Jews that might fuel antisemitism. Given this careful scrutiny of Jewish content, studios chose the safe route of minimizing the Jewish presence on-screen. In addition, after the rise of Hitler in 1933, films featuring Jewish characters were certain to be banned in Germany, an important foreign market.[46]

As his films became more formulaic, Cantor enjoyed the space to unleash his freewheeling stage style through the emerging medium of radio: a form in which he exerted more artistic control. Cantor hired most of the writers, chose the stories, and managed the scripts with limited network and sponsor intervention. Starting in the fall of 1931, Cantor's rollicking *Chase and Sanborn Hour* blended songs, skits, humorous monologues, and casual banter between the star and announcer James Wallington. At home, from the comfort of their living rooms, listeners across the country enjoyed a free, weekly combination of music, comedy, and star power unlike anything else on the air.

Cantor was one of many film and Broadway stars who participated in experimental broadcasts and took guest slots throughout the 1920s. However, before Cantor's long run on *The Chase and Sanborn Hour*, most of these appearances by stage stars were short-lived. In adapting his theatrical persona to radio, Cantor created a format and a formula for radio comedy. He took advantage of the fact that radio was relatively new. The industry was open to experimentation in 1931. Broadcasters needed more big names and talent. NBC was established as the nation's first national radio network, reaching from New York west to Kansas City, only five years earlier. NBC added a second network, "NBC Blue," in 1927 and began coast-to-coast broadcasts in 1928. In 1930 a little under fourteen million households, representing 45 percent of all homes, owned radio sets. As more stations came online during the 1930s, programming improved, receiver prices fell, and the industry boomed. Millions of Americans purchased radio sets for cheap entertainment during the Great Depression, and radio became central to American life. By 1940 radio ownership had risen to over 80 percent of all American households, plus more than seven million cars were equipped with radios.[47]

It is impossible to determine whether Cantor's program induced people to purchase radio sets, or whether Cantor merely figured out a way to capitalize on the growing medium, but he soon became one of the biggest stars of the air. During his initial 1931–1932 season, the *Chase and Sanborn Hour* averaged a Crossley rating of 28.9, second only to *Amos 'n' Andy*. The next year, Cantor's show averaged a 55.7 rating, which remains the highest mark ever for a weekly, prime-time network program. At least twenty-five million Americans spent an hour with Cantor each Sunday night during the early 1930s.[48] A May 1933 survey of listeners conducted by *Variety* named Cantor America's favorite radio performer. The survey further divided the audience into five geographical regions. Cantor placed first everywhere except for the Northwest, where he was second to Jack Pearl, one of the many Jewish stage comics who migrated to radio in the wake of Cantor's success. Others who followed Cantor included the Marx Brothers, Jack Benny, Al Jolson, George Burns, and Ed Wynn.[49]

Variety recognized that Cantor's radio popularity enhanced the marketability of his films to rural audiences: "Every country store and farmhouse has [a] radio set now. And, while Eddie Cantor was just a picture

Cantor, a master of promoting himself across media, adds an NBC microphone to this publicity photo for the film *Roman Scandals* (1933).

on a calendar two years ago, he's an idol now to farmhands."[50] Cantor provided a model for other stars, from Jack Benny to Bob Hope, by using his NBC radio show to promote himself across media, constantly plugging his films and books. With its national reach, radio was an ideal medium for Cantor to purvey his post-crash persona of a wise guy who had been burned by the stock market and politicians, but retained his faith in himself, his fellow Americans, and the country's institutions.

During Cantor's first broadcast, on September 13, 1931, announcer James Wallington touts the headliner's most recent book, in which Cantor campaigns for president: "The Cantor five-year plan for removing the depression, as outlined in Eddie's new book, *Yoo-Hoo Prosperity!*, has been hailed by right-thinking citizens everywhere as pretty darn nifty. Already, the word goes 'round, 'What about Cantor in 1932?'" Cantor then arrives to deliver jokes about the Depression. He takes a shot at Secretary of the Treasury Andrew Mellon: "We found out what Mellon meant when he said, 'The country is on a solid foundation.' It had to be. It hit rock-bottom!" However, on the air, Cantor refuses to takes sides between Roosevelt and Hoover, instead urging listeners to "elect Cantor" because "Cantor sings songs."[51]

An experienced faux candidate, having been nominated as a prospective cabinet member during his friend Will Rogers's satirical 1928 presidential campaign, Cantor mined the absurd idea of a "President Cantor." In 1931 national voters would not have elected even a serious Jewish politician, let alone an energetic former vaudevillian and son of Russian immigrants. Cantor did not explicitly reference his religion during the campaign, but his appeals had an urban, Jewish flavor. For example, later in the debut episode, Cantor again promotes *Yoo-Hoo Prosperity!*, sounding like the fast-talking Lower Manhattan tailor he portrayed on Broadway, while also paying tribute to his sponsor: "Now of course I could say to you, if you want to know about Cantor's plans, go buy Cantor's book. But I wouldn't do that. After all, what would Chase and Sanborn think? We are selling coffee tonight, not books. So I wouldn't say you can get Cantor's book for a dollar. Anyhow, who's got a dollar?" He then shares his recovery plan for free. "Cantor for President" became a running joke from the time of the September 1931 broadcast until the 1932 election.[52]

As a network radio star, Cantor parodied the empty promises of politicians and used his performance skills to animate the kind of humor that appeared in his books. In December 1931, he introduced an upbeat song, "When I'm the President," that became part of his repertoire, changing the verses on each broadcast. A typical line: "I'm not a politician, so what I say is true / If you send me to Washington, here's what I promise you." Cantor pledges to rid the country of such menaces as landlords, taxicabs, and doughnut holes. The refrain, "We Want Cantor," became a staple of Cantor's radio, film, and stage performances.[53] The pretend candidate, a Jewish populist from the East Side, resonated with listeners, who embraced Cantor's distinctive combination of anger, parody, and patriotism. In October 1931, three weeks after Cantor's debut, a *New York Times* column reported that many listeners took the campaign seriously and pledged to support Cantor for president.[54]

Cantor took an eight-month hiatus from radio starting in February 1932 to prepare and shoot *The Kid from Spain* in Hollywood. But he and Freedman kept the faux presidential campaign alive with a new book, *Your Next President!*, released in March of that year. *Your Next President!* targets politicians' pompous speeches, pandering to voters, and outrageous plans to stimulate the economy. With the 1932 election approaching, Cantor reserves the sharpest barbs for Hoover and his cabinet. In the book's longest routine, Cantor bursts into a White House lunch in which Hoover is meeting with "the leading men of the country." Similar to the financiers in *Caught Short!*, the politicians and presidential advisers sitting around the table are out of touch with the rest of the nation and obsessed with their personal comforts. Mellon, one of the wealthiest men in the world, decides that "the issue for the campaign" should be "'Buy Now!' If we could get enough people to buy stocks I could unload! What do you say gentlemen?" The inept Cabinet members respond, looking forward to dessert, "Oooh! Pie!"[55]

Cantor did not campaign for Roosevelt in the 1932 election, but the many barbs at Hoover in his books made his political sympathies clear. Cantor starts *Your Next President!* with a speech accepting a presidential nomination and reviewing the problems and weaknesses of each candidate, including Hoover. When it is Roosevelt's turn, however, Cantor is enthusiastic, offering his first public endorsement of his fellow New Yorker: "Franklin D. Roosevelt has no chance at all. He's honest, capable, will not be dictated to and is quick on finding a solution to any problem. This disqualifies him at once."[56]

Cantor and announcer James Wallington on *The Chase and Sanborn Hour,*
circa 1932.

On radio, Cantor and the head writer, Freedman, walked a fine line in
crafting topical routines without appearing overly political, especially
before an election. Radio attracted a large, diverse, national audience.
The network and sponsor gave Cantor the freedom to joke about the
Depression. Listeners expected this kind of satirical commentary from
Cantor. But it was not in anybody's interests to alienate a significant

portion of the socially and politically diverse national radio audience. Freedman explained that when they presented Cantor as "Uncle Sam's adviser — Eddie Cantor, U.S.A. . . . his comedy became timely." Yet the writer also declared politics a taboo subject because you "step on too many toes."[57] Cantor still occasionally made fun of his favorite print targets: banks, Wall Street businessmen, and Mellon. But compared with his books, Cantor presented fewer political routines and softened his satire. He did not need to remind the country about the problems with banks and politicians. More than two thousand banks failed in 1931, as depositors lost confidence in the banking system and the nation's prominent bankers. In addition, the Depression took a great political and personal toll on Hoover and his administration. Mellon resigned as treasury secretary in February 1932, and the unpopular president appeared exhausted and frail during his unsuccessful campaign against Roosevelt.[58]

Cantor rallied the country with an appealing combination of youthful energy and optimism. In a December 1931 skit, Cantor is the "Depression Doctor." His patient is Uncle Sam, who feels weak. Cantor reminds Uncle Sam that the country has suffered similar attacks, referencing panics in 1872, 1893, and 1907. When Uncle Sam protests that this one is worse, Cantor replies, "That's what you say every time. Why, compared to that internal trouble you had in 1865 which nearly upset your whole system, you haven't even got a bad cold now!" Cantor is confident that Uncle Sam will "pull through" and "boom" again. The doctor tells his patient to smile, choose the right candidate in the 1932 presidential election, stop making trips to Europe, and remember that he has "the power and wealth to be the biggest nation on earth." The sketch was such a success that, responding to listener demand, Chase and Sanborn published the "Depression Doctor" script in a 1932 promotional pamphlet for the program.[59]

In assessing the stock market crash and its aftermath, Cantor faulted weak politicians; greedy, shortsighted business leaders; and gullible investors, including hard-working people like him, who believed that the market offered a fast route to wealth. Cantor empathized with his listeners. He knew things were tough. But he urged people to have faith that life would get better. Cantor believed in America with the fervor of a child of poor immigrants, who started with nothing and achieved enormous success. He referenced his working-class background, inspiring listeners to remain hopeful about their own lives. However, Cantor did not use his rags-to-riches story to condone laissez-faire capitalism and social Darwinist ideology, which put the onus on individuals, rather than the government, to pull themselves up from poverty.[60] Instead, he supported relief through a combination of government assistance, private charitable aid, and neighborly kindness that people expressed among themselves. Cantor also advocated thrift, resourcefulness, and faith that conditions would improve. For example, in his season debut from October 1932, Cantor introduced a new song with a story about his proposal to Ida when they were both penniless. The sweet and wistful "If I Only Had a Five Cent Piece," is about a man who is "not so big on education" and doesn't have a "single thing" to give his lover, but he dreams of what he would share if he only could: "If I only had a five cent piece, enough to get a cup of coffee, I'd drink water instead, and go begging for bread, but I'd give the nickel to you."[61]

Cantor made the upbeat "Now's the Time to Fall in Love," from his film *Palmy Days*, his theme song, singing it each week during the first season and returning to it periodically throughout the decade. Cantor added hopeful verses on many programs. An early December 1931 version advises: "When Christmas is coming / Then business is humming / Now's the time to fall in love / All our worries and hard luck are bound to go now / Get your girl to stand by the mistletoe now / And tell her that Cantor / Says 'Yes' is the answer / Now's the time to fall in love."[62] On his December 27, 1931, program, Cantor introduces the song with a New Year's poem for girls to deliver to their "fellows." Marriage "is a lot of fun / And two can live as cheap as one." In fact, "any girl who really loves a man can support him."[63]

These sentimental songs and sketches, which did not have the sting of his sharper barbs aimed at bankers and politicians, became more central to Cantor's on-air persona during the early 1930s. Through the relatively new medium of radio, he demonstrated the way comedy could provide people with hope during a difficult time, promoting an optimistic faith in Americans' decency and resilience very much in line with that of President Roosevelt's. The *New York Times* radio critic Orrin E. Dunlap Jr. later recognized the importance and prescience of Cantor's light music and stories: "He stepped up to the microphone just when the depression caused no end of people to relish a comedian."[64] The radio writer B. F. Wilson similarly commended Cantor for using "his comic talent in an effort to cheer the public . . . Week after week, despite bank closings, threats of civil revolution, unemployment, stock exchange scandals, a new hope brought about by laughter and the spreading of the gospel truth of not taking life too seriously swept over the air."[65] More than sixty years after Cantor's 1930s programs, the actor Jerry Stiller referenced the lyrics to "Now's the Time to Fall in Love" in his 2000 autobiography. "Even my mother's anguish subsided when Eddie Cantor sang 'Potatoes are cheaper,'" wrote Stiller, who grew up in the Jewish working-class Brooklyn neighborhood of East Brownsville during the Depression. "More than anyone else, Eddie Cantor made us aware that the entire country was in a depression and we weren't alone."[66]

The romantic radio star who sang about missing nickels and enduring marriages sharply contrasted with Cantor's 1920s stage persona. Public taste changed quickly after the market crash, and Cantor adapted accordingly. Risqué hits from only a few years earlier, such as "Hungry Women" and "Makin' Whoopee," were seldom part of Cantor's early 1930s radio repertoire. Cantor also softened the rough stage persona of the 1920s through his sincerity and humility, especially in the inspirational messages with which he ended programs. He continued to present a range of music and comedy sketches on the show. Aspects of his manic, farcical, aggressive Broadway style remained. But Cantor was also using his program to present a more sober image that fit the times and the intimate medium of radio. The actor tempered his frantic energy for the listeners across the country who welcomed him into their homes for a full hour each week.

As Cantor later wrote, he believed that his fans were interested in "serious things, life, death, politics, religion, and taxes. We knew our audience, we had a sampling of them each week face to face, and they wanted a thought as well as a laugh."[67] Cantor created long sketches on crime, juvenile abandonment, automobile safety, and other issues that, he remembered, "a comedian had never tried to talk about before." During an especially powerful November 1933 piece, Cantor convinces an angry and despondent unemployed man not to commit suicide.[68] The character in Cantor's sketch was fictional, but the problem was real. In his 1934 primer on broadcasting, the critic Robert West cited this program, which generated many grateful letters from listeners, as an example of the "added moral quality" of Cantor's comedy.[69]

President Roosevelt and the New Deal occasionally became a subject of Cantor's topical segments. After the 1932 election, Cantor endorsed Roosevelt's policies while building a friendship with the president and some of his staff. Cantor's fervor for the president marked him as a New York Jew as clearly as his accent or Yiddish inflections did. In 1932, 80 percent of Jewish voters backed Roosevelt. A vote for Roosevelt represented a vote against Hoover, Mellon, the banking establishment, Prohibition, limited government, and older ways of addressing social and economic problems. The president won an even higher percentage of Jewish votes in each subsequent election. Jews embraced the president's personality and policies to alleviate their economic pains.[70]

Roosevelt appointed Jews to civil service positions at every level of the government, including senior advisory roles in his administration, while also promoting public welfare initiatives and supporting unions. New Deal programs provided federal relief funds that local Jewish social welfare agencies administered, easing the strains on these charities and affirming that the government could effectively partner with private Jewish philanthropies.[71] Roosevelt's politics appealed to Cantor. In addition, the actor may have recognized aspects of himself in the president: an ambitious, optimistic, savvy New Yorker who knew a thing or two about using radio to charm mass audiences.

As the president of the newly formed Screen Actors Guild (SAG) from 1933 to 1935, Cantor lobbied the Roosevelt administration. Since the 1919 Equity strike, Cantor had taken mostly honorary positions in professional organizations and guilds without becoming involved in union politics or causes; however, a series of moves by the studios to slash wages and exert more control over performers' careers impelled Cantor and his Hollywood cohorts to organize. In the fall of 1933, Cantor led the actors' fight against a set of tentative regulations, drafted by the producers, that were slated to become part of the new federal National Recovery Administration (NRA) code for the industry. He secured an audience with Roosevelt at the president's vacation home in Warm Springs, Georgia, on November 22, 1933. Cantor took the train south from New York accompanied by Marvin C. McIntyre, Roosevelt's longtime appointments secretary. McIntyre and Cantor remained friends and occasional correspondents over the next several years. The influential *Motion Picture Herald* was incensed that, of the thousands of people who had attempted to see the president about the NRA code, Roosevelt chose Cantor: a "merry, whimsical song-and-dance man." Perhaps, the trade paper condescendingly editorialized, Cantor will be funnier than the many others who were more qualified to represent the industry.[72] *Motion Picture Herald* underestimated Cantor. The comedian successfully made his case. After the meeting, Roosevelt suspended the sections of the code most objectionable to actors, including provisions that would have weakened the actors' negotiating positions and limited their salaries.[73] The next year, Cantor attributed the SAG's founding and growth to the Roosevelt administration, which created a political environment in which the union could flourish. He commended the president's "sympathy for all employees of the nation and his definite determination to improve the working conditions in every walk of life."[74]

Cantor maintained a friendly relationship with the president by supporting Roosevelt's favorite charity, the Georgia Warm Springs Foundation. On November 29, 1933, Roosevelt wrote to Cantor, thanking him for his "most generous check" to the foundation and inquiring whether Cantor might be able to conduct a live broadcast of his radio show from Warm Springs.[75] Though Cantor was unable to move his program to Georgia, he continued to raise funds for the charity by participating in Roosevelt's annual "Birthday Balls."

After their Warm Springs meeting, the actor backed Roosevelt on prime time. His broadcasts combined patriotic support for the chief executive with partisan enthusiasm for Roosevelt's leadership and the soundness of his policies. In his December 31, 1933, program, Cantor performed a variation of his "Depression Doctor" skit from 1931. This time, Uncle Sam is in the hospital, nervously preparing to give birth to a new year. Cantor assures Uncle Sam that "Doctor" Roosevelt is as good as George Washington or Abraham Lincoln: "If anybody can accomplish wonders, he can. I've seen him work. He doesn't give much medicine, either. He's got that magnetic personality—the minute he walks into a sickroom, the patient feels better already." An actor playing Roosevelt appears later in the skit to deliver Uncle Sam's baby. The scene ends triumphantly, with a baby crying and Cantor excitedly making plans for

Cantor and Shirley Temple shake hands at President Roosevelt's birthday celebration, a fund-raiser for the president's Georgia Warm Springs Foundation that was held at the Biltmore Hotel in Los Angeles (January 1937).

the new year: "Let's celebrate. We'll give a party and invite a hundred and twenty million people to the christening. We'll change the baby's name from Happy New Year to Happy New Deal." After the broadcast, President Roosevelt read a script of the program and thanked Cantor, through a letter from appointments secretary McIntyre.[76]

The following November, in an Armistice Day radio show, Cantor defended Roosevelt from charges by Senator William Borah (R-Idaho) that the administration was using federal relief funds wastefully, to achieve political ends. Before the broadcast, Cantor proudly alerted McIntyre, his contact in the White House, that the evening's program would "use a half dozen lines to answer Senator Borah."[77] In the skit, Cantor reunites with two likable old buddies from the East Side who had served in the war. The talk turns to politics, including government spending. Cantor says, "I know their argument . . . some of the money is wasted. What if it is? It's impossible to keep track of every penny in your own home. Are millions who are in need of help to be denied it, because some of the money is lost in the process of distribution." After a friend agrees, Cantor continues, "I know if our country needed us tomorrow we would all gladly answer the call—but honestly, aren't we better off spending money to feed men rather than to feed cannon? Isn't it better to spend our billions on Life instead of Death?"[78] The day after the broadcast, McIntyre informed Cantor that Stephen Early, Roosevelt's press secretary, listened to the program and "thought it was a fine contribution, helpful, effective, and appreciated."[79]

By the early 1930s, celebrity political endorsements were not new. Stars began to appear at rallies for presidential candidates during the 1920s, and Cantor himself was part of a Broadway committee endorsing Al Smith in 1928. But Cantor reached a larger audience over the air than he ever had at campaign rallies. Cantor's pro-Roosevelt radio routines illustrated the potential of radio comedy as a vehicle for social and political commentary. Will Rogers, Freeman Gosden and Charles Correll (*Amos 'n' Andy*), Fred Allen, Jack Benny, Gertrude Berg, and Burns and Allen also used current events as program fodder during the first years of the Depression. For example, the early *Amos 'n' Andy* programs presented an optimistic take, similar to Cantor's, on the economic crisis as well as Roosevelt's leadership.[80]

Later in the decade, the Federal Communications Commission (FCC), networks, and advertising agencies monitored content more closely and banned political commentary in entertainment programs. But before 1935, regulators were less concerned about the occasional political jibes on variety shows than they were about more flagrant abuses of public standards of "good taste," defined broadly to include everything from deceptive advertising to risqué jokes to obscene language.[81] Cantor and other popular radio comedians were not political radicals. While Cantor's occasional support of the New Deal may have irritated Republican listeners, he had the leverage with the network and sponsor to present this political material because of his popularity. Carroll Carroll, a longtime advertising executive who wrote for *The Chase and Sanborn Hour* as an employee of the program's agency, later recalled that "Cantor swung a lot of weight at NBC and that power brushed off on all those associated with him."[82]

In late 1937 Roosevelt formed a new organization, the National Foundation for Infantile Paralysis, and turned to Hollywood for support. Cantor led the effort. Serving as the "radio and stage" chairman of the fund-raising committee, Cantor came up with the idea of the "March of Dimes" as a theme for the fund-raising appeal. Early the next year, when the campaign launched, Cantor and other celebrities took to the airwaves, urging listeners to send dimes directly to the president. White House mail clerk Ira R. T. Smith later wrote, "We had been handling about 5,000 letters a day at that time. We got 30,000 on the day the March of Dimes began. We got 50,000 the next day. We got 150,000 the third day. We kept on getting incredible numbers, and the Government of the United States darned near stopped functioning because we couldn't clear away enough dimes to find the official White House mail."[83] *Variety* reported that an entire room of the White House was "stripped of furniture" so that it could hold all of the mailbags loaded with dimes. The 1938 campaign generated a total of 2,680,000 dimes. In reviewing his relationship with Roosevelt, Cantor remembered that his "real closeness to the President came about through the March of Dimes . . . Mr. Roosevelt was deeply thrilled with the response" to Cantor's idea.[84]

Cantor's fame had transcended the world of the stage by 1938. He comfortably mingled with politicians, including the president. His social commentary inspired audiences nationally, across all demographic lines. While many listeners probably connected Cantor's liberal politics with his working-class Jewish background and experiences, even those who did not recognize his characteristic Jewish politics could not mistake the Jewish music and comedy elsewhere in his program.

7   RADIO WITH A JEWISH ACCENT
(1931–1938)

As the star of the biggest radio program in the country during the early 1930s, Cantor created a template for presenting American Jewish comedy to a national broadcast audience. He achieved enormous success on radio while cleverly referencing his Jewish background on and off the air. Cantor was radio's most influential Jewish figure, but not its first. Samuel Rothafel, better known as Roxy, produced and hosted several popular variety shows between 1923 and 1935. More important, Gertrude Berg casually discussed common American Jewish practices on *The Rise of the Goldbergs*, later titled *The Goldbergs*, which veered between comedy and soap opera in chronicling the family's life during its long broadcast run from 1929 to 1945.[1]

When *The Rise of the Goldbergs* debuted, broadcasters shunned Jewish and other ethnic comedy. They did not want to offend listeners and organizations monitoring ethnic stereotypes and caricatures. *Variety* reported in 1929 that *The Rise of the Goldbergs* broke this barrier concerning Jewish programming and stimulated "a constant stream of requests for more Hebe comedy."[2] Still, the networks did not immediately satisfy this demand. Broadcasters worried that a show about a Jewish family might not appeal to non-Jewish audiences. The series creator, writer, and star Gertrude Berg remembered that when she first proposed her program, the "radio studio big-wigs" objected that there would not be an audience outside of large cities for her program.[3] These doubts lingered even after *The Rise of the Goldbergs* debuted. To address questions about the audience for Jewish programming, in 1932 NBC conducted an internal study of *The Rise of the Goldbergs* which confirmed, to the network's satisfaction, that "there is a large audience for good programs of a Jewish type . . . this popularity is not restricted to any geographic region."[4] Combined with the high ratings and voluminous listener mail generated by *The Rise of the Goldbergs* and Cantor's *Chase and Sanborn Hour*, the report provided important evidence that

Jewish performers and material would attract non-Jewish listeners. It also gave performers the latitude to develop Jewish content on their programs.

In establishing themselves on radio during the early 1930s, Berg and Cantor each accentuated Jewish practices that were compatible with broader American tastes and values. Berg's stories about warm holiday rituals and Cantor's playful routines punctuated by colorful Yiddish expressions invited listeners to appreciate Jewish culture. However, Cantor mixed his gentle affection for Jewish holidays and Yiddish with the brash confidence of a Broadway star. He was no Molly Goldberg, evoking an immigrant world and navigating the challenges of everyday life by using common sense and a moral compass rooted in Judaism. Instead, Cantor played the powerful celebrity, bursting into America's living room during prime time on Sunday nights. He proudly presented a quick, aggressive, irreverent style associated with Jewish comedy, but he seldom marked his lines and routines as "Jewish." Instead, the popular performer relied on listeners to decode the ways in which he drew on Jewish culture, experiences, and approaches.

Starting with the premiere episode of *The Chase and Sanborn Hour* on September 13, 1931, Cantor underscored the difference between himself and other radio personalities through parody. In his first routine, Cantor mocks a popular radio program on another network, CBS's *Camel Quarter-Hour*, which featured host Tony Wons and singer Morton Downey. Wons shared homespun wisdom in an intimate style, punctuated by his signature phrase: "Are you listenin'?" Cantor welcomes listeners with a slight Southern accent and a false sense of intimacy: "Are you listenin' in, folks . . . huh? This is your ol' pal Eddie Cantor just a callin' round for a good ol' visit with you all. Draw yourself up an easy chair by the good ol' fireplace, folks, and we'll smoke a herring together."[5]

Cantor's punch line, sharing the smelly fish loved by Eastern European Jewish immigrants and their families, signals that he is not going to become another Tony Wons. Cantor then warbles Downey's "Carolina Moon," the theme song of Wons's CBS program. Jimmy Wallington, the announcer who bantered with Cantor throughout each episode, constantly interrupts Cantor's performance. Wallington tells the star that he wants to "build up" a big entrance. Cantor replies, using phrasing and a rhetorical question typical for a Jewish New Yorker. "Okay, so go on building," he laughs. "In these times, I should stop someone from building?"

The actor from the Lower East Side did not imitate the strong, geographically neutral delivery of popular announcers, such as Wallington. Nor did he possess the melodious tones of established radio crooners, such as Downey and Rudy Vallee.[6] On his debut broadcast, Cantor refers to his house band as "Mr. Rubinoff and his Brooklyn Yankees," a pointed contrast to Vallee and his orchestra, the Connecticut Yankees. In an October 1931 newspaper interview for the American Jewish press, Cantor self-effacingly recognized his vocal limitations, suggesting that listeners to his new program might change the station as soon as they recognized his "golden baritone."[7] Cantor's distinctive voice punctured the polished façades of the smooth crooners and staid announcers. Cantor and the other Jewish comedians who debuted on radio during the early 1930s combined swagger, nervousness, and self-deprecation. Despite their successes on the stage, they were outsiders as radio personalities. Rather than attempting to elide his differences from the Connecticut Yankees of the broadcast world, Cantor used his sharp wit and quirky persona to charm audiences with an alternative vision of radio entertainment.

The Jewish-inflected parodies did not stop with Wons, Downey, and Vallee. Later in the debut episode, Cantor satirically conflates Jewish and American culture in "I Love Potato Pancakes," a jaunty tribute to the iconic Jewish dish. In Cantor's surreal fantasy, the greasy, pungent fried potato treats hold mythical power. Paul Revere rides through the streets urging people to try potato pancakes. Patrick Henry declares, "Liberty and death comes second / Give me potato pancakes." At Gettysburg, Abraham Lincoln offers a modified address, "By the people, for the people, of the people / Who wants people? / I want potato pancakes." Meanwhile, back in Hollywood, Cantor sings, "Movie queens have tried to court me / Even offered to support me / But I want potato pancakes." Cantor dreams of a nation whose founding figures and movie starlets share his people's passion for potato pancakes, but he includes no explicit Jewish references in his performance. Some listeners would have understood and appreciated the fantasy of the Jewish comedian from New York. Others might have simply seen "I Love Potato Pancakes" as a silly song about a strange kind of pancake.

After he finishes singing "I Love Potato Pancakes," Cantor addresses the radio audience, imagining the critical reaction of a Midwesterner: "Did I hear a gentleman in Columbus, Ohio, say, 'Phooey?' Come, come now . . . let's have cooperation here. Let's give Cantor a chance. After all, if Mr. Sanborn is satisfied, should you complain?" The rhetorical question targeted skeptical advertising and network executives more than the hypothetical Columbus listener. Cantor and his fellow show business veterans didn't need NBC market research reports to know that their music and comedy worked on multiple levels. Even audience members who didn't have a rich knowledge of Jewish culture enjoyed this style of humor. George Jessel, who served as a summer replacement for Cantor on *The Chase and Sanborn Hour*, observed, "The people who liked me in the theatre are the same people who listen to the radio. And the ancient idea that the guy in Altoona, Pennsylvania, or Hitching Post, Kentucky, still wears wooden shoes and doesn't know what's going on is absurd."[8]

Though Cantor lived in New York and Southern California for his entire life, he toured the country with a theatrical show every year from 1911 to 1931. The itinerary varied depending on the show, but the trouper typically remained on the road for about nine months a year, stopping in cities or towns for a week at a time to give multiple performances. Regional hubs such as Kansas City, Missouri, were more than dots on the map or lines in audience ratings reports for Cantor. He appeared in the city five times from 1913 to 1926. As he later explained in his 1957 autobiography, *Take My Life*, "It was never a matter of standing up before a cold mike wondering what kind of people were out there. I could see the Fort Worths and the San Antonios, the Kansas Citys, Omahas, Detroits, and Clevelands, all the places I'd played on the road." In 1935 Cantor also pioneered a new method of gauging popular reaction to his radio programs. Adapting a common theatrical practice of holding previews, Cantor conducted a dress rehearsal with an audience before each broadcast to see which lines earned the most laughs. At the previews and in sessions before and after shows, Cantor invited visitors, including tourists from around the country, to ask him about everything from the movie industry to politics. These queries and comments served as market research for Cantor. He wrote, "We knew our audience, we had a sampling of them every week face to face."[9]

On the air, Cantor spiced his routines with quick, seemingly impro-vised Yiddish asides, using common words and phrases that listeners familiar with Jewish culture would have understood or at least recog-nized as Yiddish. In a 1933 skit, Cantor and his cohorts take a trip to the North Pole, where they encounter a "native" named Moe Iceberg, one of "God's frozen people," according to Cantor. Iceberg greets Cantor in broken English, "Howsa youga?"

Cantor answers, "Howsa youga, they're *mushuga*," referring to his crazy partners on the journey.

Cantor asks Iceberg how to eat the local food. The native responds in Yiddish, "*Ich no farshteyn.*"

The star translates for his audience, "He doesn't understand." He then tells Moe, "Eat, eat. Chew, chew."

Moe mistakes the request for assistance for a sneeze and responds with the Yiddish (and German) "*gesundheit.*"[10]

In another sketch, from 1936, Cantor plays a farmer who breaks into song, to the tune of "She'll Be Coming 'Round the Mountain." Cantor's version prefigures later parodists such as Mickey Katz and Allan Sher-man: "Though the place is in Nova Scotia / As long as the food is kosher / I'll be coming 'round the mountain when I come."[11] With the surprising bit about kosher food, Cantor makes the classic American song a little more Jewish and gives a metaphorical wink to audience members who understood the kosher reference.[12]

Cantor similarly ends a 1934 episode with a story about a dinner with the family of David Rubinoff, his bandleader and a running character on the show. Rubinoff's mother makes the men matzo balls because she knows it is the dish "that all you Jewish boys love." The audience laughs, perhaps in recognition of the pleasures of matzo balls or the stereotyp-ical Jewish mother making the food for her boys. Cantor continues, "I got the greatest kick of my life . . . I ate about five or six of those matzo balls. And they weren't very large. Each one was like a grapefruit, you know." Cantor concludes by recommending the heavy dumplings as a cure for insomnia, since, with a belly full of matzo balls, "You can't toss around. You lay in one place."[13]

Cantor's warm, nostalgic references to matzo balls and Yiddish brought the Eastern European Jewish culture of his youth into millions of American homes via radio, presenting Jews and their practices as funny, warm, and appealing. Cantor did not make these jokes so central to his program and his persona that he alienated listeners who were not literate in basic Jewish culture. Yet he spoke about his Jewishness casually and unapologetically, as if he expected audiences to understand and share in his appreciation for matzo balls and Yiddish.

In a 1931 broadcast, which aired as Yom Kippur began, Cantor inserted one of the few references to Judaic religious practice by any prime-time comedian, informing listeners: "As you know, ladies and gentlemen, this is the eve of Yom Kippur, the Day of Atonement. All over the world the sacred song 'Kol Nidre' is being played and sung tonight. Rubinoff is going to play it for us now."[14] Cantor was not in a position to postpone a network radio program for Yom Kippur, as he did on the 1925 opening night of *Kid Boots*. However, this kind of recognition of "Kol Nidre" on the leading network radio program held great symbolic importance for American Jews because it suggested that all Americans should at least be aware of the Jewish High Holiday.

It is impossible to determine how many Jews were sitting near their radio sets, rather than their synagogue bimahs, to hear Cantor's broadcast. However, through his many on-air Jewish references, Cantor contributed to his position as a respected figure who took pride in Jewish culture and holidays. As the actor Jerry Stiller later recalled, "Eddie Cantor let us all know that he was Jewish." The fact that the top radio celebrity openly identified as a Jew buttressed Stiller's identification with him: "My mind danced when Eddie was on. I wanted to be Eddie Cantor. I thought he could change the whole world. I too could change the world if I were a comedian."[15]

American Jews showed their enthusiasm for Cantor by tuning in to his program and taking any opportunity to see him in person. In 1933 Cantor and Jessel caused a riot when they went to eat at a kosher restaurant after a performance in Atlanta. The city's Jewish newspaper reported that "news of Cantor's presence electrified the temperamental neighborhood." A mob formed, hoping for a glimpse of Cantor. Police rushed in to restore order. "The worldly cops recognized Eddie Cantor and expressed little wonder at the cause of the commotion . . . Cantor, Jessel, and their party elbowed their way through the admiring mass of humanity and sped amidst wild shouts of cheer back to the theater."[16]

While Jewish audiences embraced Cantor's music and comedy, they grew to admire him even more for his tireless philanthropic support of Jews in the United States and globally. In September 1929, Cantor donated five hundred dollars and arranged for a special performance of *Whoopee* to benefit the Palestine Relief Fund.[17] The fund aided victims of Arab rioting in August 1929, which left 133 Jews dead and four hundred more injured. Later that year, Cantor signed on to the Zionist Roll Call, an effort "to enroll 500,000 American Jews as a demonstration of faith in the rebuilding of Palestine as the Jewish National Homeland." In both cases, Cantor was the only prominent actor to support these Zionist efforts.[18] A relatively small number of American Jews were active in the Zionist movement. In 1929 the Zionist Organization of America (ZOA) included fewer than twenty thousand members; however, many American Jewish communal leaders who were not Zionists, and did not support a separate Jewish state, still funded settlement and relief efforts in Palestine, including the emergency appeal of 1929.[19]

Cantor showed little interest in the political debates and factions swirling around the American Zionist movement in 1929, and he did not label himself a "Zionist." Yet he felt a kinship with other Jews internationally. Cantor explained his support of Zionism in terms of group loyalty and Jewish self-defense. According to his ethical code, forged on the Lower East Side city streets, if Arabs attacked his people, he was obliged to act. In a 1930 interview, Cantor explained how Zionism could help Jews fight prejudice: "I'm not a Zionist, but I believe that any movement which furthers the welfare of any portion of Jewry deserves the entire support of any honest Jew regardless of his personal views on the subject. Zionism, like all good things in life, is hard. Then, again, it's hard to be a Jew, but it's worthwhile fighting to get into places where you're not wanted."[20]

During the early 1930s, Cantor was more active in Jewish charities than any other entertainer. His favored recipients included orphanages, federations, and local chapters of national organizations, such as the United Palestine Appeal (UPA) and the Young Men's Hebrew Association (YMHA). Cantor saw charity as central to Jewish communal identity and a vehicle for fighting charges that recent immigrants burdened taxpayers. "The Jew has a mission . . . We've always taken care of our poor and sick. That's a good example for the rest of the world," he said, after headlining a welfare fund luncheon in 1930. Cantor also recognized the social component of philanthropy: "Another good thing about charity —it brings Jews closer together. Gives one a chance to say to the other, 'Here, you son-of-a-gun, you can't let us down on this cause.'"[21]

Over time, the fund-raisers enabled Cantor to solidify friendships among his fellow Jews that lasted throughout his career. He worked alongside leading rabbis and the businessmen who led campaigns. Jewish weeklies reported on these efforts, as did the local big-city dailies. For example, in 1930, Cantor appeared in a short sound film benefiting the Federation for the Support of Jewish Philanthropic Societies. His distinguished costars in the fund-raising piece, which screened at a dinner before two thousand Federation supporters, included Albert Einstein, banker Felix M. Warburg, and Adolph S. Ochs, publisher of the *New York Times*.[22]

In 1932 Cantor introduced Warburg during another Federation for Support of Jewish Philanthropic Societies event that also featured Morton Downey. They appeared before an audience of 750 "men and women, among them the most eligible debutantes New York Israelites still flaunt." WOR radio in New York broadcast the program live. The *Jewish Criterion* columnist Martha Neumark praised Cantor, "Eddie has the poise, the dignity and the phraseology of a seasoned trouper and generous contributor to numerous funds." But hinting at the lingering antipathy toward popular entertainers among the Jewish establishment, Neumark bemoaned the fact that the federation, "which once got its money easily and quickly, now has to resort to the most flagrant ballyhoo."[23]

The organized Jewish community's ambivalence about actors was reflected in a December 1932 survey conducted by the Seven Arts Feature Syndicate, which distributed articles to English-language Jewish newspapers. The syndicate asked eighty-four editors and publishers to identify the leading American Jews. Cantor finished a respectable, but not outstanding, eleventh in the survey—the highest for any entertainer on a list headed by Supreme Court Justice Louis D. Brandeis and filled with politicians, rabbis, and businessmen.[24]

Most Jewish commentators appreciated Cantor's dedicated fund-raising, though some viewed this activity as self-serving: a charge that dogged Cantor throughout his career. Introducing a 1934 interview with Cantor in the *Jewish Criterion*, S. Sidney Kalwary took issue with unnamed "portly columnists that ridicule Cantor, and misleadingly impress the public that his philosophical attitude is just a theatrical pose, for the benefit of crowding show houses and selling dated coffee." Kalwary defended the actor's sincerity and seriousness: "Eddie Cantor is more than a mere comedian, a mere entertainer whose lines are forgotten the moment he finishes his song. Eddie Cantor is doing and has done more for the New Deal through the medium of radio than any other artist on the air."[25] In the context of an article about Cantor's philanthropy, Kalwary's New Deal reference signaled to readers that the actor saw private Jewish charities and public federal programs as compatible vehicles for promoting social welfare.[26]

Cantor continued to support Jewish philanthropies for the rest of his career through personal appearances, newspaper articles, and the occasional public service broadcast. But starting in the mid-1930s, Cantor's prime-time radio program featured less explicitly Jewish humor, such as Yiddish phrases and jokes about Jewish food. Changes in sponsorship, writers, the broadcast industry, and Cantor's public image influenced his presentation of Jewishness on prime time.

When his contract with Chase and Sanborn ended in 1934, Cantor agreed to headline a thirty-minute program for a new sponsor, Pebeco toothpaste, at one of the highest rates in broadcasting: $10,000 per week. The switch to Pebeco brought several additional changes to Cantor's program. He moved from NBC to CBS and doubled his salary for starring in a shorter program that required less work. Cantor also altered his writing team to lower his expenses, since the writers were under contract to him, rather than to the network or sponsor. As part of this cost cutting for the Pebeco show, Cantor ended his partnership with David Freedman, who had received 10 percent of Cantor's weekly salary under a verbal agreement. Freedman commanded $500 per week with Chase and Sanborn and would have earned $1000 per week with Pebeco. Other experienced comedy writers earned only $200 per week[27]

Freedman responded by suing Cantor for $250,000. The writer claimed that he was entitled to 10 percent of Cantor's earnings for as long as the performer remained on the air. Cantor denied that he and Freedman had a contract. The actor minimized his former partner's contributions to the program. Cantor explained that he wrote with Freedman and "anywhere from four to a dozen [additional] collaborators."[28]

The trial reached the New York State Supreme Court on December 7, 1936. The next day, with testimony set to resume, Freedman's attorney, Samuel Leibowitz, rose with the shocking announcement that his client had died of a heart attack earlier that morning. The judge declared a mistrial, and Freedman's widow declined to pursue further litigation.[29]

Philip Rapp, a former Freedman assistant, became the head writer of Cantor's new Pebeco program. In contrast to Freedman, who was steeped in Lower East Side Yiddish culture, Rapp was born and raised in England and came to America with his family at the age of sixteen, settling in the Bronx in 1923. Rapp's son later remembered, "Dad didn't do a lot of Jewish things, but when I was young, we went to temple. But it was [a synagogue] for a reformed type of Jew, the one who went once a year."[30] Rapp's scripts offered fewer Jewish jokes and references. Cantor probably did not mind this less overt Jewish style. During the mid-1930s, the star began to shift his broadcast image from a jittery, unpredictable urban wise guy to a more relaxed, confident showman and philanthropist. The nervous references to listeners in Ohio or Yiddish punchlines from *The Chase and Sanborn Hour* no longer fit this persona. Perhaps learning from his friend Jack Benny, Cantor and his writers presented a cooler style with an ensemble of quirky regulars and big-name guest stars.

Cantor did not hide his Jewishness on or off the air, but he found different ways of expressing it. He distinguished himself from the stereotypical heavily accented Jewish immigrant through his routines with two ethnic zanies: the Greek Parkyakarkus (1934–1937), played by Harry Einstein, and the Mad Russian (1937–1948), played by Bert Gordon. In these sketches, Cantor presented himself as the smooth-talking star with a firm command of the language and cultural mores, patiently correcting his wacky sidekicks. Cantor did not respond forcefully to the other actors' barbs and malapropisms, preferring to let the supporting players have the biggest laughs and the last word before affectionately sending them offstage. Einstein and Gordon stole the spotlight as sympathetic immigrants who used puns and humor to demonstrate their charm, intelligence, and ability to hold their own in American society.

Cantor may not have wanted to identify the religion of his radio characters, fearing that he would advance stereotypes of Jews as pushy greenhorns or foreigners; however, the funny accents and sharp banter of the Jewish actors who played Parkyakarkus and the Mad Russian suggested that there was some Jewish blood in these characters. Einstein, Gordon, and Cantor were Jewish comedians pretending to be Greeks, Russians, or even comfortably acculturated Americans, enjoying their success and inviting audiences to share their pleasure. The actors also drew on a tradition of ethnic comedy from vaudeville and Broadway, including some of Cantor's previous stage work, featuring seemingly naïve immigrants and outsiders who overturned authority with surprisingly quick wit. Other radio programs also cast similar characters who used puns, clever wordplay, and a sharp attitude to get the best of the headliners and charm audiences. The "linguistic slapstick" that pervaded 1930s radio comedy "threw verbal pies in the face of Victorian gentility: it showcased hostility, not politeness," wrote the historian Susan Douglas. "This was the humor of resentment and retaliation." When he debuted on the air, Cantor played the Jewish outsider, taking shots at Tony Wons, Rudy Vallee, industry insiders, and audience members who might not have liked his accent and style. During the mid-1930s, Cantor made himself into an establishment figure as a comfortable, successful radio star. But through his costars, he continued to present the humor of angry iconoclasts.[31]

Einstein was writing advertising copy for the Kane Furniture Company in Boston and dabbling in radio with his Greek dialect routine when Cantor discovered him performing at a luncheon in 1934.[32] Einstein brought his character, Parkyakarkus, to *The Chase and Sanborn Hour*, still written by Freedman, on February 1, 1934, injecting energy into the weekly program through his irreverent verbal jousting with Cantor. In a typical routine from 1934, Parkyakarkus bursts onto the stage as Cantor finishes a song. The Greek illustrates his disrespect for the star by mangling Cantor's name, "Eddie Scranton," and judging the song "good and rotten." In Parkyakarkus's world, orchestra leader David Rubinoff is "Rubin-nuts." Announcer Jimmy Wallington is "Jimmy Wilmington" or "Jimmy Washingboard."[33] Einstein remained with Cantor until early 1937, when he moved to *The Al Jolson Show* and, later, his own program, *Meet Me at Parky's* (1945–1947). Two of Einstein's children, Albert Brooks, and Bob Einstein, also known as Super Dave Osborne, followed their father into show business comedy.

Bert Gordon (born Barney Gorodetsky), the Mad Russian, was a product of Jewish Lower Manhattan.[34] Gordon's big ears and bushy hair provided comic fodder for the live audience and listeners familiar with his appearance. Gordon commanded attention through his rapid delivery, strange phrasing, and vaguely Russian accent, with a slight Yiddish inflection, developed during his years as a dialect comedian. The Mad Russian's manic greeting, "How do you doo?," caught on with listeners and became the title of a low-budget 1945 film starring Gordon.[35] The Mad Russian may not have known much about American history or English grammar, but he refused to be intimidated by the successful and well-spoken actors with whom he shared the radio microphone. Cantor remembered that "pitting Bert [Gordon] against anyone who had a certain amount of dignity was sure fire."[36] The host served as Gordon's most frequent target. In a 1938 episode, for example, the Mad Russian teaches Cantor to sing, referring to Cantor as a "Crosby singer." The skit cleverly plays on the words "Crosby" and "cross between" to transform a compliment into an insult:

> CANTOR: Tell me, what's a Crosby singer? I sing like Bing Crosby?
> MAD RUSSIAN: No, you're a cross between a foghorn and a peanut whistle.
> CANTOR: Why don't you let me sing a few notes and tell me what's wrong?
> MAD RUSSIAN: Go ahead. I have to take an aspirin anyway.[37]

Parkyakarkus and the Mad Russian took particular joy in skewering Cantor's vanity, performance skills, and masculinity. The star provided an easy target. From 1933 to 1936, he frequently wore outlandish costumes as a gimmick, and he sometimes dressed as a woman. Cantor allowed his costars, including the Mad Russian and a weekly assortment of guest singers and actors, to poke fun at his manhood, confident that he could rebound with a quick line, song, or scene that would reestablish his talent, authority, and masculinity. While these sketches did not seriously challenge gender roles, they enabled Cantor to demonstrate a self-deprecating aspect of his persona. In an exchange from December 1935, Cantor, dressed in overalls and carrying a mop, plays an apartment building superintendent. The Mad Russian is a tenant who needs help with his heater. The Russian asks Cantor, "Ain't you the gender?"

Cantor with Bert Gordon, the Mad Russian, on NBC radio during the 1940s.

Cantor corrects him, "Not gender. Janitor. Gender is am I male or female?"

The Mad Russian replies, "Well, make up your mind," as the audience roars with laughter.[38]

In the next scene, Cantor gives a smooth performance of "Calabash Pipe," a light Harold Arlen–Lew Brown song about settling down in a small town for the simple life. The announcer Wallington informs listeners that the song will appear in Cantor's forthcoming film *Strike Me Pink*: another reminder that Cantor was no mere janitor.

During the 1938–1939 season, Cantor's *Camel Caravan* added a new character, Mr. Guffy, played by Sid Fields, a former vaudevillian who also wrote for the program. With his aggressive, funny, cleverly confrontational wit and the distinctive syntax of an English speaker who grew up with Yiddish, Guffy was Jewish in style, even though the program never referenced his religion or ethnicity. The argumentative complainer knew how to put the host on the spot. In a typical episode, Guffy complains about his billing: "His [Cantor's] name he puts in lights —but mine he whispers!"

Cantor tries to mollify Guffy: "I won't whisper—I'll shout it! . . . GUFFY IS ON THE EDDIE CANTOR PROGRAM! . . . GUFFY IS ON THE EDDIE CANTOR PROGRAM!"

The disgruntled sidekick is not satisfied: "That's fine—I promised my wife I wouldn't mingle with riff-raff—and he has to advertise that I'm here!"

Cantor responds, "I don't advertise anything."

Guffy triumphantly defends the sponsor's cigarettes, "Oh—Camels are nothing!"[39]

Cantor's sketches with the supporting players highlighted the distance that the star had traveled from his working-class immigrant origins. His many radio routines about the Lower East Side served a similarly nostalgic function for Cantor and his audience, especially Jewish listeners. As they looked back, Cantor and other actors fondly recalled the warm city streets on which a fraternity of quirky, talented kids overcame hardships and began to build show business careers. Irving Berlin, who also grew up on the Lower East Side, appeared with Cantor in a January 1937 program that draws on the entertainers' shared history and connects their memories to a broader American story. Berlin reminds

Irving Berlin and Cantor: two skinny guys from the Lower East Side, circa 1936.

Cantor that they both started their careers as singing waiters in Lower Manhattan. After more reminiscing, jokes, and music, the show turns serious for a moment. "Honestly, you know, I'm thrilled with your being here tonight," Cantor tells Berlin. "It gives me a warm feeling to know that two skinny guys who started out from the east side of New York many years ago are playing here together tonight in front of millions of people. Irving, this is truly a land of opportunity."[40] There is nothing unusual about "two skinny guys" finding success in America. Berlin and Cantor became symbols of the American dream not because they overcame being "skinny," but because they ascended from poor, immigrant,

Jewish households. While Cantor and Berlin do not explicitly identify their religion, they do not need to do so. Audience members, especially Jewish listeners, knew the histories of Cantor, Berlin, and the Lower East Side. They also knew the unspoken rules of network radio and stardom: that popular entertainers rarely used the words "Jew" or "Jewish" on the air. Cantor and Berlin were household names, yet popularity had its costs and limitations. Cantor could only express his gratitude to America using coded language.

The networks and sponsors, so sensitive to potential criticisms from listeners and the FCC, discouraged open discussion of immigration, discrimination, and Jewish identification on popular entertainment programs. Jewish performers and industry executives acquiesced to these rules and practiced a form of self-censorship, rather than asserting their Jewishness. By the late 1930s, Cantor had become especially frustrated with his fellow Jews in show business. On October 26, 1937, Cantor hosted a party for six hundred Hollywood insiders at the Ambassador Hotel to celebrate his twenty-fifth year in show business and to promote his new film, *Ali Baba Goes to Town*. The tribute featured a parade of top studio executives, politicians, and entertainers, including Louis B. Mayer, Darryl F. Zanuck, California governor Frank F. Merriam, Judy Garland, Jimmy Durante, Sophie Tucker, and Jack Benny. CBS broadcast the event live from Los Angeles. Because of the time difference, the nighttime program aired from 12:30 a.m. to 2 a.m. on the East Coast. Given the time slot and the lack of sponsorship, it is unlikely that the network vetted the script, if the speakers used one, or monitored the broadcast very closely.[41]

Cantor used the occasion to parody his familiar life story while making a more serious point about Jewish timidity in the face of antisemitism. His old friend George Jessel starts the show by breaking a show business taboo, pretending to slip and calling Cantor by his given name, "Izzy." Regardless of their ethnicities, many performers of the 1920s and 1930s took stage names, seldom acknowledging their given names in public. For example, in his 1928 autobiography, Cantor says nothing about his early years as an "Itzkowitz."[42] Having established his familiarity with "Izzy," toastmaster Jessel chronicles his old friend's "humble beginnings on the East Side of New York," marveling at how high the night's honoree had risen.

Later that night, Cantor took the stage to thank the audience in a routine that substitutes subtle satire for his usual manic energy. He begins by denying the history and heritage in Jessel's routine: "This thing that you say about the east side is a very fantastic thing to me. Personally, I think it was all a publicity stunt in the earlier days. I know very little about the east side, ladies and gentlemen." Cantor imagines himself as a stereotypical upper-class gentile: "I first saw the light of day at my mother and father's summer home at Southampton." The audience laughs loudly at the surprising direction of the monologue. Cantor continues, "On the day that I was born, my father had bought his second string of polo ponies. I spoke very little English up to the time I was seven or eight years old, having been brought up by a very well bred, educated French governess, Fifi Levine."

Cantor then skewers the practice of changing names to evade antisemitism, addressing Jessel's earlier comments directly: "Of course, Georgie, when you said with a slip of the tongue, 'Izzy.' I know very little about that. I have heard you say on other occasions that my name was not 'Cantor,' which is not true. My name is 'Cantor.' People have said that at one time in my life I was called 'Izzy Itzkowitz.' Well, I was called that for a time. My father gave me the name Itzkowitz when I went to Fordham and he thought that I would make the football team." The crowd erupts at the image of Cantor, under an even more Jewish-sounding moniker, playing for the Jesuit football power, which was anchored by a powerful offensive line nicknamed the "Seven Blocks of Granite." Cantor moves forward with his deadpan personal history, explaining how he returned to his more famous name: "Of course, later on, when I missed making the team, he asked me not to use the name. Take the name of 'Cantor.' He didn't want me to use 'Itzkowitz,' knowing that later in life I would have trouble getting into certain hotels."

Cantor's daring joke about the social practice of excluding Jews from hotels reminds his audience that antisemitism remained a problem, especially for those Jews who did not change their names or reach the social echelons of many in the crowd that night. Names were primary markers of Jewishness during an era when Jews encountered tacit prejudice at schools, jobs, resorts, and social clubs. The Itzkowitzes of the world had a harder time than the Bennys and Tuckers. Yet Cantor also implies that changing a name doesn't make a person less Jewish in the eyes of non-Jews. While American society offered possibilities for re-invention, Jews who hid their backgrounds were not fooling anybody. Cantor, always sensitive to his audience, knew that many of the show business executives and performers attending his tribute—including featured speakers Mayer, Benny, and Tucker—had Americanized their names. He may have wanted to reach this audience. By flaunting his Jewishness, Cantor challenged others to do the same, rather than allowing antisemites to uncover influential Jews and spread the canard that Jews secretly controlled the entertainment industry and other American institutions. During a time when Hollywood studio heads and prominent actors hid or minimized their Jewish identifications, Cantor advocated visibility and pride.

Reflecting Cantor's growing frustration with Jewish invisibility, and his desire to be more open about his heritage within the strictures of network radio, the star included a brief reference to his given name in a sketch from a 1938 episode of his prime-time program. In the scene, Cantor watches while his announcer, Walter King, decides to live like a "big shot" celebrity. As part of this transformation, King hires a high-class British tailor and introduces the tailor to Cantor.

> TAILOR: Oh—I'm glad to know you, Mister Cawntor.
> CANTOR: Look. It's spelled C-A-N-T-O-R—is that Cantor or
>   Cawntor? How do you pronounce my name?
> TAILOR: Itskowitz!
> CANTOR: He knows me! There's a spy in the troupe.[43]

Like many of Cantor's Jewish radio scenes, the section is short, it moves quickly, and it uses coded language. Talk of "Itskowitz" and spies would have made little sense to listeners who didn't know Cantor's history or the implications of the reference to his given name. In unexpectedly blurting out "Itskowitz," the high-class tailor unmasks Cantor, and himself, as Jewish. Cantor must choose whether to acknowledge or deny the tailor's exposure of him. Rather than being ashamed or defensive, Cantor reacts with a combination of surprise and pleasure at the airing of his given name as well as the discovery of a fellow Jew in his "troupe." The "spy" becomes an ally through the secret code word: "Itskowitz."[44]

Between his debut on *The Chase and Sanborn Hour* in 1931 and the routines on name changing several years later, Cantor became more serious about his political opportunities and responsibilities as a Jew. He believed that it was time for Jews, especially celebrities, to become more visible in the fight against antisemitism: a struggle that consumed Cantor during the late 1930s.

8 THE FIGHT AGAINST NAZISM
(1933–1939)

hen Cantor gathered with his friends and radio listeners for the party to celebrate the release of *Ali Baba Goes to Town*, he was a respected broadcast star, comedian, philanthropist, and moral voice. At age forty-five, however, he was stuck playing ridiculously naïve movie buffoons half his age. What's more, as Cantor became increasingly passionate about politics, the film roles diminished his credibility as a serious thinker and advocate for Jews. He could not break from his cinematic typecast. Cantor left two different studios — United Artists in 1936 and Twentieth Century-Fox in 1938 — because he was unhappy with the formulaic films that producers offered him. In a prepared statement that he released after breaking with Fox, Cantor explained, "I want to play something else besides an insipid character which the audience does not believe."[1] During a time when many actors made four or five films a year, Cantor did not appear on-screen between the fall of 1937 and the spring of 1940, when MGM released *Forty Little Mothers*. By the late 1930s, Cantor's film career had become less important to him. Instead, Cantor focused his energies on his popular network radio program and offstage commitments that combined politics and philanthropy. Cantor made speeches and published articles emphasizing the problem of domestic antisemitism. In addition, he raised funds to help European refugees, especially children, resettle in Palestine. Others in Hollywood also opposed fascism or occasionally performed at benefits for Jewish relief organizations, but no other star matched Cantor's commitment to addressing social and political problems while identifying as a Jew and examining these problems from particular Jewish perspectives.

Cantor's response to Nazism evolved over time and across different media platforms from 1933 to 1941. Between 1933 and 1936, Cantor said nothing on his prime-time radio program about Germany or domestic antisemitism. He made a handful of political statements off the air, however, including a 1935 speech in which he questioned the patriotism of Father Charles Coughlin, the prominent antisemitic priest. Starting in 1936, Cantor intensified his opposition to Nazism. The actor prudently crafted and coded his appeals, depending on the audience. He delivered veiled anti-German comments on his prime-time radio program, but he also firmly asserted his isolationism as he made these comments. In 1936 Cantor began his association with Hadassah: the Women's Zionist Organization of America. Through Hadassah, he raised funds to facilitate immigration to Palestine and spoke against Nazism during a time when many other public figures, within and outside the Jewish community, were more reserved. Cantor's political use of his position as a celebrity carried costs. Cantor underestimated the power and intensity of the backlash that his activism provoked.

As an entertainer who advocated for causes associated with Jews, Cantor navigated the constraints imposed by the radio industry and public opinion. During the 1930s, antisemitic organizations became more visible in the United States, and incidents of physical abuse against Jews increased. According to the historian Leonard Dinnerstein, more than one hundred antisemitic organizations were established between 1933 and 1941. Father Coughlin used his radio program to rail against "communistic Jews." His followers established a Christian Front organization that attacked Jews on the streets of New York and Boston and assailed Jews as warmongers and communists. The German American Bund staged a pro-Nazi rally in Madison Square Garden on February 20, 1939. As Jews listened to the radio, read newspapers, and encountered discrimination in their daily lives, they were reminded that antisemitism was not confined to the social and political fringes. Polls indicated that many Americans held low opinions of Jews and opposed changes to immigration policy that would have admitted more European Jews.[2]

The belief that Jews held too much power, and they were conspiring to take over the government of the United States, stood at the heart of antisemitic ideology. Prominent American Jews such as Cantor walked a delicate line. They attempted to use their positions to assist and defend their fellow Jews without fueling antisemitic charges of dual loyalties or disproportionate influence. Jewish leaders disagreed among themselves about how they could best help their coreligionists abroad while neutralizing antisemitism at home. Communal organizations devised multiple strategies to pressure Germany, facilitate immigration of European refugees to Palestine and the United States, and promote greater awareness of antisemitism in Europe and the United States.[3]

Starting in 1933, the year the Hitler took power, Cantor paid attention to the Nazi threat, but he did not yet share his views publicly. In November 1933, Congressman Samuel Dickstein, conducting public hearings on domestic Nazi propaganda, telegrammed Cantor with a request: "AM INFORMED THAT YOU ARE IN POSSESSION OF A GREAT DEAL OF NAZI LITERATURE AND PROPAGANDA STOP ARE YOU ABLE TO GET IT TOGETHER FOR ME WITH A STATEMENT HOW YOU ACQUIRED IT AND FORWARD SAME TO WASHINGTON FOR MY COMMITTEE STOP IT WILL GREATLY HELP THE CAUSE."[4] Cantor responded that the materials were forwarded from Los Angeles to Richard Gutstadt, director of the Anti-Defamation League (ADL), based in Chicago. "HE [Gutstadt] WILL BE ABLE TO GIVE YOU MATERIAL," Cantor wrote to Dickstein.[5]

The most likely source of Cantor's propaganda collection was Leon L. Lewis, a Los Angeles attorney and community activist who worked closely with the ADL and Gutstadt during this time. Lewis established the Los Angeles Jewish Community Committee (LAJCC) in late 1933, with financing from executives at the Hollywood studios, to gather intelligence about the Nazi threat in Southern California and share this information with authorities. Cantor supported Lewis and the LAJCC. Throughout the 1930s, the two men discussed strategy and exchanged information. Cantor passed odd, threatening antisemitic letters that he received to Lewis. The prominent actor also asked Lewis to vet organizations that sent Cantor ideas or speaking invitations. In her history of the LAJCC, Laura Rosenzweig notes that Cantor "was not a member of the LAJCC board, but could be relied on by Lewis when needed."[6]

The telegram exchange with Dickstein illustrates Cantor's early involvement in the Hollywood anti-Nazi effort, his concern about antisemitic propaganda, and his caution about affiliating with the Jewish anti-Nazi movement in late 1933. At this point, Cantor preferred to operate behind the scenes, like the Hollywood executives who bankrolled Lewis. Testimony by Cantor before Congress, or other open support of the campaign against the Nazis in Southern California, would have provoked a combination of public disapproval and derision that the Jewish comedian was involved in a serious domestic espionage operation.[7]

Instead, Cantor gradually became more vocal about the domestic Nazi threat over the next several years.

In July 1933, Cantor announced that he was leading an effort to finance the immigration of thirty thousand German Jews to Palestine.[8] The next year, he served on the planning board for *Night of Stars*. The annual *Night of Stars* production featured hundreds of celebrities in support of the United Jewish Appeal (UJA), a joint campaign of the United Palestine Appeal (UPA) and the American Jewish Joint Distribution Committee (JDC). Though celebrity benefits were not new, the scale of *Night of Stars* was striking, as was its anti-Nazi agenda. A crowd of thirty-five thousand flocked to the debut of *Night of Stars*, held at Yankee Stadium on September 20, 1934. The orchestra played "Hatikvah," the Zionist anthem, and UJA officials made short speeches about the organization's relief work. More than three hundred celebrities smiled, waved, and performed short sketches or musical numbers. The stars included Jack Benny, George Jessel, Bill Robinson, George Burns, and Gracie Allen.[9] In 1935 the show moved to Madison Square Garden, where it remained for the next several years. Nathan Strauss, the 1935 event chairman, explained that *Night of Stars* was not merely a fundraiser; it also served the broader political purposes of protesting against discrimination in Germany and offering "moral support" to the victims of Nazi persecution. After serving on the *Night of Stars* planning board for several years, Cantor appeared in the 1938 and 1940 productions.[10]

Cantor made his first anti-Nazi statements in response to German bans of his films. In June 1934, *Der Angriff*, the newspaper owned by the Nazi propaganda minister, Joseph Goebbels, attacked *Roman Scandals* (1933), in which Cantor starred. The film, asserted *Der Angriff*, "illustrates the Jewish sadism which prevails in American films."[11] During a January 1935 trip to London, Cantor indicated that he didn't mind losing access to audiences in Germany: "Why should I send my films to Germany and make people laugh who make my people cry?" Cantor repeated the remark in discussing the Nazi ban of another film, *The Kid from Spain* (1932), at a 1935 benefit for the Catholic Actors Guild in New York.[12] In an evening filled with light entertainment, Cantor's statement stood out.

As someone who understood the persuasive power of the mass media, Cantor was especially concerned about Father Coughlin. The priest enjoyed a large radio following, and he mobilized supporters through his political organization, the National Union for Social Justice. Though Coughlin became blatantly antisemitic later in the decade, he alarmed Jewish communal leaders in 1935. The charismatic speaker employed familiar tropes charging that there was disproportionate Jewish power in politics, banking, and the media, while denying that he was antisemitic.[13]

On July 1, 1935, Cantor targeted Father Coughlin in an address at the Biltmore Hotel in Los Angeles before one thousand B'nai B'rith convention delegates and guests, including the California governor Frank Merriam and Hollywood executive Irving Thalberg. "Father Coughlin is a great orator, but I doubt that he has a sincere atom in his entire system," said Cantor, whose appearance was described by *Time* as "sober and articulate." Possibly anticipating that Coughlin, or the priest's followers, would accuse him of being anti-Christian, Cantor continued: "We Jews have nothing to fear from good Christians . . . but I am afraid of people who pretend to be good Christians. I am also afraid of Jews who are not good Jews." Cantor recognized the political dangers of domestic antisemites such as Coughlin: "We are living in precarious times. You know the situation in Europe as far as Jews are concerned; but I doubt if many of you know how close to the same situation we are in America."[14]

Cantor's speech stimulated debate at the B'nai B'rith convention that mirrored broader discussions in the Jewish community regarding how to address domestic antisemitism. Some Jewish leaders did not see domestic antisemitism as a significant problem, or they believed that calling attention to antisemitism only alienated Jews from other Americans. The evening's next speaker, the San Francisco judge I. M. Golden, reflected these views as he disagreed with Cantor, claiming that "we need have no fear concerning our position in this country. We may well be assured that the American people are sound to the core and that they will tolerate nothing un-American in these matters." Yet Governor Merriam, who was not Jewish, pointedly affirmed Cantor's warning about the dangers facing all Americans and the importance of preserving "the fundamental principles under which this government was founded." Cantor's link between antisemitism in Europe and in the United States was risky for a prominent Jewish figure. It made him vulnerable to charges that he placed global Jewish interests ahead of his support for America and faith in its people.

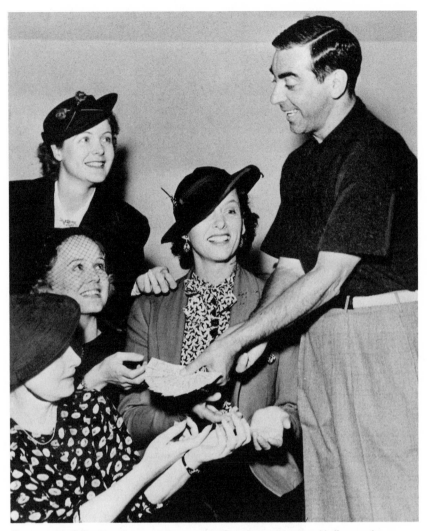

Cantor playfully distributes tickets to an October 20, 1936, Hollywood Anti-Nazi League rally at which he spoke. Clockwise from left: Gloria Stuart, Jean Muir, Dorothy Parker, Gail Sondergaard, and Cantor.

Starting with this 1935 B'nai B'rith address, Cantor used appearances for Jewish charities to deliver strong and potentially divisive statements about antisemitism that he could not present in his commercial films or radio programs. The B'nai B'rith convention provided a safe audience of other Jews with whom Cantor could discuss antisemitism. Yet over the next several years, Cantor's bold and occasionally controversial criticisms of public figures such as Father Coughlin and Henry Ford made news outside of the Jewish community. The mainstream press's coverage of Cantor was not always positive. For example, *Time* magazine's short article on the B'nai B'rith event subtly questioned the actor's loyalties by emphasizing his Jewishness, rather than Coughlin's antisemitism. The article noted that Cantor was born "Izzy Iskowitch [*sic*] on Manhattan's East Side," characterized him as a "good Jew," and cited his work for Jewish charities, including a fellowship that he had supported at Hebrew University in Jerusalem.[15]

Outside of the Jewish community, in 1936, Cantor spoke at two rallies for the Hollywood Anti-Nazi League for the Defense of American Democracy (HANL), an alliance of film industry communists, leftists, and liberals like him.[16] Addressing an audience of five hundred at the Wilshire Ebell Theatre in Los Angeles on July 23, 1936, Cantor discussed the German government's propaganda campaign in America and repeated his earlier statement that he did not want his films shown in Germany. When HANL filled Los Angeles's Shrine Auditorium at another event later that year, Cantor "pleaded for a concerted movement to thwart the ravages of Hitlerism and appealed for moral and financial support to help carry on the work."[17]

After 1936 Cantor limited his involvement with HANL for several reasons. Throughout his life, Cantor embraced capitalism and core American institutions. Leftist critiques of the government and corporations conflicted with Cantor's liberal Democratic politics. In addition, association with Hollywood radicals would have jeopardized Cantor's image and his ability to promote Jewish causes during a time when antisemites marginalized Jewish progressives by linking them with communist subversion.[18] Cantor and HANL also opposed Nazism from different perspectives. Cantor saw Nazism as a particular threat to Jews in the United States and Europe. In contrast, though HANL condemned Germany's policies, it did not highlight the Jewish dimensions of the antifascist struggle or the problem of antisemitism in America. The group placed anti-Jewish prejudice alongside suppression of free speech, exploitation of workers, opposition to the Spanish Loyalists, and other right-wing offenses. Even though many on the Hollywood left were Jewish, they identified more strongly as communists than as Jews and did not affiliate with Jewish religious and communal groups.[19]

Cantor preferred to work through Jewish organizations based in New York that were not connected with the political left. He also injected sly anti-German commentary into his popular network radio programs.

On commercial radio, Cantor walked a thin line in criticizing Germany without upsetting broadcasters. Changing industry standards stifled political messages. Starting in the mid-1930s, advertising agencies and broadcasters exerted more control over broadcast content and censored material that could offend listeners. Believing that the public associated radio stars with particular networks and sponsors, executives did not tolerate behavior that jeopardized corporate brands or ratings.[20] Comedy-variety, the most popular and profitable radio genre, drew particularly close scrutiny. In March 1937, *Variety* reported that sponsors, agencies, and networks had "clapped so many rules and regulations on jokes about news events" that it had become impossible for comedians to present topical material. Prohibited subjects included Congress, Roosevelt, Hitler, Mussolini, the Spanish Civil War, and domestic politics.[21]

Cantor carefully opposed Nazism within the constraints of the radio industry. He broadcast more anti-Hitler comments than any other comedian of the late 1930s, but he did not allow politics to intrude on the music and humor that provided the foundation for each episode. Instead, Cantor implicitly referenced the world situation through songs and remarks delivered during the closing segments of episodes: a space that he had already established for more serious statements. As with his comments about Henry Ford onstage during the 1920s, he relied on short, quick lines. Cantor also wrapped his allusions to German aggression around peaceful, popular, and patriotic statements about the virtues of America and the dangers of military intervention.

Cantor had to be judicious in his political expression because he could not afford to alienate listeners. During the late 1930s, a majority of Americans opposed involvement in Europe's conflicts. This isolationism continued until December 1941, when the Japanese attack on Pearl Harbor dragged America into World War II. Isolationist groups such as America First routinely employed antisemitic rhetoric, accusing Jews of pushing the country toward war and placing Jewish interests ahead of American interests. The weight of public opinion and accusations of warmongering compelled Jewish organizations to accept President

Roosevelt's official policy of neutrality. At the same time, Cantor and Jewish communal leaders attempted to increase popular opposition to Nazism and align Jewish and American interests.[22]

In 1936 Cantor sponsored and promoted a contest offering a $5,000 scholarship for the best essay on ways that America could avoid war. He also performed the noninterventionist "(If They Feel Like a War) Let Them Keep It Over There," written by Tin Pan Alley veterans Howard Johnson and Willie Raskin, on at least four radio broadcasts between 1936 and 1939.[23] On his December 20, 1936, program, Cantor contrasted the peace in America with the gathering storm in Europe: "When you read the newspapers every day and you watch the newsreels and you learn of these dictators in foreign lands working feverishly day and night, getting ready to pour millions of sons of mothers into war, we ought to get down on our knees and thank God that we're Americans, living in America, the land of the free, where Santa Claus comes every single day of the year." Listeners would have recognized who was guilty of pushing the world to the brink of war. During 1936, Germany backed its militaristic, nationalist rhetoric by reoccupying the Rhineland, in direct violation of the Treaty of Versailles, and sending combat troops to support Francisco Franco in the Spanish Civil War. So that he didn't stand out as a Jewish celebrity attacking "dictators in foreign lands," Cantor ended the segment by noting that he had just returned from Chicago, where he felt the "Christmas spirit" while performing at a benefit for the city's Christmas fund.[24]

Cantor introduced a similar antiwar song, "My Land and Your Land," in April 1938 and reprised it the next month. The song contrasts wholesome American values, including peace, with German militarism: "You know, it's nice to live in a country where we're busy preparing for another world's fair / Instead of another world war / Let them fight over there—it's none of our affair."[25] Later in 1938, Cantor planned to use a similar line; however, the sponsor blocked Cantor's plan. The original script for the November 21, 1938, program, which aired three days before Thanksgiving, implicitly references the September 29–30 Munich Conference, at which the Allies appeased Hitler by allowing Germany to annex the Sudetenland of Czechoslovakia. Cantor observes, "It's really great to live in a country where people gather around a table to carve up a turkey, instead of a map." He then expresses gratitude for America's isolation from Europe, but implies that Germany won't stop with the Sudetenland: "Let's be thankful that there's nothing between us and the aggressive nations — except water."[26] Before the broadcast, the advertising agency censored the quip about carving a turkey, claiming that "some people" might not like the joke. The agency's decision to delete the line signaled heightened broadcaster sensitivity about political content as well as the advertising agency's frustration with Cantor's subtle political jabs at Germany. Ironically, the resourceful Cantor soon found a way to use the line even more effectively.[27]

In a November 24, 1938, national radio address, President Roosevelt claimed to have received a "Thanksgiving telegram" from his "old friend" Eddie Cantor. The president liked the telegram enough to share it with the nation. Roosevelt approvingly read a variation of the Thanksgiving benediction that the sponsor blocked: "I am thankful that I can live in a country where our leaders sit down on Thanksgiving Day to carve up a turkey instead of a map."[28] Audiences recognized the anti-Nazi implications in Cantor's telegram. The New York Times, for example, led its coverage with the statement: "President Roosevelt tonight again implied his abhorrence of Nazi policies by reading a Hollywood telegram contrasting the state of affairs on Thanksgiving day in this country and Central Europe."[29]

Through Marvin McIntyre, the president's appointments secretary, Cantor made a private appeal to Roosevelt the next year, asking the president to support the Wagner-Rogers bill of 1939, which would have greatly increased the number of German children admitted to America. Perhaps hoping to use his charity work as leverage, Cantor wrote to McIntyre indicating that he wanted to meet with Roosevelt to discuss two matters: the infantile paralysis drive and the problem of Jewish refugee children from Europe. The remainder of the letter emphasized the urgency of admitting additional children and the practicality of the plan proposed under the Wagner-Rogers bill. Cantor also appealed to Roosevelt's emotions and ego: "For generations to come, if these boys and girls were permitted entry into this country they would look upon our leader as a saint. They would bless the name of Franklin D. Roosevelt."[30] McIntyre forwarded Cantor's letter to Undersecretary of State Sumner Welles with a reminder to Welles that "Eddie has been a very ardent worker" for Roosevelt's National Foundation for Infantile Paralysis.[31]

Welles responded to Cantor: "It would be inadvisable to raise the question of increasing quotas or radical changes in our immigration laws during the present Congress." The White House ultimately did not take a public stand on the politically controversial legislation. The bill failed after a series of heated hearings.[32]

Cantor did not speak publicly about the Wagner-Rogers bill. In addition, his prime-time comments on Germany focused on the nation's militarism, rather than its treatment of Jews. Even if a more thorough, explicit condemnation of Germany had cleared network and sponsor censors, such content would have been too divisive, and too explicitly Jewish, for his radio audience. Instead, Cantor spoke directly about antisemitism and Jewish refugees through his tireless appearances for Hadassah: The Women's Zionist Organization of America, and its Youth Aliyah campaign.

In 1933 Youth Aliyah was founded in Germany. The organization helped Jewish teenagers immigrate to Palestine, where they continued their education and participated in kibbutz life. From 1933 to 1945, Youth Aliyah trained and resettled approximately fifteen thousand children from Germany, occupied countries, and transit countries to which youths escaped during the war.[33] In early 1936 Hadassah became the chief American supporter of Youth Aliyah. Raising funds for German emigration and resettlement represented a new kind of enterprise, different from the building of schools, playgrounds, and medical facilities in Palestine that had been Hadassah's focus. The organization continued to finance public health projects, including a new hospital, during the late 1930s, but Hadassah made Youth Aliyah an institutional priority. Hadassah recognized that the campaign to save children filled a pressing need and also had the potential to increase its membership because the cause resonated with American Jews. Hadassah raised vast sums of money for Youth Aliyah, including more than $250,000 from 1935 to 1937, which was used to acquire land, develop homes, build schools, and train the refugee youths.[34]

In February 1936 Tamar de Sola Pool, president of the New York chapter of Hadassah, interrupted Cantor's breakfast at the posh Hollywood Beach Hotel in South Florida with a proposition. De Sola Pool wanted Cantor to promote Youth Aliyah. Cantor did not disappoint her. Cantor's involvement offered Youth Aliyah credibility as a "big-time campaign," wrote Marian G. Greenberg, Hadassah's first Youth Aliyah chairperson.[35]

At his first appearance for Youth Aliyah, a luncheon held at the Waldorf-Astoria on March 26, 1936, Cantor announced that he had raised $4,400, and he would continue to support the organization.[36] Working with Hadassah's leadership, Cantor developed a fund-raising plan. He addressed small "gatherings" of potential donors around the country and promised to "secure contributions from the Hollywood world," an audience that Hadassah had not been able to reach.[37] It was unprecedented for one of America's biggest celebrities to crisscross the country, meeting with local chapters of a relatively small religious charity, but Cantor proved to be a dedicated and successful fund-raiser. In several cities, he drew on his network of friends and businessmen for pledges, making all arrangements and paying travel expenses for these meetings out of his pocket. However, Cantor did not focus exclusively on big donors. Recognizing the realities of fund-raising during the Depression, he employed the strategy that he turned to later with the March of Dimes, soliciting smaller contributors both in person and over the air. Cantor pledged "to go to any city for [Hadassah] and address any function where the sponsorship of a minimum of ten children [$3,600] will have been underwritten prior to his arrival." In fact, Cantor's events generated up to $20,000, a powerful testament to Cantor's popularity among American Jews and the importance of Youth Aliyah. Hadassah members adored Cantor, designating him their "number one boyfriend" at their 1938 national convention.[38]

Hadassah fit well with Cantor's 1930s persona. The actor was never a conventional romantic lover, and by this time in his career, he had smoothed over the rough edges of his Broadway characters. The proud husband of Ida and father of five girls, Cantor eagerly promoted the women's organization, greeted fans, and planned campaigns with local or national leaders. With three hundred chapters across the country and between fifty thousand and sixty thousand members during the late 1930s, Hadassah provided Cantor with a strong infrastructure for raising funds and meeting supporters.[39] His philanthropic appearances around the country solidified the connection between the actor and American Jews. Cantor met hundreds of people at every stop, signed autographs, posed for photographs, learned about their lives, and showed them that he cared deeply about the plight of Jews. Fueled by Cantor and Youth Aliyah, Hadassah's membership grew from 54,200 in 1938 to nearly 243,000 in 1948.[40] For the rest of Cantor's career, this generation of American Jews, roughly Cantor's age and affiliated with Hadassah or other communal organizations, constituted a reliable core audience. They stood by him during times of crisis, attended his live shows, and bought his books.

Along with personal appearances, Cantor used public service radio broadcasts to reach potential donors. Hadassah was able to secure free airtime from stations because it was a religious, nonprofit organization. Whereas radio networks and sponsors vetted Cantor's commercial broadcasts, he had more freedom to raise funds and speak about the European situation in his Youth Aliyah appeals. The networks did not monitor this content closely because the programs were unsponsored. In addition, the broadcasts aired during unpopular times in the schedule (usually Sunday afternoons) and did not attract large audiences. Still, Jewish organizations used radio to promote education, fundraising, and various religious or political agendas.[41] From 1936 to 1943, Cantor made five national Youth Aliyah radio appeals.[42] In mid-1938 he also paid for large advertisements in the *New York Times* and *Variety* to support Youth Aliyah, emphasizing that this "appeal is urgent."[43] Later that year, Cantor launched a highly publicized tour of England, raising a staggering $500,000 in fifteen days. Henrietta Szold, Hadassah's cofounder and former president, recognized Cantor's commitment to the cause as well as his fund-raising prowess. She wrote to her colleague Greenberg, "The man is a wizard!" In a telegram to Szold, Cantor modestly reported that he wanted his efforts to serve "as some slight indication of hope to our people."[44]

The actor did not underestimate the value of "hope." Earlier in the decade, Cantor made optimism a key element of his persona as he crafted inspiring music, humor, and stories to help people cope with the economic Depression. He developed a different style and new tactics to convince people that they had power, through their donation, to rescue European Jews during the late 1930s. In his Hadassah speeches, Cantor decided not to sing or joke. Instead, the actor projected the intelligence, maturity, and stability appropriate for the subject. These charity appearances also enabled Cantor to add nuance and gravity to a more familiar comic persona.[45] The actor apologized during his first Youth Aliyah address in March 1936, warning his audience, "If you came here thinking you were going to have a great deal of fun out of Eddie Cantor, you are in for a disappointment. With what we have facing us right now and in the very near future, it would be sacrilege to tell you jokes that you can hear on the radio every Sunday night anyway."[46]

Later that year, in an October 1936 talk that was broadcast nationally on CBS radio, Cantor recognized that he was using his star skills in a new forum: a speech before a religious organization that was airing as a public service. What's more, he was selling political ideas rather than sponsoring products: "It's a bit strange that I should be talking on the radio without attempting to sell coffee or toothpaste or gasoline, but on second thought, I have something else to sell and there are many, many people who should buy."[47] The public usually encountered Cantor and other actors through their roles and press pieces generated by network and studio publicists, but Cantor presented his Youth Aliyah work as more personal, authentic, and philanthropic: a glimpse of the real man behind the comic image.

Despite their shared fund-raising goals, Cantor's political priorities were different from Hadassah's. In its organizational appeals, Hadassah stressed the value of the education and training, in everything from agriculture to citizenship, that Youth Aliyah participants received in Palestine.[48] More broadly, Hadassah and Youth Aliyah advocated Jewish nationalism and fought restrictive British immigration policies regarding Palestine. These Zionist organizations built political, economic, and social structures for a future Jewish state. Cantor said nothing about Zionist ideas and activities. Because of his celebrity status and his success at raising money, Hadassah apparently did not write Cantor's speeches or expect him to promote a particular ideological position. Instead, Cantor was able to speak about issues that he understood well and cared deeply about. His focus on antisemitism and European refugees resonated widely with American Jews, regardless of their feelings about Zionism.

From the time of his initial March 1936 Youth Aliyah talk at the Waldorf-Astoria, Cantor warned audiences that the fate of the Jews in America and in Europe was interconnected: "Anything that you do for the Jews on the other side is insurance for you here in America. They are waiting for us, those antisemitic groups here and all over the world, to see whether or not we fail there, and we dare not fail."[49] Given the political climate, Cantor could not openly advocate war with Germany or major changes in United States immigration quotas. But contributions to Youth Aliyah represented a concrete action that he could endorse without challenging government policy and public opinion. For Cantor, Youth Aliyah enabled American Jews to make a symbolic statement to the world that they cared about the plight of their fellow Jews internationally. In addition to demonstrating communal strength, these donations brought children to safety in Palestine.

Cantor urged his audience to understand the grave dangers that Jews in America and around the world faced. This was war. Jewish lives, including his own, were at risk. At a Hadassah fund-raiser, he spoke about American Nazi threats to his family, confessing, "I tell you I am a little bit frightened." The actor had good reason to be frightened. He was constantly participating in public events with little or no protection from potentially violent people in the crowd. It would not have been difficult for Nazis to attack Cantor or his family. The threats began in 1934 and increased through the end of the decade. They were serious enough to merit local and federal investigations. In 1937 antisemites planned to bomb the homes of several Jewish movie stars, including Cantor's. The next year, Cantor reported that Nazis called Ida, warning him "to get out of Los Angeles before he is carried out in a pine box." In addition, Nazis threatened his sponsor, R. J. Reynolds, claiming that ten million German Americans would boycott the company's Camel cigarettes if Cantor remained on the air. Cantor viewed the threats as confirmation of the importance of his message urging international Jewish solidarity. "They are threatening me only for one reason," he said. "Because I believe that the Jews must have some form of unity."[50]

In describing the magnitude of the battle against antisemitism, Cantor argued that Germany was bankrolling the Nazi movement in the United States and using prominent Americans to spread propaganda. As an example of Nazi influence, Cantor cited Henry Ford's acceptance of the Grand Cross of the Supreme Order of the German Eagle, the highest decoration given to foreigners, at a ceremony in Detroit on July 30, 1938. As a German consular representative presented Ford with the medal and conveyed Hitler's personal congratulations, Cantor was aboard the

SS *Normandie,* returning from a Hadassah fund-raising tour of Great Britain, where the dangers of Germany and its propaganda machine were inescapable. Soon after he returned, on August 3, 1938, he spoke at a Hadassah luncheon that recognized his work with Youth Aliyah. Cantor warned his fellow Jews that, if they did not oppose antisemitism, they would lose their jobs and businesses. He also asserted that the German government had "reached people in the highest places" in America, and the Nazis were doing "a good job" of spreading propaganda over domestic airwaves and presses. Cantor accused Ford of being a tool for this propaganda: "Mr. Henry Ford, in my opinion, is a damned fool permitting the world's greatest gangster to give him this citation," Cantor said. "Doesn't he realize that the German papers, reporting the citation, said all Americans were behind Nazism? Whose side is Mr. Ford on? I question Mr. Ford's Americanism and his Christianity."[51]

Ford's acceptance of the award sparked protests by other American Jews, including Roosevelt cabinet member Harold L. Ickes, but Cantor stood out as the most prominent critic of Ford and Germany.[52] In addition, Cantor's remarks went beyond a condemnation of Ford. Cantor used the industrialist to exemplify the extent to which Germany had infiltrated American institutions, including the media. Cantor's message was radical during a time when Jewish leaders rarely tied antisemitism to broader social and political structures or predicted that America could become like Nazi Germany. Daily newspapers, including wire services, widely reported on Cantor's shot at Ford. The press coverage helped Cantor spread his warning; however, it also provided fodder for his opponents.

The idea that a Jewish comedian from the Lower East Side of New York would question the patriotism and Christianity of a heroic Midwestern capitalist offended many people. Cantor received and saved approximately fifty letters from writers expressing their anger over his criticism of Ford. The letters provide powerful evidence of the range of antisemitic responses, some more brutal than others, with which Cantor contended. Several writers defended Ford's acceptance of the Nazi medal as a business decision and warned that Cantor's criticism of Ford would provoke additional antisemitism in America. One writer praised Ford as "one of the greatest living Americans." He advised Cantor, "You are doing the Jewish people a great disservice by your remarks . . . Let's

Cantor arrives in London for a fund-raising tour (July 1938).

not start anything that may lead to a hatred of the Jews in America."[53] Others relished the possibility that the situation Jews faced in Germany would be replicated in America. A typically venomous antisemitic writer ended his rant against Cantor and Jews: "Your [sic] just a clown and a poor one . . . and you try to tell Mr. Ford what to do. I hope the day comes and it isn't far away when the people of the United States will know the truth and act accordingly. As soon as you're wiped off the globe, the better it is for the other race."[54]

Many lectured Cantor about why Jews were unpopular all over the world, repeating stereotypes about the manners, ethics, and business practices of Jews. Cantor's questioning of Ford's "Americanism" struck a particular nerve with this group of people. Their responses attacked Cantor's allegiance to the United States, linking Jews with Russians and communists. Writers were incensed that Cantor had criticized Ford, especially after the actor had traveled abroad in support of European Jews rather than Americans who needed help during the Depression. One person wrote, "What I can't understand is your running over to England raising money for German and Polish Jews and then come back here and attack Ford who is putting American men to work to make a living. That's your answer why we have so many anti-Jew movements in this country. You boys bring it on yourselves."[55] Throughout his professional life, Cantor prided himself on his patriotism as well as his ability to win the approval of public audiences and critics, yet now he was receiving piles of antisemitic hate mail. Cantor may have worried that the public was turning against him and his fellow Jews.

Some of the missives, which included boycott threats, went to Cantor's network, CBS, and sponsor R. J. Reynolds. The letters illustrate how the public collapsed distinctions between Cantor's off-air politics and his radio persona. Cantor himself blurred the lines between activism and commercialism by delivering anti-Nazi quips and impromptu speeches during informal performances before and after the thirty-minute programs. Network and advertising agency executives did not silence the actor because these comments usually did not attract attention.[56] Cantor found himself in trouble, however, for a post-broadcast routine in which he imagined a conversation between a rabbi and Hitler. During the March 27, 1939, performance, an audience member, Charles Gollob, began to heckle Cantor. Gollob then caused further commotion when he and his wife, Elsie, left the studio theater while Cantor was still onstage. The Gollobs claimed that they were then beaten and called "Nazis" by men outside the studio, identifying one of the alleged assailants as Bert Gordon, the Mad Russian. The trade press and daily newspapers widely covered the sensational story, including the Gollobs' subsequent call for criminal battery charges against Gordon. After the district attorney's office refused to issue a complaint, the Gollobs remained in the spotlight by bringing a $751,000 civil lawsuit against Gordon, Cantor, CBS, and sponsor R. J. Reynolds.[57]

Cantor and the other parties in the lawsuit suffered no legal damages; nevertheless, the episode further politicized Cantor's public image and created additional friction between Cantor and his employers. Cantor's remarks about Hitler, coupled with the alleged assault of audience members, were "very disgusting to the broadcasting company officials and he [Cantor] is becoming increasingly unpopular in radio circles," according to an FBI informant who worked in the radio industry. The FBI source also anticipated Cantor's future problems with his sponsor, disclosing that R. J. Reynolds wanted to cancel Cantor's contract immediately after the Gollob incident, but that it was not able to do so legally.[58]

Many listeners believed the Gollobs' allegations and sent furious letters to Cantor, the network, and the sponsor. This mail, which included boycott threats, gave CBS and R. J. Reynolds evidence that Cantor was alienating listeners and generating too much controversy. Several letter writers saw themselves as protectors of the Gollobs, "good Americans" who were victims of Jewish aggression. An "anti-Jew organizer" wrote to Cantor: "The thing that happened last night is the best thing that could have happened, when your henchmen beat up two good white people, to wake up the Christian people to run all you Hebes back where you belong—the middle of the ocean." Others charged that Cantor was no better than Hitler in the way he treated those who disagreed with him. One man wrote, "No Nazi storm-trooper ever administered a more callous beating, or with less provocation." Another saw the alleged altercation as an example of "how intolerant your anti-Hitler crowd can be."[59]

Throughout the late 1930s, Cantor found a haven in the Jewish community and its newspapers, which were filled with articles covering his work with Youth Aliyah, including detailed accounts of his speeches. Commentators praised Cantor's strength and success in supporting Jewish causes. A *Pittsburgh Jewish Criterion* tribute, published in 1937 to commemorate Cantor's twenty-fifth anniversary in show business, chronicled the celebrity's work fighting antisemitism. "To Jewry and its institutions, he [Cantor] has given time, money, thought, and selfless service, for Cantor's record of participation in and help to things Jewish is unsurpassed by any other figure in the entertainment world."[60] In a weekly column from 1938, the *Jewish Criterion* editor Milton K. Susman wrote that, though he was not a fan of Cantor's acting, he was raising his voice "in a loud huzzah for the magnificent work he [Cantor] has done to help relieve the suffering of our sorely harassed people in other parts of the world."[61] Similarly commending the more serious Jewish activism beneath the comic façade, the *Jewish Advocate* lamented, "Few people know the humane, gentle, earnest Eddie Cantor. They do not see beneath the wise-cracker's shell. He is a courageous American . . . a generous Jew."[62]

With the support of Hadassah and the Jewish press, Cantor continued speaking about the dangers of American Nazi propagandists. On the afternoon of June 13, 1939, Cantor addressed the New York chapter of Hadassah at the World's Fair Temple of Religion. Though the talk from the Palestine Pavilion was not broadcast, daily newspapers covered it, and the Jewish press published a transcript of the speech under Cantor's byline. Using even stronger language charging Nazi manipulation of American institutions than he had the previous year, when talking about Henry Ford, Cantor warned, "The whole business now going on over there [Germany] can be transferred over here. Some people have told me that I seem to be getting a little panicky . . . They don't know what important industrialists are behind this business." Cantor identified Father Coughlin and Senator Robert Rice Reynolds of North Carolina in particular as two public figures supported by industrialists. "These men," he continued, referring to the figures behind Coughlin and Reynolds, "are the enemies of not only the Jews, but of all Americans."[63] Cantor did not name the prominent businessmen or provide supporting evidence for his accusation, but he may have had Henry Ford in mind. Ford and other car manufacturers were rumored to be subsidizing Coughlin.[64] The Jewish actor left himself vulnerable to charges that he was paranoid or disloyal in challenging the patriotism of a senator and warning that Americans were susceptible to Nazism. Moreover, while Coughlin's influence had diminished, the priest still had an active and vigilant following in 1939. In addition, Cantor probably did not endear himself to the powers at R. J. Reynolds, the North Carolina–based tobacco company that sponsored his program, by singling out the state's junior senator. In short, Cantor may have gone too far.

Two weeks after Cantor's World's Fair speech, the radio season ended. R. J. Reynolds and the William Esty advertising agency announced that they would not renew Cantor's contract for his *Camel Caravan* show, even though the star attracted a large audience. Cantor averaged a 17.3 rating during the 1938–1939 season, making his *Camel Caravan* the sixth-most-popular program on radio; and he placed highly in a June 1939 *Radio Guide* poll of more than seven hundred thousand listeners.[65] There was surprisingly little press coverage of R. J. Reynolds' decision to drop the star, and no explanation for this decision in the major daily newspapers and trade journals. Phineas J. Biron, who covered both show business and anti-Nazi politics in his syndicated column for Jewish newspapers, and frequently ran items on Cantor, was one of the few to speculate on the reasons for Cantor's absence from the air. Alluding to the actor's charges against Senator Reynolds, Biron wrote, "It will be denied, and we'll never be able to prove our contention, but we have more than a suspicion that the reason why Eddie Cantor and his radio sponsor, Camel cigarettes, have split had something to do with Cantor's attack on the un-Americanism of a well-known figure who, in turn, has some connections with Camels."[66]

No other sponsor hired Cantor. He missed the entire 1939–1940 radio season, becoming one of the first radio performers to lose work on account of political activity. Cantor did not comment publicly on his troubles at the time, but he later confirmed that he was taken off the air because of his politics. In a 1943 interview, Cantor recalled that during the 1930s, sponsors warned him to stop commenting on dictators. His principled reply: "'Long after I'm through as a comedian, I'll still be a man."[67] In his 1957 autobiography, Cantor wrote that the 1939 World's Fair address "not only cost me $585,000," his salary for a season of radio, "but threatened my radio career for good."[68]

Camel replaced the Cantor show with a situation comedy, *Blondie*, based on the popular comic strip and film series. It ran on radio for eleven years. R. J. Reynolds continued to sponsor another network program, *Camel Caravan* with Benny Goodman, which moved from CBS to NBC starting with the 1939–1940 season. Both shows were cheaper to produce and may have seemed fresher to audiences than Cantor's show. More important, these replacements did not feature an outspoken star who threatened network and sponsor corporate images by expressing controversial political views.

Without a sponsor, Cantor responded to the crisis in the summer of 1939 the way he always had when he was in trouble: by working hard, generating publicity, and retooling his image.

9 CANTOR GOES TO CHURCH
(1939–1941)

ow off the air, Cantor began to rehabilitate his image. He chose his associations with Jewish groups carefully, curtailing his activities for Hadassah, the United Palestine Appeal (UPA), and other Zionist groups. When Cantor received an honor from B'nai B'rith in November 1939, he emphasized his pride in the fraternal organization's patriotism, rather than B'nai B'rith's long history of Jewish communal service: "I belong to an organization of American citizens that stands for Americanism, that preaches and practices Americanism, and whose program of activity is permeated by love of country."[1] In December 1939, Cantor joined the board of the American Jewish Joint Distribution Committee (JDC), the largest humanitarian relief organization aiding Jews overseas.[2] Most important, after June 1939, Cantor tempered his rhetoric about the threat of Nazism in the United States. He had learned that assailing the loyalties of right-wing Nazi sympathizers and supporters left him vulnerable to questions about his own patriotism. After he lost his radio program, Cantor used different tactics and worked with new partners to oppose domestic antisemitism and aid Jews abroad.

Cantor was not entirely absent from radio during the 1939–1940 season. He made a handful of guest appearances in unsponsored blockbuster tributes to other stars and charity benefits for popular organizations such as the March of Dimes and the American Red Cross. The highlight of this period was a short scene in a New Year's Eve 1939 production of the *Gulf Screen Guild Theater* in which Cantor parodied his dull and desperate life without a sponsor.

In the sketch, two producers call on Cantor at his home because every other comedian is working. The former headliner is not doing well. The Salvation Army drops off a care package for the family. Cantor has a neon sign in the window beneath a Christmas wreath. Instead of "Merry Christmas," it says "Make Me an Offer."

Bea Benedaret portrays Ida, and other actresses play Cantor's daughters.

One daughter asks plaintively, "Mama, how about some butter?"

Ida replies tiredly, "How many times have I told you girls? We can't have butter until your father gets a sponsor."[3]

As Cantor tried to regain a more permanent spot on radio, he still had name recognition, the affection of a large audience, and the versatility to star in several different media. In March 1939, before he lost his radio sponsorship, Cantor signed a contract with MGM for a one-picture movie deal. The unnamed film developed into *Forty Little Mothers* and was released in April 1940. Mostly, Cantor remained busy performing live. On June 29, 1939, three days after his last *Camel Caravan* program aired, the Loew's State Theatre on Broadway hosted Cantor and his radio costars for a week. They played six shows a day between screenings of the film *It's a Wonderful World*. Cantor opened the crowd-pleasing performance with a short monologue and bantered with Bert Parks about their trip to the Lower East Side, where Cantor introduced the young announcer from Atlanta to such Jewish delicacies as matzo balls, kreplach, and bagels. Cantor also acted in sketches with radio costars Sidney Fields and Bert Gordon and sang a medley of his hit songs. Cantor closed with his familiar line expressing gratitude that, with Europe at war, "we are living in the land of the free." The star added a line criticizing all radicals, not only those on the right, explaining that he had "no sympathy with the guys who stand up on soap boxes and tell us what is wrong with this country . . . the greatest democracy on the face of this earth."[4]

Cantor and his troupe gave a total of forty-one performances over the week, shattering the house record for the number of shows and the box office gross. Cantor split the take, reportedly a little over fifty thousand dollars, with the Broadway theater. For an enthusiastic Loew's publicist, Cantor's sold-out engagement in the midst of the New York World's Fair demonstrated that "Broadway is still alive. Broadway can still compete with the Fair." During the show's run, Cantor managed to find time to return to the Lower East Side for a rally on public safety and accident prevention that demonstrated his undiminished popularity in the neighborhood. Nearly twenty thousand people showed up for the

Crowds flock to one of Cantor's shows at the Loew's State Theater
on Broadway in the summer of 1939. Courtesy of UCLA Library Special
Collections.

event, which was held in a high school auditorium that only accommodated two thousand. Fifty policemen, including two emergency squads, managed the crowd.[5]

That fall, Cantor went on the road, presenting a series of one-week engagements in Pittsburgh, Boston, Brooklyn, Washington, DC, Chicago, and Cincinnati. The touring show was similar to the one in New York, though Cantor now closed with his old isolationist radio hit, "Let Them Keep It over There." He repeated the grueling New York schedule of five or six performances a day, maintaining a steady audience flow while also impressing critics. In Chicago, *Variety* reported that he generated "zowie coin" of $52,000, with mobs of fans demanding that Cantor add more shows. A *Pittsburgh Post-Gazette* reviewer, Harold W. Cohen, marveled that Cantor "is the top salesman-showman of his time, a comedian who continues to be good to the public that has been good to him for more than twenty years. Perfection is a pretty unapproachable commodity; Mr. Cantor achieved it some time ago and is still improving upon it."[6]

On previous tours, Cantor found time between commercial engagements to appear at local fund-raisers for Jewish federations, synagogues, or Hadassah. In Pittsburgh, Cantor's main offstage event was held at the First Baptist Church. He appealed for the preservation of democracy and Christianity before eighteen hundred people, advocating "church attendance and strict adherence to Christian principles to keep subversive influences of dictatorial governments from destroying the American rights of 'life, liberty and the pursuit of happiness.'" Cantor saw "Christian prayer" as an important weapon against the dual threats of fascism and communism: "Christianity and Democracy go hand in hand. Go to church and practice true Christianity, because edifices like the one we are in tonight will live long after Hitler and Stalin are forgotten." The speaker even had conciliatory words about Father Charles Coughlin. Cantor still "resented" unspecified remarks by Coughlin, but he believed that the radio priest's influence could be used for good and promised that he "would be the first to fight for his [Coughlin's] right to free speech."[7]

From 1939 to 1940, Cantor took every opportunity to emphasize his affinity with Christians. Cantor tied religious faith to American values, reestablished his patriotism before skeptics, and aligned himself with major Jewish communal organizations. Groups such as the American Jewish Committee and the National Conference of Christians and Jews (NCCJ) extolled America's value as a country that fostered multiple forms of religious expression. Before Cantor stood atop the church pulpit, the NCCJ sent "tolerance trios" to thousands of communities throughout the 1930s. Comprising a minister, a priest, and a rabbi, the trios combated prejudice and promoted interfaith goodwill.[8] American Jews emphasized the importance of religious freedom as central to democracy and looked for other affirmations of this freedom. In October 1936, for example, shortly before both the Jewish New Year and the presidential election, the Seven Arts Feature Syndicate distributed a long article under President Roosevelt's byline to Jewish newspapers.

The article compiled segments from speeches in which the president spoke about religious "tolerance" and "understanding" as fundamental to American democracy.[9]

By the late 1930s, the interfaith movement had become a crucial vehicle through which mainstream Jewish organizations fought prejudice and defined antisemitism as un-American. In highlighting similarities between Christianity and Judaism, American Jews asserted that people of different faiths shared common values: respect for freedom, defense of minority rights, and appreciation of the value of prayer and organized religion. Jewish leaders contrasted American tolerance of religious diversity with Nazi persecution, insisting that all good Americans, not only Jews, should oppose Hitler. For example, the General Jewish Council (GJC), an umbrella organization that four major Jewish groups formed in 1938, publicized German actions against Protestants and Catholics. The GJC stressed that the Nazis held no regard for basic human rights.[10]

As someone who was mindful of Jewish communal politics, including interfaith efforts, Cantor occasionally referenced the Bible and Christian prayer in his radio program during the late 1930s. In a 1936 episode, for example, Cantor's surrogate radio son, Bobby Breen, complains that the Bible is not interesting or relevant. Cantor disagrees, "No matter what you've ever read, you'll find it written much better in the Bible." The wise host proves his point by linking Bible stories to more contemporary literature and events.[11] Three years later, Cantor ended a 1939 broadcast by speaking of church as offering shelter from storms: a metaphor to which he returned in subsequent talks about religion. He concludes, "We are extremely fortunate to live in a country where we can worship as we please, when we please. Let's make the most of this blessing. Go to church . . . Whatever your race or creed . . . You'll meet old friends and make new ones."[12] Starting with his 1939 stage show and offstage appearances, Cantor made these kinds of appeals more frequently and followed the blueprint for interfaith cooperation of the GJC and related organizations, especially the American Jewish Committee and B'nai B'rith.

During his time in Pittsburgh, Cantor spoke with a reporter from the city's Jewish newspaper, the *Jewish Criterion*. He continued to espouse the power of faith and the importance of social engagement:

Cantor and Cobina Wright Jr., one of his costars during his engagement at the Loew's State Theater, pose with a large copy of the American Declaration of Tolerance and Equality. The declaration was displayed at the Loew's State Theater and other theaters on July 4, 1939.

"Entertainment, comedy, is just froth. On the other hand, the audience goes home and remembers the serious things I say." For the benefit of the reporter, Cantor dictated a letter to a fan who had asked the actor to write her young son a letter. This fan wanted the boy to appreciate "the man, Eddie Cantor." Though Cantor was speaking with a Jewish newspaper, he responded in the voice of a generic, patriotic clergyman, rather than a Jewish comedian and activist: "I am doing what I can for my country and what it stands for. We have so much to be thankful for but we are all too busy to remember God—what a pity! I hope your boy will grow up to have the same kindly soul which you possess."[13]

After Pittsburgh, Cantor arrived in the nation's capital, where he kept a busy schedule of five shows a day starting on October 26, 1939. As in Pittsburgh, he mixed stage comedy, social commentary, and philanthropy. Cantor presented himself as a patriotic and benevolent grandfather concerned about the country's youth, rather than a fiery Jewish activist. In a typically clever, unobjectionable quip from the show, Cantor commented on young people: "I would rather have them hailing band leaders than heiling bund leaders."[14] Offstage, he extended his traffic safety campaign, taking the time to appear on a local radio show at 11 p.m., so he could present an award to a courteous driver. Cantor told the station, "I'll even cancel a scheduled call to my grandson to take part" in the broadcast.[15] The line epitomized Cantor's persona as a nonthreatening family man and his eagerness to accept practically any opportunity to showcase this image.

While in Washington, Cantor visited the local YMCA and a branch of the Boys' Club of Washington.[16] The father of five daughters also met a group of female high school journalists for a backstage press conference and photo opportunity. The publicity event buttressed his image as a mentor ahead of the release of *Forty Little Mothers*, in which Cantor played a high school teacher at an all-girls school.[17] More seriously, Cantor held short meetings with President Roosevelt and House Speaker William Bankhead. He also accepted an honorary parchment, with "The American's Creed" printed on it, from the House of Representatives. The *Washington Post* theater critic Nelson B. Bell, who accompanied Cantor as the actor toured Capitol Hill, praised Cantor's "Americanism, humanitarianism, and all around broad thinking." Bell hinted that some critics were skeptical about the comedian's motives and loyalties, but he defended Cantor: "This deep-seated patriotism of Eddie's is no idle or counterfeit pose, nor any specious sort of 'flag-waving.'"[18]

Cantor continued to speak of communism and fascism as dual threats during his fall 1939 interviews and closing statements from the stage. He told the *Jewish Criterion*, "I am out of patience with those left-wing groups which stand on our street corners and decry the government of this country."[19] Even at the height of the Depression, Cantor never advocated communism. He held himself up as an exemplar of the American Dream and fervently supported a combination of individual initiative, private charity, and Roosevelt's New Deal as vehicles for pulling the nation out of the economic morass. However, Cantor was vulnerable to accusations of communist sympathies because of his record as a liberal, Jewish antifascist. He associated with leftists in movies, labor unions, and political organizations such as the Hollywood Anti-Nazi League. The loss of his radio program signaled the power of conservatives to besmirch Cantor's patriotism and punish him for his political activism.

Several events, in America and internationally, further fueled Cantor's anticommunism. Washington grew increasingly interested in Hollywood communists during the late 1930s. In May 1938, Congress established the House Committee for the Investigation of Un-American Activities (abbreviated for purposes of pronunciation as HUAC) to investigate domestic fascism and communism. When hearings began on August 12, 1938, the committee heard testimony from witnesses who exposed American Nazi activity. But on the third day of the hearings, HUAC turned its attention to communism on the West Coast, including Los Angeles. Committee investigator Edward F. Sullivan reported that communist activities were "rampant" in the film industry. Sullivan also asserted that communists branded any opponents as Nazis or fascists, and Jewish organizations were overreacting to the Nazi threat.[20]

On August 6, 1938, shortly before the hearings began, HUAC chairman Martin Dies attempted to make an appointment with Cantor to support the committee's antifascist work. Like Congressman Dickstein five years earlier, Dies wanted Cantor to deliver information on domestic Nazism that was compiled by Leon L. Lewis of the Los Angeles Jewish Community Committee. Cantor waited to see how the hearing developed before he replied to Dies's invitation. By August 25, 1938, following Sullivan's testimony, he had seen enough to decline the meeting with Dies. Cantor wrote to Lewis, "It looks as if he [Dies] has been reached by the Nazis. I can't understand his dropping that phase of the investigation after a mere two days of examination."[21]

Through 1939 and 1940, communist subversion in Hollywood continued to interest the Dies committee and its chairman. In two *Liberty* magazine articles from February 1940, Dies charged that Hollywood was "used as a dupe and vehicle for Communist activity and propaganda." The HUAC chairman, a conservative Democrat, expressed particular distaste for the Hollywood Anti-Nazi League, which he asserted was "under the control of Communists." Dies further explained that, as Jews, Hollywood producers sympathized with any anti-Nazi group or organization. He alluded to Lewis's anti-Nazi program as an example of the ways in which Hollywood Jews overreacted to the Nazi threat. Dies expressed interest in conducting more extensive investigations of communism in the film industry, though HUAC did not formally convene hearings on the subject until 1947 under a new chairman, J. Parnell Thomas.[22] Cantor disliked HUAC, but he also understood the investigative power of the committee and its chair. Cantor remained out of the crosshairs of conservatives by affirming his anticommunism. This position did not conflict with his beliefs, especially given recent developments in Europe.

Cooperation between Stalin and Hitler in the summer and fall of 1939 shattered the Popular Front coalition of liberals and communists. In August 1939, Germany and Russia signed two pivotal agreements: one providing the Nazis with Russian raw materials in exchange for German goods and the second a nonaggression pact. Nine days after signing the agreements, Hitler invaded Poland. War had begun in Europe. After the events of August 1939, committed anti-Nazis such as Cantor became more vocal in opposing communism.

In October 1939, an interfaith audience of more than sixteen hundred people packed Washington, DC's downtown First Congregational Church, where Cantor delivered a variation of his Pittsburgh address. Speaking on a podium filled with fresh flowers and American flags, Cantor heralded religion as the only defense against Stalin and Hitler. Church loyalty, he believed, could counter Nazi propaganda. Cantor also praised religious tolerance, appreciating that a Christian house of worship would welcome Jewish speakers. Acknowledging that critics saw him as a "professional flag waver," Cantor defended his patriotism, asserting, "We don't wave the flag enough."[23] After the sermon, he told reporters, "If I can make one Christian feel more kindly toward the Jews, I shall be glad to preach many times again."[24]

In an interview with Dr. Arnold A. Roback, a prominent psychologist who wrote a column for the *Boston Jewish Advocate*, Cantor explained that his earlier devotion to "exclusively Jewish interests" was hurting his career. He had to "Americanize his activities." Cantor cited fundraising for Catholic refugees and speaking directly with people who held anti-Jewish ideas as examples of ways in which he was broadening his appeal while still resisting Nazism. Roback rejected Cantor's effort to "appease" and neutralize antisemites.[25] Other commentators did not echo Roback's criticisms. Jewish organizations, churches, and interfaith groups welcomed Cantor into the coalition of prominent Jews and Christians seeking to cross religious lines, find common values, and strengthen the role of prayer in American life. For the rest of his career, Cantor continued to emphasize the value of religious pluralism and the dangers of bigotry as fundamentally un-American and antidemocratic.

Cantor's next major role had no social or political commentary, but *Forty Little Mothers* (1940), his first film appearance since *Ali Baba Goes to Town* (1937), cemented his growing image as a seasoned, reliable star. In the comedy, which opened in April 1940, Cantor plays a shy, unmarried teacher who takes care of an abandoned baby while managing a classroom full of unruly girls at a boarding school. With only one song and a contemporary setting, *Forty Little Mothers* featured a more subdued style from Cantor, compared with his films of the 1930s. In addition, his character is mature and conscientious. Cantor told the *New York Times* that he welcomed the opportunity to portray someone his own age, rather than "striving for youth in a romance with a girl who could be his granddaughter."[26] Cantor received positive reviews in his straight role, letting costar Baby Quintanilla steal several scenes.[27]

Following the release of *Forty Little Mothers*, Cantor continued to use public service events to remain in the public eye and polish his patriotic image. In May 1940 he took the train from Los Angeles to a football stadium in Tulsa, Oklahoma, where he was the featured speaker at a rally celebrating newly naturalized citizens. In remarks broadcast live over the NBC Blue network, Cantor praised the ceremony as a "baptism of citizenship." He connected religious diversity with national identity: "True, some of us belong to different faiths and creeds. Some of us come from different races and different countries. But all of us give reverence to the one great, all embracing religion that unites us in a common brotherhood. The great religion of Americanism."

Cantor also commended FBI Director J. Edgar Hoover's work confronting domestic threats and echoed Hoover's statements that "if we use our heads today, we may not be forced to use our rifles, our airplanes and our battleships tomorrow." Cantor explained that Hoover "has been faced with the job of meeting and conquering those forces that are challenging our democracy from within. And he has done that job well."[28] Though he was not specific about what aspects of Hoover's work he appreciated, or how vigilance would keep America out of the war in Europe, the statement enabled Cantor to reaffirm his opposition to war while also endorsing the nation's powerful symbol of law-abiding patriotism. Hoover responded with a friendly letter thanking Cantor for the "kind references" in the speech. "It was a real source of encouragement to hear that you thought we had done our job well," wrote Hoover. The next week, Cantor and Hoover each addressed a B'nai B'rith convention in Boston. It is not clear whether they met or appeared together during the three-day event.[29]

Cantor occasionally worked with Hoover over the next several years, cementing a connection that helped both men. Hoover used Cantor's celebrity to enhance the agency, while Cantor's association with the FBI helped insulate him from questions about his loyalty and patriotism. In 1945 Hoover served as one of three judges in an essay contest that Cantor sponsored on juvenile delinquency. Cantor returned the favor by performing a long sketch in which he talks about having lunch with his "pal," J. Edgar Hoover. The comedian then fantasizes that he is an FBI agent. The FBI director wrote to Cantor after the broadcast, commending the comedian's work as a "G-man." Hoover continued, "The program was grand and I do appreciate your continued interest and friendship."[30]

In May 1940, shortly after his citizenship speech in Tulsa, the more politically moderate Cantor signed a contract for a new radio program to begin in the fall. Sponsor Bristol-Myers, makers of Sal Hepatica laxative and Ipana toothpaste, slotted Cantor to replace Abbott and Costello on the Wednesday evening comedy show *It's Time to Smile*. Cantor's old friend Jack Benny, radio's biggest star, helped him return to prime time. Benny asked his former producer Tom Harrington, the vice president in charge of radio for the Young and Rubicam advertising agency, to offer Cantor a contract. As Young and Rubicam prepared to launch the new Cantor show, Bill Thomas, the agency's publicity director, wrote a long memo to Harrington, listing the "distinct handicaps" in promoting Cantor. Thomas maintained, "Cantor's non-comedy activities of recent years have tended to present him as a serious-minded person, making it difficult for listeners to appreciate him as a person to be laughed at. These activities include his work for war refugees." Thomas also lamented Cantor's "unfortunate attack on Father Coughlin." Working with Cantor's personal publicist and representatives from NBC, Young and Rubicam decided to "present Cantor to the public strictly as a funny man, and [to] try to avoid any publicity that would indicate that Cantor ever has a serious thought or is guilty of a serious deed." Thomas insisted, "If Cantor does some kind deed for the poor, or for the war refugees, etc., it should be in private and without publicity."[31]

Thomas's memo reflected industry concerns about political activity, especially the Jewish advocacy for which Cantor was known; however, Thomas misjudged the risks from Cantor's politics. The actor's recent focus on finding common ground with Christians, fighting prejudice, and opposing both communism and Nazism resonated with audiences. In addition, by the summer of 1940, many Americans shared Cantor's antipathy toward Nazi Germany, though they did not want the United States to join the war in Europe.[32] As President Roosevelt told the nation in his Fireside Chat of September 3, 1939, delivered two days after Germany invaded Poland: "This nation will remain a neutral nation, but I cannot ask that every American remain neutral in thought as well. Even a neutral has a right to take account of facts. Even a neutral cannot be asked to close his mind or his conscience."[33]

Jewish listeners, who remained loyal to Cantor, recognized his return to radio as an important symbolic victory. Now that Cantor was back on prime time, asked Dr. G. George Fox, rabbi of Chicago's Reform South Shore Temple, "Are we going to stand back and permit the hooligans to shower his sponsor with their filthy screed again?" Instead, Rabbi Fox urged his readers to send Bristol-Myers supportive letters and to use

Ipana. The rabbi explained, "That toothpaste is probably as good as any other. It tastes better than some that we have tried."[34]

After Cantor secured the new radio deal, he began speaking more freely about politics off the air. Though he did not strictly follow the guidelines in Thomas's memo, the actor continued to frame the fight against fascism in terms of American values, rather than the perils that Jews faced. For example, in a July 1940 interview, he told *Variety* that antisemitism and other "hates" weaken America and would make it easier for a dictator to "conquer" this country.[35] Indicative of his more measured discussion of specifically Jewish problems and perspectives, Cantor appeared at a November 1940 benefit for the Zionist Mizrachi Women's Organization of America. He used the occasion to announce that he was "devoting all his time to refugee work and to the Bundles for Britain," a relief organization with no religious or political affiliation. Responding to the German bombing of London, Cantor pledged to house one hundred British children on his estate in Great Neck, as soon as transportation could be arranged for the refugees. "We must do all we can to aid what looks like the next-to-last democracy," Cantor said, though he was also clear that "we should never send troops."[36]

In August 1941, after a season back in prime time, Cantor felt comfortable enough to make an anti-Hitler quip in public for the first time since 1939. Appearing on *Millions for Defense*, a Treasury Department program that hosted big-name talent selling bonds, host Barry Wood prods Cantor: "I am sure that in these times you are only too happy to give all that you can to the man with the grey whiskers."

Cantor replies, "Uncle Sam? Of course, I figure it's much better to have the fella with the grey whiskers than wait for that guy with the little black moustache."

The studio audience responds with a long, approving cheer.[37]

Two months later, Cantor joined a diverse group of other celebrities in front of seventeen thousand people at the "Fun to Be Free" anti-Hitler revue and rally in Madison Square Garden. The actor Bill Robinson, wearing gold pants, tap-danced on Hitler's coffin as the band played "When That Man Is Dead and Gone." Feisty Brooklyn Dodgers manager Leo Durocher, whose team had lost Game Four of the World Series against the Yankees earlier in the day, proclaimed, "We don't want Hitler." More astonishingly, he praised his crosstown rivals: "The Yankees are a great ball club. Even if we lose, we'll be losing in a free country." Cantor did his part by donning a hoopskirt to present a parody of Irving Berlin's "Easter Parade" with his friend Jack Benny.[38]

Cantor remained cautious about expressing anti-Hitler or pro-intervention sentiments on *It's Time to Smile*, his commercial radio program, from the NBC show's premiere in October 1940 until after America entered World War II. His new program retained the style and format of the 1930s broadcasts. *It's Time to Smile* featured a popular new singer, Dinah Shore, along with seasoned supporting player Bert Gordon. Cantor still bantered with big-name guests such as Joe DiMaggio, Humphrey Bogart, and Tallulah Bankhead. The *New York Times* critic John K. Hutchens wrote of Cantor, "If he depends largely on guest artists, it is also true that he has a way with them, even to the extent last week of almost making an actor out of Joe DiMaggio."[39] While recognizing that Cantor's "comedy is standard as ever," *Variety* praised the 1940 debut episode's "skillful" pacing and Cantor's appeal as a "resourceful showman."[40]

The familiar star achieved solid ratings for several years, with his show finishing among the top twenty programs. In 1940, *It's Time to Smile* aired on Wednesday nights directly against Fred Allen's popular *Texaco Star Theater*. Cantor typically earned a fifteen rating (15 percent of all homes with radios): slightly higher than Allen's number. More than 4.5 million homes tuned to Cantor each week. With weaker competition, his ratings rose in later seasons.[41]

When Cantor returned to the radio in 1940, the forty-eight-year-old headliner filled his program with jokes about his age, supporting the more mature, authoritative image that he presented in *Forty Little Mothers* and his offstage charity work. He also solidified his image as a family man and American success story through sentimental skits celebrating birthdays, wedding anniversaries, and show business landmarks. The veteran entertainer still enjoyed talking fondly about his working-class Jewish origins on the Lower East Side, minimizing the violence and indigence that were central to his earlier childhood reminiscences. Cantor helped to establish the Lower East Side as the romantic embodiment of the Jewish immigrant experience through his nostalgic recollections on national radio and television during the 1940s and early 1950s.[42] He cemented his identification with the neighborhood through sketches with guest stars. Cantor and other actors strayed from the historical facts as they imagined the East Side's immigrant community of the 1910s.

In a June 4, 1941, broadcast celebrating Cantor's twenty-seventh wedding anniversary, guest star Al Jolson goes back in time with Cantor to around 1910: "The days," says Jolson, "when we were both kids on the Lower East Side of New York." The sketch continues with the two tough-talking young men, affecting thicker New York accents than usual, hanging around the city streets causing trouble. In reality, Jolson grew up in Washington, DC, not New York, and he did not know Cantor as a teenager. Jolson, six years older than Cantor, was touring the country as a vaudeville headliner when the radio skit takes place. Yet listeners easily imagined the two boys growing up together, given the centrality of a childhood on the Lower East Side to American Jewish identity. It was especially easy for Jolson to pass for a Lower East Side kid because of his long association with New York, including his successful Broadway career and his screen role as Jakie Rabinowitz/Jack Robin in *The Jazz Singer* (1927), a film loosely based on Jolson's biography.[43]

Ida Cantor, the neighborhood girl who became Eddie's wife, was a staple of these routines. "Ida, Sweet as Apple Cider," a love song that Cantor first sang in vaudeville, remained one of his signature numbers on radio, on records, and in live shows. Though she rarely appeared on the air with him, Cantor constantly talked about Ida, their long marriage, and their five girls. The star's longtime union with his Lower East Side sweetheart charmed fans, especially Jewish audiences, and established the actor as an authority on love and family. While Cantor portrayed a happily married man, he occasionally flirted with the actresses and singers who appeared as guests on the show. Cantor was not as sexual on radio as he had been onstage earlier in his career. His risqué radio banter usually ended with the young woman reminding Cantor of his age or his marital status.

Cantor made a nostalgic and much-anticipated return to Broadway to star in a new musical, *Banjo Eyes*, on December 25, 1941.[44] The title alludes to Cantor's big, bulging eyes, which became more central to his persona during the 1930s, as film close-ups enabled the actor to showcase a wider range of facial expressions. Later, newspaper writers occasionally used "Banjo Eyes" as a nickname for Cantor. In the play, "Banjo Eyes" is the name of a horse. Cantor plays Erwin Trowbridge,

Eddie, Ida, and their five daughters at the Stork Club in New York, 1943.
Standing, from left to right: Natalie, Edna (who lights the cigarette), and Janet.
Seated, from left to right: Marilyn, Ida, Eddie, and Marjorie.

a meek greeting card writer. The horse appears in Erwin's dreams and delivers winning selections. Gangsters find out about Erwin's powers and force him to share the winners with them. Like Cantor's Broadway plays of the 1920s, *Banjo Eyes* allowed the star to step out of character and perform a scene in blackface through a thin plot device: Erwin decides to imitate "Eddie Cantor." *Banjo Eyes* evoked Cantor's earlier stage and screen work with its blackface scene and a breezy plot mixing gangsters, girls, and Cantor as a naïve young man. But the late-1941 play also highlighted the distance that the headliner had traveled in only a few years. As Theodore Strauss of the *New York Times* wrote, "Today, Eddie is something more than a frantic little buffoon; he is perilously close to being a national institution."[45] America's entry into World War II marked a new phase in Cantor's career. He added the patriotic war song "We Did It Before and We Can Do It Again," which included a Pearl Harbor reference, to *Banjo Eyes*.[46] But the star was ready to move on.

Cantor closed *Banjo Eyes* in April 1942, citing his doctor's orders to stay off his feet for several weeks following a minor operation. He also was busy with his radio show and wartime benefits. Cantor may have found the rigors of starring on Broadway for eight live performances per week too much. In addition, even though *Banjo Eyes* remained popular, and the producers refunded more than thirty-five thousand dollars in advance sales, the light comedy did not speak to the concerns of a nation at war.[47]

10 IT'S TIME TO SMILE AGAIN
(1941–1945)

I n an interview with the *New York Herald Tribune* published on December 21, 1941, Cantor recognized that "things are different now." For the first time, he went on the record about why he had lost his sponsorship, still angry at those who had driven him from broadcasting: "I was off the air for a year, though, for saying the kinds of things everybody is begging me to say these days. In my broadcasts I used to tell people that Hitler would strike us when it suited him. Well, he has. Was I right?"[1] After seeing the *New York Herald Tribune* article, Cantor's friend James G. McDonald, a prominent diplomat and advocate for Jewish refugees, sent Cantor a telegram expressing "DELIGHT" in the reference to "YOUR EARLIER EXPERIENCE WHEN FARSIGHTED DENUNCIATION OF HITLER LED TO YOUR WITHDRAWAL FROM THE AIR . . . THOSE OF US WHO IN THOSE DAYS FORESAW THE MENACE WERE STIGMATIZED AS WAR MONGERS."[2] Two weeks later, the *New York Times* also reported that Cantor's political activism had cost him his radio program. Cantor blasted isolationists who suddenly supported the war after Pearl Harbor "as if to be pro-American were a fad like a new kind of hat or a pencil-striped suit."[3]

According to the *New York Times*, Cantor remained "a little bitter." After many years of sounding alarms about the profound problem of Hitler and Nazism, yet curbing calls for intervention because of the domestic political climate, Cantor felt entitled to claim his moment of vindication. But he soon dismissed his lingering anger. Cantor costarred in radio and movie productions with conservative actors such as Adolph Menjou and George Murphy. He also donated his time to an extraordinary range of charities. America's entry into the war presented an opportunity for Cantor to proudly oppose fascism, while boosting his patriotic image.

In 1942, with the country at war, Cantor became the first radio comedian to joke about the enemy. Others built routines around rationing, victory gardens, and life in the military. Cantor told his share of these kinds of jokes, but he also ridiculed Germany constantly, recognizing that popular culture played an important role in the war effort. In January 1942 he published an article in *Variety* contrasting the warm Allied leaders with the Axis "sourpusses" Hitler, Mussolini, and Hirohito. "That trio is awful funny," Cantor wrote, "only they don't realize it." With his own troubles for being too outspoken still fresh in his mind, Cantor saw comedy as an important symbol of American values, implicitly linking it to freedom of speech: "Laughter is an oxygen tank for free-breathing democracy. The countries that do not permit the absolute freedom of laughter will sink first."[4] As a Jew, he recognized the power of humor to counter adversity, telling the *New York Times*, "I come from a race that has had much tragedy. It has been able to live through the Hitlers of all centuries because of two things: Its Talmud and its ability to laugh in the midst of its own misery."[5] Cantor was no Talmudic scholar, but he knew a great deal about humor as well as broadcast industry politics. He made it difficult for networks and sponsors to squelch anti-Axis programming framed in these patriotic terms.

Two months later, Cantor brought his ideas about wartime comedy to his evening radio show. On his March 11, 1942, episode, Cantor introduced a recurring routine that parodied a Nazi newscast. As the humorless, Walter Winchell–like German commentator, Cantor fires a series of bulletins underscoring Nazi propaganda, brutality, and incompetence. A typical joke: "Heil Hitler. During the fiscal year, your wonderful government has spent a hundred billion dollars. Of this figure, a hundred billion dollars was expended for military equipment. Eight cents was spent to buy a new string for Der Fuehrer's yo-yo. Another five cents was squandered to buy food for our great army. This explains why we are losing so much military equipment on the Russian front. Instead of shooting the guns, our soldiers is eating them. In conclusion, Heil Hitler."[6]

These fake news reports broadly mocking life in the Nazi dictatorship could be heavy-handed. Other weekly sketches generated more laughter with their clever wordplay, charismatic Hollywood guest stars, and familiar characters; however, live audiences enthusiastically applauded the newscast barbs. Cantor displayed a potent combination of fury at the enemy and confidence that the Axis war machine relied on a shaky foundation. Over time, the routines incorporated news of German military defeats and included a Japanese segment with similar jokes. In pointing out the Axis leadership's failures and disregard for their own people, Cantor celebrated Allied successes and provided his celebrity endorsement of an ideological rationale for fighting: this was a war to preserve freedom and democracy.

Cantor's parodies marked a new incursion of anti-Nazi politics into prime-time comedy. His tone made some network people nervous. At a March 1942 NBC War Clinic, where high-level network and station executives discussed wartime challenges and practices, Paul Morency of station WTIC (Hartford) found Cantor's humor to be in "extremely bad" taste. Morency worried that Cantor's recent "burlesque of Hitler" might encourage listeners to make light of the German threat. NBC programming executive Clarence L. Mesner countered that if NBC had tried to stop Cantor's skit in the wartime environment, the network "would have had something called down on our heads that would have been terrific, and to a lot of people in these United States, I think, we probably would have seemed wrong." As they tried to set standards for anti-German satire, other War Clinic attendees noted public criticisms of *The Great Dictator* (1940) and *To Be or Not to Be* (1942): recent films, faulted for trivializing Nazism, that influenced the tone of Cantor's wartime newscasts. NBC did not want to be in a position of defending Cantor from similar charges. Ultimately, the network hoped that the War Department would provide more guidance on "whether it is a good thing to ridicule these boys [Nazis]." Without this direction from the government, however, NBC and its sponsors allowed Cantor to continue the faux newscast. Despite the network's concerns, Cantor's sketches over the next three years did not generate controversy.[7]

The NBC discussion reflected broader debates and confusion about the role of popular media in the war effort. For example, the federal Office of War Information (OWI), which produced and regulated radio programming, praised Spike Jones's hit recording of "Der Fuehrer's Face" (1942), a novelty spoof similar in tone and style to Cantor's German newscasts.[8] Recognizing a shared aesthetic, Cantor performed his own version of the song in a 1942 broadcast before seven hundred troops, live from the Hollywood Canteen.[9] The next year, however, when the OWI issued guidelines for the radio and music industries, it cautioned writers: "Don't make the enemy an object of humor. Beware

The cast of *It's Time to Smile* from the early 1940s. Left to right: Dinah Shore (singer), Edgar "Cookie" Fairchild (band leader), Harry von Zell (announcer), Cantor, and Bert Gordon (the Mad Russian).

of ridiculing him in ways that may lead the public to underestimate his strength, to become complacent, to slacken the intensity of its effort."[10] Still, these recommendations did not stop Cantor, who had long understood the power of social and political satire. He had practiced this kind of humor from his 1916 Ziegfeld *Midnight Frolic* debut poking fun at William Randolph Hearst through later routines spoofing Henry Ford, Herbert Hoover, and Andrew Mellon.

While the network, government, and sponsors struggled to define the right tone for anti-Nazi satire, and most other comedians safely avoided jokes about the enemy, Cantor forged ahead. In addition to regularly reprising his faux German newscast, he created new anti-Hitler sketches, some more serious than others. An episode with guest star Edward G. Robinson on March 31, 1943, was devoted to mocking Hitler and Germany. The program includes an especially biting fake newscast. In a typical line, Cantor's German reporter informs his listeners: "I know, my dear German people, this past winter you were cold and didn't eat. But things will be different when it comes summer. You will be warm and not eat."[11]

Later, the tone of the episode shifts. A rousing closing segment adopts the style of such influential radio dramas as Norman Corwin's *This Is War!* (1942) and Stephen Vincent Benét's *Dear Adolf* (1942). Cantor and Robinson address a four-minute "bedtime story" to Hitler in Germany. Cantor gently taunts Hitler by warning that the tale "consists of many sounds which may keep you awake." It starts with a ticking clock, reminding Hitler that time marches on. The clock yields to the steady, thumping sound of a hammer, representing the hands of American factory workers, "welding, riveting, putting life in the ship of democracy. Carving death in the tombstone of Nazism." Next, the sound of boots, as Robinson thunders, "That's the sound of America on the march." Finally, the heart of America, beating for one goal: "Peace on earth. Good will to all men." The sounds merge and music plays. Cantor screams, "Long after Heil Hitler is dead, we'll be singing 'God Bless America.'" The piece ends with a chorus singing a portion of "God Bless America" as the audience cheers.

In a similar, but less effective, experiment from 1944, Cantor ends a raucous episode featuring actress Betty Hutton with a sober, six-minute sketch, delivered in rhymed verse, in which he puts Hitler on trial. Cantor plays a prosecutor. The twelve "jurors" represent twelve nations, each accusing Hitler of a different crime. Hitler's sentence: instead of death, he must "live forever" so that he may hear of the suffering that he has caused. Hitler protests, "If you give me a living death, millions of people will mourn." Cantor replies with a brief song snippet, playing on Hitler's final words: "Yes, but oh what a beautiful morning. Oh, what a beautiful day."[12] The sketch illustrates the difficulties that entertainers encountered in finding the right tone for opposing Hitler and the Nazis. *Variety* reproached Cantor in its review, explaining that the sketch "was neither serious drama, satire, nor entertainment. In attempting to solve the what-to-do-with-Hitler problem . . . Cantor, through his comedy, openly managed to make [the problem] appear ridiculous. This is one question that's just a bit too important to be treated with levity."[13]

A funnier, more conventional routine from 1945 finds Cantor dreaming that he joins army intelligence. With announcer Harry von Zell, he captures a cowering Hitler.

Cantor and von Zell knock on the door of Hitler's palace. One of Hitler's men announces, "A couple of Americans to see you, Herr Hitler."

Hitler whines back, "Tell them we don't need anything. There are too many Americans here already." The audience laughs and cheers.

As Cantor and von Zell prepare to capture Hitler, the dictator begs, "Listen, please. Can't we talk about all this like gentlemen?"

Then Hitler tries bluster, "I am the master of all. I will run the table."

Cantor and von Zell silence him, "Ah, shut up."

Hitler's response, "Ah, if they had only told me that ten years ago."[14]

Cantor mixed broad topical humor and sober patriotic appeals more deftly than any other radio comedian. In a 1942 *Variety* article, he disputed the conventional wisdom that popular film and radio served as "escapism" for audiences: "Maybe people today want to forget about themselves and the bitter realities of the headlines. I don't think, however, that comedy is just a sugar-coated bromide."[15] With the war never far from listeners' minds, Cantor shifted from jokes about the military or the Germans to more serious affirmations of American values. His closing segments, featuring emotional stories about the soldiers and their sacrifices to preserve freedom around the world, drew rousing cheers from the studio audience.

Cantor frequently broadcast live from military bases and played additional benefits for troops and defense workers. These audiences appreciated him. Even though many servicemen had not been born yet when Cantor first achieved national fame in the *Ziegfeld Follies*, they had grown up listening to his radio show and watching his movies. Recognizing the risks of embarrassing himself or seeming patronizing, Cantor did not copy the styles and the slang of younger performers. He had been a symbol of youth culture and now was happy to yield to newer stars, such as Frank Sinatra. In a 1943 speech to an entertainment industry group, Cantor listed his "ten commandments" for entertaining soldiers. Among his rules: don't talk down to "the kids in uniform," don't get too patriotic, and don't bring up controversial issues and subjects.[16] It also helped that Cantor toured with attractive singers, including Dinah Shore and Nora Martin, who flirted with the troops.

Cantor's charisma and stature as a celebrity eclipsed any notion that he might be dated or hokey. As the critic John K. Hutchens perceptively recognized in a 1944 essay, "On the air, he obviously has never been so great as he was in the theater . . . Still it is radio that has played the largest part in making him—like many another performer—a national asset at this particular time." Having taken Cantor into their homes each week for more than a decade, wartime listeners appreciated the familiar Cantor comedy style and references to life off the air, including his marriage, charitable work, and movie projects. Hutchens described a warm audience of fifteen hundred servicemen shouting questions about Ida during an appearance by Cantor at Mitchel Field, an Air Force base in New York. He explained, "Radio had long since made him [Cantor] an old friend."[17]

On the weekend of January 29–30, 1944, Cantor traveled to San Francisco radio station KPO to stage a twenty-four-hour war bonds broadcast that attracted national attention and provided a model for later telethons. Cantor and his troupe had only four hours of breaks during the twenty-four-hour period, from six o'clock Saturday morning to six o'clock Sunday morning.[18] The star talked, sang, joked, and even staffed the phones taking pledges. He received support from the band leader Cookie Fairchild and the singer Nora Martin.[19] Most of the marathon aired locally, though the NBC network carried a portion of the Saturday afternoon program. The thirty-minute finale on Sunday morning was broadcast on shortwave radio for troops overseas. Curious locals joined the studio audience throughout the marathon, purchasing bonds as the price of admission and bidding on various items. Cantor sold more than $37 million in bonds. A rifle captured from a Japanese sniper at Guadalcanal garnered $350,000. A San Francisco man offered a half-million dollars for the privilege of having lunch with Cantor on the radio. "People all over the United States heard me slurp my soup and crunch my celery," Cantor marveled, as he reviewed the marathon's highlights early Sunday morning. The quirky broadcast also featured Cantor crowing like a rooster, singing "Makin' Whoopee," and urging the soldiers to "keep up the good fight."[20]

Variety lauded Cantor's "unbelievable showmanship, personal courage and endurance" in presiding over "the greatest one-star bond selling show in history." The magazine assured show business skeptics that Cantor and his company did, indeed, broadcast live from the San Francisco studio for the entire time, rather than relying on prerecorded material.[21] President Roosevelt sent Cantor a congratulatory telegram after the marathon: "FINE WORK. TAKE THINGS EASY UNTIL YOU GET RESTED. BEST OF LUCK ALWAYS."[22]

Cantor did not rest for very long. In April 1944 he embarked on a month-long national tour of military hospitals. Accompanied by Martin, Fairchild, Bert Gordon, and announcer von Zell, Cantor visited wounded soldiers during the afternoons and then performed for an hour in the evenings. *Variety's* Abel Green joined Cantor on a visit to Halloran General Hospital in Staten Island, reporting on "the magic effect of a song, a gag or a silly comedy routine on the bedded soldiers." Cantor presented a set of twenty songs, but Green reported that the star's old *Ziegfeld Follies* hits were most popular with the veterans.[23] Cantor recognized that his songs took on new meanings for the wounded soldiers. He used the many requests for "I Don't Want to Get Well" to illustrate the troops' indomitable spirit and "sincere cheerfulness and spirit in the face of tragedy." He explained, "The tune dates back to the first world war. The lyrics are corny. And I hereby take an oath that nobody has ever mistaken my voice for Bing Crosby's. Yet that's the kind of kids they are."[24]

Soon after the hospital tour, Cantor enlisted the American Legion to establish "Give a Gift to a Yank Who Gave," a Christmas gift campaign for wounded soldiers that continues to this day. Founded in 1919 to serve veterans, the American Legion built a national network of member posts. Cantor's partnership with the organization bolstered his patriotic credentials among conservatives. He had established a relationship with the influential group by appearing at its annual pageants, held in outdoor stadiums before thousands of Legionnaires, in 1938 and 1939.[25] In the fall of 1944, Cantor sent a telegram to Warren Atherton, national commander of the American Legion, who had recently served as a judge in a Cantor radio contest to locate the typical "G. I. Joe." Demonstrating his typical combination of ambition, altruism, patriotism, and salesmanship, Cantor had a new proposition to solicit donations on each weekly broadcast before Christmas. Listeners would drop the packages at local American Legion posts and volunteers would deliver the gifts to hospitals. In his pitch to Atherton, Cantor highlighted his admiration for the American Legion and its work supporting soldiers.[26]

Cantor in 1942 with troops at the Santa Ana Army Air Base,
Santa Ana, California.

Within a few days of Cantor's solicitation, nineteen thousand American Legion posts became part of the campaign. Legionnaires held listening parties for Cantor's weekly program and partnered with local retailers. National department stores also recognized the promotional possibilities of "Give a Gift to a Yank Who Gave," highlighting the program in stores and delivering presents from shoppers to local posts. In its first two years, 1944 and 1945, "Give a Gift to a Yank Who Gave" received more than four million gifts, with an estimated value of over fifteen million dollars. Together, retailers and Cantor reaped cross-promotional benefits from "Give a Gift to a Yank Who Gave." For example, in 1946 Cantor used his broadcast platform to read a telegram from Jack I. Straus, president of Macy's, announcing that its flagship New York store would boost "Give a Gift to a Yank Who Gave" with full-page newspaper advertisements, window displays, and a first-floor booth staffed by American Legion volunteers. Macy's estimated that more than three hundred thousand people would visit the Manhattan store and see the booth at Christmas time.[27]

As with much of his philanthropic work, Cantor helped charitable organizations and other partners, such as retailers, while also polishing his image. The Christmas gift campaign enhanced Cantor's reputation as a generous, altruistic celebrity whose interests transcended religious and political boundaries. In addition, the actor's ongoing public identification with the American Legion through "Give a Gift to a Yank Who Gave," and his friendship with the leaders of the influential conservative organization, afforded Cantor additional insurance against potential accusations that he sympathized with communism. These connections became especially important after the war, when the American Legion compiled dossiers on liberal and leftist actors and threatened to boycott films in which alleged "subversives" appeared.[28]

By supporting the troops so vigorously, Cantor remained susceptible to criticism that he opportunistically flaunted his love of America to advance his career. These charges rarely made it into print during the 1940s. The many positive articles about Cantor, awards from countless charities, and testimonials from people in the entertainment world and beyond effectively neutralized cynics who questioned Cantor's motives. However, Cantor and his supporters occasionally alluded to accusations that the actor was overly patriotic. In a 1944 tribute to Cantor broadcast on NBC, the prominent Democratic politician Jim Farley recalled the pressures that Cantor had faced since the early 1930s for defending religious freedom and opposing Hitler. Reading from a script drafted by Cantor's writers, Farley thundered, "For years he [Cantor] stood the taunt of being a so-called 'super-patriot,' knowing within his heart that no one who lived in America could love this country too much."[29]

Cantor further defused criticisms by showing audiences that he could laugh at himself, rather than allowing others to mock his philanthropy and patriotism. He satirized his charitable image in *Thank Your Lucky Stars* (1943), a funny and underrated movie in which he plays two roles: himself and Joe Simpson, an aspiring actor who drives a tour bus. Cantor portrays himself as a vain, nasty Hollywood celebrity. The feature film provides a behind-the-scenes look at the making of a fictional all-star variety benefit and includes short appearances by Bette Davis, Humphrey Bogart, Errol Flynn, and other Warner Bros. headliners. The producers of the benefit want Dinah Shore to perform. Cantor uses his exclusive contract with Shore as leverage to control the benefit, alienating everybody else involved in the production. He tells terribly corny jokes, demanding that his sycophantic staff laugh hysterically at his every utterance. The frustrated producers must implement the star's daffy suggestions, such as the brainstorm that live elephants, zebras, and camels be part of the show. Cantor summoned a combination of self-awareness, courage, humility, and savvy to play himself in such an unappealing role, especially considering the scriptwriters.

Coming from the incestuous world of radio comedy, the writers of *Thank Your Lucky Stars* heard many negative stories and opinions about Cantor. The film gave the writers an opportunity to share this material with the public and to take a bit of revenge on the star. Cantor had a reputation as a rude, talentless taskmaster, especially among radio writers who had apprenticed in the shop of Cantor's former partner, David Freedman.[30] Everett Freeman, who co-developed the story for *Thank Your Lucky Stars*, began his career working with Freedman and Philip Rapp on several programs, including Cantor's *Chase and Sanborn Hour*. Freeman later reunited with Rapp on *Baby Snooks*.[31] Norman Panama, Melvin Frank, and James V. Kern wrote the screenplay for *Thank Your Lucky Stars*. Panama and Frank had several radio credits, including *The Bob Hope Show* and *The Rudy Vallee Show*. They worked with Cantor veterans Sid Fields and Vick Knight on the Vallee program. The characterization of Cantor in *Thank Your Lucky Stars* incorporates the worst images of the star that had circulated among industry insiders.[32]

Cantor risked antagonizing critics and filmgoers with his acidic self-portrait. *Thank Your Lucky Stars* was not a blockbuster, but it did above-average business at the box office, aided by a campaign promoting "stars, songs, and girls."[33] In a scathing review, Bosley Crowther of the *New York Times*, no fan of Cantor's, denounced the "masochistic spite" with which Cantor played himself, declaring Cantor's character "so disagreeable that it almost ruins" the film. *Variety* was more charitable, praising the "hilarious results" of Cantor's dual roles.[34] Ultimately, despite the mixed reviews, Cantor used *Thank Your Lucky Stars* to stymie potentially damaging attacks from newspaper critics and industry insiders. After *Thank Your Lucky Stars*, it was old news to knock Cantor's big ego, bad jokes, and eagerness to flaunt his patriotism in benefit performances. Cantor would not allow detractors to slow him down as an entertainer or a humanitarian.

In *Thank Your Lucky Stars* and his network radio work of the early 1940s, Cantor said little about domestic antisemitism, which remained a problem even after America went to war with Nazi Germany.[35] By supporting the war effort, rather than drawing attention to particular Jewish problems and concerns, Jewish celebrities enhanced the image of Jews as good Americans and advanced the ultimate goal of defeating Hitler.[36] In December 1942, Cantor wrote to Milton Weill, vice president of the Jewish Welfare Board, affirming that Jewish performers should counter antisemitic comments through their patriotic deeds. "The public can be told over and over again that Al Jolson flies overseas to entertain our men in service, that Jack Benny is going on such a trip in the near future, that Eddie and Ida Cantor are at present wrapping one thousand presents to give to men in service on Christmas Day at the Hollywood Canteen," Cantor wrote. "That is the propaganda we need to off-set the unfavorable jokes about us."[37]

As a role model, Cantor guarded against negative stereotypes in his program. He also monitored the way other comedians portrayed Jews. In his letter to Weill, Cantor criticized Fred Allen, who was not Jewish, maintaining that "there are very few programs on which Fred Allen doesn't, without thinking, take a crack at the Jews." Cantor cited a clothing store sketch that had aired the previous Sunday as an example of Allen's "bad taste."[38] Allen's segment was similar to Cantor's old "Belt in the Back" routine, but it featured a sales clerk with a heavier Yiddish accent and less charm than Cantor's earlier tailor.[39] The fact that Cantor objected to the sketch, closely modeled on his earlier work, illustrates the way both he and the times had changed. A skit that seemed to be an innovative, affectionate expression of Jewish culture in 1922 had become more dangerous and conservative, especially when practiced by a non-Jewish comedian, during the 1940s. Images of fast-talking, aggressive Jews selling cheap clothes no longer amused Cantor.

Though Cantor occasionally provided glimpses of the ethnic performer who spiced his act with Yiddish phrases and Lower East Side memories, Jewish audiences appreciated him more as a fund-raiser and advocate for Jewish causes. As Rabbi Stephen Wise said in a 1944 tribute, "Whenever Jews need someone who will not only give and secure help, but who will understand them, who will laugh with them, who will weep with them, for them, they turn to Eddie Cantor."[40]

Cantor still supported relief for refugees during the war, but he avoided controversy and attracted less media attention for this work than he had during the 1930s. After his experiences of alienating fans and sponsors, Cantor remained wary of appearing too radical or endorsing too many exclusively Jewish causes and organizations. He did not lobby Roosevelt or other politicians for more liberal immigration quotas and other assistance for refugees. In addition, despite his celebrity status, when Cantor participated in large anti-Nazi events that focused on the plight of Jews, he let others make headlines. In June 1943, Cantor served as an honorary chairman for a Madison Square Garden rally and pageant to support Jewish refugees. The assembly was most newsworthy because it featured two hundred rabbis and the reading of a declaration to Roosevelt, signed by one hundred thousand religious school students, expressing solidarity with Jewish children in Nazi-occupied areas.[41] Later that month, Cantor shared the podium with the German novelist Thomas Mann, now living in Southern California, at an anti-Nazi rally in San Francisco. The audience of more than eleven thousand people closed the meeting by unanimously adopting a resolution calling for the Allies to accommodate more Jews in their own counties and facilitate immigration to Palestine.[42]

Throughout the early 1940s, Cantor maintained a frantic schedule in radio, film, theater, and such wartime charities as the Red Cross and the March of Dimes. With these other priorities, he had less time for Jewish organizations. However, he still occasionally raised funds for Hadassah and the United Jewish Appeal (UJA), a refugee-relief effort of the JDC and the United Palestine Appeal (UPA). In his appearances before Jewish groups, which attracted less media attention than the large rallies, Cantor spoke clearly and directly about the particular problems facing Jews. In a September 1942 article for the Jewish press, Cantor underscored the urgency of the UJA's activities. He also recognized that fund-raisers had been turning to a relatively small pool of Jewish donors with similar appeals for a long time. "Are you getting tired of the story of Jewish misery?" Cantor asked. "If you are, you're falling into the Nazi trap . . . How can we expect to arouse the world to our plight if we ourselves are going to react with no more feeling than a scarecrow?" He aligned Jewish and American interests, maintaining that the "highest government leaders will tell you that the fullest support of the United Jewish Appeal is part of our war work as Americans." Cantor believed that his readers had a "patriotic duty," as Jews and Americans, to support European Jews resisting Nazism, Palestinian Jews "fighting for democracy," and immigrants to the United States building new lives as "good Americans."[43]

In the summer of 1943, Cantor visited several cities for Hadassah's Youth Aliyah and delivered a moving radio address that CBS aired as a public service. He described the Nazis' "violent persecution and systematic extermination" of Jews and Youth Aliyah's heroic effort to resettle children, many of them orphans, in Palestine. Recognizing that the war was causing suffering everywhere, Cantor still urged the audience to consider the particular plight of Jews: "Every people conquered by the Nazis knows the bitter taste of slavery, but the Jewish people have been promised a worse fate. Extermination. And this is one promise that Hitler means to keep."[44] In an article for the Los Angeles weekly B'nai B'rith Messenger, Hadassah member Ruth Maizlish praised Cantor as the "savior of children." Still, Cantor seemed unsatisfied by the Jewish public's response to his summer tour. He published an article that fall, for the High Holidays, imploring American Jews to "Stand . . . And Be Counted." Cantor once again emphasized philanthropy and political engagement, rather than religious observance, as the most vital expressions of Jewish identity. He particularly criticized Jews who had assimilated and denied their heritage, arguing that they would nullify the bravery and sacrifices of wartime refugees and soldiers: "The Jew who will not stand up and plead his cause has no cause. The Jew who will not stand up and fight for his reason for existence has no such reason."[45]

Cantor's appeals to Jewish audiences acknowledged the exceptional problems and responsibilities of Jews. In contrast, he continued to purvey more universal ideals on his commercial radio program. Starting in early 1945, with Allied victory seeming increasingly likely, Cantor returned to his prewar theme regarding the importance of prayer as a democratic tool. He highlighted the common moral values and goals among Jews and Christians, along with the broader virtue of religious faith as a foundation for American national identity.

Cantor and his orchestra ended his January 31, 1945, broadcast with "Just a Prayer Away," written by Ida's cousin Charles Tobias, a frequent Cantor collaborator, and David Kapp. Vocalist Nora Martin starts the wistful, sentimental hymn, promising, "There's a happy land somewhere / And it's just a prayer away."[46] Cantor adds a passionate spoken segment in which he extols the importance of religion in promoting peace and democracy. He praises the church as the only institution "resisting evil" regimes and urges listeners to attend houses of worship: "You go to yours, I to mine. Let us join in a community of prayer for the lives of those dear to us all . . . There is a house of God near you. Don't wait for its bells to ring out the victory. Its doors are always open. God is always there. And peace may come one day sooner if we will pray for it." Cantor reprised the appeal less than two weeks later on the long-running variety program *We the People*.[47]

Following the broadcasts, Cantor received hundreds of supportive letters from everyday listeners, soldiers, and Christian clergy. Many requested copies of the speech so they could use it in church sermons or Sunday school teaching. Charles R. Smyth, a Methodist minister from New Jersey, praised Cantor's "gem." He planned to print the speech in his church's newspaper. "I'm sure it will offer a lift and a challenge to our people," he wrote. "You have rendered a greater service to God and humanity than you realize in these brief words." T. Raymond Allston, field director for the Presbyterian Church's Board of Christian

Education, thanked Cantor for his "impressive spiritual plea." Allston recognized that Cantor wielded particular influence as a popular entertainer: "There are many people who will take it from you who may tend to evade the Rabbi, Priest, or Minister."[48] As a public service, Sachs Quality Furniture, "founded on faith in America's future," took out a full-page advertisement in the *New York Sunday News* referencing and reprinting portions of Cantor's January 31, 1945, radio remarks. The advertisement also included new passages, attributed to Cantor, on the importance of fighting "intolerance and bigotry and prejudices," and ending with the admonition to readers: "Be American!"[49] Capitalizing on the buzz that Cantor had created on his programs, Bing Crosby and the Sammy Kaye Orchestra each had hits with separate versions of "Just a Prayer Away" in the spring of 1945.[50]

Cantor did not observe Judaic law and practice; however, he fervently believed in the rituals and power of show business. He cited popular entertainers as models to illustrate the imperative that all Americans must fight bigotry and religious intolerance. Cantor delivered a speech in May 1945, less than three weeks after Germany surrendered, to raise funds for the General Maurice Rose Memorial Hospital, named after the Jewish division commander. Cantor observed that Hollywood stars had traveled the world to entertain troops. He continued, "And I do *not* know of a single one who has ever walked into a camp or ward and said . . . 'I want to entertain only the men of my own faith.' Catholic, Protestant, or Jew . . . each of them knows that laughter and song are universal." Cantor also used the occasion to sound what became a familiar theme coming out of the war: people of all religious faiths gave their lives to fight religious prejudice. "We here tonight . . . and all of us . . . everywhere . . . must seek out *every* enemy of tolerance and conquer every bigot who does not believe . . . *that all men are created free and equal.*"[51]

This interfaith message became even more prominent for Cantor and his audience in the postwar years.

POSTWAR STRUGGLES
   (1945–1950)

antor hit a creative low between the end of World War II and 1950. His radio show had retained a static format and style since 1934, when he moved from *The Chase and Sanborn Hour* to the thirty-minute program for Pebeco toothpaste. The war provided a jolt to Cantor's *It's Time to Smile*, offering opportunities for the star to showcase his talents in creative skits and passionate speeches. Segments in which Cantor lampooned Hitler and Germany conformed with national priorities and popular sentiments. In addition, when the writers needed lighter material, they could rely on jokes about rationing, victory gardens, and life on the home front. In the radio studios and military bases from which Cantor broadcast the program, raucous live audiences filled with boisterous troops appreciated the comedian's humor and patriotism. *It's Time to Smile* regularly attracted top stars, who promoted their films, bantered with soldiers in the audience, and showed fans a lighter side of their personalities.

Starting with the 1945–1946 season, Cantor could no longer draw on the war for material. He and his writers were unable to craft satirical comedy sketches or moving appeals about Cantor's postwar social and political priorities: religious tolerance, relief for European refugees, and support for the new state of Israel. Audiences did not share Cantor's interest in, or knowledge of, these subjects. The radio program seemed listless, with its familiar plotlines and flat jokes. For example, one episode revolves around a misunderstanding: the actor Burgess Meredith thinks that Cantor has dated Paulette Goddard, Meredith's wife. In another show, Cantor sorts through his basement wardrobe, deciding which clothes he should donate to charity. As *It's Time to Smile* spiraled downward, the show attracted fewer big-name guest stars.[1]

Cantor and other radio comedians were running out of fresh material. Bob Hope, Jack Benny, Burns and Allen, and Fred Allen still garnered high ratings, despite broadcasting for at least a decade; however, savvy stars and industry insiders saw trouble ahead. In June 1945, Fred

Allen and Cantor each used *Variety* articles to bemoan the tired state of radio, hoping that fresh writing talent could salvage the medium. Allen emphasized the speed with which weekly program production "consumes material." Cantor compared broadcasting to other industries that required innovation. As radio's most senior comedian, he urged broadcasters to subsidize new writers and programs. He cited the "comedy stooge making fun of his boss," a longtime staple of his programs, as an example of a tired technique: "Maybe the new writing blood — and that is truly the life-blood of radio of the future — if encouraged to let itself go would change that format [the stooge] completely."[2]

During the 1945–1946 season, *It's Time to Smile* was the twelfth highest-rated show on the air, usually earning a rating of between fifteen and twenty. NBC estimated that twenty million listeners tuned in to *It's Time to Smile* each Wednesday night at nine o'clock. The program benefited from its place on the schedule. *It's Time to Smile* aired directly before a popular crime drama, *Mr. District Attorney*.[3] Over the next three years, however, ratings declined dramatically, and criticisms of Cantor and other veteran comedians increased. Old stars seemed out of touch with audiences. Jack Gould of the *New York Times* observed that broadcast comedy faced "a crucial challenge. Can it overcome its repetition? Can it meet the incessant cries of its professional critics that it must develop 'something new' or 'something different,' or, like vaudeville, slowly perish from familiarity?"[4] Even though Gould identified Cantor as one of several old-style radio personalities, the veteran actor shared the critic's concerns. Like many of his fellow comedy stars, Cantor knew something was wrong, but wasn't sure how to fix it. He continued urging the industry to develop new talent, such as Jack Parr and Henry Morgan. Cantor also tinkered with his format by presenting longer sketches during his last two seasons.[5] But a combination of repetitive jokes, hackneyed scenarios, and competition from television doomed Cantor. His radio program, now sponsored by Pabst Blue Ribbon, was canceled after the 1948–1949 season. By that time, the ratings were 11.7, Cantor's lowest figure ever. *The Eddie Cantor Pabst Blue Ribbon Show* was the fifty-second most popular program on the air.[6]

In an effort to enliven the show for the 1945–1946 season, Cantor replaced singer Nora Martin with Thelma Carpenter, an accomplished African-American performer who had toured with big bands led by

Coleman Hawkins and Count Basie during the war. Several African-Americans held regular roles on radio, mostly in comedies, but Carpenter became one of the first weekly singers on a major variety series.[7] Cantor had a reputation for giving opportunities to African-American artists, such as the Nicholas Brothers, who danced in *Kid Millions* (1934) and went on tour with Cantor the following year. He recognized affinities between blacks and Jews. "I am just as anxious to see the colored people emerge from Race prejudice as I am my own Race," Cantor told the *Pittsburgh Courier* in 1935. "We have the same things to contend with that you do, but both of us will win and we will do it from the stage. We will make the people all over the world laugh and when one laughs he forgets to hate."[8]

During the late 1930s and early 1940s, Hattie McDaniel and Hattie Noel each appeared on Cantor's radio show for extended stints. The play *Banjo Eyes*, which ran from 1941 to 1942, featured dancer Bill Bailey. As the *Amsterdam News* editor Dan Burley wrote in 1942, "With Eddie Cantor, it's a simple formula: What can you do and can it be sold on the stage."[9] The black press praised Cantor and other white actors who helped African-American performers find work and demonstrate their talents. Newspapers also ran lists and features spotlighting African-American performers on the air, even though many of these roles perpetuated stereotypes. After World War II, negative images of African-Americans attracted more scrutiny and criticism.

Carpenter's role on Cantor's radio show was similar to that of the previous singer, Nora Martin. Cantor and his writers did not highlight Carpenter's race in their introductions or choices of material. Each week, Carpenter performed a pop standard, such as "How Deep Is the Ocean," "All by Myself," or "The Man I Love." On a handful of programs, she also bantered briefly with Cantor. One of these lines employed stereotypes to make fun of African-Americans. In a Thanksgiving episode, Carpenter tells the star her secret to stuffing a turkey: she uses a fried chicken. However, most of her scenes and songs were not stereotypical.[10] Carpenter participated in typical Cantor routines. In a January 1946 episode, for example, the host congratulates the singer for winning an *Esquire* magazine award. Carpenter shows her appreciation for Cantor by baking him a birthday cake in honor of his fifty-fourth birthday. The cake is topped with one candle and fifty-three vitamin pills. Carpenter explains, "If you eat them [the vitamins], you'll have strength enough to blow out the candle."[11] Any of the previous (white) singers could have made the same crack about Cantor's age and frailty, which had been a running joke for several years.

Near the end of the 1945–1946 season, Cantor decided not to renew Carpenter's twenty-six-week contract. By then, he was preparing for a new sponsor and format emphasizing situation comedy, rather than shorter sketches and musical performances. That summer he also released longtime costar Bert Gordon, the Mad Russian.[12] Nevertheless, Carpenter was not happy to be fired. She faulted Cantor's writers for not giving her a larger comedic role. In April 1946 several African-American newspapers reported the singer's claim that she lost her job because Cantor's staff "could not find a proper spot for her in the script" and gave her only forty-five seconds to sing each week. "They would have renewed her contract if she had consented to lower herself as a colored artist and poke fun at the race . . . a thing she refused to accede to," according to the *Baltimore Afro-American* writer R. R. Dier, who scolded the star. "Cantor, who was hailed as a liberal and a democrat when he signed her on his radio show, now takes his place among those who 'talk a good case' about minority groups but never do anything about it, unless it benefits their own personal interests."[13]

These articles stung Cantor, and he recognized the gravity of Carpenter's accusations. Cantor gave an exclusive interview to the *Los Angeles Sentinel* the next week, maintaining that he had made no attempt "to exploit the girl for her race. We hired Thelma Carpenter strictly because of her talent." Cantor pointed out that he had given Carpenter between ninety seconds and two-and-a-half minutes, the same amount of time as singers on other programs. He had released Carpenter because her "specialized talent" did not fit within the new show that he was planning: "Her statement that we would have renewed her contract if she would have consented to poke fun at herself and lower her race is . . . a very definite misstatement of fact."[14]

Four months later, Carpenter softened her criticism, saying that Cantor had "wanted to keep her, but other prejudiced radio people — script writers, program directors, and others, ganged up on him and forced him to cancel her contract."[15]

The major daily newspapers and industry journals did not report on

Carpenter's release from the program. Cantor relied on his reputation and the fact that Carpenter could not support her charges to defend himself and minimize the damage, but the firing of Carpenter generated significant criticism from the African-American press, and the most serious challenge thus far to his liberal credentials. Carpenter's accusation regarding demeaning parts served notice that humor incorporating blatant stereotypes was growing less acceptable.

Off the air, Cantor opposed "all forms of discrimination and bigotry," as he told a radio interviewer in 1949.[16] Rather than joining specific efforts to fight racial segregation, he worked through interfaith tolerance campaigns, such as the National Conference of Christians and Jews' annual Brotherhood Week, frequently serving as the Jewish representative in tri-faith events.[17] For example, in May 1950 the actor received a citation and shared the podium with Eleanor Roosevelt and Notre Dame football coach Frank Leahy in a well-publicized dinner, attended by fourteen hundred people and hosted by the Massachusetts Committee of Catholics, Protestants, and Jews.[18]

In its review of his 1947 season premiere, *Variety* asserted that Cantor's radio program suffered because he put too much energy into his offstage philanthropy: "That he's a force in corralling public opinion for various humanitarian efforts can't be denied. But that Cantor as a top comedian of a high budgeted entertainment package comes out a second best only accents the time-worn conclusion that one must be subordinated to the other."[19] Privately, Cantor agreed that commercial performances seemed obligatory and routine next to his passions: supporting charities, especially those that helped displaced persons (DPs) and advanced the establishment of a Jewish state in Palestine. Between his professional commitments and his range of philanthropic activities, Cantor knew that he was overextended. In 1947 he wrote to James G. McDonald: "Have been going at top speed, what with my motion picture, the weekly radio show, appearing for numerous charitable organizations, the March of Dimes now, ad infinitum. But these things must be done, and someone must do them. Will be so glad to finish the picture [*If You Knew Susie*], a very old commitment, which will leave me more time for these more important things," referring to the resettlement of DPs from Europe to Palestine.[20] Cantor and McDonald worked together on some of these efforts during the late 1940s, with Cantor

Cantor, seated between Frank Leahy and Eleanor Roosevelt, at the Massachusetts Committee of Catholics, Protestants, and Jews event in Boston in 1950. Courtesy of Franklin D. Roosevelt Presidential Library and Museum.

using his fame and personal relationships and McDonald drawing on different experience and political contacts.

McDonald was well connected with the Roosevelt administration, but not with President Truman or the new president's advisers. In late 1945, McDonald asked Cantor to help him secure two different appointments from Truman. Cantor was in good company. The diplomat also called on Senator Robert F. Wagner of New York and the financier Bernard Baruch.[21] Though McDonald failed to receive one position, assistant secretary of state, he did merit a slot on the Anglo-American Committee of Inquiry Regarding the Problems of European Jewry and Palestine, charged with issuing recommendations on the crucial issue of immigration to Palestine.

In seeking the State Department assignment, McDonald asked Cantor whether he knew President Truman, Secretary of State James F. Byrnes, or Postmaster General Robert Hannegan, a Democratic power broker and longtime Truman ally. Cantor responded guardedly, "DO NOT KNOW THE GENTLEMEN YOU MENTION BUT KNOW PEOPLE WHO DO." Cantor identified several potential contacts and devised a strategy to use his political connections and Hollywood friendships, including George Jessel, to lobby for McDonald.[22]

When McDonald next turned his attention to an appointment to the Anglo-American Committee of Inquiry, Cantor met with Harry Schwimmer, a lawyer from Missouri who enjoyed access to Truman and the president's advisers.[23] McDonald wrote Cantor a grateful letter in October 1945: "Harry Schwimmer pledged his utmost cooperation and I think he will carry through. Talking with you was, I think, his thrill of a lifetime."[24]

Though Cantor quietly sent a letter to the Roosevelt administration in support of the Wagner-Rogers bill in 1939, the strategic effort to help McDonald represented a deeper level of political involvement. It required Cantor to draw on a wide network of people close to the White House. Celebrities such as Cantor and Jessel were emerging as influential figures in national politics. Their star power and charisma enabled them to transcend the world of entertainment.

More publicly, Cantor continued raising funds, speaking against antisemitism, and promoting relief for displaced persons. In late 1946, approximately 250,000 Jews lived in DP camps and other facilities in Europe. Most Jewish DPs wanted to resettle in Palestine; but the British, who controlled Palestine, severely limited Jewish immigration. Instead, the DPs were stuck in dirty, overcrowded camps that did not meet basic needs.[25] American Jews took it upon themselves to conduct the massive philanthropic operation necessary to care for European Jews living in the camps and scattered throughout Europe. The Jewish community united to raise millions of dollars for food, clothing, medical services, and even cultural needs, such as books and religious objects. Cantor and the many others who supported these relief activities improved the material conditions of survivors, memorialized the six million killed by Hitler, and satisfied what they saw as an obligation to save what remained of European Jewry.[26]

Whereas Cantor's speeches and articles about antisemitism had generated a great deal of publicity during the 1930s, this activity made less news after the war. American Jews still contended with discrimination and bigotry in several areas, including immigration laws. But Cantor's was now one of many public voices, Jewish and non-Jewish, that condemned anti-Jewish statements and policies. On January 4, 1946, Cantor bought a large advertisement in the *New York Times* featuring the bold headline, "I Thought That Hitler Was Dead." Cantor's short essay expressed outrage over statements by Lieutenant General Sir Frederick Morgan, the British head of United Nations Relief and Rehabilitation Administration (UNRRA) efforts in Germany. The understaffed, poorly managed UNRRA operated many of the DP camps, which included Jewish and non-Jewish DPs. Morgan was skeptical about recent pogroms in Poland, claiming that a secret Jewish force was organizing an exodus of "well-dressed, well-fed, rosy cheeked" refugees. The insensitivity to Polish antisemitism from Morgan, an officer in the agency that was failing in its mission to care for Jewish survivors, incensed Cantor. He wrote, "Tell me, Sir Frederick, are you one of these 'humanitarians' who believe that the only good Jews are dead Jews? Apparently you are very sorry that Hitler didn't complete the job of extermination."[27] Cantor's caustic criticism of Morgan generated only a few lines of coverage in the Jewish press and no attention, beyond the ad space, from the larger daily newspapers.[28]

Cantor presented the plight of Jewish DPs as a humanitarian issue. In addition to raising funds to improve conditions for DPs, he proposed immigration to Palestine as a solution to the refugee problem. Cantor had many prominent allies, Jewish and non-Jewish, in this advocacy. The actor was one of eighty-four signatories to a June 1946 advertisement placed in major daily newspapers proclaiming: "THERE IS A LIMIT TO WHAT EVEN JEWS CAN ENDURE." The advertisement urged the British government to implement recent recommendations of the Anglo-American Committee of Inquiry, on which McDonald served, that would have increased Jewish immigration to Palestine. The issue united a diverse group of clergymen, publishers, journalists, labor activists, and public intellectuals. Others who signed the advertisement included Albert Einstein, Henry Luce, Walter Reuther, Norman Vincent Peale, and Major General William Donovan, head of the Office of Strategic Services during World War II.[29]

The next year, Cantor joined Paulette Goddard, Katherine Hepburn, Gene Kelly, and twenty other Hollywood figures in a letter to the editor of the *New York Times* urging the government to support the creation of separate Jewish and Arab states in Palestine. The writers decried the "degrading" deportation of Jews from British Palestine and saw a Jewish state, which would accept immigrants, as the best solution to the DP crisis.[30]

In addition to calling for Jewish statehood, stars raised funds for the UJA, which provided aid to DPs and supported Jewish immigration to Palestine. Though actors such as Al Jolson, Paul Muni, Edward G. Robinson, and Cantor were no longer top box office draws, they still commanded large followings, especially among Jewish audiences, who comprised the donor base for the UJA. In addition to appearing at UJA events, Hollywood celebrities, including many who were not Jewish, participated in unsponsored UJA radio programs and fund-raising films during the late 1940s. In April 1946, the UJA inaugurated a radio department that remained active over the next several years. *Variety*'s review of the unit's first major broadcast, *Star Spangled Way* on ABC, illustrates the UJA's star power as well as the limitations of these familiar and predictable appeals. Cantor began the program "with a talk on the virtue of giving and Palestine as the hope" of DPs. Charles Boyer, Ginger Rogers, Ingrid Bergman, Jack Benny, and Tallulah Bankhead followed with similar pitches. *Variety* criticized the show's "repetitive material."[31]

The UJA's scripted dramas were more successful than its variety fund-raisers. Top Hollywood names helped the UJA depict the dire conditions in DP camps and the efforts of agencies to provide food, medical assistance, and ultimately, safe passage to America or Palestine. The UJA hired a skillful writer, Allan Sloane, who enjoyed a long and successful career in radio and television, later winning three Emmys and six Peabody Awards and specializing in scripts about children.[32] The radio veteran Himan Brown, who produced and directed several UJA programs, recalled the shows' high production values: "They gave me a half-an-hour, a twenty to thirty piece orchestra, and we did impressive dramatic presentations of particular families, of lives, of dramatic situations which would move the audience to make contributions."[33] These unsponsored programs usually did not air during prime time and were subject to little network scrutiny. Sloane and the UJA used the public service space to tell moving stories that incorporated the recent history and ongoing struggles of Jews in Europe and Palestine.[34]

In "Time—The Present—A Day of Remembrance" (1947), a chilling drama about the Holocaust and its aftermath broadcast over the ABC network on the Saturday night between Rosh Hashanah and Yom Kippur, Cantor plays dual roles: the narrator and a Holocaust survivor named Spiegelman. As the narrator, he guides listeners through a series of vignettes highlighting the work of relief organizations in camps from Austria to Cyprus. In one scene, Cantor slips into the drama, playing Spiegelman, a famous pianist who was presumed to have been killed in Dachau. Spiegelman was Cantor's first explicitly Jewish character since his stage skits of the 1920s, such as the Jewish cab driver and the Jewish aviator. Spiegelman explains to a psychiatrist at the French DP camp that he survived by playing music for the Nazis, but he vowed never to give Europeans the joy of hearing his music ever again. Echoing a line that Cantor used when the Nazis banned his films during the mid-1930s, the musician asks, "How can I make people happy who have made my people mourn?" Spiegelman would play only in Palestine. The psychiatrist hopes to help Spiegelman immigrate to Palestine so that the world may hear his music again.[35]

"Time—The Present—A Day of Remembrance" ends with the music of Kol Nidre and an actor saying the Kaddish prayer in Hebrew. The music provides background as Cantor solemnly explains that in America, some synagogue attendees will stand up during the recitation of the Kaddish, indicating that they have lost a loved one over the past year. But in "the makeshift synagogues of Europe, and in the barracks in concentration camps, and in the new tabernacles in Zion, in Palestine—and on ships going to America and in the hospitals—there—everybody will stand up all at once. For everybody there has lost somebody, and most of them have lost everybody!" Cantor becomes more emotional, reminding listeners to make a vow during this sacred time of the year to support the UJA: "There is nobody who can help—but you. Not tomorrow—but now."[36]

The UJA's work may have held additional meaning for Cantor after he found out that he had a relative in a DP camp: a man named Jacob Wolkin, who was a first cousin of Ida's. Before the war, Wolkin worked as a barber in the town of Baranovichi, Belarus, which was under Polish rule until it was annexed by the Soviet Union in 1939. Germany captured Baranovichi in June 1941, occupying the city for more than three years. In a June 1947 letter to Eddie and Ida, Wolkin briefly sketched his wartime experiences living in the Jewish ghetto, being sent to a camp, and joining the anti-German resistance. Writing in fluent English, Wolkin also described the poor lighting, heating, and drinking water at Camp Ebelsberg in Austria. The camp was Wolkin's home during much of the time that he corresponded with the Cantors, from June 1947 to October 1948.[37]

Eddie and Ida regularly sent Wolkin large food packages and money. In addition, Eddie frequently contacted leaders of the JDC and the UJA to check on conditions for Wolkin, including the status of Wolkin's efforts to leave Austria.[38] Wolkin asked Cantor to help him immigrate to the United States. One of Wolkin's letters suggested that the Cantors provided affidavits offering to support Wolkin, an important element of a visa application.[39] Cantor also asked his contacts whether there was any possibility of getting Wolkin out of Austria, but he was unable to facilitate Wolkin's emigration during a time when quotas severely limited the number of Jewish DPs who could enter the United States. Independent of Cantor's efforts, Wolkin and his wife, Sally Dauber, settled in Canada around 1951.[40]

Eddie's private packages and letters on behalf of Ida's cousin demonstrated his commitment to helping DPs even when he was not in the spotlight. In addition, Wolkin's moving plight may have fueled Cantor's more public work conducted through the UJA. The actor's personal fortune paled compared to that of other philanthropic businessmen and family foundations, but Cantor leveraged his celebrity to become one of the UJA's leading fund-raisers. He embarked on several national tours for the UJA and occasionally traveled abroad, much as he did for Hadassah's Youth Aliyah during the late 1930s. In the summer of 1948, Cantor spent more than a month in Europe, where he promoted *If You Knew Susie*, toured DP camps, and observed the work of UJA agencies firsthand. The opportunity to see the impact of his fund-raising energized Cantor. Upon returning to New York in late August, he announced that he was embarking on a whirlwind tour of twelve cities in two weeks, including smaller locales such as Springfield, Massachusetts; Toledo, Ohio; and Camden, New Jersey. By the end of September, Cantor had raised more than $5 million.[41]

In September 1949, Cantor headlined a UJA luncheon held at the Commodore Hotel in New York that raised $1.25 million. *Variety*, always aware of box office figures, claimed that the event "established a record for one-time fundraising." Donors included the Jewish studio executives Jack Cohn and Barney Balaban. Earlier in the year, Cantor had raised $1.8 million for the UJA during another national tour. Speaking at the luncheon, Cantor proudly cited the newly independent State of Israel's recently concluded war against Arab countries as proof that the world would no longer see Jews as cowardly or defenseless.[42] The next year, at a UJA event in Pittsburgh, Cantor stressed the importance of Israel as "the only country in the entire world where Jews were free to come and rebuild their lives in an atmosphere of freedom and hope and joy."[43]

In the postwar rhetoric of the American Jewish leadership, Israel continued to hold a special place as a safe haven for Jews. But after the founding of Israel in 1948, Cantor spoke less about Israel in connection with the Holocaust and the wrenching conditions in postwar Europe. Instead, he presented Israel as a bastion of freedom, democracy, and hope in the Middle East. His UJA appeals extended a strategy that Cantor had pursued since the late 1930s when responding to Nazism, conflating Jewish and American values. For Cantor, donating to the UJA, and later Israel Bonds, gave Jews a way to celebrate Jewish statehood while advancing pro-Western democracy abroad. Other Israel advocates ranging from David Ben-Gurion to the UJA president Henry Morgenthau also highlighted similarities between the United States and Israel during the early years of the Cold War.[44]

In extolling the democratic virtues of Israel, Cantor drew on firsthand experience. He toured the country, representing the UJA, in July 1950. The American visitor spent time with Prime Minister Ben-Gurion, President Chaim Weizmann, and future prime minister Golda Meir then known as Golda Meyerson. He met a range of Israelis: new immigrants at the airport, longshoremen in Haifa, and musicians in the Israel Symphony Orchestra. Cantor reviewed troops alongside military commander Moshe Dayan, who told him that more than a thousand soldiers were once children who had immigrated to Israel through Youth Aliyah. Cantor called the nearly three weeks that he spent in the country "the most thrilling of all my life."[45]

חשבוע: "המטרה - הירח"

קולנע

75 פרוטה

שבועון מצויר לעניני קולנע תיאטרון ואמנות

Cantor holds a boy during his 1950 tour of Israel. The tour included visits to Hadassah hospitals and camps, where he met children who recently immigrated to the country.

After Cantor returned from Israel, he continued to make universal appeals that portrayed Israel as a new land of opportunity and a homeland for the world's huddled masses yearning to breathe free. He also chronicled the UJA's heroic accomplishments, including resettling more than four hundred thousand "homeless people." As he wrote in a 1950 article for the Jewish press, "The doors of Israel shall be kept open for all those who flee from persecution, and to all those who yearn for this new freedom and new democracy."[46] Cantor presented Israel as a symbol of American ideals throughout the 1950s, explaining somewhat disingenuously in his 1957 autobiography: "My interest in Israel has nothing to do with religion. The only religion I've known is the Bible." Referring to the literal definition of "Israel" as "the Jewish people," he continued, "I've explained over and over to audiences—'Forget what Israel stands for, this has nothing to do with Jewishness, who is or who isn't.'" Instead, Israel was worthy of support as "the only country with its gates wide open."[47]

The performer's associations with the UJA, and later Israel Bonds, were mutually beneficial to the organizations and Cantor. By the late 1940s, Cantor was a well-known Jewish spokesperson who was comfortable and experienced delivering the UJA's messages about refugees, Israel, America, and democracy. He raised a great deal of money and added visibility, as a celebrity, to the organization's fund-raising appeals. In so doing, Cantor advanced his own personal and professional goals. Support for DPs and Israel gave Cantor's life a fresh, meaningful focus during a time when his show business career flagged artistically and commercially. Cantor believed in these Jewish causes. The founding of Israel represented the culmination of twenty years of activism and fund-raising, frequently alongside Zionists, in support of Jewish refugees internationally. In addition, as Cantor became less relevant in popular entertainment during the late 1940s, he won many awards and attracted large audiences at appearances for Jewish organizations in communities across the country.

In 1950 Cantor launched a new plan to leverage his popularity, especially among Jews, and raise even more funds for Jewish organizations while revitalizing his show business career.

12 THE LAST COMEBACK
(1950–1952)

uring the early 1950s, Cantor revitalized his career through a one-man theatrical show (*My Forty Years in Show Business*) and a television variety program (*The Colgate Comedy Hour*). While both of these formats were new for Cantor and most audience members, his performances featured an older style. The show business veteran sang hits from the 1920s and reminisced about his landmark roles. Cantor established himself as the consummate entertainer and a proponent of traditional values. He reflected on the importance of hard work, the opportunities that America offered a poor immigrant, and the transformative power of show business. The actor presented a mythical, simpler time in American history, but he occasionally broke the nostalgic spell to comment on Cold War politics or to advocate for Israel. Cantor's focus on his show business history carried risks along with benefits. After 1951, network executives, critics, and audience members increasingly found the actor to be out of touch with changes in the entertainment industry and the broader culture. Aspects of Cantor's style, especially his use of blackface, became less socially acceptable.

In January 1950, Cantor introduced a new live act, *My Forty Years in Show Business*, featuring material that he had polished over several decades. By March he was filling Carnegie Hall. The road to Carnegie, and his last great comeback, began on a winter weeknight in Orono, Maine. Despite a blizzard that piled eighteen inches of snow along the roads, Cantor sold out two shows at the University of Maine, with twenty-five hundred fans at each performance. University officials expressed "amazement" at the crowd, especially given the weather conditions. Cantor visited a handful of other colleges that winter, including the University of Arizona and William and Mary, before his March 21, 1950, Carnegie Hall engagement. The headliner demonstrated that even during a low period, he could still pack houses across the country, including smaller cities and college towns. He may have hoped that television executives would note his ticket sales and wide appeal among different age groups and geographic regions. In addition, the star followed the traditional theatrical practice of testing a new show out of town before bringing it to New York. This trial was especially important for *My Forty Years in Show Business* because it inaugurated a new form of celebrity-driven theater.[1]

Cantor pioneered a format that others later adapted: a one-man exhibition in which he was the star and the subject, seamlessly interweaving stories and music. Reviewing the Carnegie Hall performance, Abel Green of *Variety* predicted that the Cantor show "could set a pattern for similar cavalcades by any of the contemporary greats of now and yesteryear, blending nostalgia and the present into a socko evening's entertainment."[2] After Cantor's success, Danny Kaye and Milton Berle each announced that they would mount one-man shows along the lines of Cantor's; though, perhaps learning that Cantor made this kind of complex production look deceptively easy, Kaye and Berle never completed their plans.[3] Over time, such performers as Groucho Marx, Elaine Strich, Billy Crystal, and Jerry Lewis built their own versions of the one-person autobiographical production. The countless actors mounting recent tribute shows to iconic celebrities, from Al Jolson to Elvis Presley, also owe a debt to Cantor for demonstrating the creative and economic potential of this kind of production.

My Forty Years in Show Business required compelling material so that a single headliner, accompanied by two piano players, could hold an audience's attention. Working only with notes that he had onstage, the actor put himself in a perilous situation more akin to that of a later stand-up comic than any theatrical performer from 1950. If Cantor flubbed lines, encountered hecklers, or simply had an off night, there was no other actor onstage to help him. Nor was there an orchestra to share the burden or divert attention. Like most of his contemporaries, Cantor had occasionally performed short music and comedy acts solo; however, no other celebrity had the combination of nerve, talent, ego, and top-flight material to pull off a two-hour production like *My Forty Years in Show Business*.

The March 1950 Carnegie Hall performance was so popular that after it sold out, two hundred seats were added in the space near the stage, apparently providing an obstructed view of the show. Cantor used the unusual arrangement as an opportunity to commiserate with theater-goers about their poor seats: "I think if you people on the stage paid the same money that you people paid out here, then you have been cheated and I'd like to give you back some of the money." He then delights the crowd by taking dollar bills from his pocket and passing them out. He continues, "My accountant tells me that this is deductible."[4]

Cantor did not attempt to sustain this high energy, which had always been a trademark, over the course of the entire performance. He would have grated on the audience, and taxed his body, if he had played the frantic singer, dancer, and joker all night. Instead, the fifty-eight-year-old star paced himself and demonstrated his underrated sense of comic timing in moving through his repertoire of entertaining anecdotes, which he animated with deft impressions of show business legends such as Jolson, Durante, and Ziegfeld. Critics praised the veteran's command of the stage. *Variety* recognized that Cantor's life story, "by now more or less public information, requires no gilding, hence his raconteuring has greater authority by underplaying." *Billboard* agreed that Cantor managed to find an effective tone for his one-man show: "He gave a warm human touch to the routine that was the essence of showmanship."[5]

Cantor opened his nostalgic Carnegie Hall show with a surprising contemporary political reference, promising to evoke "memories of a much more pleasant day, a day without the H-bomb or Senator Mc-Carthy or other evil things that want to destroy mankind."[6] Five weeks earlier, on February 9, 1950, Joseph McCarthy, then a little-known senator from Wisconsin, made headlines with a speech in Wheeling, West Virginia, in which he fumed against the "traitorous actions" of government workers and claimed to have a list of 205 Communist Party members who were working in the State Department.[7] Over the next several weeks, McCarthy continued to garner media attention with his charges that "card-carrying Communists" had infiltrated the State Department and his call for the resignation of Secretary of State Dean Acheson.[8] On March 17, 1950, four days before Cantor spoke against McCarthy at Carnegie Hall, the influential *Washington Post* columnist Stewart Alsop condemned McCarthy's vicious tactics: "guilt-by-association, occasional fuzzy mindedness labeled disloyalty, reputations ruined by unsupported charges hurled from behind the comfortable protection of congressional immunity."[9] These tactics were the "evil things" to which Cantor was referring. Over the next four years, many American Jews similarly associated McCarthy's tactics with demagoguery, authoritarianism, and antisemitism. Several organizations launched anti-McCarthy campaigns, though Cantor was one of the earliest to oppose McCarthy.[10]

During the national tour of his one-man show, Cantor made principled statements against the increasingly common practice of blacklisting. A coalition of sponsors, broadcasters, government agencies, and legislative committees, most notably HUAC, determined who would be blacklisted and what kinds of associations disqualified a person from work. Radio and television actors also fell under the scrutiny of anti-communist organizations such as the American Legion and conservative watchdogs. For example, a small group called American Business Consultants published *Red Channels* (1950), an influential manual that listed 151 alleged left-wing Hollywood personnel and detailed their tainted progressive political affiliations, dating back to the 1930s. Jean Muir, an actress named in *Red Channels*, became the first television casualty of the blacklist. On August 27, 1950, sponsor General Foods abruptly fired Muir and canceled the season premiere of *The Aldrich Family*, the television program in which she was slated to appear. The sponsor cited Muir's "controversial" presence in explaining its actions.[11]

Cantor swiftly condemned the sponsor's decision and defended Muir, who was active in the Screen Actors Guild when Cantor headed the organization from 1933 to 1935. He called her dismissal "one of the most tragic things that ever happened in show business," adding that Muir never had a chance to defend herself. At the time that Muir was fired, Cantor was about to debut as the host of a new NBC television program, *The Colgate Comedy Hour*. He defiantly told the *New York Times*, "If I had a part for her, I'd put her on in a minute and take my chances on being fired."[12] Cantor affirmed his opposition to the blacklist even more urgently in a letter to Syd Eiges, NBC vice president in charge of publicity: "If we are to live as free people, things like that [Muir's firing] cannot go on. If a few phone calls and telegrams can drive a person out of their profession, then I'd want to quit this whole business. I'm not being heroic, but I have principles and if I suffer for them, I'd do it gladly."[13]

Cantor continued his campaign against the emerging blacklist in his one-man shows over the next three months, condemning the unfairness of the proceedings and the inaccuracy of the charges. He urged a Milwaukee audience not to "convict actors of communistic leanings based on hearsay."[14] He closed an October performance in Oklahoma City by taking an even stronger stand against the self-appointed promoters and enforcers of the blacklist: "When I'm judged, I want it to be by someone bigger than a bigot." The star then specifically defended Muir and Irene Wicker, who was also listed in *Red Channels*, from the "untrue and unfair" accusations that resulted in their being blacklisted.[15]

In Boston, Cantor advised the crowd at Symphony Hall to "stamp out communism, but take pains not to stamp out American liberties." More than a decade later, the copublisher of the *Boston Jewish Advocate*, Joseph G. Weisberg, still recalled Cantor's admonition about the dangers of anticommunist excesses and the performer's defense of civil liberties, describing the Boston show as an "historic occasion in the history of entertainment, when fellow Americans came to pay honor to the best loved performer of his generation, whose brightness as a star was secondary to his radiance [as] an apostle for peace."[16]

Some audience members and critics did not like this intrusion of current politics on a light, nostalgic evening. Madelaine Wilson, in her review of the Oklahoma City show, asserted that the estimated forty-two hundred people came to hear Cantor sing. She was disappointed that, after his short statement about Muir and Wicker, "the little fellow marched quickly off the stage with no song as his farewell."[17]

Cantor did not let concerns about his political expression deter him. He delivered what had become a standard closing speech in defense of blacklisted actors the next month at a Camden, New Jersey, performance benefiting St. Bartholomew's Catholic Church, a predominantly African-American parish. Cantor scheduled the benefit as a favor to Frank Folsom, president of NBC's parent corporation, RCA. Folsom supported the church and attended the show. By late 1950, Cantor was starring on NBC's *Colgate Comedy Hour*. With his boss in the crowd, the performer declared his opposition to Stalin, whom he compared to Hitler, but cautioned his audience "to make sure you protect the rights of others." Cantor extolled the "great American tradition" that people are innocent until proved guilty and pointed out that Wicker's son gave his life for the country during the war.[18]

Singer Rudy Vallee initially joined Cantor in supporting Muir, as did the ACLU, but the industry quickly institutionalized the blacklist and silenced opposition. To avoid a repeat of the Muir controversy, networks and advertising agencies conducted background checks on potential performers before they were hired, rather than firing actors who were already cast. CBS installed a "security officer" to screen potential network personnel for communist ties. It also required loyalty oaths for its employees and guest performers. NBC had required similar loyalty statements since the mid-1940s and continued to use its legal department to vet actors.[19]

Networks and sponsors opposed even seemingly innocuous ideas with potential connections to communists. As he prepared for the new *Colgate Comedy Hour*, Cantor wanted to feature European entertainers from countries that were receiving aid under the Marshall Plan. Colgate did not like Cantor's proposal because it seemed to support a "controversial" political program and could provide work to "foreign artists" who were difficult to vet. Colgate also reminded NBC of its corporate policy regarding "using communists" and sent the network a copy of a 1949 policy memo stating: "This is a request to avoid in every way possible using any one who is known to be Red or 'pink' on any of our programs or in any way in which they could be associated with this Company."[20]

As a prominent Hollywood Jew with a history of antifascist activism, Cantor was vulnerable to attacks on his loyalty. Throughout the postwar era, vocal conservatives continued to conflate Jews and communism. Most infamously, from the House floor, the HUAC member John Rankin of Mississippi called out the "real names" of Cantor, Danny Kaye, Edward G. Robinson, and Melvyn Douglas: Jewish actors who supported the Committee for the First Amendment, a Hollywood group that defended ten writers and directors called before HUAC in 1947.[21]

Cantor had always watched his associations with people and organizations on the political left, and he was especially careful after he lost his weekly radio slot before the 1939–1940 season. Over the years, he cultivated relationships, based on common charitable goals unrelated to politics, with powerful conservatives such as J. Edgar Hoover and anticommunist organizations such as the American Legion. In addition, starting in the fall of 1939, Cantor bolstered his altruistic image with extensive support of interfaith and wartime charity efforts. After years of listening to his radio pitches and seeing him everywhere from churches to parades to military bases, most Americans did not view Cantor as a dangerous subversive. Nevertheless, even with this patriotic reputation, Cantor needed to be cautious, especially given the changing political climate. News of communist treachery and advances throughout late 1949 and 1950 seemed to support conservatives' warnings about the Red Menace. Headlines included the conviction of Alger Hiss for perjury related to espionage charges, the arrest of Julius and Ethel Rosenberg for conspiracy to commit espionage, the fall of China, the first successful atomic explosion by the Soviet Union, and the outbreak of the Korean War.[22] In the spring of 1951, HUAC resumed its investigation of Hollywood, further cementing the blacklist and providing conservatives with another vehicle for pressuring actors who had even a tenuous connection to the Hollywood left of the 1930s. HUAC investigations and industry blacklists derailed the careers of Cantor's friends and associates from the Screen Actors Guild and the Hollywood Anti-Nazi League, such as Muir, Lionel Stander, Gale Sondergaard, and Edward G. Robinson.

In this environment, Cantor said little explicitly about the domestic communist threat, Joseph McCarthy, or the blacklist. Like many anticommunist liberals, Cantor disapproved of the spurious accusations, bullying tactics, and rushes to judgment of the McCarthyites; however, he was unable to defend accused leftists without appearing soft on communism. Cantor chose not to continue his explicit criticisms of McCarthyism as violations of free speech and general principles of fairness after 1950. Instead, he opposed McCarthyism more subtly by tempering his anticommunist rhetoric. Cantor also countered the tone and tactics of rabid anticommunists by espousing decency, equality, interfaith cooperation, and tolerance as central to American democracy.

The actor protected himself and advanced his ideals by working with organizations that attracted supporters across political lines. Cantor donated the proceeds of several *My Forty Years in Show Business* performances to the March of Dimes, local hospitals, interfaith groups, or Jewish communal organizations. In early 1952, he went on a seven-city tour at his own expense, attracting several thousand fans at each stop. The price of admission was a pint of blood for the Red Cross, which needed to replenish its reserves during the Korean War. Cantor's audiences provided 110,000 pints, earning the performer universal plaudits.

From the floor of the United States Congress, Republican Bernard W. (Pat) Kearney of New York, a staunch anticommunist who served on HUAC, commended Cantor's "valiant assistance" to the Red Cross. The blood drive also pleased Folsom, the head of RCA, who praised his star: "You are doing one of the most magnificent jobs that any man ever did in your work for the Red Cross."[23]

In the fall of 1950, Cantor crisscrossed the country, playing twenty-eight engagements. Yet, in the absence of an established circuit for a one-man show such as *My Forty Years in Show Business*, he chose to draw on a different kind of network: Jewish charities. Cantor partnered with B'nai B'rith for several dates, working with the communal organization's local lodges. In making the B'nai B'rith chapters into theatrical producers, Cantor charged the charities 50 percent of gross receipts, rather than the 70 percent that he received from commercial promoters, with a minimum guarantee of $2,500 to Cantor for each show. The headliner's payments frequently exceeded this guarantee. He also supported B'nai B'rith by donating his time to appear at a fund-raising dinner before each performance. Always a savvy operator, he kept his expenses low for the one-man show, paying for only his travel, two piano players, and a portion of the publicity.[24]

The tour was a success, with Cantor usually appearing in five-thousand-seat auditoriums. Smaller Southern cities such as Birmingham and El Paso booked the biggest venues, testifying to Cantor's national appeal, though he commanded higher ticket prices in the North and Midwest. The top Chicago ticket sold for a whopping ten dollars a seat. In most other venues, prices started around three dollars. Cantor grossed more than nine thousand dollars for a show in Oklahoma City. He topped $12,000 in St. Louis and New Orleans, and $35,000 in both Chicago and Detroit. The syndicated columnist Bob Considine cited Cantor's box office figures and full houses in describing "one of the more astonishing comebacks in theatrical history." Abe Lastfogel, Cantor's agent at William Morris, tallied the box office figures for a particularly busy week, which took Cantor from Oklahoma City to Toronto for a total of seven shows. In a letter to Cantor, Lastfogel marveled, "I doubt if anyone, anywhere, at any time, has ever touched your receipts . . . $121,507 for seven performances without scenery, costumes, with just a pair of pianos is truly amazing." Even allowing for the hyperbole of an agent complimenting his client, Cantor made the industry notice him and the potential of his new format.[25]

Cantor's fall 1950 tour represented an important advance in celebrity philanthropy beyond the occasional brief appearance at a single event or at a series of luncheons, such as those that Cantor headlined for Hadassah during the 1930s. Other performers, such as Molly Picon and Sophie Tucker, occasionally played benefits for Jewish organizations while on tour. But before Cantor, no other star melded commercial entertainment and charity fund-raisers on this scale. Jewish organizations became active production partners and important sources of revenue because they helped publicize events among the core audiences that adored Cantor. The entrepreneurial celebrity inaugurated a new form of fund-raising, booking big-name Jewish stars a little past their prime, that later became standard for synagogues, community centers, and federations. Together, Cantor and B'nai B'rith also earned favorable publicity for their charitable work. Daily newspapers noted that B'nai B'rith planned to use profits from the shows to support local hospitals and youth organizations conducting interfaith work.[26]

The fact that Cantor was back on television in September 1950 starring on *The Colgate Comedy Hour* helped ticket sales for the live performances. Always a master of promotion, Cantor used his video platform to generate excitement over the touring show and announce the lucky cities where he would soon be appearing. In 1950, television, a rapidly growing medium, was supplanting radio's cultural influence, though radio still reached more people. Approximately 9 percent of American living rooms housed television sets in 1950, with the highest concentration in the Northeast. By 1955 this figure had jumped to 65 percent of all homes, with even higher market penetration in big cities. Radio ownership remained steady, at around 95 percent, during this time. In 1950, television broadcasters had two related goals: sell television sets and attract sponsors. A new receiver cost at least $150, about two weeks' wages for the average worker, though appliance stores made the sets more affordable by offering easy credit. Networks and local stations had to provide something of value that consumers couldn't receive from other media. Comedy-variety shows gave viewers the opportunity to view top-quality entertainment for free in the comfort of their living rooms. With most network shows originating from Midtown

Manhattan studios, talent from nearby theaters and nightclubs dominated early television.[27]

NBC designed its big-budget *Colgate Comedy Hour* to cut into the audience of Ed Sullivan's *Toast of the Town*. In a July 1950 pitch meeting, NBC executives assured Colgate president E. H. Little that "we had a mutual interest at stake to lick Sullivan."[28] The Sunday night CBS variety show was the second most-popular program on television, regularly attracting more than 60 percent of all viewers. Only Milton Berle's Tuesday evening *Texaco Star Theater* was bigger. Berle and Sullivan set the standard for many others, creating a genre that the industry termed "vaudeo": video programs that followed the vaudeville model of combining a variety of music, dance, theater, comedy, and novelty acts. Because of the popular taste for nostalgia and the technical demands of the live medium, these shows revitalized the careers of several old vaudevillians and stage comics such as Ed Wynn, Bobby Clark, and the team of Smith and Dale.

Following the template from Berle's *Texaco Star Theater*, *The Colgate Comedy Hour* featured big-name entertainers performing lavish comedy skits and musical numbers. It employed a rotating cast of hosts who also starred in several sketches. Cantor, Fred Allen, Bob Hope, Jackie Gleason, Martin and Lewis, and Abbott and Costello each headlined episodes of *The Colgate Comedy Hour* during the first season. Versatile stars such as Cantor, with stage experience and name recognition from radio, were well suited for live television. Just as Cantor had helped to popularize radio comedy nearly twenty years earlier, NBC used him in its strategy for selling television comedy. When he pitched the new program to Colgate executives, NBC vice president for television programming Pat Weaver boasted, "There will be nothing as good on Broadway as Cantor and Allen." Weaver also appreciated Cantor's reputation for nurturing talent and building new stars on his radio program, expecting the veteran actor to do the same on television. Maybe Cantor would discover the next Deanna Durbin or Dinah Shore. NBC and Colgate needed Cantor as much as he needed the network to revitalize his career for a new medium.[29]

Cantor hosted twelve *Colgate Comedy Hours* during the premier 1950–1951 season and the same number of episodes the next year, 1951–1952. Nobody else helmed as many episodes. Initially, *The Colgate Comedy*

Hour was a commercial and critical smash, accomplishing the network's goal of stealing viewers from Sullivan while garnering praise for bringing slick entertainment into America's living rooms. On his debut, September 10, 1950, Cantor's program scored a rating of 32.1, nearly five points better than Sullivan, even though his CBS rival featured the popular singers Frankie Laine and Patti Page along with the comedian Victor Borge. Cantor reached 2.3 million homes and 32 percent of the viewing audience. Over the full 1950–1951 season, Cantor had higher ratings than Sullivan nine times.[30]

In an internal memo after the first season, the NBC programming executive Fred Wile made a strong argument to re-sign Cantor, both because of the star's popularity and fear that the competition would snap him up: "Since he is in the hit class—perhaps not to the extent of Martin and Lewis or Sid Caesar or Berle, but nevertheless a hit—I feel that there is a better than even chance he could make a CBS deal real fast." NBC made a good decision. In 1951–1952, Cantor achieved higher ratings than Sullivan in all twelve episodes that he hosted.[31]

Cantor appealed to audiences with a combination of talent, versatility, and familiarity from his many years as a star. The actor energetically dusted off physical comedy skills from decades earlier without missing a step. In one sketch, from early 1952, the sixty-year-old star does a variation of the old osteopath routine. A burly football player, played by the six-foot-four character actor Michael Ross, throws Cantor onto a smoldering chair. Cantor keeps thrusting his body up, as the athlete commands him to sit down. Cantor escapes when his captor inadvertently takes sleeping pills and staggers around the room, while Cantor joins Ross in a slapstick fight that devolves into a slow dance.[32] Other skits from this season found Cantor leaping into the arms of costars, silently playing the straight man to an intractable bull (ably portrayed by an unbilled actor in a cheap costume), and drinking wine out of a shoe as he parodies handsome leading man and guest star Cesar Romero.

Physical comedy enjoyed a revival through Cantor and other variety program hosts such as Berle, Sid Caesar, and Jackie Gleason. Slapstick worked better on television than radio. Despite the best efforts of writers, announcers, and sound effects engineers, radio shows could not replicate the full impact of an unexpected fall, a chaotic pie fight, or the expression of a shocked victim of a practical joke. The slapstick on early

Cantor portrays a college student alongside burly Michael Ross on *The Colgate Comedy Hour* (1952). Courtesy of UCLA Library Special Collections.

television variety also coincided with popular appreciation of the artistry of silent film comedy. For example, in September 1949, *Life* magazine featured the forgotten actor Ben Turpin on the cover, supporting the influential critic James Agee's long essay extolling "Comedy's Greatest Era," from 1912 to 1930.[33]

Cantor distinguished himself from other television personalities because, in addition to the comedy sketches, he could draw upon his rich background in theater and deep catalog of popular music standards. Cantor usually opened *The Colgate Comedy Hour* with a long, splashy number. Surrounded by young dancers, Cantor and his company might pay tribute to New York or Hollywood, using a combination of old songs and newer pieces written for the routine. The veteran performer frequently poked fun at his age and nostalgic image. In a September 1951 *Colgate Comedy Hour*, Cantor's writers crafted a number that celebrated his forty-second anniversary in show business as well as the new technology of television. AT&T had recently completed construction of the coaxial cable that enabled networks to transmit live programs from coast to coast. This episode of *The Colgate Comedy Hour*, originating from Hollywood, became the first commercial program to take advantage of the national distribution vehicle. In the routine, Cantor names cities and towns that he has visited over the years on tour and promises that he will now reach even more people via television: "It's no fairy tale or fable / It's tee vee's coaxial cable / Reaching everywhere from Hollywood and Vine."

A telephone call interrupts Cantor. An elderly woman seems to cue Cantor for more nostalgic reverie: "Are you the Eddie Cantor who played with Gus Edwards's *Kid Kabaret* forty years ago?" she asks.

Cantor answers, "Yes."

The caller keeps asking about Cantor's career until the star enthusiastically interrupts her, perhaps getting ready to sing a medley of his hits: "Yes, the same Eddie Cantor who played in *Kid Boots*, in *Whoopee*, the same Eddie Cantor who is in radio and now television."

The caller snaps, "Look, isn't it time already you quit and gave someone else a chance?"[34]

Behind this self-deprecating humor lurked the valid question of whether Cantor had overstayed his welcome as an entertainer. *The Colgate Comedy Hour* episodes that Cantor hosted achieved solid ratings during the 1951–1952 season, but he could not keep recycling old routines and telling nostalgic stories. Cantor and his writers tried to create more contemporary sketches and running characters for the actor. His most successful new character was Maxie the Taxi, a likable New York cab driver. Maxi served as a straight man and source of advice to the outlandish guest stars who hailed his cab, including, in one case, a chimp voiced by Mel Blanc. But the nostalgic performances remained central to each episode that Cantor hosted. Faithful renditions of old music and comedy from 1920s Broadway seemed breezy and fun when Cantor debuted in 1950. By 1952 these routines, especially Cantor's use of blackface, appeared anachronistic and offensive to many critics, viewers, and network executives. Popular objections to blackface and racial stereotyping increased dramatically during the early 1950s.

Cantor usually wore blackface in the elaborate musical routines that closed *The Colgate Comedy Hour*. He sang his hits and paid tribute to the *Ziegfeld Follies*, vaudeville, or Tin Pan Alley songwriters. As in his one-man show, energetic songs such as "Ma, He's Making Eyes at Me," "How Ya Gonna Keep 'Em Down on the Farm," "If You Knew Susie," and "Ida (Sweet as Apple Cider)" pleased the crowd. In 1950, NBC executives and the Colgate sponsors appreciated Cantor's nostalgic act, including the blackface. At a production meeting for the first episode of *The Colgate Comedy Hour*, for example, the executives eagerly anticipated the way the finale would "bring back the minstrel days."[35] Critics also praised the extravagant closing dance numbers on *The Colgate Comedy Hour* as highlights of the episodes, either neglecting to mention the blackface or noting it only in passing. The makeup was a natural and expected element of Cantor's routines.[36]

During the early 1950s, NBC paid more attention to negative images of African-Americans. The network quickly responded to changing attitudes about race in the country, as it consulted with the National Association for the Advancement of Colored People (NAACP) and other civil rights organizations, while acknowledging the increasing importance of black consumers. The network's Community Acceptance department, which policed NBC content, required producers to expunge derogatory material. The weekly Community Acceptance Radio and Television (CART) reports that the department head Stockton Helffrich wrote for other NBC departments chronicled the changes that the network made to programs and registered critical comments from viewers.

Helffrich proudly recorded an alteration to a 1952 *Gangbusters* script that eliminated stereotypes of a black janitor: "The Hollywood office skillfully called for avoidance of a showing of the Negro as scared along stereotyped lines and deleted [the] reference to the Negro janitor as being hopped up as a result of gin drinking."[37]

From 1950 to 1952, Community Acceptance received no complaints about Cantor's blackface performances. The CART reports recorded only three negative but vague phone calls about a Cantor dance routine from September 9, 1951, "presumably feeling [the dance] to be stereotyping." In fact, this particular program did not include a dance scene stereotyping African-Americans, though Helffrich may have made his judgment about stereotypes based on segments from earlier episodes and Cantor's reputation as a blackface performer. Helffrich added a parenthetical observation to his CART report: "There does seem to be inconsistency between Eddie Cantor's obvious effort on behalf of tolerance in American life and his inclusion of somewhat dated versions of Negro life." The NBC executive did not pass these thoughts to Cantor. Images and stereotypes on other programs seemed more dangerous than the actor's "somewhat dated" characterizations.[38]

In October 1951, Helffrich received complaints about blackface on two different programs: Milton Berle's *Texaco Star Theater* and *The Kate Smith Hour*. In his CART report responding to these complaints, Helffrich "strongly recommended" that the network ban blackface. Referencing changing popular attitudes, he found it "increasingly apparent" that blackface damaged "the good will of the public."[39] The report indicates that the Community Acceptance department was paying more attention to racial stereotypes, but this relatively small item in a weekly memo did not immediately change prime-time programming. Since Cantor remained popular in blackface and his programs did not generate significant criticism, he continued to wear the makeup through the January 20, 1952, *Colgate Comedy Hour*. This episode ends with an elaborate tribute to George Gershwin featuring Cantor and costar Robert Clary in blackface together. After the music fades and Clary leaves the stage, Cantor stretches to fill the last few minutes of the live broadcast. Still in blackface, the headliner names the show's supporting players. Cantor then announces that he is about to travel from Los Angeles across the country for two reasons: to help the March of Dimes and to celebrate his upcoming sixtieth birthday at the Commodore Hotel in New York. Cantor describes the birthday party: "A thousand people are paying a million dollars to buy bonds for the State of Israel." The studio audience cheers.[40]

New industry practices made it clear that Cantor would have to battle if he wanted to keep appearing in blackface. Instead, he quietly retired this look.[41] There was no honor in being the last blackface actor on television. Furthermore, as Helffrich observed, blackface undercut Cantor's liberal, charitable persona. By 1952 the makeup also hurt his image as he worked with the National Conference of Christians and Jews (NCCJ) and other groups fighting prejudice. Cantor could not support one minority while continuing to wear a costume that denigrated another. Even though Cantor did not view blackface as an insult to African-Americans, he was sensitive to appearances and the changing tastes of audiences. With blackface less central to his image, it was easier for Cantor to participate in events such as the NCCJ's annual Brotherhood Weeks and a March 1952 NAACP gala held at Madison Square Garden.[42] Though the show business veteran understood that it was time to curtail the use of blackface, he could not reverse a bigger problem: he was growing older and running out of fresh material for his music and comedy routines.

Cantor seemed more socially relevant in advocating for Israel. His sixtieth birthday celebration, the Israel Bonds fund-raiser that he promoted before a supportive audience on *The Colgate Comedy Hour*, symbolized the broader ascent of Jewish entertainers to the highest strata of American life. The orphan kid from the Lower East Side ghetto was feted by eighteen hundred people. Speakers included Vincent Impellitteri, mayor of New York, and Alben Barkley, vice president under Truman, who presented Cantor with a plaque on behalf of Israel Bonds. Cantor also received a leather-bound volume filled with birthday telegrams from friends in entertainment, philanthropy, and politics. David Ben-Gurion praised Cantor's "heart rich in humor and humanity." Jack Benny found it appropriate for Cantor to spend his sixtieth birthday helping Israel. Younger performers such as Martin and Lewis, Danny Kaye, and Sid Caesar cited Cantor as an "inspiration" because of his commitment to humanitarian causes. In a further testament to the popularity of Cantor and Israel Bonds, twenty-eight state governors and two Supreme Court justices also wished Cantor well.[43]

Newspapers across the country, especially the Jewish weeklies, paid tribute to Cantor's tireless "furtherance of humanitarian ideals and charitable causes."[44] The *Hartford Jewish Ledger* wrote admiringly that in Cantor "there is a synthesis of Jew and American and he is a complete personality, unfrightened, unsplintered, whole Jew and whole American, respected and honored and loved for what he is."[45] In a more secular vein, from the floor of the House of Representatives, Democratic congressman John Dingell Sr. of Michigan commended Cantor's "spotless character" and "exemplary" family life. He noted that the "foremost men and women of America" were preparing to celebrate the birthday of this "little dynamo of energy."[46]

In a long essay that he wrote for a commemorative booklet, Cantor explained why he supported Israel. He used this well-publicized birthday celebration to advance the views of Israel that he and the UJA first expressed in 1948. Though Cantor saw the birth of Israel as a victory against Hitler and "Hitlerism," Cantor did not focus on Israel as a haven for Jews after the genocide. Instead, in keeping with the Cold War rhetoric of the time, he emphasized the ideological connections and historical parallels between Israel and the United States. Israel represented a "tiny America, following our way of life . . . there is no Statue of Liberty in the Harbor of Haifa, but there is just as deep an appreciation of the meaning of liberty by the people of Israel." Cantor described Israel as a land of opportunity for immigrants, a "pioneering country—the way America used to be a hundred years ago," and a "new democracy," modeled on the government of the United States. In eliding the distinctions between "Jewish" and "American" interests, Cantor wrote, "to be a good American you should also be a good Jew, and vice versa."[47]

Cantor's sixtieth birthday party capped the last great phase of his career. He hosted a popular television program and regularly packed theaters when he took his one-man show on the road. Cantor also raised public awareness and a great deal of money for the new State of Israel: a richly meaningful cause for a performer who had spent his career advocating for the Jewish people. Leading politicians, Jewish philanthropists, fellow performers, and newspaper writers eagerly praised Cantor for his work on and off the stage. While Cantor held a special place of honor among Jews, his fame cut across religious, geographic, and generational boundaries.

These good times did not last.

13 FADING AWAY
(1952–1964)

At the age of sixty, Cantor showed no interest in modifying his schedule or retiring. He began his third season as a featured host of *The Colgate Comedy Hour* on September 28, 1952.

Shortly before he went on the air that evening, Cantor felt pain in his left arm and his chest. But the trouper ignored the pain and delivered "an hour of sock entertainment that set a high mark for the others in the series to shoot at," according to *Variety*. After the five o'clock broadcast from Hollywood, a doctor examined Cantor and found no problems. That evening, Cantor attended synagogue for Kol Nidre services. Early the next morning, on Yom Kippur, Cantor had a major heart attack in his home and was rushed to Cedars of Lebanon Hospital, where he spent the next six weeks.[1] As he recovered, Cantor canceled several commitments, including television appearances and an Israel Bonds tour, before resuming his monthly hosting duties on *The Colgate Comedy Hour* in January 1953.

In a *Look* magazine article, Cantor described his recent medical ordeal, mocking himself while offering cautionary advice. He took the blame for pushing himself too hard and ignoring the medical signs of heart trouble, explaining ruefully: "You can't slow down if you're going to jump up and down and clap your hands and be Eddie Cantor." As he recuperated, Cantor humbly admitted that various television programs and benefits to which he had previously committed were fine without him: "I wound up learning, the hard way, how to act my age. And I came face to face with some 'heart truths' I'd like to share with other foolish mortals . . . You can be replaced, your heart can't."[2]

After the heart attack, Cantor no longer demonstrated his characteristic youthful energy and enthusiasm. Given his condition, he modified his acting style. Cantor spent more time seated when he performed on *The Colgate Comedy Hour*. He also filmed some segments, such as his Maxi routines, so that he could work at a slower pace. The *Comedy Hour* directors edited the film pieces into the live broadcasts. The star explained his new techniques as natural and logical adaptations after the heart attack: "I'm not jumping around the stage any more. When a routine lends itself to a stop-and-go kinescope [film] method, we do this and I have another few minutes when I can relax. I'd rather settle for half a loaf than gorging a few months, and then rocking on the front porch the rest of my life."[3] The sponsor did not share Cantor's easygoing acceptance of the new style. In a letter to the production supervisor Samuel Fuller, Colgate's Leslie Harris sniped, "You might remind Cantor when he is reminiscing about 'Kid Boots' that they didn't open the show with him dangling his legs over the footlights."[4]

As Cantor moderated his activity, his costars became more important. Since the fall 1950 debut of *The Colgate Comedy Hour*, Cantor had featured a mixture of established entertainers and newer talent, which the host had a reputation for boosting. For example, Joel Grey and Sammy Davis Jr. each performed on Cantor's program before they were well known nationally. Davis already was headlining top nightclubs in New York and Los Angeles as part of the Will Mastin Trio, alongside Mastin and Sammy Davis Sr. The Will Mastin Trio also toured the country with Jack Benny before the dance group made one of its earliest television appearances on the February 17, 1952, *Colgate Comedy Hour*. This episode has earned a place in show business lore because of Davis's electrifying performance and Cantor's response to Davis. Cantor is so moved by Davis's athletic tap dancing and vocal gymnastics in a series of impersonations that he runs onto the stage to wipe Davis's brow for three seconds between numbers. At the end of the routine, Cantor returns to congratulate the group. He puts his arm around Davis and delivers a short benediction: "Am I right? Is this the greatest hunk of talent that you've seen in years?" The audience cheers. Cantor continues, "And Sammy, I have news for you. I'll probably get killed for this, but you're coming back here on my next show four weeks from tonight."[5]

In his 1965 autobiography, Davis reported that the appearance triggered "an avalanche" of hate mail from racist viewers offended that men of different skin colors would touch onstage. Davis's agent claimed that the sponsor did not want him to return to the *Comedy Hour*. The young performer assumed that his television career was over. Later, Davis received word that Cantor, not one to be pushed around, had successfully pressured the sponsor into bringing Davis back on the remaining programs that Cantor was hosting through the end of the season. Davis recalled, "Here there were people going out of their way to kick me in the face with nothing to gain by doing it, then along comes a man like Eddie Cantor with everything to lose, but he deals himself into my fight."[6] As Cantor promised, the Will Mastin Trio appeared on the next *Colgate Comedy Hour* featuring Cantor, in March 1952, and on two additional episodes during the 1952–1953 season. Davis and Cantor remained friends beyond this time.

Davis probably exaggerated the volume of hate mail as well as Cantor's influence with the sponsor and network. Colgate and NBC would have banned the Will Mastin Trio from the program, despite Cantor's protests, if the racist viewer hate mail and reactions that Davis described truly concerned the corporations. Cantor did not have enough leverage to reverse this kind of decision. NBC's detailed Community Acceptance division reports do not mention any viewer complaints or problems with the February 1952 *Colgate Comedy Hour* episode on which the Will Mastin Trio appeared. Over the previous year, the department registered only a handful of complaints about blacks and whites appearing together onstage, including pro-segregation comments by the governor of Georgia, Herman Talmadge, published in *Variety*. But NBC and the other networks affirmed their commitment to presenting the best talent, regardless of skin color.[7] As Helffrich, the Community Acceptance department head, wrote in an internal report, "Broadcasting is certainly reaching new frontiers, and the resistance to the joint featuring of performers regardless of their skin pigmentation has been infinitesimal."[8]

Still, Davis's story illustrates the larger truth that the public friendship and warmth of liberal white celebrities such as Cantor held significant symbolic weight in the fight against racism and segregation. Cantor supported costars and friends, regardless of their race. The African-American press commended Cantor for advancing the careers of Davis and other performers. In March 1952, the *Amsterdam News* praised Cantor as "one of the few white entertainers who has gone out of his way to 'make' Negro entertainers and stars."[9] The following year, the *Chicago Defender* commented on a *Colgate Comedy Hour* appearance by Davis: "If you were looking, you saw Cantor giving [Davis] plenty of opportunities to display his fine talent. WONDER IF ANY other emcee would have been as liberal with Sammy or any other Sepian, however

Cantor with his arm around Sammy Davis Jr. during an appearance of the
Will Mastin Trio on *The Colgate Comedy Hour* (1952). Courtesy of UCLA
Library Special Collections.

great his talents."[10] The longtime *Baltimore Afro-American* columnist and activist Sam Lacy noted that "for many, many years [Cantor] has been admired for his liberal attitude toward entertainers of all races."[11]

When Cantor casually suggests that he'll "be killed" for inviting the Will Mastin Trio back so quickly, he may have been referring to the riskiness of supporting lesser-known entertainers, regardless of race. NBC and Colgate condoned Cantor's work with Davis, Lena Horne, and other popular African-American artists, but network and sponsor executives regularly knocked Cantor's guest stars and bemoaned the lack of big names on his programs. William Morris, the agency that represented Cantor, booked the acts. The network paid Cantor and William Morris a flat rate of a little over $40,000 per episode, which included fees for guest stars. NBC executives believed that Cantor was saving money by hiring cheaper supporting players.[12] Some Cantor episodes devolved into talent shows, with Cantor introducing a series of undistinguished singers, dancers, and comedians. As early as January 1952, before Cantor's heart attack, Colgate complained to NBC that recent episodes hosted by Cantor, Donald O'Connor, and Abbott and Costello were "little better than amateur hours."[13] These criticisms only intensified from January 1953 through Cantor's last broadcast in May 1954. By 1953 ratings had slipped for all *Comedy Hour* hosts except for Martin and Lewis. The expensive program was not producing the audience that the sponsor needed, though Cantor still occasionally topped CBS rival Ed Sullivan.[14]

Cantor pointed to his respectable ratings in defending his approach to booking talent. In March 1953, he wrote to NBC's head of programming, Charles ("Bud") Barry, that he had outdone Sullivan on twenty-one of their twenty-five competing episodes since the show's 1950 debut. The show business veteran also questioned the relationship between stars and ratings, citing examples of particular NBC radio and television programs with marquee celebrities that fizzled with audiences. Cantor further blamed NBC for insufficient promotion of the show and noted that his production budget, used to pay guests' appearance fees, was lower than that of other *Colgate Comedy Hour* hosts. "It is too easy to put the blame on a star. Let's fluoroscope the situation and come up with a true picture," he wrote.[15]

Critics recognized Cantor's emphasis on newer artists, but they did not share the harsh assessment of NBC and Colgate executives. As *Va-*

riety wrote, "Cantor, after these many years, knows what to do with talent and he gives newcomers a major showcase." Another *Variety* reviewer praised the "freshness" of a "standout" May 10, 1953, episode featuring young entertainers along with more experienced artists who were not top names, such as opera singer Jan Peerce.[16] Testing the theory that Cantor was too old, the veteran *New York Daily News* radio and television columnist Ben Gross, not always a fan of Cantor's, watched the program with his "hep young assistant" Kay Gardella. Explaining Cantor's appeal across generations, she praised the star's "ability to find young talent" and his "old time songs." Gardella, who went on to a long career as a television columnist, explained, "I always get a lift out of these sentimental journeys."[17]

Even in these showcases for younger performers, Cantor favored safe, traditional, familiar acts: cute kids, energetic dancers, and smooth vocalists who purveyed popular styles but did not challenge audiences artistically or politically. He liked and understood these kinds of performers. Cantor booked African-American dancers and singers such as Davis, Horne, and William Warfield, but no contemporary jazz or rhythm and blues bands. It was not until the fall of 1954 that a younger late-night host, Steve Allen, gave bebop and cool jazz a national television platform. In addition, the vibrant country music of figures such as Hank Williams and Lefty Frizzell eluded Cantor, even though these influential musicians appeared elsewhere on network radio and television. Similarly, Cantor did not appreciate the more low-key, observational comedy coming into vogue during the mid-1950s. In a 1953 new-talent program that Cantor hosted, George Gobel, soon to star on his own NBC show, performed a quirky, meandering, stand-up routine about his frustrating search for a lost bowling ball. Gobel's deadpan story had a foundation in the style of humor depicting everyday experiences gone awry that Cantor and other stage comedians popularized during the 1920s. But Gobel's bowling ball monologue provided a narrower focus on the mundane than Cantor's earlier satires of clothing stores and chiropractors. After watching Gobel, Cantor seemed befuddled. The host withheld his usual praise for a guest comedian.[18]

By the 1953–1954 season, public nostalgia for the Jazz Age had faded. Former vaudevillians no longer found easy work on television, as networks moved away from variety shows to filmed dramas and situation comedies. These formats seemed fresher and offered writers more possibilities than the familiar songs and routines that served as the foundation for weekly variety hours. Milton Berle was no longer at the top of the ratings charts, supplanted by *I Love Lucy*. *The Colgate Comedy Hour* slipped to number ten in the national Nielsen ratings, its lowest position ever.[19] Still, Cantor hoped that the new film biography of his life, *The Eddie Cantor Story*, would revive his career, as a similar biopic had for Jolson in 1946. In fact, Cantor chose Sidney Skolsky, the Hollywood gossip columnist who produced *The Jolson Story*, to work on his film. Cantor shrewdly publicized *The Eddie Cantor Story* on television, including on *The Colgate Comedy Hour*. An episode of *This Is Your Life* starred Cantor and featured coverage of the December 23, 1953, New York premiere of the film. The program reached thirty million viewers and "proved to be one of the most successful promotion tie-ups in motion picture–TV relations," according to *Motion Picture Daily*.[20]

Other television promotions that Cantor and his studio planned were not as successful. NBC rejected several short *Eddie Cantor Story* commercials because they included clips of the actor Keefe Brasselle, who portrayed Cantor, in blackface. The network also forced Cantor to eliminate a tribute to Al Jolson slated for *The Colgate Comedy Hour*. Cantor would have appeared in blackface for the first time since 1952, dancing alongside another actor portraying Jolson, who died in 1950. NBC's internal memos indicate that the network eliminated the sketch because it found the blackface "flatly unacceptable." But NBC executives may have been concerned that censorship of Cantor's nostalgic tribute to Jolson for this reason could cause controversy. Many viewers had fond memories of both Cantor and Jolson in blackface. Instead, NBC created a more innocuous rationale for the programming decision. Network executives told Cantor that he had mentioned Jolson too frequently in earlier episodes of the series.[21] In his 1957 autobiography, Cantor angrily recalled the cancellation of the Jolson tribute, complaining that he was never told the reason for NBC's veto. By this time, he probably suspected that blackface was the problem. Cantor's description of the Jolson routine focused on the blackface makeup and arbitrary standards of broadcasters.[22]

Cantor's energetic promotion of *The Eddie Cantor Story* was hindered by another problem, in addition to the blackface: the film was not very good. The upbeat biography's thesis is that the orphan boy goes into show business because he needs the love and approval of audiences. After neglecting his family for the fame and fortune of the stage, and giving himself a heart attack from working too hard, Cantor slows down. He learns to appreciate Ida and to be more charitable. The film ignores Cantor's Jewish identity and political activism. Though critics liked the music, featuring a new soundtrack by Cantor to which the actor Keefe Brasselle lip-synched, they savaged the clichéd narrative and Brasselle's performance. As Alton Cook of the *New York World Telegram-Sun* wrote, "Keefe has been made so intent on a few mannerisms, such as constantly bulging eyes, he is merely making faces, not making a man. Lifeless treatment of the central figure of a story that was wooden to begin with reduces the narrative sections of the film to a series of tedious interludes."[23] Despite these reviews, the public remained interested in Cantor and his biography. The film did well at the box office.[24]

In an effort to invigorate *The Colgate Comedy Hour*, NBC modified the format for the 1954–1955 season, mixing variety with hour-long productions of popular musicals. The network saw a more limited role for Cantor, penciling him in for only two episodes.[25] Instead of signing with NBC, Cantor decided to leave the network where he had started on radio in 1931 and remained for most of his broadcast career. Cantor hosted his final *Colgate Comedy Hour* on May 16, 1954. That summer, he began work on *The Eddie Cantor Comedy Theatre*, a new series of thirty-minute filmed programs syndicated by the Ziv Company. Ziv reportedly paid Cantor a minimum of more than a million dollars to star in twelve episodes and provide brief introductions to twenty-four additional programs. Based on the star's drawing power, Ziv was able to sell *The Eddie Cantor Comedy Theatre* to 180 markets — a solid figure for a syndicated program, but short of the national imprint of the major network shows.[26] *The Eddie Cantor Comedy Theatre* premiered in late January 1955 and aired at a different time in each city, so Ziv could not promote the program or tabulate ratings nationally. Viewership varied dramatically based on the station, airtime, and competition. According to one industry estimate, *The Eddie Cantor Comedy Theatre* ranked tenth among syndicated programs, with a respectable average rating of 15.7 in the larger markets.[27]

The episodes featuring Cantor offered musical routines and sketches similar to *The Colgate Comedy Hour*. The format and jokes seemed stale, despite the occasional split screens and other editing tricks. The *New York Times* critic Jack Gould wrote, "The Cantor on TV film just wasn't the Cantor of live TV; the well-known bounce of the little man with the rolling eyes just didn't survive the artificiality of the production."[28] Ziv canceled *The Eddie Cantor Comedy Theatre* in late 1955, after one season and thirty-six episodes, though the films remained available to stations for several years. In 1957 Cantor looked back on his "fatal" experience with Ziv, asserting that he did not have artistic control over the series and that the syndicator cared only about producing programs quickly, striving for an "assembly line, not a quality product." Cantor wrote, "For once in my life I allowed my better judgment to be swayed by the money involved. I'd give all the money back if I could take back the shows, which are still running."[29]

As Cantor struggled through the longest and most difficult slump of his show business career, his Jewish identity remained central to his public persona. When Cantor was the subject of *This Is Your Life* in December 1953, the popular program ended its parade of highlights from Cantor's career with a dramatic, emotional visit from a young woman named Dvora Eckheiser who immigrated to Israel with Youth Aliyah. Eckheiser tells Cantor her story: "Like many, many others, I was rescued from Hitler countries, but Youth Aliyah helped us to become proud and dignified citizens of our country. To you and the others who worked with you, we want to say, simply, thank you." Cantor responds, "It's been a great joy."[30]

In addition to referencing his long history supporting Youth Aliyah and other Jewish causes, Cantor engaged in contemporary politics. In October 1954, he purchased a full-page advertisement in the *New York Times*. His open letter to Secretary of State John Foster Dulles criticized the State Department's growing support of Arab nations. Cantor worried "as an American" and "as a Jew." He fumed, "Hitler removed several million of my co-religionists from the world. Less than two million of the remnants have found a refuge in Israel. I would not be human if I did not feel a special responsibility to that handful that has remained."[31] With the midterm elections coming, *Life* magazine blasted Cantor's' "full-page bleat . . . obviously aimed at the Zionist-influenced vote." Cantor was so disturbed by *Life*'s dismissal that he considered replying to the magazine, but James G. McDonald persuaded him that "the publishers of *Life* are tough," and a response by Cantor would only provoke a "much more virulent attack."[32] Though *Life* opposed Cantor, his letter to Dulles did not set off the kind of venomous antisemitic assaults on his patriotism that similar statements had elicited during the 1930s. Jewish advocacy was neither controversial nor surprising by 1954. In fact, four days after Cantor's letter was published, the heads of sixteen national Jewish organizations met with Dulles to express similar concerns directly. In addition, Cantor told McDonald that several supportive newspapers printed the letter for free. For example, the Pittsburgh Jewish newspaper columnist Milton K. Susman, a longtime Cantor supporter, reprinted the piece along with a proud introduction: "We've never loved Mr. Cantor quite so much as we did for having written that [letter]."[33]

Cantor's continuing health problems squashed any chance for a final comeback. In November 1955, he canceled a guest appearance on Milton Berle's program because of a reported kidney infection, which hospitalized him for a month and required additional rest and recuperation at home in Beverly Hills.[34] By May 1956, Cantor was well enough to travel east. He spoke at an Israel Bonds fund-raiser in Boston, where he urged the State Department to allow the sale of military equipment to Israel and introduced a Carnegie Hall performance by the Hungarian cantor Bela Herskovits. Cantor also prepared to star in two television dramas, playing characters close to his own age.[35] The roles did not require the kind of conditioning of his kinetic comedy from a few years earlier, but they still represented significant achievements because of the physical and artistic demands of these live productions. In "George Has a Birthday," Cantor played the title character, a mild-mannered elevator operator who is slated to inherit $500,000. George must contend with two sisters who plot to kill him for his money. The sixty-minute production aired on NBC's low-rated but ambitious *Matinee Theater*, which presented a new play each afternoon. He delivered another skillful performance in "Sizeman and Son," part of the prestigious *Playhouse 90* series. Cantor portrayed a successful Jewish clothing manufacturer who clashes with his idealistic, politically radical son (Farley Granger). Even though "George Has a Birthday" and "Sizeman and Son" did not attract the kind of press and public attention that Cantor had received during his heyday, the roles enabled the veteran performer to showcase his skills while reminding fans that he remained active.

Cantor promoted "Sizeman and Son" and his forthcoming autobiography, written with Jane Kesner Ardmore, by appearing beside Ida on Edward R. Murrow's *Person to Person* in October 1956. The couple shared stories and gave viewers a tour of their Beverly Hills home. Murrow interviewed them from a television studio. Cantor does not seem completely settled in his semiretired domesticity.

Murrow asks Ida if she helps her husband relax.

Ida replies with a laugh, "Oh, no. He hasn't relaxed in years. No, I can't make him do that."

Murrow then wonders whether Eddie helps around the house.

Ida answers, "Oh, he makes a pretense."

Eddie defends himself: "Don't say I make a pretense." He then self-deprecatingly describes his skills at making tea.

He is more confident discussing his future and crafting his legacy. Murrow asks, "What do you regard as the best in your life?"

Cantor replies by referencing his offstage philanthropy: "The best in my life, I believe, are the things that happened when the curtain dropped. Not in the theater. Not as an entertainer. But the things that I have done, well, as a man."

Murrow's follow-up: "What is the plan for the rest of Eddie Cantor's life?"

Cantor answers: "The rest of my life, Ed, I would like to devote to making for a better relationship between people. All kinds of people. All kinds of races and colors." Before he died, Cantor wanted to see "a more peaceful world. A more peaceful America. An America that is unified."[36]

Cantor had few opportunities to continue his charitable work and participate in the burgeoning civil rights movement. Though civil rights leaders did not condemn Cantor, they also did not court the aging former blackface performer. More important, Cantor's weak heart limited his public appearances on and off the stage.

On January 12, 1957, Cantor starred in an all-star television spectacular, similar in format to *The Colgate Comedy Hour*, celebrating his sixty-fifth birthday. Friends and former collaborators such as Eddie Fisher, George Jessel, Lucille Ball, and Burns and Allen performed short routines. Eddie and his daughter Marilyn sang a duet, a sweet musical comedy sketch looking back on Cantor's career.

The birthday celebrant did not seem well. He spoke slowly, sat down

Cantor with some of the awards for his philanthropic work.
Courtesy of UCLA Library Special Collections.

frequently, and appeared uncharacteristically sloppy, wearing a baggy suit and crooked bow tie. During a big, multicamera production number at the end, Fisher, Cantor, and Connie Russell take turns singing snippets of Tin Pan Alley favorites, accompanied by the respective composers. After Cantor's turn, the camera lingers a little too long. Perhaps not knowing that he is still on air, Cantor wipes his nose with his hand, and then shakes his head in disgust as he waves his hand at the camera to move on. Still, Cantor is ready for his next number, and he gamely appears with his fellow singers when they unite for the big finish, "Lullaby of Broadway." After a commercial, Cantor prepares to welcome his old friend Jessel. Cantor pauses: "You don't mind if I sit down," he says as he grabs a chair, not well enough to stand for the routine. Then, as Jessel tells a story about their time together with Gus Edwards, Cantor calls for a glass of water, which a stagehand delivers. Jessel stands over Cantor's chair, wraps his big arms around his old friend, and tells viewers about an Israel Bonds birthday celebration for Cantor slated for early February. The man of honor looks down and fidgets uncomfortably. As Jessel leaves, Cantor summons a final burst of energy, popping up and smiling to welcome the comedian Pinky Lee. After some brief banter with Lee, Cantor closes by gamely thanking the sponsors and each of his guests.[37]

When the show ended, Cantor collapsed into a chair at the studio. He was rushed to Cedars of Lebanon Hospital in Los Angeles, where he remained for three days. Cantor's personal physician, who accompanied him to all public performances, attributed the collapse to "exhaustion," but the star had actually suffered another heart attack during the program. The fact that he soldiered on and performed as well as he did, despite the glitches, is a testament to his pride and professionalism. Perhaps sensing that this would be his last splashy broadcast appearance, Cantor was determined not to step aside or show weakness on national television. While the January 1957 heart attack was not as serious as his 1952 ordeal, it squashed any further hope of starring in a live production.[38]

Cantor recovered well enough to board a flight from Los Angeles to Miami for the February 16 Israel Bonds gala in honor of his sixty-fifth birthday. More than two thousand people filled the Grand Ballroom of the Fontainebleau Hotel, while additional Israel supporters gathered in thirteen other cities to watch the event via closed-circuit television. Cantor's birthday party raised nearly $20 million in bond sales.[39]

Cantor received congratulatory telegrams from prominent figures in politics and show business, including many of the same well-wishers from a similar birthday gala held five years earlier. Several actors and politicians who were not part of the 1952 celebration also sent greetings. John Wayne proclaimed himself a "fan," as did Richard Nixon.[40] On the other side of the political aisle, former President Harry S. Truman, the featured speaker at the event, paid tribute to Cantor: "For about four decades now he had helped us to laugh—in bad times as well as good . . . Eddie Cantor has always worked to bring happiness into the lives of others. It is only natural that one of his abiding interests should be the State of Israel." Truman made news that night for his strong statement faulting the Eisenhower administration's "drift and procrastination" in the Middle East.[41]

Given the purpose of the event, Cantor downplayed his great skills and influence as a performer over the course of his career. Instead, he reminded his friends and followers of the value of supporting Israel. In a souvenir booklet essay, Cantor cited this philanthropic work as his greatest legacy. "I have lived a pretty full life. I have been blessed with a wonderful family. I have enjoyed a respectable amount of recognition," Cantor modestly reflected. "But I have found the greatest joy in my work for democracy and for the State of Israel. The existence of the State of Israel has taken the Jew off his knees and put him on his feet."[42] Cantor's statement about the importance of his work for Israel, and the way Israel brought pride and security to him and other Jews, was not empty rhetoric. Cantor found a meaningful and welcoming American Jewish community during his later years. He also raised a great deal of money for Israel: a country and a cause in which he believed. By the mid-1950s show business no longer provided similar financial and spiritual satisfaction. Stage fame may have seemed fleeting or inconsequential. As long as his health allowed him to do so, Cantor continued to appear at Israel Bonds events and to write articles in support of Israel.[43]

Eddie and Ida each dealt with medical scares related to their hearts while in Miami Beach. Eddie began looking pale the night before the gala. Ida treated her husband by giving him amyl nitrate to sniff. Eddie went to bed early that evening. He had recovered by the time of the event. The day after the party, Ida Cantor entered the Miami Heart Institute. Her diagnosis: an insufficient heartbeat. She remained in the hospital for three days. Eddie and Ida flew back to Los Angeles when Ida was able to travel again.[44]

Four weeks after the Cantors returned from Miami Beach, in March 1957, Cantor briefly fainted backstage before receiving an honorary Oscar as an "Ambassador of Goodwill." When he accepted the award, the actor made a humble fifteen-second statement: "I could mention the names of a hundred individuals in this industry to whom you might have given this award tonight. I feel that I am a symbol. For them and for myself, thank you." Cantor then walked off to a polite reception from the audience. It was the last time that he heard the applause of a large crowd. Cantor limited his future television appearances to short filmed guest spots.[45]

As he became more physically frail, Cantor rarely traveled. Working from his home in Beverly Hills and recording studios in Southern California, he still did what he could to generate income and remain in the public eye. Cantor made a series of short, syndicated radio pieces, *Ask Eddie Cantor*, covering everything from Los Angeles Dodgers pitchers to Lucy and Desi's divorce. He also published a new book, *The Way I See It* (1959), an engaging and likable summary of his life philosophy and lessons. Cantor ends the book with an upbeat meditation on how lucky he has been. He starts to list things he might have changed if he had his life to live over again: he would have "looked after his health" better or stayed out of the stock market during the 1920s. Then he stops himself: "No, I wouldn't! What I did was *me*. And what's the point of wondering. We can't go back. And anyway, I want to see what's up ahead. Thank you, Mr. God, for everything."[46]

Cantor faced a difficult life "up ahead." In May 1959, as he was finishing *The Way I See It*, his eldest daughter, Marjorie, died of cancer at age forty-four. Marjorie's death weakened the Cantors physically and emotionally. Ida suffered another heart attack in December 1959. Eddie was hospitalized in the late summer and fall of 1960, at the age of sixty-eight, following a heart attack. Ida, weakened by a bad heart, died in the Cantor home on August 8, 1962, at the age of seventy. Eddie was at home when Ida died, but he was staying in a different room. When Cantor received the news about his wife of forty-eight years, he collapsed in grief and went into a state of shock. A doctor placed him under sedation. Though Cantor had toured the world, by this time he could not even travel from his Beverly Hills home to nearby Hillside Memorial Park for Ida's funeral. Doctors believed that he was too weak and his body would not handle the stress of the funeral service.[47]

After Ida's death, Eddie stayed home even more, writing and watching television. He walked around the neighborhood for exercise, usually without being recognized. As the Los Angeles Times television critic Hal Humphrey noted, many people did not even know that he was still alive. During these years, Cantor's speech was slow and slurred, even though he retained sharp memories from his career. Bob Thomas, another reporter who visited Cantor, recalled that the actor "moved with a deliberateness of a man who knew he was existing on borrowed time." At the mention of Ida, "he dissolved in tears and had to leave the room."[48]

Shortly after his seventy-second birthday, on February 3, 1964, Cantor received a formal commendation from President Lyndon B. Johnson for his lifetime of humanitarian service. Since Cantor could not travel to Washington, the California governor, Edmund G. Brown, visited Cantor's home and personally delivered the citation. President Johnson sent a warm letter to Cantor, describing himself as a "devoted fan" and thanking Cantor for "making the world a happier place in which to live."[49]

On October 11, 1964, the New York Times tucked a small United Press International article in the corner of its front page, under more prominent coverage of the World Series, Queen Elizabeth's visit to Quebec, and South Vietnam's new constitution. Eddie Cantor had died of a coronary occlusion the day before, on October 10. He was seventy-two. Honoring Cantor's wishes, the family held a small, private funeral service in Los Angeles. The impersonal New York Times obituary reminded readers that Cantor was a "banjo-eyed vaudevillian whose dancing feet and double takes brought him stardom in movies, radio, and television."[50] Inside, the newspaper ran a short but insightful three-paragraph appreciation of Cantor that recognized his "greatness" as a comedian as well as his "special place in New York hearts."[51] The Washington Post buried an Associated Press article about the "banjo-eyed comic" on its back pages, next to the weather and a more prominent obituary for a local builder.[52] Other large daily newspapers similarly ran wire-service

California Governor Edmund G. (Pat) Brown reads a citation on behalf
of President Lyndon B. Johnson as Cantor (right) listens, in 1964.

articles. The modest obituaries illustrate how far Cantor had fallen off
the public radar after making headlines for so long.

Editors did not uniformly neglect Cantor. Speaking for Cantor's many
longtime fans, the *Hartford Courant* explained, "Entertainers like Mr.
Cantor hold a special place in the hearts of the American people because a special bond develops that makes most people feel they know
them personally. This was true particularly of Eddie Cantor."[53] *Variety*

similarly lauded Cantor and his generation of showmen: "They outlived and outlasted many a fleeting fad and/or catastrophic event because the warmth of their talent was long held in such high esteem as part and parcel of the American conscience."[54] With Cantor's death closely following those of Harpo Marx and Gracie Allen, the *Los Angeles Times* observed, "Suddenly it seemed that a whole golden era of show business had passed away, as indeed it had, for these three were irreplaceable veterans of a day when good humor characterized much of America's stage, films, and radio."[55]

Jewish newspapers claimed Cantor as a model Jew on and off the stage. The *Jewish Criterion* published a 150-word appreciation, concluding: "The happy go-lucky song and dance man exemplified a winning trait of the Jewish people—the ability to laugh at oneself and the world."[56] In the *Boston Jewish Advocate*, the copublisher Joseph G. Weisberg praised Cantor's "warn and capacious heart" and cataloged years of local charity appearances.[57] Writing in the *Southern Israelite*, Martin Silver chronicled Cantor's courageous battles against Nazism and his savvy contributions to Israel Bonds campaigns, noting that Cantor provided suggestions on campaign strategies in addition to appearing at the fund-raising events.[58] Nine different organizations, most of them Jewish, purchased obituary notices in the *New York Times* paying tribute to Cantor.[59] As Cantor had presciently recognized, his good deeds and charitable work offstage, especially for Jewish organizations, overshadowed his many years of performing as a headliner. For American Jews, Eddie Cantor was much more than the "banjo-eyed comic" of the wire-service obituaries.

EPILOGUE
EDDIE CANTOR'S LEGACY

P eople who grew up with Cantor and followed his long career in the public spotlight mourned his death and recognized the contributions that he had made to American life over the course of his career; however, the actor had become less culturally relevant by the 1960s. Cantor's nostalgic television routines from the 1950s rendered the show business veteran hopelessly outdated to younger critics and performers, who increasingly became cultural arbiters. His old songs, charitable appeals, self-promotion, need for audience approval, and faith in established Jewish and American institutions fell out of fashion. With his sentimental sketches and corny jokes, Cantor also epitomized a particularly Jewish style of comedy from which younger Jewish comics such as Lenny Bruce and Shelley Berman were distancing themselves. The fact that Cantor performed in blackface for so many years, and he remained associated with blackface even after he stopped wearing the burnt cork makeup, only made him appear more antiquated and unappealing.

Popular tastes in comedy shifted during the late 1950s. A new generation of comedians built their acts on improvisation, personal stories, sharp political satire, and unfiltered honesty.[1] In addressing current social and political issues, these fresh comics made show business icons such as Cantor, George Burns, Jack Benny, and Bob Hope seem like relics from another era. The new "rebel comedians" either ignored Cantor entirely or, in the case of Lenny Bruce, casually used Cantor as fodder for a hipper style of comedy. Bruce takes a sharp jab at Cantor's Jewish persona in his canonical "Jewish-goyish" monologue, introduced in 1961, three years before Cantor died.

Bruce divides the world into two categories: "Jewish" and "*goyish*" (Yiddish for non-Jewish). Bruce classifies the things that he likes as "Jewish." He uses the "goyish" label for bland, boring, archetypal American symbols. After defining "Jewish" and "goyish," Bruce begins his quirky typology: "Dig: I'm Jewish. Count Basie's Jewish. Ray Charles

George Jessel, George Burns, Cantor, and Jack Benny when they appeared together on an NBC special, *George Burns in the Big Time* (1959).

is Jewish. Eddie Cantor is goyish. B'nai B'rith is goyish. Hadassah, Jewish." Bruce then continues to assess everything from lime Jello (goyish) to Eugene O'Neill (Jewish). The monologue satirizes the Jewish need to demarcate insiders and outsiders even as it delineates an aesthetic for hipster Jews.[2]

Bruce's routine has had a long cultural life. The "goyish" pronouncement from Bruce has not helped Cantor's reputation over the years. Recent critics and performers have taken Bruce's cue in disassociating themselves from Cantor or dismissing him. For example, in a 2016 essay analyzing Bruce's monologue, the *Jewish Currents* editor Lawrence Bush speculates about why Bruce labels Cantor "goyish." Bush highlights Cantor's political and artistic conservatism, explaining that Cantor "rolled his eyes like a black-face comic, and he dealt in unsophisticated immigrant humor with little social bite."[3] Through a collective silence, many others have implicitly shared Bush's assessment or have simply found no reason to revisit Cantor's body of work.

Cantor certainly wore blackface and referenced Jewish immigrant culture, as Bush suggests. But Cantor's humor, especially on Broadway and radio, was sophisticated and socially relevant to national audiences. Cantor merits a more central place in the history of American comedy. From the late 1910s through the early 1940s, he provided a model for expressing Jewish identity in popular entertainment. Countless performers since the 1950s have presented Jewishness in similar terms to those of Cantor: as a form of cultural expression rooted in urban immigrant experiences from the early twentieth century. Like Cantor, more recent comedians have signified Jewishness through jokes referencing the Lower East Side, Jewish foods, and religious holidays. They have delivered this comedy with a New York accent, spiced with Yiddish. Cantor also developed a range of recognizably Jewish characters that have remained central to Jewish comedy, though Cantor's importance in popularizing these archetypes during the first decades of the twentieth century has been lost or forgotten. For example, Cantor crafted a template for Lenny Bruce's aggressive rebel; Woody Allen's neurotic nebbish; Jerry Lewis's or Andy Kaufman's nut job; Sarah Silverman's wide-eyed ingénue with a surprisingly lewd side; Larry David's angry crank railing against everyday indignities; Rodney Dangerfield's victim who can't win respect; and Jon Stewart's secular Jew casually joking about Jewish holidays and foods before non-Jewish audiences.

Mel Brooks, one of the few comedians of the 1960s and 1970s to cite Cantor as an influence, was old enough to remember Cantor's fresh, innovative radio work from the 1930s. In a 1994 interview, Brooks described Cantor as a "great entertainer," citing Cantor's "fast and furious" radio sketches as well as his "genius at comic timing."[4] The two performers also shared a fondness for parodies of Hitler and Nazism. In fact, Brooks's *The Producers* (1967) took this humor to a level that would have been impossible for Cantor during World War II.

Since the 1960s, Jewish comedians have enjoyed more options for expressing themselves as Jews, and explicitly discussing Jewish culture and politics, than Cantor did during the first half of the twentieth century. Yet Jewish celebrities continue to struggle with the questions of how much to identify as Jews and what it means to "act Jewish." Many entertainers today deploy the familiar codes signifying Jewish identity without addressing more difficult and potentially controversial issues. For example, Jewish performers rarely use the tools at their disposal to combat antisemitism. They have not followed Cantor's model by force-fully responding to attacks on Jews and the proliferation of antisemitic conspiracy theories in the United States and globally.[5] In addition, recent celebrities have not matched Cantor's tireless commitment to Jewish communal organizations and his principled engagement with politics from an explicitly Jewish perspective. Instead, entertainers ad-vance their favored social and political issues through groups without Jewish affiliations. As Cantor's career demonstrated, Jewish-identified activism is difficult and risky, on and off the stage.

The television program *Broad City* (Comedy Central, 2014–) illustrates the way contemporary comedians explore Jewish social life without ap-pearing "too Jewish." Abbi Jacobson and Ilana Glazer, two Jewish ac-tors, created *Broad City*. Jacobson and Glazer also co-write the episodes and star as Abbi Abrams and Ilana Wexler. The likeable lead characters frequently reference their Jewish identities, yet they are unenthusias-tic about Jewish institutions and the kind of Jewish political advocacy that Cantor practiced offstage and occasionally incorporated into his commercial productions. In two raunchy April 2016 episodes filled with insider Jewish jokes, Jacobson and Glazer parody Birthright Israel, a program that sponsors free trips to Israel for Jewish adults between the ages of eighteen and twenty-six. The comedians present Birthright Is-rael as a misguided, ridiculous effort to counter endogamy.[6] On the one hand, the *Broad City* episodes epitomize how much the media landscape has changed since Cantor's heyday. A prime-time parody of a relatively obscure Jewish communal program would have been impossible during Cantor's time on radio and television. On the other hand, *Broad City's* comedy is safe. Like many other recent comedians, Jacobson and Glazer poke fun at conventional aspects of American Judaism, such as Jew-ish consumerism, religious observance, character types (especially the Jewish mother), Holocaust remembrance, and support for Israel. This humor allows Jacobson and Glazer to distance themselves from other Jews, especially those who conform to more traditional models or seem to fit the *Broad City* stereotypes. The *Broad City* stars affirm their Jew-ishness through jokes about contemporary Jewish life that appeal to like-minded viewers. But the program does not promote a coherent or viable American Jewish social identity, beyond the wisecracks targeting mainstream Jewish practices and institutions.

Music writers and performers have been kinder to Cantor than have those who focus on his postwar radio and television comedy. While Cantor's use of blackface still influences popular perceptions of him, writers have considered this blackface alongside other elements of his persona. In his *Visions of Jazz*, Gary Giddins recalls that he learned to "look anew" at Cantor and "a generation of performers I had reflexively rejected" after an interview with the African-American actor Avon Long. Giddins asked Long whom he had most admired when starting out. Long replied, "Eddie Cantor." Giddens continued, "I grimaced and asked if he wasn't offended by the blackface. He sat up and asked heatedly, 'Do you think black people are stupid?' 'Of course not,' I sputtered. 'Well,' he crowed, 'don't you think *we* can appreciate genius, too?'"[7] Will Friedwald, author of the definitive *Biographical Guide to the Great Jazz and Pop Singers* (2010), similarly recognizes that Cantor's use of blackface did not negate his power as a performer. Friedwald observes that "where blackface makes Al Jolson seem surreal, like a harlequin figure, Cantor comes across as a real person, one with contagious enthusiasm, bouncing all over the stage like a man on a trampoline." In surveying Cantor's recordings, Friedwald praises Cantor as a "great entertainer, a colossal figure in American vernacular culture." He points to Cantor's "laid-back, semi-sung approach" in "Makin' Whoopee" as "a textbook model of how to put over a lyric."[8]

Cantor's versions of "Makin' Whoopee" circulate on Jazz Age compilation CDs and playlists.[9] Artists as varied as Cyndi Lauper (with Tony Bennett), Norah Jones, and Harry Nilsson have covered the Gus Kahn–Walter Donaldson composition. Allan Sherman's "Taking Lessons" (1966) provides new lyrics to the familiar melody, transforming the target of parody from marriage to the modern family and consumerism. Michelle Pfeiffer's slinky version of the song remains a highlight of *The Fabulous Baker Boys* (1989), though self-described "punk cabaret" singer Amanda Palmer's wry 2012 duet with husband Neil Gaiman best captures the spirit of Cantor's original.[10]

As the continued popularity of "Makin' Whoopee" suggests, Cantor has found champions among aficionados of popular entertainment from the first half of the twentieth century. Cantor has many fans on Facebook. One Facebook group, the Eddie Cantor Fan Club, is devoted strictly to Cantor. Another group, on vaudeville, frequently includes posts about him.[11] Cantor's daughter, Janet Cantor Gari, has published two family memoirs. Cantor's grandson, Brian Gari (Janet Cantor Gari's son), has released twelve CDs and six DVDs compiling rare Eddie Cantor music, radio shows, and television programs.[12] In addition, Martin Scorsese and his collaborators on the TV series *Boardwalk Empire* (HBO, 2010–2014) use Cantor as a character in several episodes to evoke the Jazz Age. Though Cantor tried to distance himself from criminals during his lifetime, the fictional Cantor of *Boardwalk Empire* provides a light touch amid the violent world of Atlantic City gangsters. The series revived obscure Cantor songs and performances that capture the spirit of the 1920s.

Cantor remains a particular favorite among American Jews. Synagogues and community centers frequently host Great American Songbook discussions and performances. The smooth, witty music, including Cantor's Broadway hits from the late 1910s and the 1920s, represents an enduring Jewish contribution to American popular culture. Similarly, Cantor and his contemporaries figure prominently in nostalgic public programs that cover everything from Jewish comedy to Broadway musicals to the Lower East Side. Old photographs of Cantor appearing at local events hold valued places in family and communal archives, alongside Cantor's recordings, sheet music, and autographs. Cantor provides Jews today with a symbolic link to American Jewish history and the cultures of parents, grandparents, and great-grandparents. The process of remembering celebrities from Cantor's era, including the sharing of music and video clips from these performers, also connects American Jews with each other. In *Entertaining America*, a landmark 2003 Jewish Museum (New York) exhibit and catalog, the cocurators, J. Hoberman and Jeffrey Shandler, highlighted the symbolic importance of entertainers in enabling fans to create a "collective Jewish experience."[13] The exhibit chronicled the history of Jews and Jewish discourse in popular culture. Hoberman and Shandler placed Cantor in their "Star Gallery" of twenty-two celebrities who each provided different perspectives on Jewish stardom in American film and broadcasting.

Like Hoberman and Shandler, the members of the Idelsohn Society for Musical Preservation suggest ways in which the history of Jewish popular culture, including Cantor's work, may inform contemporary efforts to construct Jewish identities. The group collects and reissues

Jewish music from throughout the twentieth century. The Idelsohn Society's mission is "to incite a new conversation about the present by listening anew to the past." This statement appears at the end of the liner notes to *Jewface* (2006), a compilation of "Hebrew comedy" songs and routines released between 1906 and 1924. The liner notes, written by Jody Rosen, acknowledge the obvious stereotypes of the music. But Rosen also appreciates the artistry of the songs and examines how the dialect music appealed to Jewish audiences and influenced later performers. *Jewface* includes a version of "My Yiddisha Mammy" co-written by Cantor and recorded by Irving Kaufman.[14] Another Idelsohn Society release, *'Twas the Night before Hanukkah: The Musical Battle between Christmas and the Festival of Lights* (2012), compiles two discs of music. One disc presents Hanukkah music, with liner notes connecting the songs to postwar American Jewish social history. The second disc features Christmas songs written or performed by Jews. The release epitomizes the way the Idelsohn Society blurs standard categories and provides surprising, fresh perspectives on Jewish musical history. *'Twas the Night before Hanukkah* includes Cantor's obscure 1939 release, "The Only Thing I Want for Christmas." The CD's liner notes commend Cantor's subtlety in delivering the "socially conscious" plea for peace instead of the usual holiday "consumer blitz."[15]

Cantor's presence in recent popular music, Facebook pages, television programs, museum exhibits, and Jewish music CD compilations illustrates how a range of creators and consumers of popular culture have been inspired by different aspects of Cantor's music and acting. These complimentary responses to Cantor in the years since his death in 1964 balance a less-flattering image of Cantor as nostalgic, assimilationist, and stereotypical. Attempts to grapple with Cantor's history, including negative appraisals, demonstrate Cantor's ongoing relevance as an entertainer and a Jew. Cantor's life and work also resonate more subtly in Jewish magazines, such as *Tablet*, and public programs at museums, community centers, and synagogues. Cantor shaped the twentieth-century Jewish history and culture that fuels these continuing efforts to redefine Jewish identity and build community in contemporary America. He provides a model for negotiating Jewish identities while making Jewish voices and perspectives central to American social, cultural, and political life.

This book has been a journey of recovery and rediscovery: taking a figure who has been largely forgotten, understanding him in the context of his times, and assessing Cantor's influence as a Jewish entertainer, social commentator, and political activist. The world has changed since Cantor died in 1964. But the challenges and possibilities of reimagining and reaffirming American Jewish politics and culture remain vital.

NOTES

INTRODUCTION

1 Neal Gabler's widely cited *An Empire of Their Own: How the Jews Invented Hollywood* remains the most thorough examination of the ways in which "Hollywood Jews effaced their Judaism as a means of being accepted." Gabler focuses on Hollywood executives and the films that they made during the first half of the twentieth century, but he also argues that, under the Hollywood system, actors were forced to hide their Jewishness. See Neal Gabler, *An Empire of Their Own: How the Jews Invented Hollywood* (New York: Crown, 1988), 168, 303.

2 For more on "coded" Jewish performances in popular entertainment, see Henry Bial, *Acting Jewish: Negotiating Ethnicity on the American Stage and Screen* (Ann Arbor: University of Michigan Press, 2005), 3, 16-21. Bial focuses on ethnic coding from 1947 to 1997.

3 "President Franklin D. Roosevelt Reads a Telegram from Eddie Cantor," track 20, *Pals: Eddie Cantor and George Jessel*, produced by Brian Gari, Original Cast OC-9918, 1999, compact disc; Felix Belair Jr., "Roosevelt Carves Turkey, Not Map," *New York Times*, November 25, 1938.

4 Richard Nixon to Eddie Cantor, February 11, 1957, box 74, Eddie Cantor Papers, UCLA Library Special Collections, Los Angeles, CA; hereafter, cited as Cantor Papers UCLA.

1. IMMIGRANTS, CRIMINALS, AND ACTORS (1892–1908)

1 Eddie Cantor as told to David Freedman, *My Life Is in Your Hands* (1928; repr., New York: Cooper Square Press, 2000), 9. Cantor biographer Herbert Goldman claims that Cantor was born "on Rosh Hashanah," a holiday that encompasses three calendar days, in September 1892. See Herbert Goldman, *Banjo Eyes: Eddie Cantor and the Birth of Modern Stardom* (New York: Oxford University Press, 1997), 4. Goldman does not provide a specific birth date or indicate the evidence for this claim. There is no extant birth certificate for Cantor. I take the spelling, "Iskowitz," from the earliest extant Cantor family document: the 1894 death certificate for Meta Iskowitz. See Death Certificate for Meta Iskowitz, July 25, 1894, no. 25373, State of New York, certified copy in possession of author. Cantor and others spelled his surname several different ways over the years, and I retain these spellings when quoting from these materials. For example, Cantor calls himself "Isidore Itzkowitz" in Eddie Cantor with Jane Kesner Ardmore, *Take My Life* (1957; repr., New York: Cooper Square Press, 2000), 13.

2 Gur Alroey, *Bread to Eat and Clothes to Wear: Letters from Jewish Migrants in the Early Twentieth Century* (Detroit: Wayne State University Press, 2001), 9; Annie Polland and Daniel Soyer, *Emerging Metropolis: New York Jews in the Age of Immigration, 1840–1920* (New York: New York University Press, 2013), 111–13.

3 The available information on Esther Kantrowitz's life before she arrived in the United States is murky and contradictory. Here, I use the birth year of 1834, taken from Eddie Cantor's writings. This birth year also appears in Esther Cantor's burial record and in Herbert Goldman's biography of Cantor. See Cantor and Freedman, *My Life Is in Your Hands*, 15; Cantor and Ardmore, *Take My Life*, 12; Esther Cantor, burial record, JewishGen Online Worldwide Birth Registry, online database, www.jewishgen.org; Goldman, *Banjo Eyes*, 3–5. Census sources list other birth years for Esther. The United States Census of 1910 gives the year as 1849, and the New York State Census of 1915 reports it as 1840. See p. 14a [handwritten], line 29, Enumeration District 0053, New York, NY, *Thirteenth Census of the United States, 1910* (National Archives Microfilm Publication T624, roll 1007), Records of the Bureau of the Census, Record Group 29, online database, www.ancestry.com; p. 25 [handwritten], line 24, Assembly District 8, New York, NY, *State Population Census Schedules, 1915*, New York State Archives, Albany, NY, online database, www.ancestry.com.

4 Cantor and Freedman, *My Life Is in Your Hands*, 13–14.

5 Cantor and Ardmore, *Take My Life*, 12; Cantor and Freedman, *My Life Is in Your Hands*, 6, 11. In his biography of Cantor, Herbert Goldman speculates that Mechel abandoned Eddie and Esther after the death of Meta. In contrast, Eddie Cantor's grandson, Brian Gari, who has conducted research on his family's history, discovered that a man named Max Itzkovitz died in 1896. Gari suggests it is "quite possible that this was the Michael Cantor that Eddie named in his books." Gari also found evidence that Eddie had a younger sister, Lena, who died as an infant shortly after their mother Meta passed away. Eddie never mentioned the younger sister. See Goldman, *Banjo Eyes*, 5; Brian Gari, addendum to *My Life Is in Your Hands and Take My Life*, by Eddie Cantor with David Freedman and Jane Kesner Ardmore (New York: Cooper Square Press, 2000), 289–90.

6 Jewish charities and social workers began to focus on the problem of desertion in 1900. The National Council of Jewish Charities founded the National Desertion Bureau (NDB) in 1911 to locate deserters and provide financial support to the families they left behind. The NDB handled nearly ten thousand cases during its first six years. See Reena Sigman Friedman, "'Send Me My Husband Who Is in New York City': Husband Desertion in the American Jewish Immigrant Community 1900–1926," *Jewish Social Studies* 44 (1982): 9–10; Jenna Weissman Joselit, "Modern Jewish Family in the United States," in *Jewish Women: A Comprehensive Historical Encyclopedia*, ed. Paula Hyman and Dalia Ofer, Jewish Women's Archive, 2006, www.jwa.org/encyclopedia; Polland and Soyer, *Emerging Metropolis*, 142–43.

7 Cantor and Ardmore, *Take My Life*, 13–15; Goldman, *Banjo Eyes*, 13–14; see also p. 14a [handwritten], line 29, Enumeration District 0053, New York, NY, *Thirteenth Census of the United States, 1910*; p. 25 [handwritten], line 24, Assembly District 8, New York, NY, *State Population Census Schedules, 1915*.

8 Polland and Soyer, *Emerging Metropolis*, 114; David Nasaw, *Children of the City: At Work and at Play* (Garden City, NY: Anchor Press, 1985), 9.

9 Cantor and Ardmore, *Take My Life*, 11. Also see Cantor and Freedman *My Life Is in Your Hands*, 16, 35.

10 Cantor and Freedman, *My Life Is in Your Hands*, 20–22.

11 Cantor and Ardmore, *Take My Life*, 16–19.

12 Eddie Cantor, *The Way I See It*, ed. Phyllis Rosenteur (Englewood Cliffs, NJ: Prentice-Hall, 1959), 77; Cantor and Freedman, *My Life Is in Your Hands*, 161.

13 Cantor and Freedman, *My Life Is in Your Hands*, 26–27.

14 US Bureau of the Census, *Bicentennial Edition: Historical Statistics of the United States, Colonial Times to 1970*, pt. 2 (Washington, DC: Government Printing Office, 1976), 379; Neal Gabler, *Winchell* (New York: Knopf, 1994), 16. Polland and Soyer, *Emerging Metropolis*, 122; Nasaw, *Children of the City*, 46–47; Stephan F. Brumberg, *Going to America, Going to School: The Jewish Immigrant Public School Encounter in Turn-of-the-Century New York City* (New York: Praeger, 1986), 184–89.

15 Cantor and Freedman, *My Life Is in Your Hands*, 48.

16 Cantor, and Ardmore, *Take My Life*, 14.

17 Ibid., 19.

18 Cantor and Freedman, *My Life Is in Your Hands*, 41, 72–73.

19 Ibid., 39.

20 See, for example, Arnold M. Auerbach, *Funny Men Don't Laugh* (Garden City, NY: Doubleday, 1965), 26. Auerbach used the pseudonyms Jerry Wilson (for Cantor) and Lou Jacobs (for writer David Freedman); Bob Weiskopf, interview, in Jordan R. Young, *The Laugh Crafters: Comedy Writing in Radio and TV's Golden Age* (Beverly Hills, CA: Past Times Publishing, 1999), 143–45; Harry von Zell, interview, *Same Time, Same Station*, syndicated, original airdate May 21, 1972, MP3 file, author's private collection.

21 Von Zell, *Same Time, Same Station*.

22 Cantor and Ardmore, *Take My Life*, 13; Cantor and Freedman, *My Life Is in Your Hands*, 76. In rare cases, Cantor may have performed entire monologues in Yiddish early in his career. See George Jessel, *So Help Me* (Cleveland, OH: World, 1946), 12.

23 Cantor and Freedman, *My Life Is in Your Hands*, 47.

24 Ibid., 75–76, 91.

25 "Last of Historic Playhouse," *Dramatic Mirror*, Oct 30, 1912, 13; Robert W. Snyder, *The Voice of the City: Vaudeville and Popular Culture in New York* (1989; Chicago: Ivan R. Dee, 2000 ed.), 99; John E. DiMeglio, *Vaudeville USA* (Bowling Green, OH: Bowling Green University Popular Press, 1973), 66–67.

26 Cantor and Freedman, *My Life Is in Your Hands*, 79.

27 When and where Cantor changed his name is murky. Cantor claimed that when he was six and his grandmother registered him for school, Esther became flustered

and misstated her name as "Kanter." When he later transferred schools, young Izzy changed the spelling of his last name and also adopted the Americanized first name of Eddie. See Cantor and Ardmore, *Take My Life*, 13. The Kantrowitzes probably changed their names more deliberately around 1900. Esther is listed as "Ida Cantor" in the 1910 United States Census and the 1915 New York State Census. She was buried in 1917 as "Esther Cantor." Eddie's uncle, Saul Cantor, also Americanized his name. See p.14a [handwritten], line 29, Enumeration District 0053, New York, NY, *Thirteenth Census of the United States*; p. 25 [handwritten], line 24, Assembly District 8, New York, NY, *State Population Census Schedules, 1915*; Esther Cantor, JewishGen Online Worldwide Birth Registry; "News from the Dailies," *Variety*, May 8, 1929, 58.

28 Cantor and Freedman, *Take My Life*, 81.

29 Joe Laurie Jr., *Vaudeville from the Honky Tonks to the Palace* (New York: Henry Holt, 1953), 86, 193; Frank Cullen, *Vaudeville, Old and New: An Encyclopedia of Variety Performers*, vol. 1 (New York: Routledge, 2007), 447–48.

30 Cantor and Freedman, *My Life Is in Your Hands*, 82–85.

31 Schenck, "Inside Vaudeville," 33; Laurie Jr., *Vaudeville from the Honky Tonks*, 245–46; "2,000 Small-time Theatres in Vaudeville Next Season," *Variety*, July 3, 1909, 4.

32 George Burns, *All My Best Friends* (New York: Putnam, 1989), 41.

33 Cantor earned five dollars a week as a runner in a brokerage house and seven dollars a week as a clerk at a clothing retailer: two short-term jobs at which he worked circa 1910. See Goldman, *Banjo Eyes*, 25; Cantor and Freedman, *My Life Is in Your Hands*, 68–70. For more on work, wages, and expenses on the Lower East Side during this time, see Polland and Soyer, *Emerging Metropolis*, 118–23.

34 Trav S. D., *No Applause, Just Throw Money* (New York: Faber and Faber, 2005), 177; Joseph M. Schenck, "Inside Vaudeville," *Variety*, December 20, 1912, 33; Snyder, *The Voice of the City*, 45–47.

35 Minnie Marx is quoted in Charlotte Chandler, *Hello I Must Be Going: Groucho and His Friends* (New York: Simon and Schuster, 2012), 51; Simon Louvish, *Monkey Business: The Lives and Legends of the Marx Brothers* (New York: St. Martin's Press, 1999), 21. According to Chandler, Marx came to America in 1880; according to Louvish, she arrived in 1879.

36 Snyder, *The Voice of the City*, 52; Lawrence J. Epstein, *Gorge Burns: An American Life* (Jefferson, NC: McFarland, 2011), 17–21.

2. A VAUDEVILLE EDUCATION (1908–1916)

1 Cantor and Freedman, *My Life Is in Your Hands*, 88–89. Cantor remembers being stranded in Shenandoah, Pennsylvania; but according to Goldman, the company played additional dates in Pennsylvania and West Virginia before the manager abandoned the company. The *New York Dramatic Mirror* reports that *Indian Maidens* played in several Pennsylvania theaters in January 1909, but the newspaper does not include information on the small West Virginia venues that may have presented

......

the show. See "Correspondence," *New York Dramatic Mirror*, January 9, 1909, 20; "Correspondence," *New York Dramatic Mirror*, January 30, 1909, 24; Goldman, *Banjo Eyes*, 22, 317–18.

2 Cantor and Freedman, *My Life Is in Your Hands*, 96.

3 Ibid., 99.

4 Ibid., 96–101; see also Jimmy Durante and Jack Kofoed, *Night Clubs* (New York: Knopf, 1931), 83.

5 Cantor and Freedman, *My Life Is in Your Hands*, 97.

6 Ibid.,105–10.

7 "His Persistency Made Him a Star," *Philadelphia Inquirer*, November 28, 1920. Cantor's autobiographies are incomplete and inconsistent with other evidence and sources covering his employment from 1909 to 1911. Cantor recalls working for a short time at two different companies, J. C. Weir and the National Cloak and Suit Company, at around age sixteen, before he began his stage career in 1909. It seems more likely, however, that he worked at these jobs when he was a little older. Cantor provides detailed information about these positions in his autobiographies, suggesting that he held the jobs for several weeks or months. The 1910 United States Census indicates that Cantor worked as a stock runner in a broker's office: the kind of work that he did at J. C. Weir. See p.14a [handwritten], line 30, Enumeration District 0053, New York, NY, *Thirteenth Census of the United States, 1910*; Cantor and Freedman, *My Life Is in Your Hands*, 68–71; Cantor and Ardmore, *Take My Life*, 20. In his biography of Cantor, Herbert Goldman asserts that Cantor worked at J. C. Weir from October 1909 to June 1910 and National Cloak and Suit from August 1910 to January 1911. See Goldman, *Banjo Eyes*, 24–26, 318.

8 George Jessel, *So Help Me* (Cleveland, OH: World, 1943), 8–12. At the Edwards audition, Jessel recognized Cantor as having been a frequent performer at the Imperial. Cantor does not mention performing at the Imperial in his memoirs.

9 Jessel, *So Help Me*, 11–15. Jessel remembers the audition for *Benches in the Park* and Cantor's first appearance with Bedini and Arthur as having occurred in 1909, though contemporary sources indicate that the events took place in 1910. *Variety* published two short pieces in 1910 on the casting of *Benches in the Park*. See [no headline], *Variety*, July 2, 1910, 5; [no headline], *Variety*, July 9, 1910, 5. Jessel recalls seeing Cantor a few days after their Gus Edwards audition at the New Brighton Theatre, where Cantor was assisting Bedini and Arthur. Jessel lists the entire bill, in order of appearance. These acts performed together at the New Brighton Theatre on May 16, 1910. See Jessel, *So Help Me*, 14–15; "News of the Theaters," *Brooklyn Daily Eagle*, May 8, 1910; [no headline], Variety, May 14, 1910; "Paris Nightlife in Vaudeville Pantomime," *New York Herald*, May 17, 1910. In his biography of Walter Winchell, a singing partner of Jessel's, Neal Gabler also dates the first Edwards performances to 1910, not 1909. See Gabler, *Winchell* (New York: Knopf, 1994), 15, 18.

10 Sime Silverman, review of "Madame Ten," *Variety*, June 4, 1910.

11 Burns, *All My Best Friends*, 42.

12 "The Hippodrome," *Utica Sunday Tribune* (Utica, NY), March 3, 1911.

13 Cantor and Ardmore, *Take My Life*, 64–65; Goldman, *Banjo Eyes*, 29. Cantor also wore blackface for at least one of his earlier upstate New York engagements, at the Burtis Grand Theatre in Auburn, New York. See "In the Playhouses," *Auburn Citizen*, March 1, 1911.

14 David Nasaw, *Going Out: The Rise and Fall of Public Amusements* (New York: Basic Books, 1993), 49–54; Allen Woll, *Black Musical Theatre: From Coontown to Dreamgirls* (Baton Rouge: Louisiana State University Press, 1989), 50–51; Snyder, *Voice of the City*, 121; DiMeglio, *Vaudeville USA*, 113–16.

15 Laurie Jr., *Vaudeville from the Honky Tonks*, 139.

16 Cantor and Freedman, *My Life Is in Your Hands*, 114–15.

17 Burns, *All My Best Friends*, 36.

18 Laurie Jr., *Vaudeville from the Honky Tonks*, 139; see also review of "Frank Tinney," *Variety*, June 4, 1910, 22.

19 Cantor and Freedman, *My Life Is in Your Hands*, 122.

20 For more on female impersonation, see Susan Glenn, *Female Spectacle: The Theatrical Roots of Modern Feminism* (Cambridge: Harvard University Press, 2000), 110–11; Robert C. Allen, *Horrible Prettiness: Burlesque and American Culture* (Chapel Hill: University of North Carolina Press, 1991), 168; Eric Lott, *Love and Theft: Blackface Minstrelsy and the American Working Class* (New York: Oxford University Press, 1993), 159–68; Robert C. Toll, *Blacking Up: The Minstrel Show in Nineteenth Century America* (New York: Oxford University Press, 1974), 142–45.

21 Dash., "Fifth Avenue," *Variety*, March 2, 1912, 18.

22 Mark., "Henderson's," *Variety*, July 5, 1912, 17.

23 Eric L. Goldstein discusses how Jewish racial ambivalence troubled white Americans. See Goldstein, *The Price of Whiteness: Jews, Race, and American Identity* (Princeton, NJ: Princeton University Press, 2006), 41–42. Michael Alexander argues that blackface helped Jews express and navigate their positions as social outsiders. See Alexander, *Jazz Age Jews* (Princeton, NJ: Princeton University Press, 2001), 277.

24 Cantor and Ardmore, *Take My Life*, 65–67. Early references to Cantor's cobilling appear in "What Is Going on in the Theatres," *New York Sun*, February 25, 1912; "Eva Fay Humorist," *Syracuse Post Standard*, March 12, 1912. Additional reviews of Bedini and Arthur from the late spring and summer of 1912 mention Cantor's assistance. See, for example, "Eva Tanguay," *Buffalo Morning Express*, April 9, 1912; "Varieties, Roofs, and Parks," *New York Tribune*, June 23, 1912; "Keith's Union Square," *New York Clipper*, June 29, 1912, 7.

25 Burns, *All My Best Friends*, 43.

26 Goldman, *Banjo Eyes*, 318; "Eva Tanguay," *Buffalo Morning Express*, April 9, 1912; "Eva Tanguay at Orpheum; 'Madame X' at Greenpoint," *Brooklyn Daily Eagle*, May 19, 1912; "Bills Next Week," *Variety*, December 9, 1911, 23; "Hammerstein's Roof Opens,"

New York Dramatic Mirror, June 12, 1912, 13; "Eddie Cantor's Farewell to a Friend," *Daily Variety*, May 2, 1957, 11.

27 See, for example, Groucho Marx, *Groucho and Me* (1959; repr., New York: Manor Books, 1974); Jessel, *So Help Me*; Cantor and Ardmore, *Take My Life*, 104; Cantor and Freedman, *My Life Is in Your Hands*, 134; "Edmonton, Canada," *New York Clipper*, July 5, 1913, 19; "'Kid Kabaret' Is Headline," *Oregonian* (Portland), July 5, 1913.

28 Cantor and Freedman, *My Life Is in Your Hands*, 134.

29 Cantor and Ardmore, *Take My Life*, 80.

30 Goldman, *Banjo Eyes*, 37–41, 320; "The Week's Play Bills," *Washington Herald*, September 15, 1912; unsigned review of *Kid Kabaret*, *New York Clipper*, September 7, 1912, 11; "Palace" (Chicago), *New York Clipper*, October 12, 1912, 13; Jolo, review of *Kid Kabaret*, *Variety*, September 6, 1912, 25; "Lyric," *Oregonian* (Portland), July 15, 1913; Cantor and Freedman, *My Life Is in Your Hands*, 132.

31 Ibid., 140–42; Goldman, *Banjo Eyes*, 42, 322.

32 Ibid., 43; Cantor and Freedman, *My Life Is in Your Hands*, 158.

33 In his 1957 autobiography, Cantor claimed that he wrote all of the act's material because he could not afford a writer; but in several trade magazine advertisements, Madison listed Cantor and Lee among his clients. See, for example, James Madison, advertisement, *New York Dramatic Mirror*, October 23, 1915, 21; James Madison, advertisement, *New York Dramatic Mirror*, February 26, 1916, 22; James Madison, advertisement, *Variety*, April 7, 1916, 39; Jack, "Vaudeville Whispers," *Billboard*, October 17, 1914, 75.

34 Cantor and Ardmore, *Take My Life*, 97.

35 Cantor and Freedman, *My Life Is in Your Hands*, 144–46.

36 Unsigned review of Cantor and Lee, *Variety*, November 21, 1914, 20.

37 Cantor and Freedman, *My Life Is in Your Hands*, 145. Cantor and Ardmore, *Take My Life*, 97.

38 Cantor and Freedman, *My Life Is in Your Hands*, 147.

39 Unsigned review of Cantor and Lee, *Variety*, November 21, 1914, 20.

40 "Colonial," *New York Clipper*, October 30, 1915, 11.

41 "'Canary Cottage' Will Return to Victory November 22," *San Jose Evening News*, November 16, 1916.

42 Ken Bloom, *The Routledge Guide to Broadway* (New York: Routledge, 2007), 176.

3. THE JEWISH WISE GUY (1916–1919)

1 Rennold Wolf, review of *Midnight Frolic*, *New York Telegraph*, October 4, 1916.

2 Cantor and Ardmore, *Take My Life*, 118.

3 Unsigned review of *Midnight Frolic*, *New York American*, October 4, 1916; see also unsigned review of *Midnight Frolic*, *Variety*, October 20, 1916, 18; Ethan Mordden, *Ziegfeld* (New York: St. Martin's Press, 2008), 143–44.

4 M. L. A., review of *Ziegfeld Follies*, *Dramatic Mirror*, June 30, 1920, 18; New York Pub-

lic Library for the Performing Arts, *The Great American Revue: How Florenz Ziegfeld, George White and Their Rivals Remade Broadway* (New York: New York Public Library, 2012), 4; unsigned review of *Midnight Frolic*, *New York Times*, October 4, 1916; "Ziegfeld Midnight Frolic in Roof Garden Like Lively Cabaret at Close Quarters," *New York Herald*, January 7, 1915; "New 'Midnight Frolic' Affords Tonic for Tired Business Man," *New York World*, June 25, 1916.

5 Cantor and Ardmore, *Take My Life*, 117–18.

6 Ibid., 118; see also Heywood Brown, review of *Midnight Frolic*, *New York Tribune*, October 9, 1916.

7 Unsigned review of *Midnight Frolic*, *Dramatic Mirror*, October 14, 1916.

8 See, for example, unsigned review of *Midnight Frolic*, *Variety*, October 20, 1916, 18; unsigned review of *Midnight Frolic*, *New York Evening Telegram*, October 3, 1916; unsigned review of *Midnight Frolic*, *New York Times*, October 4, 1916; Peter M. Robinson, *The Dance of the Comedians* (Amherst: University of Massachusetts Press, 2010), 64–65; Cantor and Freedman, *My Life Is in Your Hands*, 155.

9 "The Story of Eddie Cantor," *New York Times*, June 29, 1919; Cantor and Ardmore, *Take My Life*, 118–19.

10 Cantor and Freedman, *My Life Is in Your Hands*, 158–59, 177; "Ziegfeld Girls Leaving," *Variety*, February 2, 1917, 1; "Players Engaged," *New York Clipper*, February 7, 1917, 23.

11 Cantor and Freedman, *My Life Is in Your Hands*, 157.

12 See, for example, "Obituaries," *Variety*, February 1, 1918, 24; "Obituaries," *Variety*, January 31, 1920, 25; "Obituaries," *Variety*, September 17, 1920, 6.

13 Cantor and Freedman, *My Life Is in Your Hands*, 157.

14 Descriptions of the *Ziegfeld Follies* shows from 1917 to 1919 are taken from contemporary reviews. See also Ann Ommen van der Merwe, *The Ziegfeld Follies: A History in Song* (Lanham, MD: Scarecrow Press, 2012), 107–35; Gene Buck and Victor Herbert, "Can't You Hear Your Country Calling" (New York: T. B. Harms and Francis, Day, and Hunter, 1917).

15 Cantor and Ardmore, *Take My Life*, 44; Roberta W. Grossman, *Funny Woman: The Life and Times of Fanny Brice* (Bloomington, IN: Indiana University Press, 1991), 105–6.

16 Edward Foote Gardner, *Popular Songs of the Twentieth Century*, vol. 1: 1900–1949 (St. Paul, MN: Paragon House, 2000), 75–76.

17 Sime Silverman, review of *Ziegfeld Follies*, *Variety*, June 15, 1917, 18; see also The Playgoer, review of *Ziegfeld Follies*, *New York Evening Sun*, June 13, 1917; unsigned review of *Ziegfeld Follies*, *New York Evening Telegram*, June 13, 1917.

18 Broadway Music Corporation, advertisement, *Variety*, February 22, 1918, 27.

19 For more on middle-class Victorian attitudes toward leisure and pleasure, see Michael McGerr, *A Fierce Discontent: The Rise and Fall of the Progressive Movement in America* (New York: Oxford University Press, 2003), 60–61.

20 Eddie Cantor, vocal performance of "That's the Kind of a Baby for Me," by J. C. Egan

and Alfred C. Harriman, recorded July 12, 1917, Victor 18342, digital file, National Jukebox, Library of Congress, www.loc.gov/jukebox.

21 Historian Eric L. Goldstein discusses stereotypes of Jews and blacks as sexual predators in connection with the Leo Frank case (1913–1915) in Goldstein, *Price of Whiteness*, 43.

22 Grossman, *Funny Woman*, 107–33.

23 Cantor and Freedman, *My Life Is in Your Hands*, 156.

24 Ann Douglas, *Terrible Honesty* (New York: Farrar, Straus, Giroux, 1995), 328; Eddie Cantor, *As I Remember Them* (New York: Duell, Sloan, and Pearce, 1963), 48–49.

25 Cantor and Freedman, *My Life Is in Your Hands*, 159–60; Cantor, *As I Remember Them*, 49; unsigned review of *Ziegfeld Follies*, *New York Sun*, June 13, 1917.

26 For more on youth and college during the late 1910s and the 1920s, see Paula Fass, *The Damned and the Beautiful* (New York: Oxford University Press, 1977), 139, 172, 191, 202–3.

27 Unsigned review of *Ziegfeld Follies*, *Boston Globe*, September 18, 1917; see also, for example, unsigned review of *Ziegfeld Follies*, *Washington Post*, November 20, 1917; unsigned review of *Ziegfeld Follies*, *Baltimore Sun*, November 13, 1917; Percy Hammond, "Ziegfeld and His Follies," *Chicago Tribune*, December 24, 1917. For more on ticket sales and the popularity of the *Ziegfeld Follies*, see "Chicago," *Variety*, January 4, 1918, 31; Arthur Schalen, "Montreal," *Variety*, April 5, 1918, 36. Buffalo was one of the few cities with slower sales, which *Variety* attributed to the high cost of tickets. See "Buffalo," *Variety*, April 12, 1918, 35.

28 David A. Jansen, *Tin Pan Alley: An Encyclopedia of the Golden Age of American Song* (New York: Routledge, 2003), 256–57, 355–56.

29 David Blight, *Race and Reunion* (Cambridge: Harvard University Press, 2001), 9, 381–90.

30 Eddie Cantor, vocal performance of "The Dixie Volunteers," by Harry Ruby and Edgar Leslie, 1917, on Eddie Cantor, *The Early Days (1917–1921)*, produced by Brian Gari, Original Cast Record 885767219236, 1998, compact disc; see also van der Merwe, *The Ziegfeld Follies*, 110.

31 C. Morris Horowitz and Lawrence J. Kaplan, *The Jewish Population of the New York Area 1900–1975* (New York: Federation of Jewish Philanthropies of New York, 1959), 22.

32 B. G. De Sylva and Arthur J. Jackson, "But After the Ball Was Over" (New York: J. H. Remick, 1918).

33 Unsigned review of *Ziegfeld Follies*, *Variety*, June 14, 1918, 14.

34 Cantor and Freedman, *My Life Is in Your Hands*, 187.

35 "Whiteface" had multiple meanings. The term also described performers who wore all-white makeup.

36 Cantor and Freedman, *My Life Is in Your Hands*, 187; see also "How the 'Follies' Are Written," *New York Times*, June 22, 1919.

37 Unsigned review of *Ziegfeld Follies, New York Journal*, June 19, 1918; see also Irving J. Lewis, review of *Ziegfeld Follies, New York Telegraph*, June 19, 1918.

38 Cantor and Freedman, *My Life Is in Your Hands*, 187. See credits in *Ziegfeld Follies*, program, n.d. [1919–1920], 3, Joseph Urban Papers, Rare Book and Manuscript Library, Columbia University Libraries, www.library.columbia.edu/locations/rbml; unsigned review of *Ziegfeld Follies, New York Clipper*, June 18,1919. "How the Follies Are Written," *New York Times*, June 22, 1919, describes the collaboration between Wolf and Cantor. *Broadway Brevities, Kid Boots, The Chase and Sanborn Hour, Palmy Days, Thank Your Lucky Stars*, and *The Colgate Comedy Hour* each include versions of the osteopath sketch.

39 For more on LeMaire, see *Travalanche*, "Stars of Vaudeville #884: George LeMaire," blog entry by Trav S.D., December 22, 2014, travsd.wordpress.com.

40 T. E. Oliphant, review of *Ziegfeld Follies, New York Evening Mail*, June 17,1919.

41 Shawn A. Silver, "Thanks, But No Thanks: How Denial of Osteopathic Service in World War I and World War II Shaped the Profession," *Journal of the American Osteopathic Association* 112, no. 2 (2012): 93–95.

42 Rennold Wolf and Eddie Cantor, "At the Osteopath's," *Ziegfeld Follies of 1919* (n.p.: Theatre Arts Press, 2015), 70–73. A slightly different version of the sketch, apparently scanned from a script deposited for copyright purposes, is available on the Library of Congress website. See "At the Osteopath's," *Ziegfeld Follies of 1919*, script, 1919, act 2, 8–21, Rare Book and Special Collections Division, Library of Congress, Performing Arts Encyclopedia, www.memory.loc.gov/diglib/ihas/loc.rbc.varsep.s53282/default.html.

43 Scott Balcerzak and Margaret T. McFadden each explore ways in which Cantor's "effeminate character" in his 1930s films represented the actor's general refusal to assimilate and his identification with "a variety of displaced populations regardless of race and ethnicity." See Scott Balcerzak, *Buffoon Men* (Detroit: Wayne State University Press, 2013), 93–95; Margaret T. McFadden, "'Yoo Hoo, Prosperity!': Eddie Cantor and the Great Depression, 1929–1936," *Studies in American Humor*, no. 4 (2015), 272–73.

44 Goldman, *Banjo Eyes*, 58.

45 George Chauncey, *Gay New York: Gender, Urban Culture, and the Making of the Gay Male World, 1890–1940* (New York: Basic Books, 1994), 328.

46 Ted Merwin, *In Their Own Image: New York Jews in Jazz Age Popular Culture* (New Brunswick, NJ: Rutgers University Press, 2006), 43.

47 Ruth R. Wisse, *The Schlemiel as Modern Hero* (Chicago: University of Chicago Press, 1971), 51; Franklin Foer, "Nerd vs. Nebbish: Who's the Biggest Loser," *Slate*, July 12 1998, www.slate.com; Leo Rosten, *The New Joys of Yiddish*, revised by Lawrence Bush (New York: Three Rivers Press, 2001), 264–66, 344.

48 Cantor and Freedman, *My Life Is in Your Hands*, 187.

49 Heywood Broun, review of *Ziegfeld Follies, New York Tribune*, June 22, 1919; John Corbin, review of *Ziegfeld Follies, New York Times*, June 17, 1919.

50 Philip Furia and Michael Lasser, *America's Songs* (New York: Routledge, 2006), 70; unsigned review of *Ziegfeld Follies*, *New York Sun*, June 17, 1919.

51 Eddie Cantor, vocal performance of "You'd Be Surprised," by Irving Berlin, 1919, on Eddie Cantor, *The Early Days (1917–1921)*.

52 Cantor and Ardmore, *Take My Life*, 69–73.

53 Alexander Woollcott, *The Story of Irving Berlin* (New York: G. P. Putnam and Sons, 1925), 147; Charles Hamm, *Yesterdays* (New York: Norton, 1983), 336–37; Laurence Bergreen, *As Thousands Cheer: The Life of Irving Berlin* (New York: Viking, 1990), 171; Gardner, *Popular Songs of the Twentieth Century*, 81. Extant royalty statements in the Irving Berlin Collection at the Library of Congress provide a lower, though still impressive, figure of approximately 600,000 copies of sheet music sold. See Royalty Statement, December 1 to December 31, 1919; Royalty Statement, January 1 to June 30, 1920; Royalty Statement, July 1 to December 31, 1920, box 464, Irving Berlin Collection, Library of Congress, Music Division, Washington, DC.

4. A SNAPPY HEADLINER (1919–1923)

1 For more on Cantor and the strike, see Benjamin MacArthur, *Actors and American Culture, 1880–1920* (Philadelphia: Temple University Press, 1984), 213–21; F. T. Vreeland, "The Actors' Strike," *Nation*, August 23, 1919, 243; Sean P. Holmes, "All the World's a Stage: The Actors' Strike of 1919," *Journal of American History* 91, no. 4 (2005), 1313; "Ziegfeld Suit Starts," *Variety Daily Bulletin*, August 22, 1919, 24; "Cantor Enjoined," *Variety*, September 5, 1919, 4; "1919," Equity Timeline, Actors' Equity Association, www.actorsequity.org/AboutEquity/timeline/timeline_intro.html.ad

2 Cantor and Ardmore, *Take My Life*, 126.

3 "Eddie Cantor's Position," *Variety Daily Bulletin*, August 22, 1919, 29.

4 Sime Silverman, "Actors' Equity Benefit," *Variety*, August 22, 1919, 18.

5 Cantor and Freedman, *My Life Is in Your Hands*, 209.

6 Vreeland, "The Actors' Strike," 244.

7 Cantor and Freedman, *My Life Is in Your Hands*, 209–10.

8 "Equity Benefit," *New York Dramatic Mirror*, August 28, 1919, 1355; see also Holmes, "All the World's a Stage," 1304–5; "Actors Parade a Great Success," *New York Dramatic Mirror*, August 28, 1919; "Show Raises $6,000," *New York Clipper*, August 20,1919, 36; "Benefit Performances Start," *Billboard*, August 23, 1919, 8; Lexington Theatre, advertisement, *New York Times*, August 18, 1919.

9 Holmes, "All the World's a Stage," 1314.

10 Cantor and Ardmore, *Take My Life*, 126; see also Mordden, *Ziegfeld*, 187, 196; "Cantor Enjoined," *Variety*, September 5, 1919, 4.

11 "News of the Dailies," *Variety*, April 9, 1920, 31; "Cantor Leaves Follies," *Variety*, July 9, 1920, 9; "Dates for Cantor Instead of Show," *Variety*, August 13, 1920, 14; Goldman, *Banjo Eyes*, 83; Cantor and Freedman, *My Life Is in Your Hands*, 211; Mordden, *Ziegfeld*, 196. Other press reports from mid-1920 indicate that Ziegfeld planned to

have Cantor star in another unnamed musical, not *Sally*, or a revue later that year. See "Stars Selected by Mr. Ziegfeld for Next Season," *Sun and the New York Herald*, May 3, 1920; "Cantor to be Starred," *Philadelphia Evening Public Ledger*, May 8, 1920.

12 "Ziegfeld and Cantor Quarrel," *New York Clipper*, August 11, 1920, 7; "Eddie Cantor Signs Record Breaking Contract," *Variety*, February 27, 1920, 5. *Variety* incorrectly reported that the contract was with the Brunswick label; Goldman, *Banjo Eyes*, 78. Cantor moved to Columbia Records after Emerson went into receivership in 1921.

13 "Ziegfeld and Cantor Quarrel," *New York Clipper*, August 11, 1920; "Cantor Quits Ziegfeld," *Billboard*, September 4, 1920, 6; "Cantor and Ziegfeld Split," *New York Clipper*, September 1, 1920, 1; "Cantor Going with Shuberts," *New York Clipper*, September 8, 1920, 4.

14 Cantor and Freedman, *My Life Is in Your Hands*, 211.

15 Goldman, *Banjo Eyes*, 80–82; Herbert G. Goldman, *Jolson: The Legend Comes to Life* (New York: Oxford University Press, 1988), 127; Mordden, *Ziegfeld*, 188; Gregory Koseluk, *Eddie Cantor* (Jefferson, NC: McFarland, 1995), 78; "Cantor Going with Shuberts," *New York Clipper*, September 8, 1920; "Cantor with Shuberts at $1,450 Weekly Pay," *Variety*, September 17, 1920, 1; Lee Shubert and J. J. Shubert, contract with Eddie Cantor, n.d., General Correspondence 1910–1926, box 304, Shubert Archive, New York, NY; unsigned review of *Make It Snappy*, *Variety*, April 21, 1922, 17. The average worker earned between $1,200 and $1,400 annually during the early 1920s. See Scott Derks, *The Value of a Dollar: Prices and Income in the United States, 1860–2004* (Millerton, NY: Grey House, 2004), 154; US Bureau of the Census, *Bicentennial Edition*, 168.

16 The trade press published conflicting reports on whether the Shuberts had an interest in *Broadway Brevities*. For more on the production and ownership of *Broadway Brevities*, see "What's in a Name' Held Up," *New York Clipper*, September 29, 1920, 4; "Brevities Attached, Plays On," *New York Clipper*, December 8, 1920, 34. Examples of the critical reception include unsigned review of *Broadway Brevities*, *New York Clipper*, October 6, 1920, 19; Lait., review of *Broadway Brevities*, *Variety*, October 8, 1920, 17; unsigned review of *Broadway Brevities*, *Sun and the New York Herald*, September 30, 1920; J. Ranken Towse, review of *Broadway Brevities*, *New York Evening Post*, September 30, 1920. On the box office take and the business of the show, see "Brevities Does $26,000," *New York Clipper*, October 6, 1920, 1; "Seven Outstanding Hits in Season's 44 Productions," *New York Clipper*, October 13, 1920, 5; "Brevities Attached, Plays On," *New York Clipper*, December 8, 1920, 34.

17 Unsigned review of *Broadway Brevities*, *New York Clipper*, October 6, 1920; see also Lait, review of *Broadway Brevities*; Towse, review of *Broadway Brevities*; unsigned review of *Broadway Brevities*, *Sun and the New York Herald*, September 30, 1920.

18 Unsigned review of *Midnight Rounders*, *Hartford Courant*, March 15, 1921. Other reviews also commented on Cantor's "blue" or "indelicate" humor. See, for example, Sheppard Butler, review of *Midnight Rounders*, *Chicago Tribune*, September 8, 1921;

unsigned review of *Midnight Rounders*, *Detroit Free Press*, April 25, 1921. For more on New York as a symbol of moral corruption, see Fass, *The Damned and the Beautiful*, 22.

19 For more on Victorian social mores, see David Scobey, "Nymphs and Satyrs: Sex and the Bourgeois Public Sphere in Victorian New York," *Winterthur Portfolio* 37, no. 1 (2002), 43–66; McGerr, *A Fierce Discontent*, 248–78.

20 For more on Anthony Comstock, the New York Society for the Suppression of Vice, and other local efforts to monitor or censor stage content, see Joshua Lambert, *Unclean Lips: Obscenity, Jews, and American Culture* (New York: New York University Press, 2013), 3–6; Andrea Friedman, *Prurient Interests* (New York: Columbia University Press, 1990), 72–73, 101; M. Alison Kibler, *Censoring Racial Ridicule: Irish, Jewish, and African American Struggles over Race and Representation, 1890–1930* (Chapel Hill: University of North Carolina Press, 2015), 111–32.

21 Irving Howe, *World of Our Fathers* (New York: Harcourt Brace Jovanovich,1976), 179; Lawrence J. Epstein, *At the Edge of a Dream: The Story of Jewish Immigrants on New York's Lower East Side, 1880–1920* (San Francisco: Jossey-Bass, 2007), 56.

22 "Eddie Cantor's Try at 'Whiteface' Converts Him from Minstrelsy," *New York Tribune*, October 31, 1920; "The Stage Door," *New York Tribune*, October 6, 1920.

23 "Cantor Finds Jokes Go Better in Black," *New York Tribune*, April 23, 1922; Columbia Records, advertisement, *Brooklyn Standard Union*, July 7, 1922; Emerson Records, advertisement, *Philadelphia Inquirer*, May 9, 1920; Emerson Records, advertisement, *Washington Times*, May 3, 1920.

24 "Gossip of Plays and Players," *Brooklyn Daily Eagle*, June 3, 1923.

25 Quoted in Sime Silverman, review of *Make It Snappy*, *Variety*, April 21, 1922, 17.

26 Cantor performed several hundred songs over the years, but he received fewer than forty songwriting or co-writing credits. See James Fisher, *Eddie Cantor: A Bio-Bibliography* (Westport, CT: Greenwood Press, 1997), 175–95; American Society of Composers, Authors and Publishers (ASCAP), www.ascap.com.

27 Alex Gerber, Jean Schwartz, and Eddie Cantor, "My Yiddisha Mammy" (New York: N. Witmark and Sons, 1922). "Yiddisha" meant "Jewish" and did not refer to only Yiddish speakers. Cantor did not perform "My Yiddisha Mammy" every night, alternating it with another song, "Don't (Stop — Loving Me Now)," during opening week. See Silverman, review of *Make It Snappy*. On "Eli, Eli," see Jeffery Melnick, *A Right to Sing the Blues: African Americans, Jews, and American Popular Song* (Cambridge: Harvard University Press, 1999), 179–81; Snyder, *The Voice of the City*, 112.

28 While Dixie songs were not a significant part of Cantor's repertoire, his photo appears on the cover of sheet music for at least four of these songs from 1921–1922, during his stint with the Shuberts. Cantor did not record the songs, and they are not referenced in reviews of his shows. See Geo. B. Wehner and Louis Breau, "I Want My Mammy" (New York: Shapiro, Bernstein, 1921); Albert Von Tilzer and Lew Brown, "Dapper-Dan (The Ladies Man from Dixie Land)" (New York: Broadway

Music, 1921); Bert Kalmar, Harry Ruby, and Herman Ruby, "My Sunny Tennessee" (New York: Waterson, Berlin and Snyder, 1921); Roy Turn and J. Russel Robinson, "I'll Be in My Dixie Home Again Tomorrow" (New York: Waterson, Berlin and Snyder, 1922).

29 On Cantor's repertoire of songs, see Cantor to J. J. Shubert, telegram, April 9, 1923, General Correspondence 1910–1926, box 304, Shubert Archive, New York, NY. The telegram is dated, by hand, April 9, 1924, but other contextual materials in the archive and other sources indicate that Cantor sent the telegram on April 9, 1923; "Eddie Cantor Pursued by Composers of Popular Songs," *Washington Post*, December 17, 1922; Cantor and Ardmore, *Take My Life*, 165; Ben Yagoda, *The B-Side: The Death of Tin Pan Alley and the Rebirth of the Great American Song* (New York: Riverhead Books, 2015), 34.

30 Cantor first sang the song in a special Sunday night concert at the Winter Garden and then brought it into *Midnight Rounders*. See Cantor and Ardmore, *Take My Life*, 163.

31 Eddie Cantor, vocal performance of "Margie," by Con Conrad, J. Russel Robinson, and Benny Davis, recorded December 1920, Emerson 10301, on *1921: Make Believe and Smile*, Archeophone 9002A, 2004, compact disc.

32 Shubert Press Department, "WINTER GARDEN AGAIN BECOMES HOME OF THE AMERICAN REVUE WHEN EDDIE CANTOR APPEARS THURSDAY NIGHT IN 'MAKE IT SNAPPY,'" undated (circa April 12, 1922), Show Series, "Make It Snappy," Shubert Archive; Burns Mantle, "Gossip of the Stage," *Salt Lake City Tribune*, April 30, 1922, provides a good description of the taxi scene; Alexander Woollcott, review of *Make It Snappy*, *New York Times*, April 14, 1922; Gilbert Seldes, "The New York Theaters," *Washington Post*, April 25, 1922; Robert C. Benchley, "Drama," *Life*, July 26, 1923, 82.

33 Eddie Cantor, "Taxi Scene," *Make It Snappy*, script, n.d. (performed 1922–1923), n.p., box 35, Cantor Papers UCLA; Sime Silverman, review of *Make It Snappy*, *Variety*, April 21, 1922.

34 David L. Lewis, *The Public Image of Henry Ford: An American Folk Hero and His Company* (Detroit: Wayne State University Press, 1976), 135–40; Leo P. Ribuffo, "Henry Ford and *The International Jew*," in *The American Jewish Experience*, ed. Jonathan D. Sarna, 176–84 (New York: Homes and Meier, 1986); Library of Congress, "From Haven to Home: 350 Years of Jewish Life in America," online exhibit, www.loc.gov /exhibits/haventohome.

35 The quotation is from "The Jewish Aspect of the 'Movie' Problem," *Dearborn Independent*, February 12, 1921, and "Jewish Supremacy in the Motion Picture World," *Dearborn Independent*, February 19, 1921, in J. Hoberman and Jeffrey Shandler, *Entertaining America: Jews, Movies, and Broadcasting* (Princeton, NJ: Princeton University Press, 2003), 51; on links between Ford, antimodernity, and antisemitism, see Goldstein, *Price of Whiteness*, 121; Jeffrey Shandler, "Henry Ford," in Hoberman and Shandler, *Entertaining America*, 51.

36 Max H. Newman, "Among the Clubs," *Boston Jewish Advocate*, December 14, 1922, 10.

37 For more on the comic "stage Jew" during the early twentieth century, see Merwin, *In Their Own Image*, 72–73, 79; the music and liner notes to *Jewface*, curated with liner notes by Jody Rosen, Reboot Stereophonic, Rb00 006, 2006, compact disc; Patricia Erens, *The Jew in American Cinema* (Bloomington: Indiana University Press, 1984), 89–95; Harley Erdman, *Staging the Jew: The Performance of an American Ethnicity, 1860–1920* (New Brunswick, NJ: Rutgers University Press, 1997), 103–6, 149–61. For more on organized Jewish efforts to eradicate negative stage images, see Kibler, *Censoring Racial Ridicule*, 111–32.

38 Deborah Dash Moore, *At Home in America: Second Generation New York Jews* (New York: Columbia University Press, 1981), 21–23; Horowitz and Kaplan, *Jewish Population*, 3, 15, 22, 26–29, 94; Merwin, *In Their Own Image*, 7.

39 Alan Dale, review of *Make It Snappy*, *New York American*, April 14, 1922.

40 The sketch was also known as "Belt in the Back" because of a recurring joke that plays on the word "belt." The customer wants a suit with a belt in the back, and Cantor threatens to hit him each time in response. The quotations here are from a version of the sketch in *Glorifying the American Girl*, directed by Millard Webb (1929; repr., Golden Valley, MN: Mill Creek Entertainment, 2005), digital video disc. Louis Sorin replaced Joe Opp in the *Glorifying the American Girl* sketch. For more on Hearn, see Frank Cullen with Florence Hackman and Donald McNeilly, *Vaudeville, Old and New: An Encyclopedia of Variety Performers in America*, vol. 1 (New York: Taylor and Francis, 1996), 498–500.

41 Gilbert Seldes, *The 7 Lively Arts* (Mineola, NY: Dover, 2001), 180.

42 Cantor performed "Joe's Blue Front" hundreds of times in *Make It Snappy* and reprised it in later theatrical, film, and radio productions. Berle and Hearn performed it on the *Texaco Star Theatre*, May 3, 1949. See"Cantor versus Hearn over 'Belt in the Back' Video Skit," *Variety*, May 11, 1949, 1, 53.

43 Scorsese quoted in Dennis Lim, "Comic Guerrilla Tries Sticking with the Script," *New York Times*, May 3, 2012. Cohen's other credits include *Da Ali G Show* (2000–2004) and *Borat: Cultural Learnings of America for Make Benefit Glorious Nation of Kazakhstan* (2006).

44 See, for example, Freeman Church Company, advertisement, *Hartford Courant*, March 15, 1921; Hickey's, advertisement, *Detroit Free Press*, May 3, 1921; Rothschild's, advertisement, *Kansas City Star*, November 28, 1921. Eric L. Goldstein describes Baxter Street as "synonymous with Jews." See Goldstein, *Price of Whiteness*, 37.

45 Sheppard Butler, "Eddie Cantor and His 'The Midnight Rounders,'" *Chicago Tribune*, September 8, 1921.

46 Sime Silverman, "Eddie Cantor," *Variety*, August 19, 1921, 16.

47 "Slang Tracked to Its Lair by Well-Known Comedian," *Salt Lake City Herald*, January 18, 1923.

48 Fass, *The Damned and the Beautiful*, 20–22. Several writers discuss the speedy, energetic, and charismatic style of Jewish performers from the late 1910s and the 1920s. See Seldes, *The 7 Lively Arts*, 191–96; Merwin, *In Their Own Image*, 60; Howe, *World of Our Fathers*, 566.

49 See, for example, Jack Reed to J. J. Shubert, January 11, 1921, General Correspondence 1910–1926, box 162, Shubert Archive; Jack Reed to J. J. Shubert, telegram, January 22, 1921, General Correspondence 1910–1926, box 162, Shubert Archive; Daniel Lipsky to J. J. Shubert, telegram, March 2, 1922, General Correspondence 1910–1926, box 304, Shubert Archive; J. J. Shubert to Eddie Cantor, March 3, 1922, General Correspondence 1910–1926, box 304, Shubert Archive.

50 Cantor and Ardmore, *Take My Life*, 126. See also Jack Reed to Lee Shubert, January 10, 1923, General Correspondence 1910–1926, box 162, Shubert Archive; Goldman, *Banjo Eyes*, 91–93.

51 Cantor and Ardmore, *Take My Life*, 126–27; Eddie Cantor, advertisement, *Variety*, March 15, 1923, 39; "Eddie Cantor Signs with Follies," *New York Times*, May 16, 1923.

5. MAKIN' WHOOPEE WITH ZIEGFELD (1923–1930)

1 J. J. Shubert to Daniel Lipsky, June 21, 1923, General Correspondence 1910–1926, box 304, Shubert Archive.

2 "News of the Dallies," *Variety*, June 28, 1923, 38. The newspaper did not quote Cantor's jokes about the KKK and Ford.

3 Another Jewish comedian, Lou Holtz, also used Cantor's Klan joke from *Kid Boots* in his act, though he claimed to have stolen the joke from a different comedian, not Cantor. See Lou Holtz, letter, *Variety*, February 28, 1924, 5; Ibee [Jack Pulaski], review of Hippodrome bill, *Variety*, February 21, 1924, 23. On the Ku Klux Klan during this time, see Rory McVeigh, *The Rise of the Ku Klux Klan: Right-Wing Movements and National Politics* (Minneapolis: University of Minnesota Press, 209), 21–27; George Lewis, "'An Amorphous Code': The Ku Klux Klan and Un-Americanism, 1915–1965," *Journal of American Studies* 47, no. 4 (2013): 973–76; Bill Bryson, *One Summer: America, 1927* (New York: Doubleday, 2013), 359; Goldstein, *Price of Whiteness*, 122–24.

4 James Craig, review of *Ziegfeld Follies of 1922: Summer Edition*, *New York Evening Mail*, June 26, 1923.

5 Eddie Cantor, "My Girl Uses Mineralava" (New York: Solax, 1923).

6 "Beauty Clay Behind Cantor?" *Variety*, July 4, 1923.

7 Goldman, *Banjo Eyes*, 339–42.

8 Unsigned review of *Kid Boots*, *Baltimore Sun*, April 13, 1926; see also Ibee [Jack Pulaski], review of *Kid Boots*, *Variety*, January 10, 1924, 16; unsigned review of *Kid Boots*, *New York World*, January 2, 1924; Cantor and Freedman, *My Life Is in Your Hands*, 229.

9 For more on Harbach, see *Internet Broadway Database*, s.v. "Otto Harbach," www .ibdb.com; Ken Bloom, *Broadway: Its History, People, and Places: An Encyclopedia*

(New York: Routledge, 2004), 216–19. For more on McGuire, see James Fisher and Felicia Hardison Londré, *The A to Z of American Theater: Modernism* (Lanham, MD: Scarecrow Press, 2008), 314; "McGuire Writes in Novel Way," *Boston Daily Globe*, October 3, 1926; Cantor and Freedman, *My Life Is in Your Hands*, 230–32.

10 Cantor and Freedman, *My Life Is in Your Hands*, 251.

11 Ibid., 234–35.

12 Ibid., 252.

13 William Anthony McGuire and Otto Harbach, *Kid Boots*, script, n.d. (performed 1923–1926), act 1, I-23, ser. 1: Scripts, Florenz Ziegfeld–Billie Burke Papers, New York Public Library for the Performing Arts, New York, NY. In fact, on September 6, 1926, the Knights of the Ku Klux Klan played a baseball game against the Hebrew All-Stars of Washington, DC. The only notable incident was a rainstorm, which forced stoppage of the game in the seventh inning, with the Klan leading 4–0. See "Klansmen Are Victors over Hebrew Stars, 4–0," *Washington Post*, September 7, 1926; Josh Perelman, ed., *Chasing Dreams: Baseball and Becoming American* (Philadelphia: National Museum of American Jewish History), 110.

14 McGuire and Harbach, *Kid Boots*, I-25.

15 Unsigned review of *Kid Boots*, *New York World*, January 2, 1924.

16 McGuire and Harbach, *Kid Boots*, II-49.

17 Cantor also sang "Dinah," which became a standard, in *Kid Boots*, but he did not record the song at this time. For more on the popularity of "Charley, My Boy" and "If You Knew Susie," see Gardner, *Popular Songs of the Twentieth Century*, vol. 1, 191–93.

18 Unsigned review of *Kid Boots*, *Chicago Daily Tribune*, September 29, 1925.

19 Goldstein, *Price of Whiteness*, 172–74.

20 Jack Lait, "The Stage—and the Jew," *Chicago Sentinel*, April 22, 1921, 16. Lait's article also appeared, without a byline, in "The Stage and the Jew," *Pittsburgh Jewish Criterion*, June 24, 1921, 14. See also "Returns from America to Propagate Anti-Semitism," *Chicago Sentinel*, August 25, 1921, 22; Harry Schneiderman, "Who the Jews Are in the United States," *Chicago Sentinel*, October 12, 1922, 7; Harry Schneiderman, "Have Jews Any Claim to Title 'American'?," *Chicago Sentinel*, December 21, 1922, 39.

21 Felicia Herman, "Views of Jews: Anti-Semitism, Hollywood, and American Jews, 1913–1947" (unpublished PhD diss., Brandeis University, 2002), 45–46 (UMI #3036416).

22 "Jewish Actors' Guild," *Pittsburgh Jewish Criterion*, September 24, 1924, 119.

23 Cantor and Ardmore, *Take My Life*, 26.

24 Walter Lippmann, "Public Opinion and the American Jew," *American Hebrew*, April 14, 1922, 575; see also Alexander, *Jazz Age Jews*, 95.

25 "Jewish Fund Gets $125,000," *New York Tribune*, May 10, 1920.

26 "Relief Drive Continues during Jewish Sabbath," *Baltimore Sun*, February 19, 1922.

27 "The Brooklyn Dinner at the Biltmore," *American Hebrew*, February 24, 1922, 402.

28 "This Is Apple Week; All Are Urged to Buy: Fruit to Be Distributed," *New York Tribune*, October 31, 1920.

29 "Benefit Concert at Colonial This Sunday," *Boston Jewish Advocate*, February 10, 1921, 8; see also Max Hart to J. J. Shubert, February 9, 1921, file 570, General Correspondence 1910–1936, Shubert Archive.

30 "Persons Talked About," *American Hebrew*, August 5, 1921.

31 Brief newspaper items published before the date was changed mention the original September 27, 1925, opening night. See "Theater," *Chicago Tribune*, August 28, 1925; "New Playbills in Chicago," *Chicago Tribune*, September 6, 1925. Advertisements and articles starting September 13, 1925, more than a week before tickets went on sale, list the new September 28, 1925, opening night. See Woods Theatre, advertisement, *Chicago Tribune*, September 13, 1925; "New Playbills in Chicago," *Chicago Tribune*, September 13, 1925.

32 "Cantor Wouldn't Open on Holiday," *Variety*, September 30, 1925, 21.

33 Rabbi S. Felix Mendelsohn, "Topics of the Week," *Chicago Sentinel*, October 1, 1925, 7.

34 Eddie Cantor, letter, *Chicago Sentinel*, October 15, 1925, 17.

35 "Eddie Cantor Owns Chicago," *Variety*, December 9, 1925, 4.

36 Robert E. Sherwood, review of *Kid Boots*, *Baltimore Sun*, October 24, 1926; Fred [Fred Schader], review of *Kid Boots*, *Variety*, October 13, 1926, 15.

37 Laurence Reid, review of *Special Delivery*, *Motion Picture News*, May 6, 1927, 1677.

38 Cantor and Freedman, *My Life Is in Your Hands*, 275.

39 Ung., "Metropolitan (Los Angeles)," *Variety*, June 29, 1927, 28. For more on the mixed reception, see, for example, "Key City Reports," *Motion Picture News*, May 13, 1927, 1841; "Key City Reports," *Motion Picture News*, May 27, 1927, 2086; "Key City Reports," *Motion Picture News*, June 10, 1927, 2283; "Key City Reports," *Motion Picture News*, June 17, 1927, 2362; "Key City Reports," *Motion Picture News*, July 1, 1927, 2559.

40 "Cantor Returns to Ziggy at $4,500 — Percentage," *Variety*, May 18, 1927.

41 Cantor and Freedman, *My Life Is in Your Hands*, 188–90.

42 Ibid., 284; Goldman, *Banjo Eyes*, 122.

43 Unsigned review of *Whoopee*, *Variety*, November 14, 1928, 55; "National Box Office Opens at Dawn to Care for Rush," *Washington Post*, November 22, 1928; "Paul Gregory Is New Singer of 'Whoopee,'" *Washington Post*, November 30, 1928; "Shows in N.Y. and Comment," *Variety*, October 2, 1929, 78; "Stock Market Influence Still Felt by B'way Drawing Shows," *Variety*, November 20, 1929, 58.

44 William Anthony McGuire, *Whoopee*, script, n.d. (performed 1928–1930), 2.5.3, Restricted Materials no. 7427, New York Public Library for the Performing Arts, New York, NY.

45 J. Brooks Atkinson, review of *Whoopee*, *New York Times*, December 5, 1928; John J. Daly, review of *Whoopee*, *Washington Post*, November 27, 1928.

46 Atkinson, review of *Whoopee*; Richard Lockridge, review of *Whoopee*, *New York Sun*,

December 5, 1928; see also Donald Mulherm, review of *Whoopee*, *Brooklyn Standard Union*, December 5, 1928.

47 McGuire, *Whoopee*, script, 1.1.24.

48 In the film version of *Whoopee*, Cantor's character refers to himself as "Big Chief Izzy Horowitz." This line does not appear in the script of the play, but the stage direction instructs Cantor's character to "gradually work into a Jewish accent, acting like a Jewish salesman" during the ad lib argument with Underwood. See McGuire, *Whoopee*, script, 2.1.15–17.

49 Victoria Saker Woeste, *Henry Ford's War on Jews and the Legal Battle against Hate Speech* (Stanford, CA: Stanford University Press, 2012), 271–80.

50 *A Ziegfeld Midnight Frolic*, Paramount Pictures, 1929. This film is widely available on YouTube and is included on the digital video disc of *Kid Boots*, produced and annotated by Brian Gari, Original Cast OC-6201, n.d., digital video disc. Working as The Happiness Boys, the popular comedians Billy Jones and Ernest Hare found similar humor in Ford's apology, releasing "Since Henry Ford Apologized to Me," by Dave Stamper, Ballard MacDonald, and Billy Rose, recorded 1927, Victor 20925, 78 rpm record.

51 *A Ziegfeld Midnight Frolic*. Stanley Green discusses Cantor's performance of these songs during his specialty routine in *Whoopee*, liner notes by Stanley Green, Smithsonian American Musical Theater Series, RCA Records DPM1 0349, 1978, LP.

52 Andrea Most examines Cantor's feminized character in Most, *Making Americans: Jews and the Broadway Musical* (Cambridge: Harvard University Press, 2004), 47–54. Eric L. Goldstein discusses images of the weak Jew as a "representative of many of modernity's ills" in Goldstein, *The Price of Whiteness*, 37.

53 Eddie Cantor with the Nat Shilkret Orchestra, performance of "Makin' Whoopee," by Gus Kahn and Walter Donaldson, Victor 21831, 1928, 78 rpm record. Cantor performs versions of the song with slightly different lyrics in the 1930 movie *Whoopee!* and later recordings of the song.

54 "Joys and Glooms of Broadway," *Variety*, June 14, 1923, 32.

55 Goldman, *Jolson*, 162, 174.

56 Jessel, *So Help Me*, 102–3, 137. On Cantor's distaste for alcohol, see Jessel, *So Help Me*, 132; Goldman, *Banjo Eyes*, 66; Janet Cantor Gari, *Don't Wear Silver in the Winter* (Albany, GA: Bear Manor Media, 2008), 26.

57 "Eddie Cantor Plans to Retire Next Year," *New York Times*, May 9, 1929.

58 Eddie Cantor, "Goodbye Broadway," *Washington Post*, January 5, 1930.

6. VOICE OF THE DEPRESSION (1929–1938)

1 Cantor and Freedman, *My Life Is in Your Hands*, 287, 299; "Cantor's Wall St. 'Blues' Just a Joke," *New York Times*, December 4, 1930.

2 "Business and Finance: Index," *Time*, December 31, 1928, 24, 26; Cantor and Freedman, *My Life Is in Your Hands*, 299.

3 Eddie Cantor, *Between the Acts* (New York: Simon and Schuster, 1930), 67.

4 Robert S. McElvaine, *The Great Depression: America, 1929–1941* (New York: Three Rivers Press, 1993), 46–48.

5 Bide Dudley, "White Way Wisdom," *Washington Post*, November 3, 1929. For more on the entertainment industry's reaction to the crash, see Goldman, *Banjo Eyes*, 133–35; "Skidding Market Skidded; B'way Legits Badly Last Wk.; Great Break Great Leveler," *Variety*, November 6, 1929, 57; "Broadway Takes the Slap," *Variety*, November 6, 1929, 1.

6 "Wall St. Lays an Egg," *Variety*, October 30, 1929, 1, 64.

7 Ibid.

8 "Skidding Market Skidded," 57.

9 See "Shows in N.Y. and Comment," *Variety*, October 30, 1929, 7; "Shows in N.Y. and Comment," *Variety*, November 13, 1929, 68; "4 Shows Out," *Variety*, November 20, 1929, 58.

10 Goldman, *Banjo Eyes*, 133; "Cantor's Market Gags," *Variety*, November 6, 1929, 57; Cantor and Ardmore, *Take My Life*, 31–32.

11 Bob Batchelor, "Psychological Impact of the Depression," in *Encyclopedia of the Great Depression*, vol. 2, ed. Robert S. McElvaine (New York: MacMillan Reference, 2004), 778.

12 Weinberg is interviewed in Studs Terkel, *Hard Times* (1970; repr., New York: Avon Books, 1971), 93.

13 "The Microphone Will Present," *New York Times*, October 27, 1929; "Jessel Dinner Catches Wits and Laughs," *Variety*, October 30, 1929, 65; Ruth Morris, "Uncommon Chatter," *Variety*, October 30, 1929, 68.

14 Richard D. White Jr., *Will Rogers: A Political Life* (Lubbock: Texas Tech University Press, 2011), 150, 154, 159.

15 "Will Rogers Says New York Has a 'Wailing' Day," *New York Times*, October 25, 1929.

16 "Wall Street's Vicissitudes Nothing to Will Rogers," *New York Times*, October 26, 1929.

17 Goldman, *Banjo Eyes*, 123–24; Fisher, *Eddie Cantor*, 165; Bob Landry, "Disk Reviews," *Variety*, November 27, 1929, 65.

18 The copyright page to the fifth printing of *Caught Short!* (November 1929) indicates that one hundred thousand copies of the book had been printed. See Eddie Cantor, *Caught Short!: A Saga of Wailing Wall Street* (New York: Simon and Schuster, 1929); Goldman, *Banjo Eyes*, 134.

19 "Cantor's Market Gags," *Variety*, November 6, 1929, 37.

20 Cantor, *Caught Short!*, 37; "Literati," *Variety*, November 20, 1929, 62.

21 "Eddie Cantor Discourses of Music Films," *New York Times*, October 25, 1931.

22 Ray Long and Richard R. Smith, advertisement, *New York Times*, April 3, 1932.

23 Eddie Cantor, *Between the Acts* (New York: Simon and Schuster, 1930), xi.

24 "Cantor Is Plaintiff in $100,000,000 Suit," *New York Times*, February 12, 1932; "Or-

......

dered to Post Bond of $500,000," *New York Times*, June 16, 1932; "Inside Stuff—Pictures," *Variety*, June 21, 1932, 47; "Cantor Ends Attack on Goldman Sachs," *New York Times*, September 5, 1936.

25 Richard Breitman and Allan J. Lichtman, *FDR and the Jews* (Cambridge: Harvard University Press, 2013), 37; Beth S. Wenger, *New York Jews and the Great Depression* (New Haven, CT: Yale University Press, 1996), 10–15.

26 "Jews in America," *Fortune*, February 1936, 130, 133.

27 Susie J. Pak, *Gentlemen Bankers: The World of J. P. Morgan* (Cambridge: Harvard University Press, 2013), 80–93; Gordon Thomas and Max Morgan-Witts, *The Day the Bubble Burst: A Social History of the Wall Street Crash of 1929* (Garden City, NY: Doubleday, 1979), 59.

28 Cantor, *Caught Short!*, 23.

29 Frederick Lewis Allen, *Only Yesterday: An Informal History of the 1920's* (1931; repr., New York: John Wiley and Sons, 1997), 250; "Topics in Wall Street," *New York Times*, October 25, 1929; "Financiers Ease Tensions," *New York Times*, October 25, 1929; "Bank Heads Confer on Stocks Debacle," *Washington Post*, October 25, 1929.

30 Cantor, *Caught Short!*, 30.

31 "A Note About the Author," in Cantor, *Caught Short!*, 9–10.

32 The $5,000 figure is from "Eddie Cantor Plans to Retire Next Year," *New York Times*, May 9, 1929; according to Goldman, Cantor earned $4,500 a week. See Goldman, *Banjo Eyes*, 134.

33 "Eddie Cantor and 'Whoopee': Gay and Gorgeous Show in Which the Popular Comedian Is at His Best," *Boston Globe*, November 26, 1929; "Theater: 'Whoopee,'" *Chicago Daily Tribune*, January 21, 1930.

34 "Sam, Flo, and Eddie Active in Hollywood," *Washington Post*, April 20, 1930.

35 Goldman, *Banjo Eyes*, 165; "Cantor's Wall St. 'Blues' Just a Joke."

36 S. N. Behrman, "Profiles: 'Chutspo,'" *New Yorker*, December 10, 1932, 27.

37 Ben Cooper, "Cantor Cures Blues in Paramount Laughie," *Atlanta Constitution*, September 29, 1930. The *Atlanta Constitution* also ran three articles previewing the film and highlighting Cantor's role. See Ralph T. Jones, "S.R.O.," *Atlanta Constitution*, September 28, 1930; "Eddie Cantor in 'Whoopee' at Paramount," *Atlanta Constitution*, September 28, 1930; "Big Week Ahead with Many Fine Attractions on Screen," *Atlanta Constitution*, September 28, 1930.

38 Sime, review of *Whoopee!*, *Variety*, October 8, 1930, 22.

39 "'Widow' and 'Whoopee' Start Daily Take of $10,000 Each on Broadway; 'Wife' at Garden $41,400—Very Big," *Variety*, October 8, 1930, 8; "'Lincoln's' $10,000—'Whoopee's' $28,000 Philly's Best—Others Are All Down," *Variety*, October 15, 1930, 9; "Bankers Bring $28,000 to the 'Whoopee' B.O.," *Motion Picture News*, October 11, 1930, 30; "Golden West to Good $12,500 in Providence," *Variety*, October 8, 1930, 8.

40 "Palace, Loop, Hits New High with $23,900 with Vaude Favs on Stage; Up-Stage Ad Stuff Hurts 'Whoopee,'" *Variety*, October 15, 1930, 9.

41 "'French Girls' $13,000. Orph $12,700 — P'tland," *Variety*, October 22, 1930, 9; "'Africa Speaks' $8,000 'Whoopee' Big, $16,100," *Variety*, October 22, 1930, 8; "'Whoopee' Is Top with $10,000 in Oklahoma City," *Motion Picture News*, November 15, 1930, 42.

42 "Managers' Round Table Club," *Motion Picture News*, December 13, 1930, 54.

43 "Managers' Round Table Club," *Motion Picture News*, November 15, 1930, 63; "Louisville, Ky.," *Variety*, November 12, 1930, 79.

44 On *Whoopee!* as a metaphor for the immigrant experience, see Most, *Making Americans*, 42. Cantor starred in *Palmy Days* (United Artists, 1931), *The Kid from Spain* (United Artists, 1932), *Roman Scandals* (United Artists, 1933), *Kid Millions* (United Artists, 1934), *Strike Me Pink* (United Artists, 1936), and *Ali Baba Goes to Town* (Twentieth Century-Fox, 1937). Precise box-office figures are difficult to determine, but Joel W. Finler's research suggests that Cantor's films were among the most popular from this time period. See Joel W. Finler, *The Hollywood Story* (New York: Crown Publishers, 1988), 276.

45 Henry Jenkins, *What Makes Pistachio Nuts?* (New York: Columbia University Press, 1992), 166, 175–83.

46 Herman, "Views of Jews," 82–90; see also "Motion Picture Code" (1930), reprinted in Leonard J. Jeff and Jerold Simmons, eds., *The Dame in the Kimono: Hollywood, Censorship, and the Production Code from the 1920s to the 1960s* (Lexington: University Press of Kentucky, 2001), 289; Thomas Doherty, *Hollywood and Hitler: 1933–1939* (New York: Columbia University Press, 2013), 45.

47 Christopher H. Sterling and John M. Kitross, *Stay Tuned: A Concise History of American Broadcasting* (Belmont, CA: Wadsworth, 1978), 533; Robert J. Brown, *Manipulating the Ether: The Power of Broadcast Radio in Thirties America* (Jefferson, NC: McFarland, 1998), 2.

48 See Jim Ramsburg, *Network Radio Ratings, 1932–1953: A History of Prime Time Programs through the Ratings of Nielsen, Crossley and Hooper* (Jefferson, NC: McFarland, 2012), 229, 316. Similar ratings numbers appear in Harrison Boyd Summers, *A Thirty-Year History of Programs Carried on National Radio Networks in the United States, 1926–1956* (Columbus: Ohio State University, 1958), 25, 31. I follow Ramsburg in using the conservative estimate of 2.5 listeners per radio home. In accounting for friends, neighbors, and family members who listened to programs together, the industry generally used a higher estimate of four listeners per home. For more on ratings, see also Elizabeth McLeod, *The Original Amos 'n' Andy: Freeman Gosden, Charles Correll and the 1928–1943 Radio Serial* (Jefferson, NC: McFarland, 2005), 167. A CBS survey from 1933 estimated 3.6 listeners per set. See "CBS Survey Claims 16,809,100 Sets Now in Use for 60,514,000 Listeners," *Variety*, February 23, 1933, 43. Audience ratings from the early 1930s, though imperfect, were widely used within the broadcast industry and provide the best data available today for measuring audiences.

49 "New Savants Up in Poll," *Variety*, May 16, 1933, 39.

50 "Bill Big Town Radio Personals 100 Miles Away for Farm Trade," *Variety*, March 14, 1933, 37.

51 *Chase and Sanborn Hour*, script, NBC Red, September 13, 1931, WEAF Master Books, NBC Collection, Recorded Sound Section, Library of Congress, 2; hereafter, cited as WEAF Master Books. An audio copy of this program also circulates among collectors and appears on *The Eddie Cantor Chase and Sanborn Radio Show, 1931–1933*, Brian Gari producer, Original Cast OC-8715, 1999, disc 1, compact disc. Gari and other collectors list the airdate as "probably December 13, 1931."

52 *Chase and Sanborn Hour*, script, NBC Red, September 13, 1931, WEAF Master Books, 8.

53 Al Lewis and Al Sherman, "When I'm the President (We Want Cantor)" (New York: Mack Stark Music, 1932).

54 Orrin E. Dunlap Jr., "Listening-In," *New York Times*, October 4, 1931. See also Martin Golde, "Highlights and Sidelights," *Pittsburgh Jewish Criterion*, October 16, 1931, 26.

55 Cantor and Freedman, *Your Next President!*, 24–25.

56 Ibid., 4, 7.

57 David Freedman, "Making Jokes," *Pittsburgh Jewish Criterion*, September 1, 1933, 4; David Freedman, as told to Lester Gottlieb, "David Freedman Tells How to Write Radio Comedy," *Radioland*, May 1935, 59.

58 McElvaine, *The Great Depression*, 131–35; Frederick Lewis Allen, *Since Yesterday: The 1930s in America* (1939; repr., New York: Harper and Row, 1968), 74.

59 *Chase and Sanborn Hour*, script, NBC Red, December 27, 1931, WEAF Master Books, 18–24; *How to Make a Quack-Quack* (New York: Standard Brands, 1932).

60 Marc Dollinger, *Quest for Inclusion: Jews and Liberalism in Modern America* (Princeton, NJ: Princeton University Press, 2000), 24–25.

61 *Chase and Sanborn Hour*, NBC Red, October 30, 1932, in *Eddie Cantor Radio Show: Season Debut of 1932*, Brian Gari producer, Original Cast OC-6037, 2002, compact disc.

62 *Chase and Sanborn Hour*, script, NBC Red, December 13, 1931, WEAF Master Books, 32. Cantor introduced the song on his fourth broadcast of the season, on October 4, 1931. See *Chase and Sanborn Hour*, script, NBC Red, October 4, 1931, WEAF Master Books, 16.

63 *Chase and Sanborn Hour*, script, NBC Red, December 27, 1931, WEAF Master Books, 32.

64 Orrin E. Dunlap Jr., "Breaking a Spell," *New York Times*, December 10, 1939.

65 B. F. Wilson, "Cantor's in the Money Now!," *Radioland*, April 1934, 66.

66 Jerry Stiller, *Married to Laughter*, large print ed. (New York: Random House, 2000), 9.

67 Cantor and Ardmore, *Take My Life*, 219.

68 *Chase and Sanborn Hour*, NBC Red, November 26, 1933, in *Eddie Cantor Chase and Sanborn Radio Show 1931–1933*, disc 2, compact disc.

69 Robert West, *So-o-o-o You're Going on the Air* (New York: Rodin Publishing, 1934), 44.

70 Breitman and Lichtman, *FDR and the Jews*, 43; Howard M. Sachar, *A History of the Jews in America* (New York: Vintage Books, 1992), 460; Leonard Dinnerstein, "Jews and the New Deal," *American Jewish History* 72, no. 4 (1983), 474; Lawrence H. Fuchs, *The Political Behavior of American Jews* (Glencoe, IL: Free Press, 1956), 101; Rafael Medoff, *Jewish Americans and Political Participation* (Santa Barbara, CA: ABC-CLIO, 2002), 185; Wenger, *New York Jews and the Great Depression*, 2, 48.

71 Wenger, *New York Jews and the Great Depression*, 133; Dollinger, *Quest for Inclusion*, 30–31.

72 "Calling Mr. Cantor," *Motion Picture Herald*, November 18, 1933, 7; "Code Is at 'Little White House' with Industry Interest Lagging," *Motion Picture Herald*, November 25, 1933, 20.

73 David F. Prindle, *The Politics of Glamour: Ideology and Democracy in the Screen Actors Guild* (Madison: University of Wisconsin Press, 1988), 24–25; Larry Ceplair and Steven Englund, *The Inquisition in Hollywood: Politics in the Film Community, 1930–1960* (Berkeley: University of California Press, 1979), 29. For more on the battle over the NRA Code, see Harvey G. Cohen, "The Struggle to Fashion the NRA Code," *Journal of American Studies* 50, no. 4 (December 28, 2015): 1039–66, journals.cambridge.org.

74 Eddie Cantor, "What the Guild Stands for . . . ," *Screen Player*, March 15, 1934, 2.

75 David M. Oshinsky, *Polio: An American Story* (New York: Oxford University Press, 2005), 39; Franklin D. Roosevelt to Eddie Cantor, November 29, 1933, PPF 1018, President's Personal File, Franklin D. Roosevelt Presidential Library and Museum, Hyde Park, NY; hereafter, cited as FDR PPF 1018.

76 *Chase and Sanborn Hour*, NBC Red, December 31, 1933, in *Eddie Cantor Chase and Sanborn Radio Show*, disc 4, compact disc; M. H. McIntyre to Eddie Cantor, January 5, 1934, "Eddie Cantor," FDR PPF 1018.

77 "Borah Demands a Relief Inquiry to End 'Scandal,'" *New York Times*, November 10, 1934; Cantor to McIntyre, telegram, November 11, 1934, "Eddie Cantor," FDR PPF 1018; see also other correspondence in "Eddie Cantor," FDR PPF 1018.

78 *Chase and Sanborn Hour*, script, NBC Red, November 11, 1934, WEAF Master Books, sect. 3, 12.

79 McIntyre to Cantor, telegram, November 12, 1934, "Eddie Cantor," FDR PPF 1018.

80 McLeod, *Original Amos 'n' Andy*, 95–101; Arthur Frank Wertham, *Radio Comedy* (New York: Oxford University Press, 1979), 39–41, 79–83, 165; J. Fred MacDonald, *Don't Touch That Dial!* (Chicago: Nelson-Hall,1979), 107; Glenn D. Smith Jr., *Something on My Own: Gertrude Berg and American Broadcasting, 1929–1956* (Syracuse, NY: Syracuse University Press, 2007), 79–80.

81 H. B. Summers, *Radio Censorship* (New York: H. W. Wilson, 1939), 25, 139–52. Michele Hilmes chronicles the problems that networks encountered in trying to control content, especially sexual innuendo, in comedy-variety programs in Hilmes,

Radio Voices: American Broadcasting, 1922–1952 (Minneapolis: University of Minnesota Press, 1997), 119–24.

82 Carroll Carroll, *None of Your Business* (New York: Cowles Book Company, 1970), 35.

83 Oshinsky, *Polio*, 55; Ira R. T. Smith, *Dear Mr. President . . . The Story of My Fifty Years in the White House* (New York: Julian Messnep, 1949), 155.

84 "Hollywood Inside," *Variety*, January 27, 1938; Scott M. Cutlip, *Fund Raising in the United States: Its Role in America's Philanthropy* (1965; repr., New Brunswick, NJ: Transaction Publishers, 1990), 386. Cantor and Ardmore, *Take My Life*, 198–200.

7. RADIO WITH A JEWISH ACCENT (1931–1938)

1 The program began as *The Rise of the Goldbergs* on November 20, 1929. In 1936, the title was shortened to *The Goldbergs*. After its continuous run ended in 1945, the show returned on CBS as a weekly comedy program for the 1949–1950 season. See J. Hoberman, "The Goldbergs: A Chronology," in Hoberman and Shandler, *Entertaining America*, 124–25; Donald Weber, "Goldberg Variations: The Achievements of Gertrude Berg," in Hoberman and Shandler, *Entertaining America*, 113–23.

2 "Yid Comedy Gets Over," *Variety*, November 27, 1929, 65.

3 Perriton Maxwell, "Mother of the Goldbergs," *Radioland*, March 1934, 41.

4 NBC Statistical Department, "A Brief Study of the Appeal and Popularity of 'The Goldbergs,'" unpublished report, July 25, 1932, box 13, National Broadcasting Company Records, Wisconsin Historical Society, Madison, WI, hereafter, cited as NBC Records Wisconsin Historical Society; Susan Smulyan, *Selling Radio* (Washington, DC: Smithsonian Institution Press, 1994), 116.

5 Quotations from this episode here and following come from *Chase and Sanborn Hour*, script, NBC Red, September 13, 1931; *Eddie Cantor Chase and Sanborn Radio Show 1931–1933*, disc 1, compact disc.

6 For more on the role of announcers in reinforcing social differences, see Susan J. Douglas, *Listening In: Radio and the American Imagination, from Amos 'n' Andy and Edward R. Murrow to Wolfman Jack and Howard Stern* (New York: Random House, 1999), 103.

7 The Dial Twister, "Tuning In," *Pittsburgh Jewish Criterion*, October 9, 1931, 7.

8 Jessel, *So Help Me*, 140.

9 Cantor and Ardmore, *Take My Life*, 219; "Radio Preview Now; Eddie Cantor's Idea," *Variety*, February 12, 1935, 78.

10 *Chase and Sanborn Hour*, NBC Red, December 17, 1933, on *Eddie Cantor Chase and Sanborn Radio Show 1931–1933*, disc 3, compact disc.

11 *Eddie Cantor Show*, CBS, December 13, 1936, MP3 file, author's private collection.

12 Historian David E. Kaufman analyzes how performers and audiences used Yiddish and other "insider's nods" to Jewish audiences. See David E. Kaufman, *Jewhooing the Sixties* (Hanover, NH: University Press of New England/Brandeis University Press, 2012), 120.

13 *Chase and Sanborn Hour*, NBC Red, March 18, 1934, on Vintage Radio Classics, n.d., compact disc.

14 *Chase and Sanborn Hour*, script, NBC Red, September 20, 1931, WEAF Master Books, 9.

15 Stiller, *Married to Laughter*, 28–32; Jerry Stiller interview, Archive of American Television, Television Academy Foundation, www.emmytvlegends.org.

16 Joseph A. Loewinsohn, "Eddie Cantor in Atlanta," *Atlanta Southern Israelite*, April 1933, 9, 13.

17 "Prominent American Jews Join Palestine Relief Fund Committee," Jewish Telegraphic Agency, September 1, 1929, JTA Archive, www.jta.org/archive.

18 "Notables Rally to Zionist Roll Call," Jewish Telegraphic Agency, November 21, 1929, JTA Archive, www.jta.org/archive.

19 Henry L. Feingold, *A Time for Searching: Entering the Mainstream* (Baltimore: Johns Hopkins University Press, 1992), 172–75; Melvin I. Urofsky, *American Zionism from Herzl to the Holocaust* (Garden City, NY: Doubleday, 1975), 323–87.

20 Raymond Dannenbaum, "Eddie Cantor Confides His Beliefs," *Boston Jewish Advocate*, November 28, 1930, 7.

21 Ibid.

22 "Workers Launch Federation's Drive for $2,221,000," Jewish Telegraphic Agency, October 20, 1930, JTA Archive, www.jta.org/archive.

23 Martha Neumark, "The Lights of New York," *Pittsburgh Jewish Criterion*, December 2, 1932, 4; see also "Today on the Radio," *New York Times*, November 15, 1932.

24 "84 Editors Select 'Ten Leading Jews,'" *New York Times*, December 31, 1932.

25 S. Sidney Kalwary, "Eddie Cantor . . . The Philosophical Personality," *Pittsburgh Jewish Criterion*, March 23, 1934, 36.

26 For more on the tensions between private and public assistance, see Wenger, *New York Jews and the Great Depression*, 146–48; Dollinger, *Quest for Inclusion*, 35.

27 Goldman, *Banjo Eyes*, 169; "Cantor's 100% Tilt to $5,000 upon Returning," *Variety*, April 11, 1933, 35; "New Cantor Air Deal Is $10,000, 30 Min. Weekly," *Daily Variety*, April 24, 1934, 1.

28 "Eddie Cantor Sued by Dave Freedman," *Variety*, April 3, 1935, 35.

29 "David Freedman, Quip Writer, Dies," *New York Times*, December 9, 1936.

30 Ben Ohmert, *The Gripes of Rapp: The Auto/Biography of the Bickersons' Creator, Philip Rapp* (Albany, GA: Bear Manor Media, 2001), 7.

31 Douglas, *Listening In*, 106.

32 Dunning, *On the Air*, 222; Cantor and Ardmore, *Take My Life*, 235.

33 *Chase and Sanborn Hour*, NBC Red, April 1, 1934, compact disc, author's private collection.

34 Frank Cullen, *Vaudeville Old and New: An Encyclopedia of Variety Performers in America*, vol. 1 (New York: Routledge, 2006), 446–47; Richard Lamparski, *Whatever Became of . . . ?*, ser. 3 (New York: Crown Publishers, 1970), 108–9.

35 *How DOooo You Do!!!* (PRC Pictures, 1945).

36 Cantor and Ardmore, *Take My Life*, 234.

37 *Texaco Town*, CBS, January 5, 1938, MP3 file, author's private collection.

38 *Eddie Cantor Show*, CBS, December 22, 1935, MP3 file, author's private collection; Douglas, *Listening In*, 114.

39 *Eddie Cantor's Camel Caravan*, unpublished script, CBS, January 16, 1939, Old Time Radio Researchers Group, www.otrr.org (punctuation in original).

40 *Texaco Town*, CBS, January 31, 1937, MP3 file, author's private collection.

41 "Eddie Cantor Anniversary Is Observed," *Boston Jewish Advocate*, October 29, 1937, 1; "H'wood's Tribute to Eddie Cantor's Silver Jubilee a Big Click," *Variety*, November 3, 1937, 4; *Eddie Cantor Testimonial Dinner*, CBS, October 28, 1937, Nostalgia Company, n.d., compact disc. Subsequent quotations from the broadcast are taken from this compact disc.

42 Here, I follow Cantor's spelling in his autobiography and pronunciation in the broadcast for "Itzkowitz," rather than the spelling on the 1894 death certificate of Cantor's mother, Meta Iskowitz. See Cantor and Ardmore, *Take My Life*, 13.

43 *Eddie Cantor's Camel Caravan*, unpublished script, CBS, May 30, 1938, 11–12, Master Settlement Agreement (MSA) Collections, Legacy Tobacco Documents Library, University of California, San Francisco, www.industrydocumentslibrary.ucsf.edu/tobacco; hereafter, cited as Legacy Tobacco Documents. "Itskowitz" is spelled slightly differently here than it is in Cantor's autobiography.

44 Josh Kun writes about this kind of unmasking in Josh Kun, "Abie the Fishman: On Masks, Birthmarks, and Hunchbacks," in *Listen Again: A Momentary History of Pop Music*, ed. Eric Weisbard (Durham, NC: Duke University Press, 2007), 50–68.

8. THE FIGHT AGAINST NAZISM (1933–1939)

1 Gregory Koseluk, *Eddie Cantor: A Life in Show Business* (Jefferson, NC: McFarland, 1995), 276; Goldman, *Banjo Eyes*, 201; A. Scott Berg, *Goldwyn: A Biography* (New York: Ballantine Books, 1990), 255; "Cantor Walks on Goldwyn Antique, Looks Like Law," *Daily Variety*, July 28, 1936; "Cantor Ends Contract with 20th Over Story Material," *Daily Variety*, August 31, 1938.

2 Dinnerstein, *Anti-Semitism in America*, 111–27; Henry L. Feingold, *A Time for Searching: Entering the Mainstream 1920–1945* (Baltimore: Johns Hopkins University Press, 1992), 228; Alan Brinkley, *Voices of Protest* (New York: Vintage Books, 1983), 266.

3 There is a vast historiography on the American Jewish response to Nazi Germany and the Holocaust. Useful summaries of the literature include Rafael Medoff, "New Perspectives on How America, and American Jewry, Responded to the Holocaust," *American Jewish History* 84, no. 3 (1996): 253–66; Steven Bayme, "American Jewish Leadership Confronts the Holocaust: Revisiting Naomi Cohen's Thesis and the American Jewish Committee," *American Jewish Archives Journal* 61, no. 2 (2009), 163–86.

4 Samuel Dickstein to Eddie Cantor, telegram, n.d. (ca. November 1933), Committee Papers, Special Committee on Un-American Activities Authorized to Investigate Nazi Propaganda, HR 73a-F30.1 (entry 9), Seventy-Third Congress, Records of the US House of Representatives, Record Group 233, National Archives, Washington, DC; hereafter, cited as Nazi Propaganda Records.

5 Cantor to Dickstein, November 7, 1933, Nazi Propaganda Records.

6 See the correspondence between Cantor and Lewis in Jewish Federation Council of Greater Los Angeles, Community Relations Committee Collection, Oviatt Library, California State University, Northridge; hereafter, cited as Jewish Federation Council collection. For more on Lewis and the LAJCC, including Lewis's respective relationships with Gutstadt and Cantor, see Laura Rosenzweig, "Hollywood's Spies: Jewish Infiltration of Nazi and Pro-Nazi Groups in Los Angeles, 1933–1941" (PhD diss., University of California, Santa Cruz, 2013), 310, 367.

7 In November 1933, Gutstadt and Lewis ultimately decided to withhold information from Dickstein's committee to protect their undercover operation. See Rozensweig, "Hollywood's Spies," 164–68.

8 "News from the Dailies," *Variety*, July 11, 1933, 60.

9 "35,000 Hear Stars to Aid Reich Jews," *New York Times*, Sept 21, 1934.

10 "'Night of Stars' Will Aid U.J.A. Campaign," *New Palestine*, September 27, 1935; "'Night of Stars' Huge Success," *New Palestine*, October 4, 1935; "400 to Play in Benefit," *New York Times*, November 6, 1938; "Woollcott Hopes to Resume Acting," *New York Times*, November 20, 1940; "Jewish Fund Aided by 'Night of Stars,'" *New York Times*, November 28, 1940. The 1938 *Night of Stars* was a benefit for the UPA. The 1940 show benefited the reconstituted UJA.

11 "Death Toll Mounts in Germany," Jewish Telegraphic Agency, July 12, 1934, JTA Archive, www.jta.org/archive.

12 "Cantor Explains Success Theory," Jewish Telegraphic Agency, January 14, 1935, JTA Archive, www.jta.org/archive; "Catholic Guild Show Raises $14,000 Fund," *New York Times*, February 18, 1935.

13 Donald Warren, *Radio Priest: Charles Coughlin, the Father of Hate Radio* (New York: Free Press, 1996), 129–60; "Warburg Plays Drums in Ship's Orchestra," *New York Times*, March 15, 1935; "Baruch Corrects Priest," *New York Times*, March 13, 1935; "Jews Urged to Aid in Defense Abroad," *New York Times*, March 17, 1935; "Warning to Europe Urged by Coughlin," *New York Times*, March 25, 1935; "Dr. S. S. Wise Replies to Father Coughlin," *New York Times*, March 27, 1935. Historian Alan Brinkley recognizes the concerns of American Jews about Coughlin during the mid-1930s, and he notes the ways in which Coughlin evoked antisemitic stereotypes by railing against "international bankers" and "money changers." Brinkley argues that antisemitism did not play a role in Coughlin's popularity until 1938, however, when the priest's rhetoric became more explicitly hostile to Jews. See Brinkley, *Voices of Protest*, 269–73.

14 "Religion: Cantor on Coughlin," *Time*, July 13, 1935, 43; Sheldon Marcus, *Father*

Coughlin: *The Tumultuous Life of the Priest of the Little Flower* (Boston: Little, Brown, 1973), 97; "Jews' Status Precarious, Cantor Warns Lodgemen," *Los Angeles Times*, July 2, 1935.

15 "Religion: Cantor on Coughlin"; "Jews' Status Precarious."

16 Thomas Doherty, *Hollywood's Censor: Joseph I. Breen and the Production Code Administration* (New York: Columbia University Press, 2007), 206–7.

17 The July 23, 1936, rally was sponsored by the Hollywood League against Nazism, a precursor to the HANL. "Nazi Policies Rapped by Filmites at H'wood Meet," *Daily Variety*, July 24, 1936; "10,000 Pack Shrine for Anti-Nazi Meet," *Daily Variety*, October 21, 1936. According to publicity before the event, Cantor was scheduled to appear at two additional anti-Nazi functions in Los Angeles: an anniversary party for the Hollywood Anti-Nazi League held on August 5, 1937, and a rally sponsored by the Los Angeles Community Conference on Democracy, a coalition of one hundred organizations including the HANL, held on January 30, 1938. Media coverage of these events suggests that Cantor did not actually appear as announced, though a telegram from Cantor was read at the January 30, 1938, rally. See "'Million Dollar' Floor Show Is Gay Spectacle," *News of the World*, August 7, 1937, 1, 6; Phyllis Marie Arthur, "Gals and Gab," *Daily Variety*, August 6, 1937; "7000 Roar OK to Collective Action against War-Makers," *Hollywood Now*, February 4, 1938.

18 Leonard Dinnerstein chronicles the association of Jews with communism during the 1930s in *Anti-Semitism in America*, 111–18; see also Steven Carr, *Hollywood and Anti-Semitism: A Cultural History up to World War II* (New York: Cambridge University Press, 2001), 154–81.

19 Saverio Giovacchini, *Hollywood Modernism: Film and Politics in the Age of the New Deal* (Philadelphia: Temple University Press, 2001), 104; Ronald Brownstein, *The Power and the Glitter* (New York: Vintage Books, 1992), 63; Gabler, *An Empire of Their Own*, 334. Thomas Doherty surveys HANL's activities and politics in Doherty, *Hollywood and Hitler*, 96–121.

20 See, for example, NBC Continuity Acceptance Department, "Radio Is Human, Too!," unpublished report, April 1938, 17, folder 357, NBC History Papers, Library of Congress; on advertiser branding of stars, see Cynthia B. Meyers, *A Word from Our Sponsor* (New York: Fordham University Press, 2014), 149.

21 "Serious Side of Comedy," *Variety*, March 24, 1937, 1; MacDonald, *Don't Touch That Dial!*, 107; "Radio Is Human, Too!," 17; West, *The Rape of Radio*, 250.

22 Dinnerstein, *Anti-Semitism in America*, 105–30; Dollinger, *Quest for Inclusion*, 72–75.

23 The first performance was on *The Fleischmann Yeast Hour*, hosted by Rudy Vallee, NBC Red, April 23, 1936. The other broadcast dates, on Cantor's program, were November 15, 1936, March 28, 1938, and March 13, 1939.

24 *Eddie Cantor Show*, CBS, December 20, 1936, MP3 file.

25 *Eddie Cantor's "Camel Caravan,"* script, CBS, May 2, 1938, 36, Legacy Tobacco Documents, legacy.library.ucsf.edu.

26 *Eddie Cantor's "Camel Caravan,"* script, CBS, November 21, 1938, 30A, Legacy Tobacco Documents, legacy.library.ucsf.edu.

27 "Cantor's Quip, Publicized by President, Was Turned Down by Radio Sponsor," *Variety*, November 30, 1938, 1.

28 "President Franklin D. Roosevelt Reads a Telegram from Eddie Cantor," track 20. *Pals: Eddie Cantor and George Jessel*, produced by Brian Gari, Original Cast OC-9918, 1999, compact disc.

29 Felix Belair Jr., "Roosevelt Carves Turkey, Not Map," *New York Times*, November 25, 1938.

30 Eddie Cantor to Marvin H. McIntyre, January 12, 1939, FDR PPF 1018.

31 M. H. McIntyre to Sumner Welles, memo, January 18, 1939, FDR PPF 1018.

32 Welles's response was sent under McIntyre's signature. See M. H. McIntyre to Eddie Cantor, January 27, 1939, FDR PPF 1018. For more on the Wagner-Rogers bill, including the significance of Welles's response to Cantor, see Arthur Morse, *While Six Million Died: A Chronicle of American Apathy* (New York: Random House, 1968), 252–69.

33 Sandra Berliant Kadosh, "Ideology vs. Reality: Youth Aliyah and the Rescue of Jewish Children during the Holocaust Era 1933–1945" (PhD diss., Columbia University, 1995), 1; Marian Greenberg, *There Is Hope for Your Children: Youth Aliyah, Henrietta Szold and Hadassah* (New York: Hadassah, 1986), 4; Erica B. Simmons, *Hadassah and the Zionist Project* (Lanham, MD: Rowman and Littlefield, 2006), 118.

34 Simmons, *Hadassah and the Zionist Project*, 115, 123, 136–37; Marlin Levin, *Balm in Gilead* (New York: Schocken Books, 1974), 120–21; Mira Katzburg-Yungman, *Hadassah: American Women Zionists and the Rebirth of Israel*, trans. Tammy Berkowitz (Portland, OR: Litman Library of Jewish Civilization, 2012), 34–35. For more on Hadassah's fund-raising and allocations among medical projects and Youth Aliyah, see the annual reports on Hadassah in the *American Jewish Yearbook*. For example, *American Jewish Year Book 5697*, vol. 38 [1936 to 1937], ed. Harry Schneiderman for the American Jewish Committee (Philadelphia: Jewish Publication Society of America, 1936), 205; *American Jewish Year Book 5698*, vol. 39 [1937 to 1938], ed. Harry Schneiderman for the American Jewish Committee (Philadelphia: Jewish Publication Society of America, 1937), 287–88.

35 Marian G. Greenberg, *There Is Hope for Your Children*, 96; Levin, *Balm in Gilead*, 130.

36 Marian G. Greenberg to Henrietta Szold, April 3, 1936, Record Group 1, box 1, Archives of Youth Aliyah: 1933–1960, Hadassah Archives at the Center for Jewish History, New York, NY, hereafter, cited as Youth Aliyah archives; Hadassah, "Eddie Cantor Pledges Aid for German-Jewish Children," press release, March 27, 1936, box 17, Youth Aliyah archives.

37 Greenberg to Szold, April 3, 1936, Youth Aliyah archives.

38 "Extract from a letter outlining the conditions under which Mr. Cantor will visit any city on behalf of the Youth Aliyah Movement," letter to Hadassah chapter pres-

idents, n.d. (circa 1936), box 1, Youth Aliyah archives; Marian G. Greenberg to Eva Stern, November 16, 1936, box 1, Youth Aliyah archives; Marian G. Greenberg to Hedwig Epstein, April 5, 1938, box 1, Youth Aliyah archives; "New Yorker Re-elected President of Hadassah," *New York Times*, November 3, 1938.

39 *American Jewish Year Book 5697*, vol. 38 [1936 to 1937], 205; Levin, *Balm in Gilead*, 127; US Bureau of the Census, *Religious Bodies: 1936*, vol. 2, pt. 1, Denominations A to J (Washington, DC: Government Printing Office, 1941), 771; Katzburg-Yungman, *Hadassah*, 309.

40 Membership figures are from Katzburg-Yungman, *Hadassah*, 35–36, 309.

41 Zev Zahavy, "A History and Survey of Jewish Religious Broadcasting" (PhD diss., Yeshiva University, 1959), 148–85.

42 The programs aired on October 20, 1936, August 3, 1938, January 9, 1943, June 29, 1943, and July 9, 1943.

43 On the *New York Times* ad, see Henrietta Szold to Marian G. Greenberg, May 24, 1938, box 9A, Youth Aliyah archives. Ads for Youth Aliyah, sponsored by Cantor, appeared in *New York Times*, April 11, 1938, and *Daily Variety*, June 25, 1938.

44 Hadassah, untitled press release, July 29, 1938, Youth Aliyah archives; Hadassah, "Hadassah Honors Eddie Cantor for Youth Aliyah Work," press release, August 3, 1938, box 17, Youth Aliyah archives; Henrietta Szold to Marian G. Greenberg, August 1, 1938, box 9A, Youth Aliyah archives. Cantor's telegram is quoted in Szold's letter.

45 Greenberg to Stern, November 16, 1936.

46 The text of the address was reprinted in several Jewish weeklies. See Eddie Cantor, "No Time for Jokes!: A Humorist Gets Serious about the Jews," *Youngstown Jewish Times*, April 3, 1936, 11; see also Eddie Cantor, "No Time for Jokes!: A Humorist Gets Serious about the Jews," *Boston Jewish Advocate*, April 3, 1936, 1; Eddie Cantor, "No Time for Jokes!: A Humorist Gets Serious about the Jews," *San Francisco Jewish Tribune*, April 3, 1936, 11.

47 *Youth Aliyah*, CBS, October 20, 1936, tape LWO 5265 1A1–2, Recorded Sound Section, Library of Congress.

48 Simmons, *Hadassah and the Zionist Project*, 126.

49 Cantor, "No Time for Jokes!," 11; Hadassah, "Eddie Cantor Pledges Aid for German-Jewish Children."

50 "Eddie Cantor, Part 1 of 6," Federal Bureau of Investigation, Freedom of Information/Privacy Acts Section, File Number 26544, FBI Records: The Vault, vault.fbi .gov/Eddie%20Cantor, hereafter, cited as Cantor FBI; Walter Winchell, *Jergens Journal*, script, WJZ [NBC Blue], November 14, 1937, WJZ Master Books, NBC Collection, Recorded Sound Section, Library of Congress, hereafter, cited as WJZ Master Books; "Cantor Says Nazis Threaten His Life," *Hollywood Reporter*, April 1, 1938; "Cantor Reveals Nazi Threat Against Him," *Daily Variety*, April 1, 1938, 3.

51 "Nazi Honor to Ford Stirs Cantor's Ire," *New York Times*, August 4, 1938; Goldman, *Banjo Eyes*, 199–200.

52 David L. Lewis, *The Public Image of Henry Ford: An American Folk Hero and His Company* (Detroit, MI: Wayne State University Press, 1976), 149–50.

53 M. E. Rozelle to Cantor, August 5, 1938, Milt Larsen private collection; hereafter, cited as Larsen Collection. In 2016 the University of California Santa Barbara Library, Department of Special Research Collections, acquired this collection.

54 Lotz to Cantor, August 8, 1938, Larsen Collection.

55 A. Burt to Cantor, August 5, 1938, Larsen Collection.

56 "In Progressive Hollywood," *Hollywood Now*, June 11, 1938.

57 "Cantor Joke about Hitler Starts Fight," *Los Angeles Times*, March 28, 1939; "Hollywood Inside," *Daily Variety*, March 28, 1939; "Mild Riot Occurs during Eddie Cantor Broadcast," *Palm Beach Post*, March 29, 1939; "Cantor Aide May Go Free," *Los Angeles Times*, April 6, 1939; "Hollywood Pair Sue Cantor for $751,000 Damages," *Washington Post*, August 1, 1939; Koseluk, *Eddie Cantor*, 366. The episode received no more publicity after the Gollobs announced that they had filed a lawsuit on July 31, 1939. This lack of additional press coverage suggests that the civil case did not go to trial.

58 R. B. Hood to Director [J. Edgar Hoover], memorandum, April 4, 1939, "Eddie Cantor, Part 1 of 6," Cantor FBI.

59 Unsigned card to Cantor, March 28, 1939; Jerry P. Marshall to Cantor, March 30, 1939; A. Carroll, postcard to Cantor, n.d. All letters in Larsen Collection.

60 Louis Pekarsky, "The Jew in Eddie Cantor," *Pittsburgh Jewish Criterion*, October 22, 1937, 8.

61 Milton K. Susman, "As I See It," *Pittsburgh Jewish Criterion*, August 5, 1938, 7.

62 Eddie Cantor, "The One-Man Americanism Campaign," *Boston Jewish Advocate*, July 7, 1939, 10 (ellipses in original).

63 Eddie Cantor, "In the Temple of Religion: I See a Challenge to Humanity," *Pittsburgh Jewish Criterion*, June 23, 1939, 2; "Cantor Warns Jews at Fair's Hadassah Day," *New York Herald Tribune*, June 14, 1939; Goldman, *Banjo Eyes*, 210–11. For more on Reynolds, including his antisemitism, see Julian M. Pleasants, *Buncombe Bob: The Life and Times of Robert Rice Reynolds* (Chapel Hill: University of North Carolina Press, 2000), 141, 165–66. Senator Reynolds was not part of the R. J. Reynolds family.

64 Warren, *The Radio Priest*, 147–48. In his diary entry of August 26, 1939, Secretary of the Interior Harold Ickes noted that "rich people," including Ford and other car manufacturers, were said to be financing Coughlin. Harold L. Ickes, *The Secret Diary of Harold L. Ickes: vol. 2: The Inside Struggle, 1936–1939* (New York: Simon and Schuster, 1954), 706.

65 Ramsburg, *Network Radio Ratings*, 79; on ratings, see also Summers, *A Thirty-Year History of Programs*, 75; "Most Popular Radio Stars Picked in Fan Poll," *Broadcasting*, July 1, 1939, 46.

66 Phineas J. Biron, "Strictly Confidential: Tidbits from Everywhere," *Pittsburgh Jewish Criterion*, July 7, 1939, 5.

67 Emily Cheney, "Only Human," *New York Sunday Mirror*, July 4, 1943.

68 Cantor and Ardmore, *Take My Life*, 224–25.

9. CANTOR GOES TO CHURCH (1939–1941)

1 "Eddie Cantor Becomes Life Member of A.Z.A.," *Ohio Jewish Chronicle*, November 17, 1939, 1; "The First Cantor in A.Z.A.," *B'nai B'rith Messenger*, November 17, 1939, n.p.

2 "Edward Warburg Named J.D.C. Co-chairman at Chicago Parley; Labor Leaders Get Posts," Jewish Telegraphic Agency, December 4, 1939, JTA Archive, www.jta.org /archive.

3 *Screen Guild Theater*, CBS, December 31, 1939, MP3 file, author's private collection; Koseluk, *Eddie Cantor*, 367.

4 Douglas W. Churchill, "Screen News Here and in Hollywood," *New York Times*, August 24, 1939; Odec., review of Eddie Cantor stage show, *Variety*, July 5, 1939; no author, "Eddie Cantor—Loew's State Theatre—Week of June 29, 1939," script, box 2, Cantor Papers UCLA.

5 "'What a Life' Ends Tomorrow Night," *New York Times*, July 7, 1939; Robert Coleman, "Cantors to Celebrate Silver Wedding All Day Today," *New York Mirror*, June 9, 1939; "Cantor Draws 20,000 to Safety Meeting," *New York Times*, June 29, 1939.

6 Scho., review of Eddie Cantor stage show, *Variety*, October 25, 1939, 45. "Durbin's 'First Love' Tees Off Chi's Palace Duals to Good $13,000, Cooper Fine 15G, Cantor Ups 'Cat' to Wow 52G," *Variety*, November 8, 1939, 7; Harold W. Cohen, review of Eddie Cantor stage show, *Pittsburgh Post-Gazette*, September 30, 1939.

7 "Eddie Cantor, in Pulpit, Makes Plea for Democracy," *Pittsburgh Post-Gazette*, October 2, 1939; "People," *Time*, October 9, 1939, 68.

8 Kevin M. Schultz, *Tri-Faith America: How Catholics and Jews Held Postwar America to Its Protestant Promise* (New York: Oxford University Press, 2011), 35–41; Wendy L. Wall, *Inventing the American Way* (New York: Oxford University Press, 2008), 76–83.

9 Franklin Delano Roosevelt, "Hands across Creeds," *San Francisco Jewish Tribune*, October 10, 1936, 35.

10 Dollinger, *Quest for Inclusion*, 55–65; Stuart Svonkin, *Jews against Prejudice: American Jews and the Fight for Civil Liberties* (New York: Columbia University Press, 1997), 45.

11 *Texaco Town*, script, CBS, September 27, 1936, 17–23, box 1, Cantor Papers UCLA.

12 *Eddie Cantor's "Camel Caravan,"* script, CBS, February 20, 1939, 31, Legacy Tobacco Documents; "Eddie Cantor Speaking," *Radio Guide*, March 18, 1939, 4.

13 Marion K. Kablet, "Entertainment Is Just Froth Says Eddie Cantor to Criterion Interviewer," *Jewish Criterion*, October 6, 1939, 7.

14 Unsigned review of Eddie Cantor stage show, *Washington Post*, October 27, 1939.

15 Howard E. Wentworth, "Eddie Cantor to Broadcast on Post-WJSV Safety Drive," *Washington Post*, October 28, 1939.

16 "Cantor Plays a Second to His Grandson," *Washington Post*, November 1, 1939.

17 "High School Scribes Corner Cantor," *Washington Post*, October 31, 1939.

18 "A Pair of Wide-Open Eyes See Washington," *Washington Post*, October 28, 1939; Pare Lorentz Center at the FDR Library, "Franklin D. Roosevelt Day-by-Day," October 27, 1939, Franklin D. Roosevelt Presidential Library and Museum, www.fdrlibrary .marist.edu/daybyday/. Nelson B, Bell, "Deanna Durbin Scores Fifth Consecutive Hit," *Washington Post*, November 2, 1939.

19 Kablet, "Entertainment Is Just Froth," 7.

20 "Declare Pro-Nazis Map War Sabotage," *New York Times*, August 13, 1938; "Federal Official Protects Bridges, Dies Aide Charges," *New York Times*, August 15, 1938; "High Federal Aids Are Linked to Reds at House Hearing," *New York Times*, August 18, 1938; Doherty, *Hollywood and Hitler*, 227–31.

21 Eddie Cantor to Leon L. Lewis, August 25, 1938, box CRC/2 17–12, Jewish Federation Council collection. See also Martin Dies, to Leon L. Lewis, telegram, August 6, 1938, box CRC/2 24–16, Jewish Federation Council collection. A digital copy of the Dies telegram is available at California State University Northridge, Oviatt Library, *In Our Own Backyard* (web exhibit), www.digital-library.csun.edu/Backyard/.

22 Martin Dies, "Is Communism Invading the Movies?" *Liberty*, February 24, 1940, 58; Martin Dies, "The Reds in Hollywood," *Liberty*, February 17, 1940, 47–48. See also Ceplair and Englund, *The Inquisition in Hollywood*, 109; Doherty, *Hollywood and Hitler 1933–1939*, 226–36.

23 "First Congregationalist Talk Warns against Propaganda for Isms; Says 'We Don't Wave Our Flags,'" *Washington Post*, Oct 30, 1939; "Eddie Cantor to Tour So. Africa for Youth Aliyah," Jewish Telegraphic Agency, October 31, 1939, JTA Archive, www .jta.org/archive.

24 Drew Pearson and Robert S. Allen, "The Washington Merry-Go-Round," *Pittsburgh Press*, November 6, 1939.

25 A. A. Roback, "Panorama," *Boston Jewish Advocate*, November 10, 1939, 4, 17.

26 "A Comic's Comeback," *New York Times*, March 24, 1940.

27 See, for example, Walt, review of *Forty Little Mothers*, *Variety*, April 17, 1940, 13; B. R. Crisler, review of *Forty Little Mothers*, *New York Times*, April 19, 1940; Richard L. Coe, review of *Forty Little Mothers*, *Washington Post*, May 11, 1940.

28 "Oath for Citizenship," NBC Blue, May 5, 1940, recording, LWO 5320 14B13–15A2, Recorded Sound Division, Library of Congress; "4,000 New Voters Hear Cantor," *Washington Post*, May 6, 1940. The FBI also summarized Cantor's Tulsa speech, bringing Cantor's references to the attention of the director. See L. B. Nichols to Clyde Tolson, memorandum, May 6, 1940, "Eddie Cantor, Part 1 of 6," Cantor FBI.

29 J. Edgar Hoover to Eddie Cantor, May 6, 1940, "Eddie Cantor, Part 1 of 6," Cantor FBI; "B'nai B'rith District 1 Holds 88th Annual Parley in Boston," Jewish Telegraphic Agency, May 13, 1940, JTA Archive, www.jta.org/archive.

30 *It's Time to Smile*, NBC, May 9, 1945, MP3 file, author's private collection; Hoover to Cantor, May 11, 1945, "Eddie Cantor, Part 2 of 6," Cantor FBI.

31 Cantor and Ardmore, *Take My Life*, 224–25; Bill Thomas to Tom Harrington, August 15, 1940, scrapbook, pf Ms. 2003.G3.1, Fred Allen Collection, Rare Books and Manuscripts, Boston Public Library. Parts of the memorandum are quoted in Robert Taylor, *Fred Allen: His Life and Wit* (Boston: Little, Brown, 1989), 284–85.

32 William D. Rubenstein, *The Myth of Rescue* (New York: Routledge, 1997), 45–47; Dinnerstein, *Antisemitism in America*, 128.

33 Franklin D. Roosevelt, "Fireside Chat," September 3, 1939, in Gerhard Peters and John T. Woolley, American Presidency Project, www.presidency.ucsb.edu.

34 Dr. G. George Fox, "From the Watch Tower," *Chicago Sentinel*, December 18, 1940, 13.

35 "Cantorisms," *Variety*, July 17, 1940, 3.

36 "Cantor Expounds on America's Need for Real Good Laugh Right Now," *Variety*, November 20, 1940, 2. It is not clear whether European refugees ever actually stayed on Cantor's estate.

37 *Millions for Defense*, CBS, August 27, 1941, LWO 5404 reel 4 B3–6, Recorded Sound Division, Library of Congress.

38 "Freedom Rally Thrills 17,000," *New York Times*, October 6, 1941; Rafael Medoff, "Leo Durocher's View of Saddam Hussein," David S. Wyman Institute for Holocaust Studies, http://www.wymaninstitute.org/.

39 John K. Hutchens, "Comedians All," *New York Times*, September 28, 1941.

40 Odec., review of *It's Time to Smile*, *Variety*, October 9, 1940, 26.

41 Ramsburg, *Network Radio Ratings*, 95, 216.

42 For more on the postwar emergence of the Lower East Side as the locus for myths about the origins of American Jewish history, see Hasia R. Diner, *Lower East Side Memories: A Jewish Place in America* (Princeton, NJ: Princeton University Press, 2000).

43 *It's Time to Smile*, NBC Red, June 4, 1941, MP3 file, author's private collection.

44 The play ran in previews in New Haven, Boston, and Philadelphia for nearly two months before the December 25, 1941, Broadway opening.

45 Theodore Strauss, "Back to Broadway Has Come a Well Familiar Face," *New York Times*, January 4, 1942.

46 Cliff Friend and Charles Tobias, "We Did It Before and We Can Do It Again" (New York: M. Witmark and Sons, 1941); Joseph Quinlan and Izzy Elinson, *Banjo Eyes*, script, n.d. (performed 1941–1942), n.p., box 1, John Cecil Holm Papers, Wisconsin Historical Society, Madison, WI.

47 Goldman, *Banjo Eyes*, 227, 352; "Show Is Terminated by Illness of Cantor," *New York Times*, April 16, 1942. Goldman asserts that Cantor had been suffering from hemorrhoids.

10. IT'S TIME TO SMILE AGAIN (1941–1945)

1 Helen Ormsbee, "Cantor, Back after 12 Years, Plans New Role as a Producer," *New York Herald Tribune*, December 21, 1941.

2 McDonald to Cantor, telegram, December 23, 1941, box 9, James G. McDonald Papers, Rare Book and Manuscript Library, Columbia University, New York, NY; hereafter, cited as McDonald Papers.

3 Strauss, "Back to Broadway."

4 "Cantor Explains Need for Comics," *Variety*, January 14, 1942, 1.

5 Strauss, "Back to Broadway."

6 *It's Time to Smile*, NBC Red, March 11, 1942, LWO 15731, reel 1, A2, Recorded Sound Division, Library of Congress.

7 NBC, *Proceedings, NBC War Clinic*, Waldorf-Astoria Hotel, New York, March 17, 1942, 31–33, folder 646, NBC History Papers, Library of Congress. For more on *The Great Dictator* and *To Be or Not to Be*, see Charles J. Maland, *Chaplin and American Culture: The Evolution of a Star Image* (Princeton, NJ: Princeton University Press, 1989), 178–85; Thomas Doherty, *Projections of War: Hollywood, American Culture, and World War II* (New York: Columbia University Press, 1993), 126–28.

8 Kathleen E. R. Smith, *God Bless America: Tin Pan Alley Goes to War* (Lexington: University of Kentucky Press, 2003), 62, 69. Walt Disney Productions used similar anti-Axis satire and the song "Der Fuehrer's Face" in its animated short, *Der Fuehrer's Face*, which won an Academy Award in 1943. See *Der Fuehrer's Face*, directed by Jack Kinney, *Walt Disney Treasures: Walt Disney on the Front Lines*, disc 1 (1943; Burbank, CA: Buena Vista Home Entertainment, 2001), digital video disc.

9 "Cantor Smile Time Is Howl Time as Banjo Wows Army," *Variety*, October 22, 1942, 4.

10 Office of War Information, *When Radio Writes for War* (Washington, DC: Office of War Information, 1943), 3.

11 *It's Time to Smile*, NBC Red, March 31, 1943, MP3 file, author's private collection.

12 *It's Time to Smile*, NBC, February 16, 1944, RWA 6294, Side B, Recorded Sound Division, Library of Congress.

13 "Follow-Up Comment," *Variety*, February 23, 1944, 32.

14 *It's Time to Smile*, NBC, February 28, 1945, MP3 file, author's private collection.

15 "Cantor Explains Need for Comics," *Variety*, January 14, 1942, 1.

16 "Eddie Cantor Lists Camp Show Don'ts," *New York Times*, July 15, 1943.

17 John K. Hutchens, "E. Cantor and Others," *New York Times*, May 14, 1944.

18 This was not the first war bonds marathon on radio. Most notably, Kate Smith attracted attention in September 1943 when she appeared on CBS for a minute or two each hour over the course of an eighteen-hour broadcast day. Cantor stayed on the air for much longer. For more on Smith's broadcast, see Robert K. Merton, *Mass Persuasion* (New York: Howard Fertig, 2004), 2.

19 "Cantor Round the World Windup," script, shortwave radio broadcast, January 30,

1944, 4–5, 9, box 3, Manning Ostroff Papers, UCLA Library Special Collections, Los Angeles, CA; hereafter, cited as Ostroff Papers.

20 "Sale of War Bonds Tops Other Drives," *New York Times*, January 31, 1944.

21 "Cantor Sells 37 Million," *Daily Variety*, January 31, 1944; "Show Biz May Be Proud of Cantor," *Variety*, February 1, 1944, 3.

22 Franklin D. Roosevelt to Cantor, telegram, January 31, 1944, box 35, UCLA Cantor.

23 Abel Green, "Cantor's Halloran Routine a Closeup of Show Biz 'M.D.'s' with Laugh Plasma," *Variety*, June 7, 1944, 2; see also "Cantor Tours Hospitals; Goes to Film Opening," *Daily Variety*, April 12, 1944; "On the Hospital Loop," *Daily Variety*, October 16, 1944.

24 Eddie Cantor to Los Angeles Advertising Club, unpublished speech, August 1, 1944, box 19, UCLA Ostroff Papers.

25 "H'Wood Comes through Legion Conv. Unscathed; Vets on Good Behavior," *Variety*, September 28, 1938, 6; "Legion's Circus Has Everything but Good Crowd," *Chicago Tribune*, September 28, 1939.

26 Cantor to Atherton, telegram, September 13, 1944, box 12, Ostroff Papers.

27 "Did You 'Give a Gift to the Yank Who Gave'?," *Macy's Star*, December 23, 1946, n.p., scrapbook, box 57, UCLA Cantor. See other articles in this scrapbook for more on the scope of the campaign.

28 Ceplar and Englund, *Inquisition in Hollywood*, 392–94.

29 *A Salute to Eddie Cantor*, script, NBC, May 7, 1944, 11–12, box 4, Cantor Papers UCLA.

30 See Arnold M, Auerbach, *Funny Men Don't Laugh* (Garden City, NY: Doubleday, 1965); Ohmart, *Gripes of Rapp*, 34–60; Bob Weiskopf, interview, in Jordan R. Young, *The Laugh Crafters* (Beverly Hills: Past Times, 1999), 140–49.

31 Carroll, *None of Your Business*, 28; Frank Buxton and Bill Owen, *The Big Broadcast 1920–1950* (New York: Avon, 1973), 50; John Dunning, *On the Air: The Encyclopedia of Old-Time Radio* (New York: Oxford University Press, 1998), 221.

32 Charles Isaacs, interview, in Young, *Laugh Crafters*, 53.

33 "The Selling Approach," *Motion Picture Herald*, September 25, 1943, 51; "Picture Grosses," *Motion Picture Herald*, October 16, 1943, 52; Red Kann, "On the March," *Motion Picture Herald*, December 18, 1943, 18.

34 Bosley Crowther, review of *Thank Your Lucky Stars*, *New York Times*, October 2, 1943; unsigned review of *Thank Your Lucky Stars*, *Daily Variety*, August 17, 1943, 4. See also Crowther's review of *Show Business*, *New York Times*, May 11, 1944.

35 For more on antisemitism during the war years, see Dinnerstein, *Anti-Semitism in America*, 128–49.

36 Marc Dollinger notes that Jewish communal leaders pursued a similar strategy. See Dollinger, *Quest for Inclusion*, 80.

37 Eddie Cantor to Milton Weill, December 2, 1942, Papers of Milton Weill, Collection P-34, box 1, American Jewish Historical Society, Center for Jewish History, New York, NY.

38 Cantor to Weill, December 2, 1942.

39 *Fred Allen Show*, November 29, 1942, CBS, MP3 file, OTR Network Library, www.otr. net.

40 "Testimonial Dinner to Eddie Cantor," unpublished transcript, May 7, 1944, Hotel Astor, New York, NY, box 37, Cantor Papers UCLA.

41 "100,000 Jewish Children Sign Declaration to Roosevelt Asking Help for Jews in Europe," Jewish Telegraphic Agency, May 5, 1943, JTA Archive, www.jta.org/archive; "'Rally of Hope' at Madison Square Garden Asks Aid for Jewish Children in Europe," Jewish Telegraphic Agency, June 7, 1943, JTA Archive, www.jta.org/archive.

42 "11,000 at San Francisco Meeting Protest Nazi Extermination of Jews," Jewish Telegraphic Agency, June 22, 1943, JTA Archive, www.jta.org/archive; "A Message to Humanity: Thomas Mann Calls for Liberalized Immigration Laws," *San Francisco Chronicle*, June 18, 1943.

43 Eddie Cantor, "No Dunkirk for Us," *Jewish Criterion*, September 11, 1942, 97.

44 *Youth Aliyah Fund Program*, CBS, July 9, 1943, LWO 5404 20B1–4, Recorded Sound Division, Library of Congress.

45 Ruth Maizlish, "Eddie Cantor, Savior of Children, Shows the Way," *B'nai B'rith Messenger*, August 13, 1943, n.p.; Eddie Cantor, "Stand . . . And Be Counted," *B'nai B'rith Messenger*, September 24, 1943, 36.

46 *It's Time to Smile*, NBC, January 31, 1945, MP3 file, author's private collection.

47 *We the People*, script, CBS, February 11, 1945, box 4, Cantor Papers UCLA.

48 Charles R. Smyth to Eddie Cantor, January 31, 1945, Larsen Collection. Allston is quoted in an undated and unsigned memorandum to Cantor with excerpts from several letters written by clergy and general listeners, circa February 1945, Larsen Collection.

49 Sachs Quality Furniture, advertisement, *New York Sunday News*, March 4, 1945.

50 Gardner, *Popular Songs of the Twentieth Century*, 132; *Buttsy's Moments to Remember*, "A Happy Land . . . Somewhere," blog entry, October 4, 2013, momentstoremember2 .wordpress.com; "Most-Played Juke-Box Records," *Billboard*, April 21, 1945, 25; "Best-Selling Popular Retail Records," April 28, 1945, 22; "Most-Played Juke-Box Records," *Billboard*, May 19, 1945, 25; "Most-Played Juke-Box Records," *Billboard*, June 2, 1945, 25.

51 Eddie Cantor, unpublished speech at General Rose Memorial Hospital Dinner, Denver, CO, May 27, 1945, box 5, Cantor Papers UCLA (emphases and underlining in original text). The speech was broadcast locally on station KOA (Denver).

11. POSTWAR STRUGGLES (1945–1950)

1 *Eddie Cantor Show*, script, NBC, December 5, 1945, box 8, Ostroff Papers; *Eddie Cantor Show*, script, NBC, February 6, 1946, box 9, Ostroff Papers.

2 Abel Green, "Radio Must Hatch Own Talent," *Variety*, June 13, 1945, 1, 44; Fred Allen, letter to the editor, *Variety*, June 13, 1945, 44.

3 Jack Hellman's "Light and Airy" column in *Daily Variety* published ratings for top programs. See, for example, Jack Hellman, "Light and Airy," *Daily Variety*, October 15, 1945; Jack Hellman, "Light and Airy," *Daily Variety*, October 29, 1945; Jack Hellman, "Light and Airy," *Daily Variety*, December 31, 1945; Jack Hellman, "Light and Airy," *Daily Variety*, March 19, 1946; Ramsburg, *Network Radio Ratings*, 229, 316. The estimate of twenty million listeners is from NBC, advertisement, *Daily Variety*, December 6, 1945. Using Ramsburg's more conservative metrics, Cantor's ratings represented approximately fifteen million listeners during the 1945–1946 season.

4 Jack Gould, "How Comic Is Radio Comedy?," *New York Times*, November 21, 1948.

5 Eddie Cantor, "What's Wrong with Radio," *Variety*, July 9, 1947, 28; Eddie Cantor, letter to the editor, *New York Times*, February 8, 1948.

6 Ramsburg, *Network Radio Ratings*, 316. Cantor had a stint as Garry Moore's replacement on the long-running Sunday night quiz show *Take It or Leave It* during the 1949–1950 season. Cantor also hosted *Show Business Old and New* (1951–1954), a thirty-minute NBC program on which he played records and talked about other entertainers.

7 Dunning, *On the Air*, 224; Harold Jovien, "Negroes Desert Stage for Screen," *Chicago Defender*, October 27, 1945, in Henry T. Sampson, *Swingin' on the Either Waves*, vol. 2 (Lanham, MD: Scarecrow Press, 2005), 569–70.

8 Bernice Patton, "Eddie Cantor, Nicholas Bros. Top Stage Bill," *Pittsburgh Courier*, August 10, 1935, A6.

9 Dan Burley, "Bill Bailey Is Dancing Star in Cantor Show, 'Banjo Eyes,'" *Amsterdam News*, February 21, 1942, 17.

10 *Eddie Cantor Show*, script, NBC, November 21, 1945, 9, box 9, Ostroff Papers; Goldman, *Banjo Eyes*, 248.

11 *Eddie Cantor Show*, script, NBC, January 30, 1946, 7, box 9, Ostroff Papers.

12 *Variety*'s review of the 1946–1947 season's first episode program notes some of these format changes and observes that singer Margaret Whiting "was slotted in just for the singing insert and not reduced to the status of stooge." See Rose, review of *The Eddie Cantor Show*, *Variety*, October 2, 1946, 35.

13 R. R. Dier, "Thelma Carpenter Tells Why Cantor Show Dropped Her," *Baltimore Afro-American*, April 13, 1946, 8. Also see "Drop Thelma Carpenter for Refusing to 'Tom,'" *Los Angeles Sentinel*, April 18, 1946, 18. The *Chicago Defender* reported that Cantor released Carpenter because of "handicaps in singing duets." See Al Monroe, "Swinging the News," *Chicago Defender*, April 13, 1946, 11. In the mid-1990s, Carpenter told writer Herbert G. Goldman that Cantor made a racist ad-lib. On a broadcast, the star joked that Carpenter cried "tears of ink." Cantor allegedly repeated the line before a group of people, including Carpenter, that evening at the Waldorf-Astoria. See Goldman, *Banjo Eyes*, 248. It is impossible to verify Carpenter's account. Other sources, including extant newspaper articles, interviews, recordings, and scripts, do

not mention Cantor's ad-lib or a similar line. In addition, Cantor rarely ad-libbed on radio. Comments that seemed spontaneous usually appeared in scripts.

14 "Eddie Cantor Denies Asking Thelma Carpenter to Uncle Tom," *Los Angeles Sentinel*, April 25, 1946, 10.

15 Ralph Matthews, "Behind the Scenes," *Baltimore Afro-American*, August 10, 1946, 3.

16 "Cantor and the ECA," *Variety*, August 31, 1949, 34.

17 Dollinger, *Quest for Inclusion*, 173, 178.

18 See, for example, "Interfaith Group Gives Citation," *Boston Globe*, June 18, 1950; "Laud Trio for Fight on Bias," *Boston Post*, May 26, 1950.

19 Rose, review of *The Eddie Cantor Show*, *Variety*, October 1, 1947, 24.

20 Cantor to McDonald, January 20, 1947, box 9, McDonald Papers.

21 James G. McDonald, *To the Gates of Jerusalem: The Diaries and Papers of James G. McDonald, 1945–1947*, ed. Norman J. W. Goda, Barbara McDonald Stewart, Severin Hockberg, and Richard Breitman (Bloomington: Indiana University Press, 2015), 18–19.

22 See McDonald to Cantor, unpublished telegram, August 6, 1945, box 9, McDonald Papers; Cantor to McDonald, telegram, August 6, 1945, box 9, McDonald Papers; Cantor to McDonald, telegram, August 9, 1945, box 9, McDonald Papers. Jessel discusses his friendship with Truman in George Jessel, *This Way Miss* (New York: Henry Holt, 1955), 167–76.

23 See Tom Evans, oral history interview, by J. R. Fuchs, Kansas City, MO, June 13, 1963, transcript, Harry S. Truman Library and Museum (Truman Library), http://www.trumanlibrary.org/oralhist/evans4.htm. According to Truman's appointment records, Schwimmer met with the president fourteen times. See "The President's Day," Truman Library, http://www.trumanlibrary.org/calendar/.

24 McDonald to Cantor, October 19, 1945, box 9, McDonald Papers.

25 Norman J. W. Goda, "Surviving Survival: James G. McDonald and the Fate of Holocaust Survivors," Monna and Otto Weinmann Annual Lecture, June 11, 2015, United States Holocaust Memorial Museum, www.ushmm.org; Dollinger, *Quest for Inclusion*, 121; Hasia R. Diner, *We Remember with Reverence and Love: American Jews and the Myth of Silence after the Holocaust, 1945–1962* (New York: New York University Press, 2009), 153; Leonard Dinnerstein, *America and the Survivors of the Holocaust* (New York: Columbia University Press, 1982), 10–14.

26 Diner, *We Remember with Reverence and Love*, 150, 170, 176.

27 Eddie Cantor, "I Thought That Hitler Was Dead," advertisement, *New York Times*, January 4, 1946; see also Dinnerstein, *America and the Survivors of the Holocaust*, 109; Diner, *We Remember with Reverence and Love*, 153.

28 See, for example, "Eddie Cantor Denounces Morgan in Paid Advertisement," *Pittsburgh Jewish Criterion*, January 11, 1946, 2; "Says Every American Citizen Condemns Morgan Attack on Jews," Jewish Telegraphic Agency, January 6, 1946, JTA Archive, www.jta.org/archive.

29 Louis Adamic et al., advertisement, *Washington Post*, June 6, 1946. The same advertisement ran in the *New York Times*, June 8, 1946.

30 Larry Adler et al., letter to the editor, *New York Times*, October 8, 1947.

31 "From the Production Centers," *Variety*, April 10, 1946, 46; Tomm, review of *Star Spangled Way*, *Variety*, May 22, 1946, 34.

32 Eric Pace, obituary for Allan Sloane, *New York Times*, May 12, 2001.

33 Himan Brown, interview by Ira Skutch, in Ira Skutch, *Five Directors: The Golden Years of Radio* (Lanham, MD: Scarecrow Press, 1998), 37. Examples of these UJA productions include "The Right to Live," NBC, May 18, 1947; "Operation Nightmare," CBS, June 9, 1947; "Operation Nightmare—Chapter Two," CBS, April 10, 1948; "Homecoming—1949," Mutual, April 3, 1949; "Operation Dawn," NBC, May 22, 1949.

34 For more on media depictions of the Holocaust in the context of Jewish organizations' fund-raising strategies, see Diner, *We Remember with Reverence and Love*, 168–69, 179.

35 United Jewish Appeal, "Time—The Present—A Day of Remembrance," script, ABC, September 20, 1947, 11–13, box 6, Cantor Papers UCLA.

36 United Jewish Appeal, "Time—The Present—A Day of Remembrance," 25–26.

37 William M. Wallace to Cantor, June 11, 1947; Jacob Wolkin to Eddie and Ida Cantor, June 28, 1947; Wolkin to Eddie and Ida Cantor, October 29, 1947; Wolkin to Eddie and Ida Cantor, November 25, 1947. All correspondence quoted concerning Wolkin is from the Larsen Collection. It is not clear why the correspondence between the Cantors and Wolkin ended in 1948. It is possible that there are additional letters from after 1948 that are not part of the Larsen Collection and have not been saved. Wolkin, a native Polish speaker, probably received assistance writing the letters in English, according to a family member. Shelley Wolkin, e-mail to author, November 10, 2016.

38 See Eddie and Ida Cantor to Jacob Wolkin, June 16, 1947; Eddie Cantor to William Rosenwald, June 16, 1947; Jacob Wolkin to Eddie and Ida Cantor, March 9, 1948.

39 Jacob Wolkin to Eddie and Ida Cantor and Children, April 27, 1948.

40 Henry Montor to Eddie Cantor, September 23, 1948; Montor to Cantor, October 5, 1949; Ernie Wolkin, telephone discussion with author, November 7, 2016; Shelley Wolkin, e-mail to author, November 11, 2016.

41 "Cantor Accepts Bid for Stockholm Airer," *Variety*, July 21, 1948, 16; "Cantor's 12-City Tour for Overseas Kids," *Variety*, August 25, 1948, 4; "Eddie Cantor Returns from Visit to DP Camps; to Tour Country for United Jewish Appeal," Jewish Telegraphic Agency, August 22, 1948, JTA Archive, www.jta.org/archive; "Eddie Cantor Honored: Gets United Jewish Appeal's Award a Second Time," *New York Times*, September 27, 1948; "Eddie Cantor Surveys Needs of Refugees in Europe in Preparation for Tour in Behalf of UJA," *Southern Israelite*, September 10, 1948, 5.

42 "Record $1,250,000 Raised by Cantor for Jewish Appeal," *Variety*, September 21, 1949, 2; "Luncheon Donates $1,253,800 for UJA," *New York Times*, September 20, 1949.

43 "Cantor Sends UJA Campaign Off to a Roaring Start," *Pittsburgh Jewish Criterion*, March 24, 1950, 5.

44 For more on American Jewish views of Israel during the late 1940s and early 1950s, including the construction of Israel as a democracy similar to the United States, see Michelle Mart, *Eye on Israel* (Albany: State University of New York Press, 2006), 56–84.

45 Eddie Cantor, "What I Saw in Israel," *Boston Jewish Advocate*, September 7, 1950, B20; "Eddie Cantor on UJF Broadcast," *American Jewish Outlook*, June 30, 1950, 11; United Jewish Appeal, *Eddie Cantor in Israel* (1950), film, posted by Spielberg Jewish Film Archive, www.YouTube.com.

46 "Message from Eddie Cantor Pleads for Cash Payments," *Pittsburgh Jewish Criterion*, August 25, 1950, 7; Cantor, "What I Saw in Israel."

47 Cantor and Ardmore, *Take My Life*, 263–64.

12. THE LAST COMEBACK (1950–1952)

1 "Cantor Boffs 'Em in Bangor as He Opens Campus Circuit," *Daily Variety*, January 25, 1950.

2 Abel Green, "Cantor's 1-Man Carnegie Show Sock Milestone," *Daily Variety*, March 29, 1950.

3 "Jack Benny Booked by Carnegie Hall," *Daily Variety*, March 29, 1950.

4 Eddie Cantor, *The Original Complete Carnegie Hall Concert*, recorded March 21, 1950, Original Cast OC-9217, 1992, disc 1, compact disc; "Cantor Clicks at Carnegie Hall, Proving Old Wine Tastes Better," *Billboard*, April 1, 1950, 4; Green, "Cantor's 1-Man Carnegie Show Sock Milestone."

5 "Cantor Clicks at Carnegie Hall, Proving Old Wine Tastes Better"; Green, "Cantor's 1-Man Carnegie Show Sock Mielstone."

6 Cantor, *Original Complete Carnegie Hall Concert*.

7 McCarthy's full speech is reprinted on American Society for the History of Rhetoric, *Advances in the History of Rhetoric*, www.advances.umd.edu/LincolnBirthday/mccarthy1950.xml.

8 "Senator Asserts Country Would Be Better Off without Secretary: Oust Acheson, McCarthy Urges," *Washington Post*, March 20, 1950.

9 Stewart Alsop, "Matter of Fact: McCarthy Past and Present," *Washington Post*, March 17, 1950.

10 Svonkin, *Jews against Prejudice*, 116–17; Dollinger, *Quest for Inclusion*, 140–41.

11 Thomas Doherty, *Cold War, Cool Medium* (New York: Columbia University Press, 2005), 24–25, 35–36; David F. Prindle, *The Politics of Glamour: Ideology and Democracy in the Screen Actors Guild* (Madison: University of Wisconsin Press, 1988), 56–57.

12 "Cantor Backs Miss Muir: Calls Her Dismissal One of 'Most Tragic Things' in Business," *New York Times*, September 6, 1950.

13 Cantor to Eiges, September 9, 1950, box 162, NBC Records Wisconsin Historical Society.

14 Walter Monfried, "Cantor Hailed in a Long Solo Show," *Milwaukee Journal*, September 21, 1950.

15 Madelaine Wilson, "Cantor Sings, Dances, Jokes, and Has Surprise for Finale," *Daily Oklahoman*, October 22, 1950.

16 Joseph G. Weisberg, "Views of the News," *Boston Jewish Advocate*, October 15, 1964, 1.

17 Wilson, "Cantor Sings, Dances, Jokes."

18 "Eddie Cantor Acclaimed by 2500 in 1-Man Show at Convention Hall," *Camden Courier*, November 18, 1950; "Cantor Resumes Tour," *Variety*, November 8, 1950, 2.

19 Doherty, *Cold War, Cool Medium*, 34–36; Robert Pondillo, *America's First Network TV Censor: The Work of NBC's Stockton Helffrich* (Carbondale: Southern Illinois University Press, 2010), 52–53.

20 James C. Douglass to Harry Floyd, July 27, 1950, box 567B, NBC Records Wisconsin Historical Society. The July 6, 1949, policy memorandum is attached to this letter.

21 For more on the image of Jew as "conspiratorial communist" during this time, see Svonkin, *Jews against Prejudice*, 112–21.

22 Ceplar and Englund, *Inquisition in Hollywood*, 362.

23 "Bowl Honor for Cantor," *Los Angeles Examiner*, September 19, 1954; B. W. (Pat) Kearney, extension of remarks, May 16, 1952, *Congressional Record: Proceedings and Debates of the 82nd Congress, Second Session*, Appendix, vol. 8, pt. 9 (Washington, DC: Government Printing Office, 1952), A3026; Frank Folsom to Eddie Cantor, May 6, 1952, scrapbook, box 71, Cantor Papers UCLA; "Cantor's Pint-Sized Plasma Pitch SRO for Red Cross in Key City Trek," *Variety*, May 7, 1952, 45.

24 Vivian M. Bowes to L. H. Williams, June 18, 1950, Larsen Collection; Vivian M. Bowes to Farrell E. Saltzman, June 29, 1950, Larsen Collection; Jack Crandell to Juliet N. Benjamin, June 21, 1950, Larsen Collection; "Excerpt from a Letter by Mr. Herbert Levy, Outlining Plan for B'nai B'rith Sponsorship of Eddie Cantor's New 'One Man Show,'" notes, n.d. (circa July 1950), Larsen Collection. See newspaper reviews of particular shows in scrapbook, box 57, Cantor Papers UCLA. Cantor also offered partnership opportunities to Hadassah, but it is not clear whether that organization chose to promote any shows.

25 Vivian M. Bowes to Marcus L. Friedman, July 10, 1950, Larsen Collection; Abe Lastfogel to Cantor, December 11, 1950, scrapbook, box 71, Cantor Papers UCLA; Bob Considine, "Sideglances at Celebrities," November 17, 1950, typescript, scrapbook, box 71, Cantor Papers UCLA; see also advertisement in *Variety*, January 3, 1951, 120, which provides box office figures. For more on ticket sales and prices in particular cities, see the articles in scrapbook, box 71, Cantor Papers UCLA. For more on prices for theater and other entertainment, circa 1950, see Derks, *Value of a Dollar*, 312.

26 See the articles in scrapbook, box 71, Cantor Papers UCLA; for example, "Welcome for Eddie Cantor Slated for Bienville Square," *Mobile Press Register*, October 15, 1950; "Eddie Cantor, Delightful as Ever, Thrills Audience with Old Songs," *San Antonio Express*, October 19, 1950; "B'nai B'rith to Present World Famous Comedian October 18," *B'nai B'rith News*, San Antonio Lodge no. 211, September 1950, 1.

27 Lawrence W. Lichty and Malachi C. Topping, *American Broadcasting: A Source Book on the History of Radio and Television* (New York: Hastings House, 1975), 521, 523; Derks, *Value of a Dollar*, 304.

28 Harry Floyd, unpublished conference report, July 27, 1950, box 567B, NBC Records Wisconsin Historical Society.

29 Harry Floyd, notes, Colgate meeting, July 25, 1950, box 567B, NBC Records Wisconsin Historical Society.

30 Robert W. McFadyen, memorandum to Edward Madden, December 12, 1950, box 567B, NBC Records Wisconsin Historical Society; "Colgate Comedy Hour," report, circa February 1953, box 368, NBC Records Wisconsin Historical Society. See also ratings in *Variety*; for example, "Toast Pops Up," *Variety*, October 11, 1950, 29; "The New TV Ratings," *Variety*, September 12, 1951, 31.

31 Fred Wile Jr. to Sylvester L. Weaver Jr., memorandum, May 2, 1951, box 119, NBC Records Wisconsin Historical Society; "Colgate Comedy Hour: Estimated Values 1953–1954 Season," report, n.d. (ca. February 1953), box 368, NBC Records Wisconsin Historical Society. Cantor also received $1,000 per week, regardless of whether he appeared on television, in exchange for granting NBC exclusive rights to his services.

32 *Colgate Comedy Hour*, NBC, January 20, 1952, digital video disc, author's private collection.

33 James Agee, "Comedy's Greatest Era," *Life*, September 5, 1949, 70–88.

34 *Colgate Comedy Hour*, script, NBC, September 30, 1951, 7–13, box 22, Cantor Papers UCLA.

35 Harry Floyd to Weaver et al., memorandum, August 22, 1950, box 567, NBC Records Wisconsin Historical Society.

36 See, for example, Jack Gould, "Cantor Scores Hit in Television Bow," *New York Times*, September 11, 1950; Harriet Van Horne, "It's Cantor for Tops on TV Fare," *New York World Telegram and Sun*, September 12, 1950. See also reviews in scrapbook, box 59, Cantor Papers UCLA. NBC's internal Community Acceptance Radio and Television (CART) report noted that Cantor's first episode gave the network "no problems." Stockton Helffrich, Community Acceptance Radio and Television (CART) report, September 15, 1950, 1, M95–105, box 1, NBC Records Wisconsin Historical Society.

37 Allison Joyce Perlman, "Reforming the Wasteland: Television, Reform, and Social Movements, 1950–2004" (unpublished PhD diss., University of Texas, 2007), 32–60; "NBC Targets Race Hate Songs," *Chicago Defender*, March 17, 1951, reprinted in Sampson, *Swingin' on the Ether Waves*, vol. 3, 884; Stockton Helffrich, Community

Acceptance Radio and Television (CART) report, September 10, 1952, 1–2, M95–105, box 1, NBC Records Wisconsin Historical Society; Pondillo, *America's First Network TV Censor*, 149–51. For more on Helffrich and NBC's policies on program content, see Pondillo's study.

38 Stockton Helffrich, Community Acceptance Radio and Television (CART) report, October 5, 1951, 1, M95–105, box 1, NBC Records Wisconsin Historical Society; *Colgate Comedy Hour*, September 9, 1951, NBC, digital video disc, author's private collection.

39 Stockton Helffrich, Community Acceptance Radio and Television (CART) report, October 31, 1951, 4, M95–105, box 1, NBC Records Wisconsin Historical Society; Stockton Helffrich, Community Acceptance Radio and Television (CART) report, November 6, 1951, 3, M95–105, box 1, NBC Records Wisconsin Historical Society.

40 *Colgate Comedy Hour*, January 20, 1952.

41 Kinescopes of several *Colgate Comedy Hour* episodes have not been preserved, so it is impossible to assert with certainty that Cantor did not appear in blackface after January 1952; however, extant kinescopes, print reviews, and other sources do not provide evidence that Cantor appeared in blackface after this date.

42 Advertisement, "NAACP's Great Night," *Amsterdam News*, March 1, 1952.

43 See telegrams published in Eddie Cantor, *I'm Glad I Spent These Sixty Years*, Eddie Cantor's Sixtieth Birthday, Hotel Commodore, New York, January 31, 1952; "$2,630,000 Israel Bond Sale via Cantor Fete," *Variety*, February 6, 1952, 2; "1,800 at Eddie Cantor's Birthday Party Buy $2,616,000 in Israel Bonds to Get in," *New York Times*, February 1, 1952.

44 "America Salutes Eddie Cantor," *American Hebrew*, January 25, 1952, n.p., scrapbook, box 54, Cantor Papers UCLA. See also other articles in this scrapbook.

45 "To Eddie Cantor at 60," *Hartford Jewish Ledger*, January 24, 1952, n.p., scrapbook, box 54, Cantor Papers UCLA.

46 John D. Dingell, "Eddie Cantor's Birthday—A Deserved Tribute," *Congressional Quarterly*, January 31, 1952, scrapbook, box 54, Cantor Papers UCLA.

47 Cantor, *I'm Glad I Spent These Sixty Years*, 9–11.

13. FADING AWAY (1952–1964)

1 Helm., review of *Colgate Comedy Hour*, *Daily Variety*, September 29, 1952; Helm., review of *Colgate Comedy Hour*, *Variety*, October 1, 1952, 101; "Cantor Progressing in Hosp. after Heart Attack," *Daily Variety*, October 1, 1952; Goldman, *Banjo Eyes*, 281; Eddie Cantor, "Me and My Heart Attack," *Look*, January 1953, 4.

2 Cantor, "Me and My Heart Attack," 4.

3 "Eddie Cantor's RX for Living," *TV Guide*, July 3, 1953, 5.

4 Leslie Harris to Samuel Fuller, May 14, 1953, box 368, NBC Records Wisconsin Historical Society.

5 *Colgate Comedy Hour*, NBC, February 17, 1952, clip uploaded by J. Fred MacDonald,

YouTube, www.YouTube.com. MacDonald provides an incorrect broadcast date of February 23, 1951. See also unsigned review of *Colgate Comedy Hour*, *Variety*, February 20, 1952, 30.

6 Sammy Davis Jr., Jane Boyar, and Burt Boyar, *Yes I Can: The Story of Sammy Davis, Jr.* (New York: Farrar, Straus and Giroux, 1965), 156–58.

7 "Webs Brush Off Talmadge Beef on Negro Talent," *Variety*, January 9, 1952, 1, 20.

8 Stockton Helffrich, Community Acceptance Radio and Television (CART) report, September 10, 1951, 5, M95–105, box 1, NBC Records Wisconsin Historical Society. See also Stockton Helffrich, Community Acceptance Radio and Television (CART) report, January 9, 1952, 2–3, M95–105, box 1, NBC Records Wisconsin Historical Society.

9 "News 'n' Notes," *New York Amsterdam News*, March 8, 1952, 14. See also "Sammy Davis Scores on 'Comedy Hour' Broadcast," *Chicago Defender*, October 18, 1952, 23; "Newest TV Star," *New York Amsterdam News*, June 6, 1953, 26.

10 "Swinging the News," *Chicago Defender*, April 25, 1953, 19 (capitalization in original).

11 Sam Lacy, "Theatrical Whirl," *Baltimore Afro-American*, October 15, 1955, 7.

12 Sam Fuller to Charles Barry, memorandum, March 16, 1953, box 368, NBC Records Wisconsin Historical Society; Charles Barry to Eddie Cantor, March 20, 1953, box 368, NBC Records Wisconsin Historical Society. See also Fred Wile Jr. to Weaver et al., April 19, 1951, box 119, NBC Records Wisconsin Historical Society; Fred Wile Jr. to Sylvester L. Weaver Jr., May 2, 1951, box 119, NBC Records Wisconsin Historical Society.

13 Leslie Harris to Ed Madden, January 21, 1952, box 567, NBC Records Wisconsin Historical Society; see also Sam Fuller to Robert Sarnoff, October 24, 1951, box 119, NBC Records Wisconsin Historical Society.

14 For example, when Cantor returned from his heart attack in January 1953, he earned a 38.8 rating to Sullivan's 22.1. Two months later, Cantor lost a close battle to Sullivan, 26.3 to 31.6. See "On Air Waves," *Daily Variety*, January 20, 1953; "CBS Weekend TVers Again Top NBC Rival," *Daily Variety*, March 17, 1953. On the ratings decline for all *Colgate Comedy Hour* hosts, see George Rosen, "How Lost Is My Weekend?," *Variety*, November 4, 1953, 42; Edward Little to David Sarnoff, telegram, November 4, 1953, box 121, NBC Records Wisconsin Historical Society; Tim Brooks and Earle Marsh, *The Complete Directory to Prime Time Network and Cable TV Shows 1946-Present* (New York: Ballantine, 1999), 1244.

15 Eddie Cantor to Charles C. Barry, March 23, 1953, box 368, NBC Records Wisconsin Historical Society. Cantor had actually hosted twenty-seven episodes of the series (not twenty-five) by March 23, 1953.

16 Jose., review of *Colgate Comedy Hour*, *Daily Variety*, May 13, 1953; Helm., review of *Colgate Comedy Hour*, *Daily Variety*, May 11, 1953.

17 Ben Gross, "What's On?," *New York Daily News*, May 16, 1953.

18 *Colgate Comedy Hour*, NBC, December 27, 1953, videotape, VA10763 T, UCLA Film and Television Archive.

19 Brooks and Marsh, *Complete Directory to Prime Time Network and Cable TV Shows*, 1243–44.

20 Pinky Herman, "Television-Radio," *Motion Picture Daily*, January 5, 1954, 7.

21 Pete Barnum quotes the telegram to Cantor explaining the network's decision in Barnum to Sam Fuller, telegram, January 27, 1954, box 380, NBC Records Wisconsin Historical Society. See also George T. Laboda to Pat Weaver, telegram, January 27, 1954, box 380, NBC Records Wisconsin Historical Society; Joseph H. McConnell to Larry Parks, January 6, 1954, box 380, NBC Records Wisconsin Historical Society; Stockton Helffrich, Community Acceptance Radio and Television (CART) report, February 5, 1954, 1, M95–105, box 1, NBC Records Wisconsin Historical Society; Pondillo, *America's First Network TV Censor*, 151.

22 Cantor with Ardmore, *Take My Life*, 248.

23 Alton Cook, review of *The Eddie Cantor Story*, *New York World Telegram-Sun*, December 26, 1953; see also unsigned review of *The Eddie Cantor Story*, *Newsweek*, December 7, 1953, 94; Archer Winsten, review of *The Eddie Cantor Story*, *New York Post*, December 26, 1953; A. W., review of *The Eddie Cantor Story*, *New York Times*, December 26, 1953.

24 For more on the film's box office figures, see, for example, "Blizzard Blitzes B'way but 'Knights' Keen 150G, 'Millionaire' Slips to 19G, 'Valiant' 11G, 'Paratrooper' 11G," *Variety*, January 13, 1954, 9; "National Boxoffice Survey," *Variety*, January 27, 1954, 3; "3 New Pix, Good Weather Help Chi; Cantor Wow $33,000 'Rifles' Sock 45G 'Sailors'—'Paint' Bangup 20G," *Variety*, February 3, 1954, 9; "'Knights' Boxoffice Leader in Feb.; 'Top Banana' and 'New Faces' Good," *Variety*, March 3, 1954, 13.

25 Fred Wile Jr. to Thomas A. McAvity, telegram, February 24, 1954, box 380, NBC Records Wisconsin Historical Society; Pat Weaver to Colgate Palmolive Company, draft of letter, February 25, 1954, box 389, NBC Records Wisconsin Historical Society; Eddie Cantor to Mannie Sacks, March 4, 1954, box 380, NBC Records Wisconsin Historical Society. *Variety* reported that NBC offered Cantor four slots over the next season. See "Cantor Switches from Live to Film in 7-Year Deal with Ziv Co.," *Variety*, June 23, 1954, 2.

26 Ziv claimed 253 markets by June 1955. See "Film Productions," *Sponsor*, January 10, 1955, 65; "Report to Sponsors," *Sponsor*, January 24, 1955, 2; "Program Service Shorts," *Broadcasting Telecasting*, June 27, 1955, 50. See also Goldman, *Banjo Eyes*, 287–88.

27 "Sponsor-Telepulse Ratings of Top Spots," *Sponsor*, August 8, 1955, n.p., scrapbook, box 59, Cantor Papers UCLA; see also "*Variety*-ARB City-by-City Syndicated and National Spot Film Chart," *Variety*, August 3, 1955, 30.

28 Jack Gould, review of *Eddie Cantor Comedy Theatre*, *New York Times*, January 31, 1955.

29 Cantor and Ardmore, *Take My Life*, 248.

30 *This Is Your Life*, NBC, kinescope, December 23, 1952, tape T:25334, Paley Center, New York, NY.

31 Eddie Cantor, "An Open Letter to the Secretary of State of the United States," advertisement, *New York Times*, October 21, 1954.

32 "The Campaign Issues—If Any," *Life*, November 1, 1954, 30; James G. McDonald to Eddie Cantor, November 1, 1954, box 9, McDonald Papers; Eddie Cantor to James G. McDonald, November 18, 1954, box 9, McDonald Papers.

33 Urofsky, *We Are One!*, 308; Milton K. Susman, "As I See It," *Pittsburgh Jewish Chronicle*, November 5, 1954, 9.

34 "Cantor Has Kidney Infection," *New York Times*, November 26, 1955, 23; Val Adams, "Berle Will Miss Show Tonight," *New York Times*, November 29, 1955, 59; "Eddie Cantor Leaves Hospital," *New York Times*, December 27, 1955, 31. According to Goldman, Cantor suffered prostate troubles and went into shock on the operating table. See Goldman, *Banjo Eyes*, 290.

35 "Cantor's Israel Speech," *Variety*, May 2, 1956, 2; Louis Biancolli, "Two Cantors and a Choir," *New York World-Telegram and Sun*, May 7, 1956.

36 *Person to Person*, CBS, October 5, 1956, inventory no. VA9975 T, videotape, UCLA Film and Television Archive.

37 "Eddie Cantor at 65," CBS, January 15, 1957, digital video disc, author's private collection.

38 Goldman, *Banjo Eyes*, 293; "Eddie Cantor Collapses after Show; In Hospital," *Los Angeles Examiner*, January 13, 1957, 1; "Cantor in Hospital: Comedian Collapses after TV Tribute on 65th Birthday," *New York Times*, January 13, 1957; "Cantor Sits Up, Feels Fine after Full Night's Rest," *Washington Post and Times Herald*, January 14, 1957.

39 "Cantor's Birthday Bond Drive Near $20,000,000," *Variety*, February 20, 1957, 53.

40 *1957 Inaugural Conference for Israel Bonds and National Celebration of Eddie Cantor's 65th Birthday*, Fontainebleau Hotel, Miami Beach, February 15, 1957 to February 17, 1957, no publisher, 11, 17.

41 "Truman Declares Doctrine Is 'Too Little, Too Late,'" *Washington Post and Times Herald*, February 17, 1957; "Text of Truman Address on U.S. Policy in the Middle East: Cites Admiration for Israel Backed U.N.," *New York Times*, February 17, 1957; "Cantor's Birthday Bond Drive Near $20,000,000," 53.

42 Eddie Cantor, "Pieces of My Life," in *1957 Inaugural Conference for Israel Bonds*, 8.

43 See, for example, "Eddie Cantor for Israel Development Corporation of America," audio recording, San Francisco, June 16,1957, Magnes Collection of Jewish Art and Life, Bancroft Library, University of California, Berkeley, www.archive.org/details/cbm_000013; Irving Spiegel, "Mrs. Meir Warns of Syria Attack: Arms from Both Russia and West Threaten Israel, Foreign Minister Says," *New York Times*, September 22, 1957; "U.S. Jewish Leaders to Set Up Plans for Israel Bonds Drive in 1959,"

Jewish Telegraphic Agency, December 16, 1958, JTA Archive, www.jta.org/archive; "$100,000 Israeli Bonds Pledged by Miss Taylor," *Washington Post and Times Herald*, February 26, 1959; Eddie Cantor, "A Very Special Bar Mitzvah," *American Jewish Outlook*, March 31, 1961, 10. Cantor was too sick to attend an Israel Bonds seventieth birthday celebration for him in Miami Beach in February 1962. See Irving Spiegel, "Israeli Stresses Desert Program: Reclamation Is Major Goal, He Tells Bond Parley," *New York Times*, February 25, 1962.

44 Goldman, *Banjo Eyes*, 294.

45 "Eddie Cantor Honorary Oscar 1957," uploaded by Brian Gari, YouTube.com; "Doctor Nixes Gala Routine," *Variety*, March 6, 1957, 2; "'80 Days' Ingrid Bergman Win 'Oscars': Brynner Top Actor—Stevens Cited as 'Giant' Director," *New York Times*, March 28, 1957.

46 Eddie Cantor, *The Way I See It* (Englewood Cliffs, NJ: Prentice-Hall, 1959), 204 (italics in original).

47 "Ida Cantor Dies; Eddie Collapses," *Washington Post and Times Herald*, August 10, 1962; "Cantor, Ailing, Is Absent from Wife's Funeral," *Washington Post and Times Herald*, August 11, 1962; Goldman, *Banjo Eyes*, 300–303.

48 Hal Humphrey, "Eddie Cantor's Left Sitting on Sidelines," *Washington Post and Times Herald*, August 23, 1963; Bob Thomas, "Cantor's Memory Unimpaired to End," *Washington Post and Times Herald*, October 18, 1964; Eddie Cantor, interview with Walter O'Keefe, *Walter O'Keefe's Almanac*, December 16, 1962, track four, *Eddie Cantor: The Later Years (1947–1962)*, Original Cast OC-5859, n.d. (circa 2013), compact disc.

49 "President Johnson Honors Eddie Cantor for Service to the Nation," Jewish Telegraphic Agency, February 4, 1964, JTA Archive, www.jta.org/archive; Lyndon Johnson to Eddie Cantor, February 19, 1964, box 74, Cantor Papers UCLA.

50 "Eddie Cantor Dead; Comedy Star Was 72," *New York Times*, October 11, 1964; Army Archerd, "Just for Variety," *Daily Variety*, October 13, 1964; "Private Service Is Planned for Cantor," *New York Times*, October 12, 1964.

51 "Eddie Cantor," editorial, *New York Times*, October 12, 1964.

52 "Eddie Cantor, 71, Banjo-Eyes Comic," *Washington Post and Times Herald*, October 12, 1964.

53 "Eddie Cantor," editorial, *Hartford Courant*, October 13, 1964.

54 "Eddie Cantor," editorial, *Variety*, October 14, 1964, 3; "Eddie Cantor Requested No Public Funeral; Star, Long Ailing, Was 72," *Variety*, October 14, 1964, 3, 23, 70; "Eddie Cantor, Five-Faceted Star Who Became an Institution, Dies at 72," *Daily Variety*, October 12, 1964.

55 "The World Loses a Little Laughter," editorial, *Los Angeles Times*, October 13, 1964; see also "Gracie, Harpo, and Eddie," *Christian Science Monitor*, October 19, 1964; "Funny and Well," *Baltimore Sun*, October 12, 1964.

56 *Pittsburgh Jewish Chronicle*, editorial, October 16, 1964, 4.

57 Joseph G. Weisberg, "Views of the News," *Boston Jewish Advocate*, October 15, 1964, 1.

58 Martin Silver, "The Real Eddie Cantor," *Southern Israelite*, December 4, 1964, 7.

59 "Deaths," *New York Times*, October 12, 1964.

EPILOGUE: EDDIE CANTOR'S LEGACY

1 Gerald Nachman, *Seriously Funny: The Rebel Comedians of the 1950s and 1960s* (New York: Pantheon Books, 2003).

2 John Cohen, ed., *The Essential Lenny Bruce* (1967; repr., New York: Ballantine Books, 1974), 41. A shorter version of the routine, which classifies both Cantor and Al Jolson as "goyish," also appears on Lenny Bruce, *Live at the Curran Theater*, recorded 1961, Fantasy Records, 1999, digital file.

3 Lawrence Bush, "Jewish-Goyish: Lenny Bruce and the Jewish Mission to America," *Jewish Currents*, Summer 2016, 23.

4 Quoted in James Fisher, *Eddie Cantor: A Bio-Bibliography* (Westport, CT: Greenwood Press, 1997), 3–4.

5 For example, in December 2016, the website Kveller, which focuses on Jewish parenting, proudly identified five "Jewish celebrities who stood up to anti-Semitism this year" in response to a dramatic rise in antisemitic incidents during the year. The celebrities—Mara Wilson, Regina Spektor, Emmy Rossum, Mayim Bialik, and Jennifer Weiner—were not household names, and their stands against antisemitism consisted of short, tame social media tweets and comments in interviews. See Joanna Valente, "5 Jewish Celebrities Who Stood Up to Anti-Semitism This Year," Kveller, December 7, 2016, www.kveller.com.

6 Abbi Jacobson and Ilana Glazer, "Getting There," *Broad City*, season 3, episode 9, Comedy Central, aired April 13, 2016; Abbi Jacobson and Ilana Glazer, "Jews on a Plane," *Broad City*, season 3, episode 10, Comedy Central, aired April 20, 2016.

7 Gary Giddins, *Visions of Jazz: The First Century* (New York: Oxford University Press, 1998), 15.

8 Will Friedwald, *A Biographical Guide to the Great Jazz and Pop Singers* (New York: Pantheon Books, 2010), 69, 71.

9 For example, *Capitol Sings Broadway: Makin' Whoopee*, Capitol, 1995, digital file; *Warner Bros.: 75 Years Entertaining the World*, Rhino, 1998, digital file; *All Time Favorites of Stage and Screen*, Halcyon, 2015, digital file.

10 Cyndi Lauper (with Tony Bennett), "Makin' Whoopee," on *At Last*, Sony Music, 2003, digital file; Willie Nelson and Wynton Marsalis featuring Norah Jones, "Makin' Whoopee," on *Here We Go Again: Celebrating the Genius of Ray Charles*, Blue Note, 2011, digital file; Harry Nilsson, "Makin' Whoopee," on *A Little Touch of Schmilsson in the Night*, BMG, 2006, digital file; Allan Sherman, "Taking Lessons," on *Allan Sherman Live! (Hoping You Are the Same)*, Warner Bros. Records, 2005, digital file; Michelle Pfeiffer, "Makin' Whoopee," in *The Fabulous Baker Boys*, directed by

Steve Kloves, originally released in 1989, YouTube video, uploaded June 2016, www.YouTube.com; Amanda Palmer and Neil Gaiman, "Makin' Whoopee," recorded live in Seattle, Washington, November 9, 2012, YouTube video, uploaded October 2013, www.YouTube.com.

11 "Eddie Cantor Fan Club," closed group, Facebook, www.facebook.com; "Vaudeville!," public group, Facebook, www.facebook.com. As of November 13, 2016, the Cantor group had 1,045 members and the Vaudeville group had 2,056 members.

12 Gari, *Don't Wear Silver in the Winter*; Janet Cantor Gari, *The Cantor Buried Tales* (Albany, GA: Bear Mountain Media, 2014). A full listing of the compact discs and digital video discs released by Brian Gari is available on the Eddie Cantor Appreciation Society website, www.eddiecantor.com.

13 Hoberman and Shandler, *Entertaining America*, 151, 156–57, 277. On the role of celebrities in enabling Jews to assert a shared culture, see Kaufman, *Jewhooing the Sixties*, 27.

14 Irving Kaufman, "My Yiddisha Mammy," by Alex Gerber, Jean Schwartz, and Eddie Cantor, on *Jewface*, curated with liner notes by Jody Rosen and Reboot Stereophonic, Reboot Stereophonic Rb00 006, 2006, compact disc with liner notes. Cantor introduced "My Yiddisha Mammy" in *Make It Snappy* (1922), but he did not record it. Reboot Stereophonic is a partner of the Idelsohn Society for Music Preservation. The group issues music under the names "Reboot Stereophonic" and the "Idelsohn Society for Musical Preservation."

15 *'Twas the Night before Hanukkah: The Musical Battle between Christmas and the Festival of Lights* includes a book with three essays and detailed liner notes. See Jenna Weissman Joselit, "Let's Hear It for Those Mirthful Maccabees" and liner notes by Idelsohn Society for Musical Preservation, *'Twas the Night before Hanukkah: The Musical Battle between Christmas and the Festival of Lights*, Idelsohn Society for Musical Preservation RSR 020, 2012, compact disc with liner notes, 13–17, 28.

INDEX

Page numbers in italics refer to illustrations.

Abbott and Costello, 158–59, 204, 216
Acheson, Dean, 197
Actors' Equity strike of 1919, 46, 47–50
advertising: control of radio content,
133–35; cross-media promotional
strategy, 94, 95; EC blackface image
in, 52–53; EC *Chicago Tribune* Ziegfeld
ad, 63; EC political advertisements,
220; EC product endorsements, 65;
EC sponsor troubles, 133–35, 138–40,
143–47, 148–49, 158–60, 165; "Joe's
Blue Front" Moe character in, 61–62;
New Amsterdam rooftop promotion,
31; taunting of radio advertisers, 110
Agee, James, 207
Akst, Harry, 45
Alexander, Jason, 44
Ali Baba Goes to Town (1937), 122, 126
Allen, Fred, 104, 161, 176–77, 181–82, 204
Allen, Gracie, 104, 129, 181, 222, 229
Allen, Steve, 217
Allen, Woody, 44, 232
Alsop, Stewart, 197
American Civil Liberties Union (ACLU),
199–200
American Jewish Committee, 71, 79–80,
152
American Jewish Joint Distribution
Committee (JDC), 129, 148, 151, 191
American Jewish Relief Campaign, 71
American Legion, 5, 172–74, 198, 200
American Red Cross, 148
Anti-Defamation League of B'nai B'rith
(ADL), 51, 58, 92, 128

antisemitism: contemporary Jewish
entertainers and, 232–33, 288n5; EC
condemnation of, 1–2, 73–74, 122–25;
Father Coughlin broadcasts, 126–27,
129–32, 159, 266n13; Holocaust denial,
188; Jewish-banker stereotype,
87–88, 266n13; Jewish press on,
70–71; *Make It Snappy* critique, 57–58,
64–65; Nazi-era antisemitism, 127–33,
139–43; post–World War II U.S.
antisemitism, 187–88, 220–21; World
War II–era U.S. antisemitism, 176–77.
See also Nazism
Ardmore, Jane Kesner, 222
Arlen, Harold, 120
Atkinson, J. Brooks, 78
Atteridge, Harold, 56, 76

Baker, Belle, 27
Balaban, Barney, 192
Ball, Lucille, 218, 222
Banjo Eyes (1941), 82, 162–64, 183
Bankhead, Tallulah, 161, 189
Bankhead, William, 154
Barkley, Alben, 210
Barrat, Robert, 66
Barry, Charles "Bud," 216
Barrymore, Ethel, 48
Barrymore, Lionel, 48
Baruch, Bernard, 186
Basie, Count, 230
Bayes, Nora, 28
Bedini and Arthur, 21, 25–27, 29–30,
243n9

Bell, Nelson B., 154–55

Benchley, Robert C., 56

Benét, Stephen Vincent, 169

Ben-Gurion, David, 192, 210

Bennett, Tony, 234

Benny, Jack, 93–94, 104, 116, 122, 129, 158–59, 161, 176, 181, 189, 210, 213, 230

Berg, Gertrude, 104, 107–8

Bergman, Ingrid, 189

Berle, Milton, 61, 196, 204–5, 218

Berlin, Irving, 13, 16, 45–46, 75, 120–22, 121, 161

Berman, Shelly, 230

Billboard, 197

Biron, Phineas J., 146

blackface: "cissy blackface" character, 26, 29–30, 39; Dixie songs, 53–55, 251–52n28; EC as nonracial character, 53, 234; EC identification with, 2–3, 18, 22–26, 24, 230, 234; EC Jewish blackface character, 25–26, 29–30, 53–54; in EC performances, 27–28, 28–30, 79, 163, 208–10, 218; EC whiteface preference, 40–42, 53, 56, 210; marketing across media, 52–53; minstrelsy, 23–25, 53; public demand for, 52–53; "That's the Kind of a Baby for Me" racial depiction, 37–38; in vaudeville, 22–23, 42. *See also* race

blacklist, 197–201

Blanc, Mel, 208

Blight, David, 39

B'nai B'rith, 130–32, 148, 152, 158, 178, 201–2, 231. *See also* Anti-Defamation League of B'nai B'rith

Bogart, Humphrey, 161, 175

Borah, William, 104

Boyer, Charles, 189

Boys' Clubs, 154

Brady, Diamond Jim, 32

Brandeis, Louis D., 114

Brasselle, Keefe, 218

Breen, Bobby, 152

Brice, Fanny, 16, 27, 31, 36, 38, 42, 58, 70

Brinkley, Alan, 266n13

Bristol-Myers, 158–60

Brooks, Albert, 117

Brooks, Mel, 61, 232

Broun, Heywood, 45

Brown, Edmund G., 5–6, 227, *228*

Brown, Himan, 189

Brown, Lew, 120

Bruce, Lenny, 230–32

Buck, Gene, 36

Bundles for Britain, 160

burlesque, 16, 18, 26, 242n1

Burns, George, 16, 22, 25, 27, 93, 104, 129, 181, 230

Burns and Allen, 104, 181, 222

Bush, Lawrence, 231

Butler, Sheppard, 62

Buzzell, Eddie, 28

Caesar, Sid, 205, 210

Camel Quarter-Hour, 108

Canary Cottage, 30

Cantor, Edna (daughter), 34, 82, 162, *163*

Cantor, Janet (daughter), 34, 82, 162, *163*, 235

Cantor, Lena (sister), 240n5

Cantor, Marilyn (daughter), 34, 82, 162, *163*, 222

Cantor, Marjorie (daughter), 34, 82, 162, *163*, 226

Cantor, Natalie (daughter), 34, 82, 162, *163*

Cantor, Saul (uncle), 241–42n27

Capone, Al, 82

Carpenter, Thelma, 182–85, 277–78n13

Carr, Frank, 18

Carroll, Carroll, 105

Carter, Frank, 40

Catholic Actors Guild, 129

Caught Short!: A Saga of Wall Street (1929), 86–89, 96

CBS, 108, 115–16, 178, 200, 204–5, 216

Charters, Spencer, 79

Chauncey, George, 43

Clark, Bobby, 204

Clary, Robert, 209

class and labor issues, 13, 39, 43, 46–50, 83–84, 98–99

Cohen, Harold W., 150–51

Cohen, Sacha Baron, 61

Cohen, Sammy, 58

Cohn, Jack, 192

Colgate Comedy Hour, The, 195, 198–99, 203–11, 206, 212–19, 215

comedy material: "At the Osteopath's," 42–45, 66, 205; "The Aviator's Test," 40–42; "Depression Doctor," 98, 102, 104; "Fresh from the Bronx" *Ziegfeld* act, 40, 245n33; Great Depression as humor subject, 85–86; Greek Parkyakarkus skit, 116–18; humor magazines, 29; *It's Time to Smile* age jokes, 161; "Joe's Blue Front," 58–62, 60, 79, 253n40, 253n42; Mad Russian skit, 116–20, 119; Maxie the Taxi, 208; "New Nut" card gag, 32–33; outdated-ness of EC comedy, 207–8, 217–18, 230; skits with Thelma Carpenter, 183–84, 277–78n13; vaudeville-era nostalgia, 204, 207, 217–18; World War I humor, 29; World War II humor, 165–70. *See also* comedy style; Jewish humor

comedy style: ironic naivety or hedonism, 43; irony in patriotic song, 39–40; multiple-audience appeal, 32; observational comedy, 217; physical/body humor, 40–42, 66, 205; rapid

banter style, 29–30, 38, 62. *See also* comedy material; Jewish humor

Committee for the First Amendment, 200

communism: EC interfaith initiative and, 151, 155–57; EC presumed association with, 2, 143, 155–56, 200; Hollywood communism, 132–33, 156; HUAC investigations of, 155–56, 197–201; Soviet pact with Nazi Germany and, 156

Coney Island, 18–20

Conrad, Con, 56

Coolidge, Calvin, 64

Corbin, John, 45

Correll, Charles, 104

Corwin, Norman, 169

Coughlin, Charles, 126–27, 129–32, 145–46, 159, 266n13

Craig, James, 65

Crosby, Bing, 118, 172, 180

Crystal, Billy, 196

Curtis, Charles, 77–78

Dale, Alan, 58

Dale, Charlie, 16

Daly, John J., 78

Dangerfield, Rodney, 232

Dauber, Sally, 191

David, Larry, 61, 232

Davidson, Max, 58

Davis, Benny, 56

Davis, Bette, 175

Davis, Owen, 77

Davis, Sammy, Jr., 213–17, 215

Davis, Sammy, Sr., 213

Dayan, Moshe, 192

Dickstein, Samuel, 128

Dier, R. R., 184

Dies, Martin, 155–56

Dillingham, Charles, 32

DiMaggio, Joe, 161

Dingell, John, Sr., 211

Dinnerstein, Leonard, 127

Donovan, William, 188

Dooley, Ray, 47

Douglas, Melvyn, 200

Douglas, Susan, 116–17

Dowling, Eddie, 47

Downey, Morton, 108–9, 114

Dramatic Mirror, 33, 48

Dressler, Marie, 48

Dulles, John Foster, 220

Durante, Jimmy, 18–19, 122, 197

Durocher, Leo, 160–61

Eaton, Mary, 66

Eckheiser, Dvora, 220

Eddie Cantor Comedy Theatre, The (1955), 219–20

Edwards, Gus, 21, 207

Egan, J. C., 37

Eiges, Syd, 198

Einstein, Albert, 114, 188

Einstein, Bob ("Super Dave Osborne"), 117

Einstein, Harry, 116–18

Emerson Records, 49, 52

Fairchild, Edgar "Cookie," *168*, 171–72

Farley, Jim, 174–75

Federal Communications Commission (FCC), 105, 122

Federation for the Support of Jewish Philanthropic Societies, 114

Fender, Harry, 66

Fields, Sidney, 120, 149, 176

Fields, W. C., 31, 40, 41, 48

film: distribution in Nazi Germany, 92, 129, 132, 190; EC discomfort with film roles, 126; Jewish characters in, 91–92; Jewish philanthropic films,

114; silent film comedy revival, 205–7; World War II–era war films, 167

financial issues: B'nai B'rith charity tour receipts, 202–3; EC Depression-era wealth, 82, 83–84, 98–99; EC product endorsements, 65; Hollywood film income, 75; *Indian Maidens* salary, 18; *Kid Boots* financial success, 74; show business financial status, 16–17; show business supplemental income, 34, 50; Shubert financial issues, 50, 62–63, 250n15; Ziegfeld contracts, 34, 49, 63, 75; *Ziegfeld Follies* ticket prices, 31, 39

Fisher, Eddie, 222–24

Flynn, Errol, 175

Fogarty, Frank, 28

Ford, Henry, 2, 57, 64–65, 68, 70, 79–80, 132, 133, 140–43, 168

Forty Little Mothers (1940), 126, 149, 154, 157–58, 161

Fox, G. George, 159–60

Fox, William, 85

Frank, Melvin, 175

Freedman, David, 76, 87, 96–98, 115–16, 175

Freeman, Everett, 175

Friedwald, Will, 234

Frizzell, Lefty, 217

Furia, Philip, 45

Gabler, Neal, 239n1 (introduction)

Gaiman, Neil, 234

Gallagher and Shean, 65

Gardella, Kay, 217

Gari, Brian, 235, 240n5

Gari, Janet Cantor (daughter), 34, 82, 162, *163*, 235

Garland, Judy, 122

"George Has a Birthday" (1956), 221

Gerber, Alex, 53–55, *54*

Gershwin, George, 209

Giddins, Gary, 234

Glazer, Ilana, 233

Gleason, Jackie, 204–5

Gobel, George, 217

Goddard, Paulette, 181, 189

Golden, I. M., 130

Goldman Sachs, 85, 87

Goldwyn, Samuel, 91–92

Goodman, Benny, 147

Gordon, Bert, 116–20, *119*, 143–44, 149, 161, *168*, 172, 184

Gordon, Cliff, 15

Gosden, Freeman, 104

Gould, Jack, 182, 220

Great Neck mansion, 83–84

Green, Abel, 172, 196

Grey, Joel, 213

Gutstadt, Richard, 128

Hadassah (Women's Zionist Organization of America), 127, 136–41, 145, 148, 178, 231

Hammerstein's Roof Garden theater, 21

Harbach, Otto, 66

Harriman, Alfred, 37

Harrington, Tom, 159

Hart, Max, 28–29, 50

Hearn, Lew, 59, *60*

Hearst, William Randolph, 32, 168

Hebrew language, 190

Hecht, Ben, 85

Helffrich, Stockton, 208–10, 214

Hepburn, Katherine, 189

Herbert, Victor, 36

Herskovits, Bela, 221

Hine, Lewis, 33

Hiss, Alger, 201

Hitler, Adolf. *See* Nazism

Hoberman, J., 235

Hollywood Anti-Nazi League for the Defense of American Democracy (HANL), 132, 155–56, 267n17

Holtz, Lou, 254n3

Hoover, Herbert, 89, 95–96, 168

Hoover, J. Edgar, 158, 200

Hope, Bob, 95, 175, 181, 204, 230

Horne, Lena, 216–17

Houdini, Harry, 27

House Committee for the Investigation of Un-American Activities (HUAC), 155–56, 197–201

Howard, Willie, 73

How DOooo You Doo!!! (1945 film), 118

Howland, Jobyna, 66, *67*

Hugo, 61

Humphrey, Hal, 227

Hutchens, John K., 161, 171

Hutton, Betty, 169

Idelsohn Society for Musical Preservation, 235–36, 289n14

If You Knew Susie (1948, film), 185, 191

immigration: EC family migration, 3, 7, 15; family separation/desertion, 7–8, 240n6; immigrant child labor, 12; immigrant relief campaign, 72; refugee resettlement, 126, 129, 135–36, 177–78, 185–94, *193*, 220; street life of young immigrants, 10, 12–14

Impelliteri, Vincent, 210

Imperial Theatre, 21

Indian Maidens burlesque show, 18, 242n1

interfaith activities, 151–60, 179–80, 185–88, *186*

Iskowitz, Isidore (Cantor birth name), 7, 76–77, 123–25, 132, 200, 239n1 (chap. 1), 241–42n27, 257n48, 265n42

Iskowitz, Mechel (father), 7–8, 77, 239n1 (chap. 1), 240n5

Israel: EC essay on, 211; EC tour of 1950, 192–94, *193*; Israel Bonds campaign, *4, 5*, 192, 194, 209–10, 221, 224–25, 229; post–World War II humor climate and, 181, 185; statehood importance, 188–89, 192. *See also* Palestine

Jacobson, Abbi, 233
jazz and bebop, 217
Jazz Singer, The (1925, play), 72
Jazz Singer, The (1927, film), 162
Jenkins, Henry, 91–92
Jessel, George, *4*, 16, 21, 22, 27–28, 82, 85, 112, 122–23, 129, 187, 222–24, 243nn8–9
Jewish humor: criticisms of vulgarity, 51–52; in EC early vaudeville roles, 22; humor as Jewish value, 166; Jewish blackface character, 25–26, 29–30, 53–54; Jewish emasculated male caricature, 44–45; Jewish humor of the 1930s, 108–9; Jewish-inflected radio parodies, 108–11, 114–16; Jewish solidarity, 56–58; "New Nut" Ziegfeld character, 32–33; *schlemiel* and *nebbish* characters, 44–45, 78–79, 91–92, 232; "stage Jew" character, 58; tough sales-man character, 58–61, *60*, 68, 80, 177; transcending of social boundaries, 37–38; wise guy character, 61. *See also* comedy material; Jewish identity
Jewish identity: EC childhood Jewish ob-servance, 10–12, 72; EC contemporary Jewish following, 235–37; EC Jewish identity model, 1–2, 70, 74, 232; food and Kosher taboos, 12, 27, 108, 109–11, 115, 149; High Holidays as political occasion, 12, 108; Holocaust and, 190; holy days observances, 10–11, 72–73, 112, 178–79, 190; Jewish invisibility and assimilation,

1, 122–25, 179, 239n1 (introduction); Reformed Judaism, 116; religious tolerance as Judaic practice, 180; transcending of social boundaries, 37–38. *See also* Jewish humor
Jewish press: on antisemitism, 70–71; on EC humanitarianism, 210–11; on EC interfaith appeal, 155; EC obituary, 229; on EC philanthropy, 113–15, 132, 178; on EC political advocacy, 57, 144–45, 220–21; Israel statehood coverage, 193–94; Jewish press reviews, 57, 70, 112; survey of leading American Jews, 114
Johnson, Howard, 134
Johnson, Lyndon, 5–6, 227, *228*
Johnson, Nucky, 82
Jolson, Al, 16, 22, 28–29, 33, 50, 55, 69, 70, 72, 82, 93, 117, 162, 176, 189, 197, 218
Jonas, Nathan S., 71, 83
Jones, Norah, 234
Jones, Spike, 167

Kalwary, S. Sidney, 114–15
Kantrowitz, Esther (grandmother), 7–11, *11*, 21, 34–35
Kantrowitz, Meta (mother), 7–8, 239n1 (chap. 1), 240n5
Kapp, David, 179
Katz, Mickey, 111
Kaufman, Andy, 232
Kaufman, Irving, 236
Kaye, Danny, 196, 200, 210
Kaye, Sammy, 180
Kearney, Bernard W. (Pat), 201–2
Kelly, Gene, 189
Kelly, Harry, *41*
Kelly, Walter, 15
Kern, James V., 175
Kid Boots (1923, play), 65–69, 72–74, 112, 207, 213, 254n3

Kid Boots (1926, film), 74–75
Kid from Spain, The (1932), 66, 96, 129
Kid Kabaret, 21, 27–28, 207
Kid Millions (1934), 183
Knight, Vick, 176
Korean War, 201–2
Ku Klux Klan (KKK), 64–65, 68, 254n3, 255n13

Lacy, Sam, 216
Lait, Jack, 70
Lasser, Michael, 45
Lastfogel, Abe, 202–3
Lauper, Cyndi, 234
Laurie, Joe, Jr., 23, 25
Leahy, Frank, 185, *186*
Lee, Al, 28–30, 245n33
LeMaire, George, 51–52
Leonard, Eddie, 22, 28
Leslie, Edgar, 39
Lewis, Jerry, 44, 196, 232
Lewis, Joe E., 82
Lewis, Leon L., 128, 155–56
Lexington Theater, 48
Lindbergh, Charles, 76
Lippmann, Walter, 71
Lipsky, Daniel, 14, 64, 90
Lockridge, Richard, 78
Loeb, Jacob, 74
Loew, Marcus, 16
Loew's State Theatre, 149–50, *150*, 153
Long, Avon, 234
Long, Ray, 87
Lorraine, Lillian, *41*
Lower East Side: EC childhood in, 7–9, 9, 11–12, 72, 83, 98–99; EC labor activism and, 47–48; in EC performances, 33, 61, 77, 161–62; exotic reputation of, 27; Jewish entertainers from, 16, 70; Jewish identity and, 72, 232; nostalgic references to, 120–22, *121*; rapid

banter style and, 62; sexual talk in, 52; street life of immigrants, 10, 12–14; visits of 1939, 149–50
Luce, Henry, 188

Madame Ten, 21
Madison, James, 29
Make It Snappy, 52–55, 57, 59, 62, 63, 68
Mann, Thomas, 177
March of Dimes, 105, 148, 185, 201, 209–10
Marshall, Louis, 79–80
Martin, Nora, 170–72, 179, 182
Martin and Lewis, 204–5, 210, 216
Marx, Groucho, 27, 196
Marx, Harpo, 229
Marx, Minnie, 17
Marx Brothers, 16, 17, 61, 93
May, Mitchell, 71
Mayer, Louis B., 122
McCarthy, Joseph (politician), 197–201
McCarthy, Joseph (songwriter), 65
McCree, Junie, 15
McDaniel, Hattie, 183
McDonald, James G., 185–88, 220–21
McGuire, William Anthony, 66, 77
McIntyre, Marvin C., 101–4
media and reviews: Depression-era media, 84, 86–87, 89–90, 90; early EC recognition, 33; EC antisemitic hate mail, 143–44; EC as celebrity, 5, 171; EC "cissy" character in, 26, 29–30; EC faux presidential campaign, 96; EC interfaith appeal and, 151–52, 154–55, 180; EC obituary and remembrance, 227–29; EC political advocacy, 64–65, 130, 132, 141–43, *142*, 188–89, 220–21; McCarthyism coverage, 197–99; radio ratings and commentary, 93, 146–47, 182, 257n48, 260n48; refugee appeals, 188–89; on sexual innuendo,

45, 51–52; slapstick comedy revival, 207; television ratings, 204–5, 207–8, 216–18; on whiteface, 41–42, 52, 56, 69; on World War II–era humor, 165, 169. PARTICULAR REVIEWS: AEA benefit show, 48; "At the Osteopath's," 45; *Banjo Eyes*, 163; *Camel Caravan*, 146–47; *The Colgate Comedy Hour*, 204–5, 216–18; *The Eddie Cantor Comedy Theatre*, 220; *The Eddie Cantor Story*, 218–19; *Forty Little Mothers*, 157; "Fresh from the Bronx," 40; *It's Time to Smile*, 161; *Kid Boots*, 66, 69, 74–75; *Make It Snappy*, 56; *Midnight Rounders*, 62; *Special Delivery*, 75; *Thank Your Lucky Stars*, 176; *Whoopee* (play), 78, 89–90; *Whoopee!* (film), 91–92; *Ziegfeld Follies*, 37, 44–45, 65. See also Jewish press; *Variety*

Meir, Golda, 192

Mellon, Andrew, 95, 96, 98, 168

Mendelsohn, S. Felix, 73–74

Menjou, Adolph, 165

Meredith, Burgess, 181

Merriam, Frank F., 122, 130

Midnight Frolic, 31–34, 46, 48, 168

Midnight Rounders, 50–51, 53, 58–62, 60, 79

Miller, Marilyn, 40, 49

Mizrachi Women's Organization, 160

Moranis, Rick, 44

Morgan, Frederick, 188

Morgan, Henry, 182

Morgenthau, Henry, 192

Morosco, Oliver, 30

Morris, William, 85

Muir, Jean, 131, 198–99

Muni, Paul, 189

Murphy, George, 165

Murrow, Edward R., 222

My Forty Years in Show Business, 195–203

My Life Is in Your Hands (1928), 7–8, 13, 35, 76–77, 83–84

National Association for the Advancement of Colored People (NAACP), 208–10

National Conference of Christians and Jews (NCCJ), 151, 185, 210

National Foundation for Infantile Paralysis, 105

National Recovery Administration (NRA), 101–2

National Union for Social Justice, 129–30

Nazism: EC condemnation of, 5, 126–28, 131, 133, 160–61, 165–70, 181, 229, 267n17; EC Nazi propaganda collection, 128, 155–56; film distribution in Nazi Germany, 92, 129, 132, 190; HUAC investigations of, 155–56; parodies of, 232; pre–World War II aggression, 133–34, 156, 159. See also antisemitism

NBC: EC influence in, 105; EC political advocacy on, 147, 157–59, 161, 167; founding of, 93; Jewish programming study, 107, 110; racial policies of the 1950s, 208–10, 213–16, 215; war bond telethon, 171–72

Neumark, Martha, 114

New Amsterdam Theatre, 30, 31, 47, 84

Newman, Max H., 57

New York City, 28, 37–38, 40, 43–45, 51, 56–59, 62, 81–82, 208, 245n33. See also particular areas and landmarks

Nicholas Brothers, 183

Night of Stars, 129

Nilsson, Harry, 234

Nixon, Richard, 5, 225

Noel, Hattie, 183

Ochs, Adolph S., 114
O'Connor, Donald, 216
Office of War Information (OWI), 167
Opp, Joe, 59, 60
Orpheum vaudeville circuit, 27

Paar, Jack, 182
Palestine, 113, 126, 129, 136–40, 178,
    186–90. *See also* Israel
Palestine Relief Fund, 113
Palmer, Amanda, 234
Palmy Days, 76, 99
Panama, Norman, 175
Parker, Dorothy, *131*
Parks, Bert, 149
patriotism, 36, 39–40, 141, 154–57,
    174–77, 179–80
Peale, Norman Vincent, 188
Pearl, Jack, 93
Pebeco Toothpaste show, 115–16, 181
Peerce, Jan, 217
Pennington, Ann, 40, 65
Person to Person (1956), 222
Pfeiffer, Michelle, 234
philanthropic support for Jews, 5, 71, 72,
    112–15, 132, 142, 151, 177, 185–92, 223
Picon, Molly, 203
political activism (of EC): American
    Declaration of Tolerance and Equality,
    153; anti-McCarthyism, 197–201;
    anti-Nazism, 5, 126–28, *131*, 133,
    160–61, 165–70, 181, 229, 267n17; faux
    presidential campaign, 95–96; non-
    interventionism, 133–35; post–World
    War II political lobbying, 185–88;
    reactionary responses to, 64–65;
    softened radio persona, 97–100, 108,
    115–16; World War II troop support,
    170–74, 176, 180, 274n18
Pollack, Lew, 55

Pollard, Annie, 9
Pool, Tamar de Sola, 136–37
Price, George, 28
Prohibition, 43–44, 45, 68

race: banjo in EC performances, 23–24;
    blackface as nonracial character, 53,
    234; Civil War commemoration and,
    39–40; EC antiracist stance, 3, 64–65,
    68, 185; EC effeminate character and,
    43, 248n43; interracial marriage in
    Whoopee, 77–78; in 1950s television,
    208–10; in post–World War II radio,
    182–85, 277–78n13; Sammy Davis,
    Jr., incident, 213–16, 215. *See also*
    blackface
radio: ethnic positioning in 1930s radio,
    116–20, *119*; Jewish fundraising
    broadcasts, 85, 114; Jewish self-
    censorship, 122; product endorse-
    ments, 65; ratings and commentary,
    93, 146–47, 182, 257n48, 260n48;
    World War II special broadcasts,
    170–74, 179, 274n18. PARTICULAR
    SHOWS: *The Chase and Sanborn
    Hour* (1931–1934), 76, 92–98, 97, 105,
    107–10, 115–17, 124–25, 175, 181;
    Pebeco Toothpaste show (1934–1936),
    115–16, 181; *Texaco Town* (1936–1938),
    118, 120–22; *Camel Caravan* (1938–
    1939), 120–22, 146–47, 149; *Gulf Screen
    Guild Theater* (1939), 148–49; *It's
    Time to Smile* (1940–1946), 158–59,
    161–62, 166–70, 174, 179, 181–82; *Star
    Spangled Way* (1946), 189–90; *The
    Eddie Cantor Pabst Blue Ribbon Show*
    (1946–1949), 182–85, 277–78n13;
    "Time—The Present—A Day of
    Remembrance" (1947), 190; *Ask Eddie
    Cantor* (1961), 225–26

Rankin, John, 200

Rapp, Philip, 116, 175

Raskin, Willie, 134

Red Cross, 5, 178, 201–2

Reid, Laurence, 75

Reuther, Walter, 188

Reynolds, Robert Rice, 145–46

Rickles, Don, 61

Riis, Jacob, 33

Rise of the Goldbergs, The, 107–8

R. J. Reynolds Corporation, 144–46

Roback, Arnold A., 157

Robinson, Bill, 129, 160

Robinson, Edward G., 168–69, 189, 200

Robinson, J. Russel, 56

Rogers, Ginger, 189

Rogers, Howard E., 45

Rogers, Will, 27, 31, 33, 36, 40, 41, 42, 78,
    86, 95, 104

Roman Scandals (1933), 66, *94*, 129

Romero, Cesar, 205

Roosevelt, Eleanor, 5, 105, 185, *186*

Roosevelt, Franklin, 2, 5, 95–96, 101–6,
    133–34, 154–55, 172, 185–86

Rosen, Jody, 236

Rosenberg, Julius and Ethel, 201

Rosenwald, Julius, 74

Rosenzweig, Laura, 128

Ross, Michael, 205, 206

Rosten, Leo, 44

Rothafel, Samuel "Roxy," 107

Rothschild, Walter N., 71

Rubinoff, David, 111, 117

Ruby, Harry, 39

Russell, Connie, 224

Rutherford, Jack, 80

Sally, 49, 63

Schenck, Joseph, 22, 47

Schwartz, Jean, 53–55, *54*

Schwimmer, Harry, 187

Scorsese, Martin, 61, 235

Screen Actors Guild (SAG), 13, 101

Seinfeld, Jerry, 61

Seldes, Gilbert, 56, 59–61, *60*

sexuality: black (caricatured), 23, 37; car-
    icatured homosexuality in *Whoopee!*
    2–3, 80, 91; Jewish emasculated male
    caricature, 44–45; New York trans-
    gressive nightlife and, 43–44, 51–52;
    sexual innuendo and vulgarity, 36–38,
    43, 45–46, 51, 80; sexual presentation
    in minstrelsy, 26; *Whoopee* depiction
    of marriage, 77–78, 80–82

Shandler, Jeffrey, 235

Sherman, Allan, 111, 234

Sherwood, Robert E., 74–75

Shore, Dinah, 161, *168*, 170, 175, 204

Shubert Brothers (Lee and J. J.), 33,
    50–51, 53, 61–64, 73

Shubert Brothers productions
    (1920–1923), 50–63

Sidney, George, 58

Silver, Martin, 229

Silver, Monroe, 58

Silverman, Sarah, 232

Silverman, Sime, 40, 62

Sinatra, Frank, 170

"Sizeman and Son" (1956), 221–22

Sloane, Allan, 189

Smith, Ira R. T., 105

Smith, Joe, 16

Smith, Kate, 274n18

Smith, Richard R., 87

Smith and Dale, 16, 58, 204

Sondergaard, Gail, *131*

songs (EC recordings and performances):
    "Automobile Horn Song," 80; "But
    after the Ball Was Over," 40; "Cala-
    bash Pipe," 120; "Carolina Moon,"
    108–9; "Charley, My Boy," 69; "Dinah,"
    255n17; "The Dixie Volunteers,"

39–40; "Eddie Cantor's Tips on the Stock Market," 86; "Hungry Women," 100; "Ida, Sweet as Apple Cider," 162; "I Don't Want to Get Well," 172; "If I Only Had a Five Cent Piece," 99; "(If They Feel Like a War) Let Them Keep It Over There," 134; "If You Knew Susie," 69; "I Love Potato Pancakes," 109–10; "I've Got My Captain Working for Me Now," 48; "Just a Prayer Away," 179–80; "Lullaby of Broadway," 224; "Makin' Whoopee," 10, 80–81, 81, 100, 171, 234; "Margie," 56; "The Modern Maiden's Prayer," 36–37, 56–57; "My Girl Uses Mineralava (That's Why I'm Her Beau)," 65; "My Land and Your Land," 134; "My Yiddisha Mammy," 53–55, 54, 58, 236, 251–52n28, 289n14; "Now's the Time to Fall in Love," 99–100; "The Only Thing I Want for Christmas," 236; "She'll Be Coming 'Round the Mountain," 111; "That's the Kind of a Baby for Me," 36–38; "We Did It Before and We Can Do It Again," 163; "When I'm the President," 95–96; "You'd Be Surprised," 45–46; "You Don't Need the Wine to Have a Wonderful Time," 45

songs (vaudeville and popular songs): "Can't You Hear Your Country Calling," 36; "Down in Bom-Bom Bay," 30; "Me and My Gal," 36–37, 39; "My Yiddisha Momme," 55; "Oh How She Could Yacki Hicki Wicki Wacky Woo," 32–33; "Pretty Baby," 36–37; "The Star-Spangled Banner," 36; "The War in Snyder's Grocery Store," 30

Southern Israelite, 229

Soyer, Daniel, 9

Special Delivery (1927), 75

St. Denis, Ruth, 38

Stewart, Jon, 232

Stiller, Jerry, 100, 112

Strauss, Nathan, 129

Strauss, Theodore, 163

Strich, Elaine, 196

Strike Me Pink (1936), 120

Stuart, Gloria, *131*

Sullivan, Ed, 204–5, 216

Sullivan, Edward F., 155–56

Susman, Milton K., 145

Take My Life (1957), 11–12, 110

Talmadge, Herman, 213–14

Tanguay, Eva, 27, 28

television: coast-to-coast transmission, 207; contemporary Jewish identity in, 233, 288n5; EC birthday celebration, 222–24; growth of television, 203–4; racial policies of the 1950s, 208–10; ratings, 204–5, 207–8, 216–18

Temple, Shirley, *103*

Thalberg, Irving, 130

Thank Your Lucky Stars (1943, film), 175–76

"That's the Kind of a Baby for Me," 36–38

This Is Your Life, 218, 220

Thomas, Bob, 227

Thomas, J. Parnell, 156

Thompson, Harry, 15

Tierney, Harry, 65

Tinney, Frank, 22, 48

Tin Pan Alley composers, 39, 134, 208

Tobias, Charles, 179

Tobias, David, 20, 71

Tobias, Ida, 13, 20, 28–29, 82, 162, 222, 225–27

Tobias, Minnie, 20

touring: annual tours of 1911–1931, 110; B'nai B'rith charity tour, 201–2; Great Depression and, 84, 89–91;

provocative humor and, 51–52; rise of nativism and, 64–65; tolerance tour of 1939, 150–54

Truman, Harry S., 4, 5, 186–87, 225

Tucker, Sophie, 16, 22, 55, 85, 122, 203

Turpin, Ben, 207

United Jewish Appeal (UJA), 129, 178, 189–94

United Nations Relief and Rehabilitation Administration (UNRRA), 188

United Palestine Appeal (UPA), 113, 129, 148, 178

Upton, Frances, 80

Vallee, Rudy, 109, 117, 175–76, 199–200

Van, Gus, 47

Variety: EC anti-Nazi writing in, 160, 166, 170; on EC celebrity, 93–95; on EC philanthropy, 105; on EC rapid banter style, 62; on Nazi-era censorship, 133; post–World War II humor climate and, 181–82, 185; racial comments in, 214; on the stock market crash, 83–84; tour of 1939 coverage, 150; on UJA, 189, 192; on World War II–era humor, 169, 172; Yizkor memorials in, 34–35. PARTICULAR REVIEWS: *The Colgate Comedy Hour*, 216–17; *The Eddie Cantor Pabst Blue Ribbon Show*, 185; "Fresh from the Bronx," 40; *It's Time to Smile*, 161; *Kid Boots*, 73–75; "Master and Man," 29–30; *My Forty Years in Show Business*, 196–97; *The Rise of the Goldbergs*, 107; *Thank Your Lucky Stars*, 176; *Whoopee!* 91; *Ziegfeld Follies*, 37

vaudeville and burlesque: blackface in, 22–23; EC competitiveness in, 13–14, 27; EC early influences, 14–16, 21–22; EC early vaudeville career, 15–17, 18–25, 19, 28–30; show business careers and, 16–17; social stigma of, 20, 71; touring circuits, 22, 25, 27, 63; vaudeville-era nostalgia, 204, 207, 217–18

von Zell, Harry, 168, 170, 172

Wagner, Robert F., 186

Wagner-Rogers bill, 135–36, 187

Walker, Jimmy, 85

Wallington, James, 92, 95, 97, 108–9, 117, 120

Warburg, Felix M., 71, 114

Warfield, William, 217

Way I See It, The (1959), 12, 226

Wayne, John, 225

Weaver, Pat, 204

Weill, Milton, 176

Weinberg, Sydney, 85

Weiner, Jennifer, 288n5

Weisberg, Joseph G., 199, 229

Weizmann, Chaim, 192

West, Robert, 100–101

whiteface, 40–42, 52

Whoopee (1928, play): comedy material in, 13, 44, 66, 77, 78–79, 79; national tours, 77, 84, 89–91; production, 77; sexuality and marriage in, 77–78, 80–82; stock market crash and, 84, 89–90; television references to, 207

Whoopee! (1930, film), 2–3, 81, 91–92

Wicker, Irene, 199

William Esty Advertising Agency, 146

William Morris agency, 202–3, 216

Williams, Bert, 31, 36, 38, 51

Williams, Hank, 217

Will Mastin Trio, 213–16, 215

Wilson, B. F., 100

Winter Garden Theatre, 50, 53–55

Wise, Stephen, 5, 177
Wisse, Ruth, 44
Woeste, Victoria Saker, 79–80
Wolf, Rennold, 43
Wolkin, Jacob, 190–91, 279n37
Wons, Tony, 108, 117
Wood, Joe, 21
Woollcott, Alexander, 56
World War I, 29, 36, 71
World War II: *Banjo Eyes* reception and,
163–64; EC anti-Nazi humor, 165–70;
EC troop support, 170–74, 173, 180;
Holocaust, 178, 188–90; isolationism,
133–34; NBC War Clinic, 167; radio
dramas about, 169; war bond
telethon, 171–72, 274n18
Wright, Cobina, Jr., 153
Wynn, Ed, 16, 93, 204

Yellen, Jack, 55
Yiddish language, 3, 9, 14, 56–58, 61, 108,
111–12
*Yoo-Hoo Prosperity! The Eddie Cantor
Five-Year Plan* (1931), 95

Young Men's Christian Association
(YMCA), 154
Young Men's Hebrew Association
(YMHA), 113
Your Next President! (1932), 87, 96
Youth Aliyah, 136–41, 145–46, 178, 192,
220

Zanuck, Darryl F., 122
Zell, Harry von, 14
Ziegfeld, Florenz, 30, 35, 43–44, 52, 197
Ziegfeld Follies: audiences, 31–32; cast of
1918, *41*; EC contracts with, 33–34, 63;
EC solo act, 30; enduring characters
from, 56; mentoring of EC in, 52;
national tours, 37, 39–40, 48–49;
nostalgic references to, 172, 208;
notable celebrities in, 27, 31; patriotic
material in, 36; sexual innuendo in,
43–46
Ziegfeld Midnight Frolic, A (1929, film), 79
Zionism, 113, 139–41, 145–46, 148, 160,
194, 220–21
Ziv Company, 219–20